# Women and Politics

Maria Freese

202-365-8681

# Women and Politics

## Paths to Power and Political Influence

### *Updated Third Edition*

Julie Dolan
*Macalester College*

Melissa M. Deckman
*Washington College*

Michele L. Swers
*Georgetown University*

ROWMAN & LITTLEFIELD
*Lanham • Boulder • New York • London*

Executive Editor: Traci Crowell
Assistant Editor: Mary Malley
Marketing Manager: Deborah Hudson
Cover Designer: Chloe Batch
Cover Art: Reuters/Alamy Stock Photo

Credits and acknowledgments borrowed from other sources and reproduced, with permission, in this textbook appear on appropriate pages within the text.

Published by Rowman & Littlefield
A wholly owned subsidiary of The Rowman & Littlefield Publishing Group, Inc.
4501 Forbes Boulevard, Suite 200, Lanham, Maryland 20706
www.rowman.com

Unit A, Whitacre Mews, 26-34 Stannary Street, London SE11 4AB

British Library Cataloguing in Publication Information Available

The Library of Congress has cataloged the previous edition of this book as follows:

Dolan, Julie.
Women and politics : paths to power and political influence / Julie Dolan, Macalester College, Melissa M. Deckman, Washington College, Michele L. Swers, Georgetown University. — Third edition.
    pages cm
Includes bibliographical references and index.
1. Women—Political activity—United States. I. Deckman, Melissa M. (Melissa Marie), 1971– II. Swers, Michele L. III. Title.
HQ1236.5.U6D635 2015
320.0820973—dc23

2015034703

ISBN 978-1-5381-0074-5 (cloth : alk. paper)
ISBN 978-1-5381-0075-2 (pbk. : alk. paper)
ISBN 978-1-5381-0076-9 (electronic)

♾™ The paper used in this publication meets the minimum requirements of American National Standard for Information Sciences—Permanence of Paper for Printed Library Materials, ANSI/NISO Z39.48-1992.

Printed in the United States of America

# Contents

# Preface

## Gender and the Pursuit of the Presidency: The 2016 Elections

### INTRODUCTION

In July 2016, Hillary Clinton made history by becoming the first woman to receive a major party's nomination for the office of the US presidency. After a hard-fought battle with Democratic rival Bernie Sanders, Clinton's victory in the California primary gave her the necessary number of party delegates to claim the mantle of party nominee, an honor she accepted one month later at the national convention in Philadelphia, Pennsylvania.

Delivering her acceptance speech from the Philadelphia convention stage, Clinton quietly paid homage to the many female pioneers who preceded her. Standing just a few miles away from the place where many suffragists were denied participation in the nation's 1876 centennial celebration 140 years before, Clinton wore a white pantsuit to honor her political sisters who also wore white to symbolize purity and the quality of their fight for suffrage (Friedman 2016). Like them, her fight was historic and raised essential questions about women's political equality. Some two hundred years after the nation's founding, why has the United States never elected a woman to the presidency?

After winning the Democratic primary, Clinton faced an unusual and controversial Republican opponent in the general election—businessman and billionaire Donald Trump. Although the vast majority of polls predicted Clinton would easily win the election and she ultimately won the popular vote by nearly 3 million votes, Trump managed to win the Electoral College

Former Secretary of State Hillary Clinton accepts the Democratic Party's presidential nomination in July 2016, becoming the first woman in American political history to become a major party presidential nominee. *Source*: Xinhua / Alamy Stock Photo.

by a margin of 77 votes (304–227).[1] How can we understand this outcome?

This preface provides a preliminary examination of the 2016 presidential elections, through a gendered lens. We argue that both Hillary Clinton's and Republican hopeful Carly Fiorina's failed candidacies illustrate the challenges of navigating gender in seeking the highest office in the land. Neither woman lost her election bid simply because of her status as a woman, but in a country that has elected only male presidents, masculinity is so thoroughly infused in the presidency that men are privileged as the default category. In both the primary and general election campaigns, both women faced gendered critiques from their campaign opponents and the media, critiques that reinforced gender stereotypes and reminded voters of the candidates' status as interlopers, attempting to tread where no woman has gone before.

What do we mean by navigating gender? As Kelly Dittmar (2015) explains,

> For most of American history, [navigating gender] has meant that presidential candidates—male *and* female—have worked to prove they are man enough for the job. Whether by emphasizing their roles as paternal protectors, displaying toughness and strength, or proving their "manliness" in campaign activities and photo-ops, candidates have long engaged in the business of gender performance to meet the masculine credentials of executive office.

But in addition to demonstrating their manliness, women, much more so than men, must also prove their femininity. Dubbed the "double bind" by

---

[1]Seven electors did not vote for either Trump or Clinton when the Electoral College votes were tallied on December 19, 2016. Two Republican and five Democratic electors refused to cast their ballots for Trump and Clinton, respectively (Schmidt and Andrews 2016).

Kathleen Hall Jamieson, the theory posits that our notions of leadership conflict with our preconceptions of what it means to be womanly, often to the detriment of women seeking entrance into the masculine world of politics. We examine the ways in which both Clinton and Fiorina "performed gender" on the campaign trail and also focus on the ways in which election opponents, voters, and the media subjected their candidacies to gendered critiques. The preface begins with an analysis of the primary campaigns in both the Democratic and Republican parties. We then discuss how the work of previous scholars on gender bias in the media and elections informs our understanding of the gender dynamics in both the primary elections and the general election campaign. Lastly, we consider how the gendered aspects of both Trump's and Clinton's presidential campaigns in terms of their messaging likely impacted the voters, through a preliminary analysis of the 2016 presidential election polls. In such a relatively close election, we maintain that the use of gendered narratives had a role to play in Trump's unexpected victory.

## GENDER IN THE PRIMARIES

We first turn our gendered lens onto the presidential primary elections, in which both parties' contests featured a prominent woman on the ballot. Republican Carly Fiorina announced her candidacy for the presidency in 2015. Fiorina had made her name and fortune as the first woman to be named the CEO of a Fortune 20 company, Hewlett Packard, in 1999, where she served in that capacity until 2005. She later became a major fundraiser for the Republican Party and in 2010 won the GOP's nomination for Senate in her home state of California, only to lose to incumbent Democratic Senator Barbara Boxer. In 2015, she decided to run for president, claiming that her status as a businesswoman and political outsider was just what the country needed. Her campaign for the nomination, however, yielded little success in a very crowded GOP field, and she dropped out of the race after finishing seventh in the New Hampshire primary. Unlike Carly Fiorina, Hillary Clinton was long presumed the frontrunner to win the Democratic nomination when she announced her candidacy early in 2015, given that she had almost become her party's nominee in 2008. Clinton went on to serve as Secretary of State during Barack Obama's first term and left office with strong approval ratings (O'Connor 2013).

Despite little in common concerning their political orientation or public policy stands, both Fiorina and Clinton faced challenges that were uniquely gendered in the presidential primaries. In the case of Fiorina, she faced questions from the media that were not addressed to her male opponents,

Hillary Clinton officially launches her 2016 presidential campaign at a rally at Four Freedoms Park on Roosevelt Island, New York City.
*Source*: Kyodo via AP Images.

such as whether she considers herself to be a feminist. She also had to endure nasty comments about her appearance from her party's eventual nominee, Donald Trump, whose "hyper-masculine" behavior became a major bone of contention during the primaries (and later general election). While Clinton would go onto secure her party's nomination, she faced a serious, unexpected challenge from Bernie Sanders, the self-described Democratic Socialist Senator from Vermont, who forced Clinton to adopt more progressive policy positions, such as a plan to allow young Americans to attend college at public universities for free. While Sanders and Clinton waged a fierce battle largely based on policy differences, Clinton arguably faced more gendered scrutiny than did Sanders—calling to mind similar challenges she first faced as a presidential candidate in 2008 (see chapter 5 for a more thorough analysis of Hillary Clinton's first attempt to win her party's presidential nomination).

## The Democratic Primaries

Five Democrats initially sought their party's nomination for president in 2016, but three contenders—former US Senators Jim Webb (Virginia) and Lincoln Chafee (Rhode Island) and former Maryland Governor Martin O'Malley—dropped out of the race before the first primary was held in New Hampshire. Many pundits assumed that Clinton would easily secure her party's nomination, given her huge initial fundraising advantage and the fact that she had earned the endorsement of most of the Democratic Party's elected officials nationally, including respected party elders such as Representative John Lewis (*Politico* 2016).

Bernie Sanders's campaign proved strong, although Hillary Clinton ultimately bested Bernie Sanders by more than 3 million votes in the primaries, securing 16.9 million votes compared to Sanders's 13.2 million votes (The

Green Papers 2016). Clinton also led Sanders in the number of Democratic "superdelegates," which are unpledged delegates, such as Democratic elected officials, who are not bound by the popular votes of their states' primary election and who make up about 13 percent of the delegates who vote for their party's presidential nominee at the Democratic National Convention (Stein 2016).

A breakdown of the votes from the primary contests shows that Sanders and Clinton pulled from different constituencies. Hillary Clinton, for example, disproportionately gained votes from racial minorities, older Democrats, and Democrats from the South, while the white vote was split evenly between the two candidates. Sanders did better in states with open primaries, in which voters registered as political independents are allowed to vote, compared with states with closed primaries, in which only registered Democrats can vote; Sanders secured the votes of close to two-thirds of Independents (Zitner, Chinni, and McGill 2016). Sanders pulled disproportionately from millennial voters as well, who were especially enthused about his proposals for universal health care, tuition-free college, and his overriding concerns about income inequality and shaking up the political status quo (Weigel 2016).

How did the women's vote break down in the Democratic primaries? Research by political scientist Barbara Norrander shows that, on average, Hillary Clinton secured 10.6 percent more votes from women in the Democratic primary contests than she got from men, which actually improved her performance against Barack Obama in 2008, when she secured 8.6 percent more votes from women compared with men (Zeller 2016). However, Clinton's advantage among women voters in the primaries was not uniform, as age played a major role in determining whether women backed Clinton or Bernie Sanders. CNN exit polls in more than half of the states that held primaries reveal that "Sanders led Clinton by an average of 37 points among women 18 to 29," while Clinton's support among older women over Sanders was also similarly lopsided (ibid.).

Given the historic nature of Hillary Clinton's nomination battle, and the importance that many older women placed on electing the nation's first female president, some feminist leaders took younger women to task for backing Bernie Sanders over Clinton. At a New Hampshire rally in early February, Madeleine Albright—who was the first female Secretary of State, serving under President Bill Clinton—essentially scolded younger women for not embracing Clinton as a revolutionary figure. Standing next to Hillary Clinton, Albright said, "We can tell our story about how we climbed the ladder and a lot of you younger women think . . . it's been done. It's not done. You have to help. Hillary Clinton will always be there for you and just remember, there is a special place in hell for women who don't help each other" (quoted in Rappeport 2016). Gloria Steinem, another feminist icon, had a different take on why many younger women were drawn to Bernie Sanders over Hillary Clinton, telling HBO host Bill Maher on his program *Real Time* that she believed younger women were drawn to Bernie Sanders because "when you're young, you're thinking, where are the boys? The boys are with Bernie" (Contrera 2016).

Both women faced backlash for their comments. For instance, Juana Summers, a columnist with mashable.com, called Steinem's suggestion that millennial women were choosing Sanders over Clinton to attract a potential mate "profoundly sexist and condescending" (Summers 2016). Angelika Nadeau, a pro-Sanders supporter from Franklin Pierce University, also rejected those sentiments, telling the *Atlantic* that although it would be great to see a woman president one day, "that doesn't mean Hillary is the right woman" (Ball 2016a). Viewing Steinem's assertion as a "sweeping condemnation of young women," many of Sanders's leading women supporters launched a petition drive to have Steinem "walk back" her statement. Steinem later apologized "for what's been misinterpreted as implying young women aren't serious in their politics" (Action Network 2016).

Yet underlying the points raised by Albright and Steinem and Hillary Clinton's many other passionate female supporters was the concern that younger women voting in the Democratic primaries failed to consider the challenges that women continue to face in the workplace and in public life, particularly when dealing with work/family balance issues. Indeed, one study found that Democratic women who "said they were discriminated against because of gender were more likely to choose Clinton over Sanders" (Poloni-Staudinger, Strachan, and Schaffner 2016). Interestingly, the study also found that *younger* Democratic women who reported experiencing gender discrimination were more likely to vote for Clinton instead of Sanders, which supports the notion that women's life experiences may have led some of them to be more willing to select Clinton because she was a woman. However, Clinton's much stronger advantage with older women voters likely came about because older women were simply far more likely than younger women, many of whom are still not mothers, to say that their "education or career had been affected by gender discrimination" (ibid.).

Turning back to Bernie Sanders, his populist message greatly appealed to younger Democratic voters, both male and female. In a few cases, however, Bernie's most ardent young male supporters—dubbed "Bernie Bros" by the *Atlantic*—were called to task for their sometimes hateful, misogynist rhetoric on social media aimed toward Hillary Clinton and her supporters (Meyer 2015). One common meme involved lambasting Clinton's female supporters for showing gender solidarity for their candidate, such as one Bernie Bro supporter who tweeted the following comment under a photo of then-New Hampshire Governor Jeanne Shaheen with Hillary Clinton at a campaign rally: "their vaginas are making terrible choices" (BBC Trending 2016). Several female reporters, such as Joan Walsh, the national-affairs correspondent with the left-leaning *The Nation* magazine, also reported receiving misogynistic hate "tweets" from Sanders's supporters after they expressed criticism of Sanders (Walsh 2016).

Bernie Sanders and his campaign quickly moved to distance themselves from such tactics. For instance, Sanders told *Ebony* magazine that some of his followers went "over the edge" in their support, apologizing for their behavior (Lemieux 2016). Sanders's Deputy Communications Director, Mike Casca, implored their followers on Twitter to "please follow the senator's lead and be respectful when people disagree with you" (Casca 2016). Still other commentators argued that the Bernie Bros phenomenon was overblown. As described by *Slate*'s Amanda Hess, the Bernie Bro argument "stretched beyond recognition by both its champions and its critics. What began as a necessary critique of leftist sexism has been replaced by a pair of straw men waving their arms in the wind" (Hess 2016). Moreover, research by Kelly Dittmar and Melissa Deckman demonstrated that Sanders's younger male supporters actually expressed more progressive views about gender equality than Clinton's younger male supporters, which suggests that the Bernie Bros likely made up only a small portion of Sanders's voting coalition (Dittmar and Deckman 2016).

Turning to their rhetorical styles, some commentators pointed to unequal treatment faced by the candidates in the Democratic primaries that was rooted in gender stereotypes. Much was made, for example, of Bernie Sanders's frank, no-holds-bar style on the campaign trail, particularly his penchant for shouting from the podium at his rallies (Healy and Berenstein 2015). While some argued that Sanders should tone down the yelling during his rallies and his debate performances, most of his supporters largely viewed Sanders's strong delivery style as a hallmark of his passionate views (Roberts 2015). As political scientist Kelly Dittmar (2016a) reminds us, voters often hold women candidates to a different standard when it comes to how they deliver their political messages:

> For example, men are expected to be assertive and loud in proving masculinity, while women's femininity is expressed by being polite, reserved, and soft-spoken.

> It's no surprise, then, that reactions to women's assertiveness can often evoke negative tropes of "nagging" wives or "lecturing" mothers. Similarly, female expressions of passion or excitement are frequently amplified as proof of emotional instability. As a result, women candidates are often coached to pay particular attention to vocal style and tone, to walk a fine line between being animated without appearing out of control and being assertive without being perceived as overly aggressive.

Hillary Clinton, herself, brought up this point at an early debate with Bernie Sanders, when the two clashed about gun control. Coming from a predominantly rural state, Sanders's record on guns was one of the few areas in which his position was more conservative than Clinton, who has always been an outspoken critic of the NRA and the pro-gun lobby. As she responded in one debate about her passion on gun control, "I've been told to stop shouting about ending gun violence. Well, I haven't been shouting. But sometimes, when a woman speaks out, some people *think* it's shouting. But I won't be silenced, and I hope you won't be either" (emphasis in original, Marcotte 2015).

Calling out such gender inequities early in her campaign marked a point of differentiation for Clinton from her 2008 campaign. Clinton also seemed far more comfortable in the 2016 race with acknowledging and even embracing the important symbolic importance of her quest to become her party's first female presidential nominee. As we detail in chapter 5, Clinton was reluctant to embrace her gender identity in her first bid for the presidency, in part because of concern that voters expect toughness from their commander in chief. However, early in the 2016 contest she told the *Des Moines Register* that she expected "to be judged on my merits," and continued, "and the historic nature of my candidacy is one of the merits that I hope people take into account" (*Des Moines Register* 2015). She routinely talked about her grandchildren on the campaign trail as well, and poked fun of critics who decried both her gender and age by telling an audience in a campaign stop in South Carolina in 2015, "Now I may not be the youngest candidate in the race. But I have one big advantage: I've been coloring my hair for years. Nooooooo . . . you're not going to see me turning white in the White House" (Karni 2015). In the primary contests, Hillary Clinton was a candidate who seemed far more comfortable embracing her feminine *and* feminist sides.

## The Republican Primaries

On the Republican side, Carly Fiorina was the sole woman to throw her hat in the ring for her party's presidential nomination, although she faced a far more crowded field than Hillary Clinton. In fact, Fiorina's own announcement for the presidency, via YouTube, took an early jibe at the Democratic frontrunner. Fiorina's video announcement begins with her clicking off a television that was airing Clinton's own presidential announcement video, turning to the cameras, and declaring that our founders "never intended for us to have a professional political class," instead wanting "citizens and leaders to step forward." She implored voters who were tired of political corruption, and who believed it is "time to declare the end of identity politics," to join her campaign.

Despite impressive debate performances, former businesswoman Carly Fiorina's campaign for the GOP nomination in 2015–2016 stalled.
*Source*: AP Photo / John Locher.

The rejection of identity politics is a theme long embraced by conservative activists, including many Republicans. Roughly speaking, identity politics can be described as a political approach employed by progressive activists who advocate for the civil rights of marginalized groups in society, based on race, ethnicity, sexual orientation, class, or gender. While liberals view such activism as vital to addressing structural or socioeconomic barriers that they believe contribute to the continued discrimination of such groups in society, conservatives argue that such an approach is divisive and misguided. When it comes to women's rights, in particular, right wing women such as Carly Fiorina take issue with liberal feminists' claims that federal regulation and more government programs are necessary for women to make greater gains in the workplace or help lift women out of poverty (Deckman 2016a). They also fiercely disagree with liberal feminists' position that the legalization of abortion is essential to women's fundamental rights.

Carly Fiorina garnered much attention in her presidential campaign for being willing to attack Planned Parenthood, a nonprofit health organization for women that is also the leading provider of legal abortions nationally. For several years, Republicans in Congress have tried to deny federal funding to the group, which also provides basic health care services to poor women nationwide; polls show that most Americans support the organization and believe the federal government should fund it (Page and Firozi 2015). Federal law already prohibits federal funding of abortion services for low-income women, but conservatives opposed to abortion believe that the organization is able to spend more on abortions because it receives federal funds to cover its other expenses. In the summer of 2015, at the start of the contentious GOP presidential race, a series of secretly filmed videos of Planned Parenthood employees suggested that the organization was selling fetal organs and tissues for profit. (A later investigation of the allegations determined them to be false.) However, Fiorina passionately took Planned Parenthood to task in an early debate over the films, and while critics denounced her claims of footage she had viewed in the film as inaccurate, she managed, in the words of *The Atlantic*'s David A. Graham (2015), to "make Planned Parenthood a national story."

Notably, during the campaign Fiorina showed a willingness to embrace the term feminist—a departure from other candidates who have previously sought the Republican Party's presidential nomination. Although a strong opponent of abortion rights, she shares with more liberal feminists the view that women often must navigate sexism in their professional lives. In one well-received video she filmed for Buzzfeed news in July 2015, titled "What If Men Were Treated Like Women in the Office?," she asked puzzled men in an office setting questions often lobbed at women workers that are never addressed to male professionals, such as "How do you walk in those shoes?" and "How do you manage the work life balance?" (Buzzfeed News 2015). In addition, Fiorina penned an essay, "Redefining Feminism," for the popular website medium.com, urging businesses and society to embrace women as leaders, noting "we still can make our country a better place by fully tapping the potential of every woman" (Fiorina 2015).

Fiorina acknowledged facing her share of sexist treatment on the campaign trail as well. In one debate, when asked by the moderator about her biggest weakness, she said "after the last debate, I was told I didn't smile enough," adding "but I also think these are very serious times" (Paquette 2015). She told the *Boston Herald*'s Herald Drive Show that her critics often called her "bimbo" and another "b word" (*Boston Herald* 2015). Many people in the media denounced her business-like, no-nonsense approach as being too unfeminine and harsh. For example, one online newsmagazine, rawstory.com, criticized Fiorina when her campaign put out a video of the candidate holding a puppy with the headline "Not Even a Room Full of Puppies Can Make Carly Fiorina Likable" (Boggioni 2015). Even the women co-hosts of the daytime show *The View* claimed that Fiorina's face looked "demented" during her performances in presidential primary debates (Richardson 2015). Fiorina called *The View* hosts to task, arguing that they would never pick on Hillary Clinton's appearance, saying conservative women politicians are often held to a different standard even than liberal women politicians.

Of course, probably the best-known dig that Fiorina had to endure during the campaign came from Donald Trump in a September 2015 article with *Rolling Stone*. In the interview, Trump maligned Fiorina, who at the time was experiencing a brief surge in the polls thanks to her strong debate performances. Of Fiorina he said, "Look at that face! Would anyone vote for that? Can you imagine that, the face of our next president?" (Estepa 2015). When Trump tried to defend his statement in the debate that followed, claiming that his comments were about her "persona" and not her looks, Carly Fiorina's response—"I think women all over this country heard very clearly what Mr. Trump said"—drew praise from the debate audience and Americans nationally (Gambino 2015). In a speech to the National Federation of Republican Women, Fiorina told the audience, "Ladies, look at this face. This is the face of a 61-year-old woman. I am proud of every year and every wrinkle. . . . And look at all of your faces—the faces of leadership" (Glueck 2015).

Despite this acclaim for her response to Trump, and what many viewed as her compelling debate performances, which showcased her strong grasp of the issues, especially foreign policy, Fiorina dropped out of the race after a disappointing performance in the New Hampshire primary. Her name did briefly reappear in the context of the primary contests—toward the end of the presidential primary, Texas Senator Ted Cruz told supporters that he would select Fiorina as his running mate if he were selected as his party's nominee, and she briefly campaigned with the senator before he conceded the race to Donald Trump in May 2016.

Trump's boorish comments and behavior about women did not stop with Carly Fiorina, however. In the first GOP debate held in August 2015, Fox news anchor Megyn Kelly asked Donald Trump about his previous statements about women:

> Your Twitter account has several disparaging comments about women's looks. You once told a contestant on the Celebrity Apprentice it would be a pretty picture to see her on her knees. Does that sound to you like the temperament of a man we should elect as president? And how do you answer the charge from Hillary Clinton—that you are part of the war on women? (quoted on Epstein 2015).

Trump's initial response was to chastise the country as being "too politically correct," and then issuing a veiled threat to Kelly while onstage: "Honestly, Megyn, if you don't like it, I'm sorry. I've been very nice to you, although I could probably maybe not be based on the way you've treated me, but I wouldn't do that" (ibid.). Later, in an interview with CNN's Don Lemon,

Trump complained that Kelly's questions were "off-base," adding, "You could see there was blood coming out of her eyes. Blood coming out of her wherever" (Wattles and Stelter 2015). Those comments got him disinvited from a conservative gathering held shortly after the debate; Trump later said that critics who claimed he was implying that Kelly's barbed line of questioning came as a result of her menstruating were "sick people."

Later, in March 2016, Donald Trump also tweeted an unflattering photo of his primary opponent Ted Cruz's wife Heidi juxtaposed against his glamorous wife Melania, a former model, telling "Lyin' Ted"—his colorful nickname for the Texas senator—that "a picture is worth a thousand words." He also defended his former campaign manager, Corey Lewandowski, who was charged with battery for grabbing a female reporter's arm during a campaign event (Miller 2016). Trump said, despite evidence to the contrary, that the reporter made up the story.

Trump also sought to shore up his masculine credentials while seeking the nation's highest office by cutting his *male* opponents down for being weak and effeminate. For instance, when former Florida Governor Jeb Bush aired an interview with his mother—former first lady Barbara Bush—shortly after his poor performance in the New Hampshire primaries, Trump maligned "poor, poor Jeb Bush," tweeting, "Wow, Jeb Bush, whose campaign is a total disaster, had to bring in mommy to take a slap at me. Not nice!" (Tani 2016).

In a series of exchanges with Florida Senator Marco Rubio, viewed by many pundits as an early GOP frontrunner for the nomination, Trump repeatedly referred to Rubio as a "lightweight" and coined the nickname "Little Marco" during one March debate. In a rally following that debate, Rubio conceded that Trump is taller physically, but questioned why his hands were so small, finishing with this quip: "And you know what they say about men with small hands? You can't trust them." In the next debate, Trump responded to this slight by raising his hands, and telling the audience: "Look at these hands. Do they look small? And, [Rubio] referred to my hands—'if they're small, something else must be small.' I guarantee you there's no problem. I guarantee" (Krieg 2016). Newspaper headlines later that evening noted that this was the first time in presidential debate history that a candidate "defended the size of his penis" (ibid.).

While such "locker room" talk may have been entertaining to millions of Americans, scholar Kelly Dittmar (2016b) describes these problematic exchanges as "the politics of emasculation," noting that the Republicans seeking their party's nomination spent "far less energy debating substantive qualifications for office than fighting to uphold stereotypical expectations of presidential masculinity" during this campaign stretch. (As we detail in the next section, Trump also brought a "hyper-masculine" style to his general election campaign against Hillary Clinton, which arguably had more impact because he was facing the nation's first female presidential nominee.)

Trump's antics early in the campaign trail during the primary season led to very high disapproval numbers among women nationally. *Politico*, the online political magazine, reported a collection of March 2016 polls from a number of independent sources showcasing extremely large disapproval ratings of him from women, ranking from 67 percent from Fox News to 74 percent from ABC News/*Washington Post* (Shepard 2016). Perhaps somewhat surprisingly, however, Trump was able to secure a plurality of women's votes during the Republican primaries and many conservative women rallied to his defense. Deckman (2016b) argues that such women were willing to overlook his offensive gendered rhetoric because of his tough stands on immigration and national security, and his criticism of the Republican Party, which resonated not just with many white working-class men, but also with conservative female activists at the grassroots. Trump supporters more generally, compared with Republicans who backed candidates such as Ted Cruz or John Kasich in the primaries, believed the country had gotten so far off track that "we need a leader who is willing to break some rules to set things right," according to a poll from the Public Religion Research Institute. This same survey also found that more than two-thirds (68 percent) of "Trump supporters, compared with 57 percent of Ted Cruz supporters, say society as a whole has become too soft and feminine" (Deckman 2016c).

Turning to the gender gap in the presidential primaries, not all the primary contests had exit polls. However, one analysis conducted by the Center for American Women and Politics showed that in twenty primary races, Trump outperformed among male voters in each race, although there was a big range in terms of gender differences. For instance, in the Alabama and Michigan contests, Trump won the men's vote by 16 percentage points; in other contests, the gender gap was only a few percentage points. Nonetheless, Trump handily secured his party's nomination, ending his most unorthodox presidential campaign ready to fight Hillary Clinton for the presidency in the general election.

## GENDER IN THE GENERAL ELECTION

Turning to the general election, Hillary Clinton had to navigate gender and politics on the campaign trail like no other candidate before her. We argue that Trump's misogyny, along with the continuing gendered media coverage of Clinton, reinforced gendered assumptions among voters that proved difficult for Clinton to overcome. Despite developing valuable experience during her 2008 run for the Democratic nomination, nothing could have prepared Clinton for the nasty and gender-infused battle that ensued in

2016. Her unpredictable opponent, Donald Trump, continued his hyper-masculine campaign style in the general election. He routinely displayed his own masculinity in crude and exaggerated ways while at the same time faulting Clinton for being insufficiently masculine. His campaign likewise called into question Clinton's femininity, referring to her as a "nasty woman" and an unfaithful wife (Ball 2016b). Clinton's treatment from the media was similarly gendered. In both the primary and general election campaigns, Clinton's media coverage was more negative than positive, almost regardless of the focus of the coverage. Discussion of her personal traits, policy positions, record of public service, and health all skewed far more negative than positive (Shorenstein Center 2016).

The general election campaign illuminated the persistence of gender-based voter stereotypes about women's capacity to govern. Despite women's continuing inroads into political office in the United States, one out of five voters polled in 2016 did not believe the United States was ready for a female president (Dutton et al. 2016). Why not? Approximately 20 percent of the American population continue to express reservations about a generic female president's ability to handle a military crisis, keep the country safe from terrorism, deal with the economy, and make difficult decisions, illustrating our stubbornly gendered notions of leadership (Associated Press 2016). As chapter 5 discusses in more detail, voters often rely on gendered stereotypes in evaluating candidate characteristics and capacities in handling particular policy issues: men are presumed to bring masculine character traits, such as decisiveness, toughness, and overall competence, to the table while women are given the edge in feminine qualities, such as compassion, honesty, and morality. When it comes to policy, men are rated as more capable in defense and foreign policy, economic matters, and crime while women have an advantage in health care, education, and social security (Rosenwasser and Seale 1988; Sanbonmatsu 2002).

Especially when seeking the office of the presidency, these stereotypes work to men's advantage and women's disadvantage. Simply put, voters especially value masculine traits and policy expertise over feminine ones in their presidential candidates (Rosenwasser and Seale 1988). Men must demonstrate sufficient masculinity to be taken seriously for the presidency, but their status as men gives them a leg up. Voters have little reason to question how their male gender affects their capacity to govern: some male presidents have performed better than others, but because only men have held the office, one particularly poor performer is not read as an indictment on all men, but reflects rather on the individual himself (see also chapter 8). By virtue of their historical monopoly on the position, male candidates benefit from being presumed competent and capable from the start, even when compelling evidence may suggest otherwise.

Because women are the anomaly, evaluating them is more complicated for a couple of reasons. For one, voters and the media typically draw on entrenched masculine notions of power and leadership to determine how women stack up. As journalist Ezra Klein (2016) argues, our societal preference for the masculine is very clearly illustrated in our notions of what distinguishes a good candidate from an inferior candidate: "presidential campaigns are built to showcase the stereotypically male trait of standing in front of a room speaking confidently . . . [c]ampaigns built on charismatic oration feel legitimate in a way that campaigns built on deep relationships do not." Klein compares Democratic rivals Hillary Clinton and Bernie Sanders to make his point, observing that "Sanders is a great talker and a poor relationship builder. Clinton is a great relationship builder and a poor talker." If both qualities were equally valued, Sanders would be faulted for lacking relationship-building skills in the same way that Clinton was criticized for her oratory skills. But he was not, because in the presidential context, feminine qualities like collaboration and relationship building play second fiddle to masculine qualities like confidence and bombast.

Second, because women candidates for the nation's highest offices are novel, voters scrutinize them more closely for how well they satisfy traditional feminine norms like compassion, honesty, and likability (Brooks 2013). Deborah Brooks terms such behavior as treating female candidates as "ladies, not leaders." The essence of treating women as "ladies" is that they are expected to exhibit both feminine characteristics as well as stereotypically masculine leadership qualities and face a formidable challenge in trying to figure out how to strike the right balance. Navigating this "double bind," as Kathleen Hall Jamieson (1995) refers to it, is unique to female candidates. And lacking any successful female predecessors in their quest for the Oval Office, both Clinton and Fiorina had to figure out how to navigate this tricky terrain on their own.

The essence of the double bind is that men are free to exhibit their full masculine selves without worrying too much about convincing voters that they also have a feminine side. As a man, Trump's masculinity was never really in doubt: he showed a willingness to humiliate his opponents, denigrate those who dared disagree with him, and brag about his ability to get away with sexual assault, as evidenced in the leaked audiotape of an interview he had done earlier in his career with *Access Hollywood*. Moreover, for his claims that he, and only he, could fix America's problems, and that he knew more about destroying ISIS than the Generals in charge of the military, Donald Trump has been referred to as an alpha male, "a cartoon of masculinity," and a "parody of machismo" (Ball 2016b). And voters appeared to give him a pass on feminine qualities, pooh-poohing his lack of empathy and compassion as well as well-documented dishonesty. At the

While many women expressed alarm at Donald Trump's misogynistic rhetoric, some conservative women enthusiastically backed the candidate, whose calls for tougher immigration policies and tougher national security measures they found appealing.
*Source*: Newzulu / Alamy Stock Photo.

end of the day, it appeared that many voters chalked up his boorish behavior and his open hostility toward women and other groups as irritating, but hardly disqualifying (Blake 2016).

Indeed, it may very well be the case that many of Trump's supporters were drawn to this hyper-masculine behavior. Melissa Deckman's analysis of PRRI data shows that two-thirds of Trump supporters believed that "society as a whole has become too soft and feminine," compared with just 17 percent of Clinton supporters (Deckman 2016c). Little wonder, then, that Trump and his vice presidential nominee Mike Pence routinely declared on the campaign trail that "broad shouldered" leadership was the only way to keep Americans safe from danger. The Trump campaign routinely cast Hillary Clinton as weak and ineffectual, and one television ad, "Dangerous," went so far as to show clips of Clinton coughing and stumbling when she went through a brief bout with pneumonia during her campaign, juxtaposed against the sound of Trump saying, "Hillary Clinton doesn't have the strength of stamina to lead in our world." As the research of Erin Cassese and Mirya Holman finds (2016), such attacks on stamina and toughness can be especially effective against female candidates who are Democrats, a party that is often viewed by voters as being weaker on national security.

Thus, Hillary Clinton faced a formidable challenge in presenting herself as sufficiently masculine. In trying to differentiate herself from Trump and give undecided voters a reason to vote for her, Clinton was caught between a rock and a hard place. If she came across as too masculine in an attempt to rival Trump, voters could dismiss her as unladylike, as a woman who has lost touch with her softer, more feminine side. Indeed, in the aftermath of Clinton's 2008 loss to Barack Obama, gender politics scholars dissecting her defeat concluded she should have run a *less* masculine and more feminine campaign (Lawrence and Rose 2014; see also chapter 5). Because voters were already convinced that Clinton was tough enough for the job, they counseled that Clinton could have gained more mileage by playing up her lifelong advocacy on behalf of women and children and reminding voters of her softer side.

Her 2016 campaign slogan of "Stronger Together" appeared crafted with such criticism in mind. Not only did it draw on Clinton's reputation as a skilled consensus builder in the Senate and as Secretary of State, but spoke to women's perceived strengths as natural collaborators. In her 2016 campaign announcement, Clinton promised to be a champion for everyday Americans. In positioning herself as someone committed to fighting income inequality in the United States, Clinton also paid special attention to policy issues that disproportionately affect women, such as pay equity, affordable day care, and paid family and medical leave (Chozick 2015). She also reminded voters that she had a shot at becoming the youngest woman president ever elected (Campaign Kickoff Speech).

Despite adopting a more distinctly feminine tone in 2016, Clinton again struggled to convince voters of her feminine strengths (see also chapter 5). Most voters readily acknowledged her impressive presidential qualifications, but evidence suggests that their final vote choices were based on factors other than her leadership capacity, no doubt shaped by her political rivals' sustained efforts over many years to paint her as cold and calculating, as quintessentially unfeminine (Gates 1996; Petri 2016). As one voter said of her, "She doesn't wear a dress ever. . . . She'll probably show up in a pantsuit for the inaugural. She's not a typical woman—she's not soft. She's so power-hungry, which is not becoming of a woman" (Ball 2016b). President Obama addressed this very issue on the campaign trail. At a campaign event in Columbus, Ohio, he specifically addressed men in the audience, saying "to the guys out there, I want to be honest. . . . You know, there's a reason we haven't had a woman president before." He continued, "[w]hen a guy is ambitious and out in the public arena and working hard, well that's okay. But when a woman suddenly does it, suddenly you're all like, well, why's she doing that?" (Kearns 2016). For many, an ambitious woman is not a likable woman.

The issue of political ambition is one that has dogged Clinton throughout her entire public career, beginning with her time as First Lady. When Hillary was tapped to head her husband Bill Clinton's efforts to reform health care in the first year of his presidency, many skeptics viewed this endeavor as political overreach, given that the traditional job of the First

Lady is to promote uncontroversial causes rather than specific public policies. After the health care task force failed miserably, she assumed a more traditional First Lady role and her approval ratings were much higher toward the end of her time in the White House. Clinton went on to easily win election as a United States Senator from her adopted home state of New York—a heavily Democratic state—in 2000 and 2006, but failed to pull similar support nationally in her first bid for the White House against Obama in 2008. During her time as Obama's Secretary of State, however, her public approval rebounded, and when she left that position, more than two out of three Americans approved of her (Pew Research Center 2015). Yet her public approval fell again when she declared her presidential candidacy in the spring of 2015 to just 41 percent, dogged by the Republican Party's relentless inquiries about her e-mail practices and handling of the terrorist attack at Benghazi, Libya, while she was Secretary of State (Dugan and McCarthy 2015). In essence, the public has always seemed more comfortable with Clinton in a supporting role, but not as a potential president (Newton-Small 2016).

Hillary Clinton was not the only unpopular presidential candidate, of course. What made 2016 such a unique presidential race is that Clinton and Trump were the two most unpopular presidential candidates nominated by their parties in years. Voters had misgivings about both Clinton and Trump's trustworthiness and likability, and even though Trump was rated as more unlikable and dishonest, these character flaws seemed much more damaging to Clinton's candidacy than Trump's (Newport 2016). The media clearly played a role in priming voters to hold such a double standard. In an analysis of 88 *Washington Post* articles that mention favorability polling numbers for the two candidates, likability is mentioned much more frequently for Clinton than for Trump. In fact, we found only two mentions of a likability problem for Trump and 21 mentions for Clinton. Journalists also framed the issue differently: they often referred to Trump's high unfavorables in polling numbers but Clinton's likability problem.[2]

Analyzing speeches at the two nominating conventions provides additional evidence that the candidates recognized these gendered standards. Trump trailed in the popularity contest, yet very few speakers at the Republican convention attempted to soften his image or vouch for his positive character traits. Instead, most people who spoke on behalf of Trump emphasized his business accomplishments and leadership skills. On the flip side, speakers at the Democratic convention spent much of their speech time attempting to humanize Clinton by telling personal stories and attesting to her good heart and character. For voters, Clinton's likability "problem" was a larger hurdle to overcome than was Trump's. For men, being

---

[2]Analysis conducted by authors, with assistance from Rose Allen.

masculine is sufficient. For women, being masculine without being sufficiently feminine is highly problematic. Or as Adrienne Kimmell, the executive director of the Barbara Lee Family Foundation, succinctly summarizes: "For women candidates, likability is linked to electability, and that's not the case for men" (quoted in Page 2016).

Donald Trump's campaign also behaved in ways that suggest he was attempting to negate any perceived advantage Hillary Clinton might have in feminine character traits, labeling her "Crooked Hillary" to cast doubt on her honesty as well as moral and ethical compass. Because women are expected to be more ethical and honest, by tagging Clinton as "crooked," Trump could continuously prime voters to scrutinize and penalize her for falling short of "ladylike" behavior while simultaneously engaging in more egregiously dishonest behavior himself. Because the public begins with lower expectations about men's honesty (Pew Research Center 2015), Trump could essentially fabricate stories to keep the issue of trustworthiness in the public eye, expecting that voters would use gendered notions of proper behavior and hold Clinton to a higher standard. As journalist Susan Page of *USA Today* suggests, "[m]ale candidates face lower expectations they will be honest, and voters are quicker to forgive them when they aren't." Adrienne Kimmell adds, "When women are pushed off of or fall off their honesty-and-ethical pedestal, it is very, very hard for them to climb back up, and that isn't the case for men" (Page 2016).

For Clinton, climbing back up on the pedestal proved nearly impossible. Months after she was cleared by the FBI of any criminal wrong-doing for setting up her own e-mail server while Secretary of State, FBI Director James Comey made the highly controversial decision to re-open the investigation a mere two weeks before the November election. The decision was particularly suspicious for a number of reasons, but particularly because Comey broke with standard protocol by commenting on an ongoing investigation and potentially violated federal law by behaving in a way that could reasonably be interpreted as attempting to influence the outcome of the presidential election (Hodges 2016). The re-opened investigation turned up absolutely nothing new, but led many Clinton campaign staff and supporters to conclude that Comey's actions sealed the deal for Trump. Not only was the timing particularly problematic as undecided voters were running out of time to make up their minds, but the narrative played perfectly into Trump's strategy of painting Clinton as fundamentally corrupt (McElwee, McDermott, and Jordan 2017).

And Trump's strategy appeared to work. Despite much evidence to the contrary, voters persisted in evaluating Clinton and Trump as about equally trustworthy (36 percent viewed Clinton as honest and trustworthy and 33 percent viewed Trump similarly). Examining nearly 400 candidate statements on the campaign trail, however, PolitiFact rated Clinton as far and away the more truthful candidate: 52 percent of her statements were rated true or mostly true while only 15 percent of Trump's received the same rating. At the other end of the spectrum, a full 70 percent of Trump's statements were rated as false, well over twice the number reported for Clinton (28 percent). In the most egregious category, statements dubbed so dishonest as to be "pants on fire," Trump was the far worse offender. Nearly one out of five of his statements received such a designation (18 percent) while a mere three out of one hundred (3 percent) of Clinton's did (Sharockman 2016).

And according to both *Washington Post* journalist Paul Waldman and scholar Thomas Patterson, the mainstream media contributed to voters' distorted assessment of the candidates' trustworthiness by employing remarkably different and unfair standards in their coverage of Clinton and Trump. Waldman (2016) suggests that the media essentially locked in on different frames for the respective candidates: Trump the crazy/bigoted one and Clinton the corrupt one. Once these frames were in place, every one of Clinton's steps was investigated and reinvestigated for evidence of corrupt wrongdoing. As he argues, "even when the new information serves to exonerate Clinton rather than implicate her in wrongdoing, the coverage still emphasizes that the whole thing just 'raises questions' about her integrity." In contrast, he continues, "when it comes to Trump . . . we've seen a very different pattern. Here's what happens: A story about some corrupt dealing emerges, usually from the dogged efforts of one or a few journalists; it gets discussed for a couple of days; and then it disappears." Political scientist Thomas Patterson (Shorenstein Center 2016) goes a step further, taking the media to task for failing to distinguish between the two candidates' weaknesses and thereby implying that both were equally flawed. As he puts it, "when journalists can't, or won't, distinguish between allegations directed at the Trump Foundation and those directed at the Clinton Foundation, there's something seriously amiss."

So how did voters respond? When we look at other public opinion measures for the two candidates, the results are initially encouraging but ultimately suggest the power of the double bind. Zeroing in on two key leadership traits, qualifications and temperament for office, reveals substantial advantages for Clinton. A majority of voters agreed that Clinton was qualified (52 percent) and had the right temperament to be president (55 percent), while much smaller minorities agreed that Trump satisfied such criteria (38 percent and 35 percent) (CNN 2016). On this score, there appears to be no double standard: Clinton undeniably possessed greater government experience than Trump and was far less combative and reckless on the campaign trail.

But when we examine how voters' assessment of both candidates affected their actual votes, we find evidence of a double standard. Trump secured 94 percent of the votes of those who thought he had the right temperament to be president and 94 percent of the votes of those who thought he was qualified to serve as president. For Trump, convincing voters that he had the right temperament and qualifications for office virtually assured their votes for him. For Clinton, these same two indicators were less telling predictors of vote choice. She secured 83 percent of the votes from those who agreed that she had the temperament to be president and 86 percent of the votes from voters who agreed she was qualified to serve as president (CNN 2016). Clinton convinced plenty of people that she possessed the necessary leadership qualities to be president, but these sentiments were not enough to sew up their votes in the way in which they were for Trump. The differences are not extraordinary, but certainly large enough to shape the final electoral outcome. These findings suggest that at least some voters downplayed Clinton's experience and qualifications, or that voters did not draw on their perceptions of the candidates' qualifications and temperament in gender-neutral ways.

The double standard is even more obvious when we examine voters who thought Trump and Clinton compared favorably on leadership traits, roughly 20 percent of the voting population. Despite such similar evaluations, these voters overwhelmingly chose Trump over Clinton. Among those who deemed both Clinton and Trump suitable in temperament, a whopping 77 percent ultimately voted for Trump and 20 percent for Clinton. A similar pattern exists when we consider voters' perceptions of the candidates' qualifications. Among those who thought both were qualified, 71 percent voted for Trump and 22 percent for Clinton (CNN 2016).

Looking at the voters who held more negative attitudes about each candidate, the same pattern persists. Among those who thought neither candidate had the right temperament to be president, 67 percent ultimately voted for Trump, more than four times the number (12 percent) who selected Clinton. For those who found neither candidate particularly qualified, 66 percent voted for Trump and 15 percent for Clinton (CNN 2016). If voters were gender neutral in their assessment of these candidates' suitability for the presidency, these numbers should be much more comparable. The fact that Trump received nearly four times more votes across all of these categories suggests that voters were using other criteria to determine their final vote choices. And since they compared favorably on feminine qualities such as trustworthiness and honesty, the evidence seems to suggest that Clinton was penalized for her perceived feminine failings while Trump was never expected to exhibit them in the first place.

Of course, the decision to cast the ballot for president involves multiple influences, not merely perceptions of the candidates' temperament, trustworthiness, and leadership qualities. For instance, voters in the same exit poll were asked whether empathy, experience, good judgment, or the ability to bring change was the single candidate quality that mattered most to them when they voted in 2016. Among the roughly 57 percent who cited the first three qualities listed above as mattering most to their vote choice, Clinton was the candidate far more likely to have been selected by such voters. Yet the single criteria that mattered most to a clear plurality of voters—roughly 4 in 10 voters—is also revealing in terms of the election's ultimate outcome: 82 percent of voters who prioritized the ability to bring change selected Trump compared with just 14 percent of these voters who chose Clinton. Moreover, as we demonstrate in more detail in chapter 3 on the gender gap in American elections, traditional factors such as partisanship mattered far more in determining vote choice than other character traits.

In sum, it bears repeating that Hillary Clinton did secure close to three million more popular votes than did Donald Trump, which is a historic achievement and demonstrates that many voters have become more comfortable with the idea of a woman president. Unfortunately for her, she was unable to win those votes in the states that mattered, and Trump handily won an Electoral College victory, in part by winning states that Obama had more easily won in 2012, including some surprises, such as Michigan, Wisconsin, and Pennsylvania, that many experts predicted were not necessarily in play for the Republican ticket in 2016. Indeed, experts say that a shift of roughly 80,000 votes in these latter three states would have been enough to shift the election results (Bump 2016). While it is impossible to know the extent to which gender alone influenced the election, our preliminary analysis and evidence suggests that longstanding gendered assumptions about women in politics, exacerbated by media narratives and the attitudes and comments of Republican candidate Donald Trump, posed a significant set of barriers to Clinton's quest to break the glass ceiling. Given the closeness of the final results, it is very likely the double standard faced by Hillary Clinton on her historic quest for the presidency mattered. How future women candidates for president navigate these tricky terrains remains an open question.

## REFERENCES

Action Network. 2016. "Walk It Back Ms. Steinem – We Aren't Here for the Boys." https:// actionnetwork.org/petitions/walk-it-back-ms-steinem-we-arent-here-for-the-boys.

Associated Press – NORC Center for Public Affairs Research. 2016. "Hillary Clinton's Candidacy and the State of Gender Discrimination in the United States." University of Chicago, NORC Center for Public Affairs Research.

Ball, Molly. 2016a. "The Kids Are for Bernie." *The Atlantic*, February 9. http://www .theatlantic.com/politics/archive/2016/02/the-kids-are-for-bernie-but-are-the -kids-alright/461925/.

———. 2016b. "What Kind of Man Is Donald Trump?" *Atlantic*, October 8.

BBC Trending. 2016. "Bernie Sanders Supporters Get a Bad Reputation Online." January 28. http://www.bbc.com/news/blogs-trending-35422316.

Blake, Aaron. 2016. "About 1 in 5 Voters Think Trump Made Unwanted Sexual Advances, but Are Still Voting for Him." *Washington Post*, October 17.

Boggioni, Tom. 2015. "Not Even a Room Full of Puppies Can Make Carly Fiorina Likable." *Raw Story*, December 15. http://www.rawstory.com/2015/12/not-even-a-room-full-of-puppies-can-make-carly-fiorina-likable/.

Boston Herald. 2015. "Carly Fiorina Joins Herald Drive." December. http://www.bostonherald.com/news/us_politics/2015/12/fiorina_blasts_gender_attacks_from_cruz_camp.

Brooks, Deborah. 2013. *He Runs, She Runs: Why Gender Stereotypes Do Not Harm Women Candidates*. Princeton: Princeton University Press.

Bump, Philip. 2016. "Donald Trump Will Be President Thanks to 80,000 People in Three States." *Washington Post*, December 1. https://www.washingtonpost.com/news/the-fix/wp/2016/12/01/donald-trump-will-be-president-thanks-to-80000-people-in-three-states/?utm_term=.5072b24df46b.

Buzzfeed News. 2015. "What If Women Talked Like Men in the Workplace." *Buzzfeed News*. July 16. https://www.buzzfeed.com/sajp/if-men-were-treated-like-women-in-the-workplace?utm_term=.dkYmvKAjR#.iil9BP5Rk.

Casca, Mike. 2016. "If You Support Bernie Sanders . . . " *Twitter*. January 25. https://twitter.com/cascamike/status/691844891652001792.

Cassese, Erin, and Mirya Holman. 2016. "Party and Gender Stereotypes in Campaign Attacks." Working Paper. https://www.academia.edu/29107953/Party_and_Gender_Stereotypes_in_Campaign_Attacks?auto=download.

Chozick, Amy. 2015. "Hillary Clinton Announces 2016 Presidential Bid." *New York Times*, April 4.

CNN. 2016. *Exit Polls 2016*. http://www.cnn.com/election/results/exit-polls

Contrera, Jessica. 2016. "Gloria Steinem Is Apologizing for Insulting Female Bernie Sanders Supporters." *Washington Post*, February 7. https://www.washingtonpost.com/news/arts-and-entertainment/wp/2016/02/07/gloria-steinem-is-apologizing-for-insulting-female-bernie-sanders-supporters/?utm_term=.dd5888b10735.

Deckman, Melissa. 2016a. *Tea Party Women: Mama Grizzlies, Grassroots Activists, and the Changing Face of the American Right*. New York: NYU Press.

———. 2016b. "Some Women Actually Do Support Donald Trump. Here's Why." *Washington Post*, April 7. https://www.washingtonpost.com/news/monkey-cage/wp/2016/04/07/some-women-actually-do-support-donald-trump-heres-why/?utm_term=.3d021bb2450a.

———. 2016c. "Why Is Anyone Sticking with Trump? His 'Alpha Male' Appeal." *Washington Post*, October 14. https://www.washingtonpost.com/posteverything/wp/2016/10/14/why-is-anyone-sticking-with-trump-his-alpha-male-appeal/?utm_term=.f0d4dcce3bd8.

*Des Moines Register*. 2015. "Clinton Hears 'Eagerness' for Talk of Female Presidency." June 14. http://www.desmoinesregister.com/story/news/elections/presidential/caucus/2015/06/14/hillary-clinton-extra-burden-president-jennifer-jacobs-des-moines-register-interview-iowa-state-fairgrounds/71224966/.

Dittmar, Kelly. 2015. "Everyone's Playing the Gender Card: The Question Is How." *Presidential Gender Watch*, August 2. http://presidentialgenderwatch.org/everyones-playing-the-gender-card-the-question-is-how/#more-3154.

———. 2016a. "Why Is Bernie Yelling at Me." *Ms*, January 19. http://msmagazine.com/blog/2016/01/19/why-is-bernie-yelling-at-me/.

———. 2016b. "The GOP's Politics of Emasculation." *Presidential Gender Watch*, February 28. http://presidentialgenderwatch.org/7010-2/.

Dittmar, Kelly, and Melissa Deckman. 2016. "In Hillary Clinton's Run, the 'Woman Card' Works in Surprising Ways. Here's How." *Washington Post*, June 10. https://www.washingtonpost.com/news/monkey-cage/wp/2016/06/10/how-do-ideas-about-gender-affect-voters/?utm_term=.f8f5b12bfd05.

Dugan, Andrew, and Justin McCarthy. 2015. "Hillary Clinton's Favorable Rating One of Her Worst." *Gallup*, September 4. http://www.gallup.com/poll/185324/hillary-clinton-favorable-rating-one-worst.aspx.

Dutton, Sarah, Jennifer De Pinto, Fred Backus, and Anthony Salvanto. 2016. "Clinton Maintains Lead after Claiming Nomination." CBS News. http://www.cbsnews.com/news/clinton-maintains-lead-after-claiming-nomination-cbs-news-poll/.

Epstein, Kayla. 2015. "Trump Responds to Megyn Kelly's Questions on Misogyny—with More Misogyny." *The Guardian*, August 6. https://www.theguardian.com/us-news/2015/aug/06/donald-trump-misogyny-republican-debate-megyn-kelly.

Estepa, Jessica. 2015. "Donald Trump on Carly Fiorina: 'Look at that Face!'" *USA Today*, September 10. http://www.usatoday.com/story/news/nation-now/2015/09/10/trump-fiorina-look-face/71992454/.

Fiorina, Carly. 2015. "Redefining Feminism: The State of Women in America." *Medium*, June 24. https://medium.com/@CarlyFiorina/redefining-feminism-19d25d8d8dfc#.ck92frl1g.

Friedman, Vanessa. 2016. "Why Hillary Wore White." *The New York Times*, July 29.

Gambino, Lauren. 2015. "Carly Fiorina Expertly Defuses Trump on 'Beautiful Face' Retort and Foreign Policy." *The Guardian*, September 17. https://www.theguardian.com/us-news/2015/sep/17/carly-fiorina-republican-debate-donald-trump-sexism-foreign-policy-women.

Gates, Henry Louis. 1996. "Hating Hillary." *New Yorker*, February 26.

Glueck, Katie. 2015. "Fiorina Finds Her Fans." *Politico*, September 13. http://www.politico.com/story/2015/09/carly-fiorina-2016-straw-poll-213580.

Graham, David A. 2015. "Carly Fiorina Makes Planned Parenthood a National Story Again." *The Atlantic*, September 18. http://www.theatlantic.com/politics/archive/2015/09/fiorina-abortion-planned-parenthood-video-debate/406168/.

Green Papers. 2016. "The Green Papers, 2016 Presidential Primaries, Caucuses, and Conventions." http://www.thegreenpapers.com/P16/D.

Healy, Patrick, and Erica Berenstein. 2015. "How Bernie Sanders Connects with His Audience." *New York Times*, October 12. https://www.nytimes.com/interactive/2015/10/12/us/politics/bernie-sanders-campaign-video-analysis.html?_r=0.

Hess, Amanda. 2016. "Everyone Is Wrong about the Bernie Bros." *Slate*, February 3. http://www.slate.com/articles/technology/users/2016/02/bernie_bros_are_bad_the_conversation_around_them_is_worse.html.

Hodges, Lauren. 2016. "Did FBI Director James Comey's Email Announcement Break the Law?" *National Public Radio*, October 31. http://www.npr.org/2016/10/31/500071704/did-fbi-director-james-comeys-email-announcement-break-the-law.

Jamieson, Kathleen Hall. 1995. *Beyond the Double Bind: Women and Leadership*. New York: Oxford University Press.

Karni, Annie. 2015. "Hillary Hair: She's in on the Joke." *Politico*, May 28. http://www.politico.com/story/2015/05/hillary-clinton-hair-118381#ixzz3c2B41NN8.

Kearns, Landess. 2016. "Obama Calls on Men to Reflect on Sexism Before Voting." *Huffington Post*, November 2. http://www.huffingtonpost.com/entry/obama-sexism-voting_us_58191a3fe4b07c97c1c53435.

Klein, Ezra. 2016. "Understanding Hillary." *Vox*, July 11. http://www.vox.com/a/hillary-clinton-interview/the-gap-listener-leadership-quality.

Krieg, Gregory. 2016. "Donald Trump Defends the Size of His Penis." CNN, March 4. http://www.cnn.com/2016/03/03/politics/donald-trump-small-hands-marco-rubio/.

Lawrence, Regina, and Melody Rose. 2014. "The Race for the Presidency: Hillary Rodham Clinton." In *Women and Elective Office: Past, Present and Future*, edited by Sue Thomas and Clyde Wilcox, pp. 67–79. New York: Oxford University Press.

Lemieux, Jamilah. 2016. "Sen. Bernie Sanders Speaks to the Issues." *Ebony*, January 21. http://www.ebony.com/news-views/sen-bernie-sanders-interview-jamilah-lemieux#axzz4V0r3Hs1Z.

Marcotte, Amanda. 2015. "Hillary Baits Bernie Beautifully." *Salon*, October 27. http://www.salon.com/2015/10/27/hillary_baits_bernie_beautifully_shouting_sexism_and_the_simple_sorry_that_would_make_sanders_look_less_jerky/.

McElwee, Sean, Matt McDermott, and Will Jordan. 2017. "4 Pieces of Evidence Showing FBI Director James Comey Cost Clinton the Election." *Vox*, January 11. http://www.vox.com/the-big-idea/2017/1/11/14215930/comey-email-election-clinton-campaign.

Meyer, Robinson. 2015. "Here Comes the Berniebro." *The Atlantic*, October 17. http://www.theatlantic.com/politics/archive/2015/10/here-comes-the-berniebro-bernie-sanders/411070/.

Miller, S. A. 2016. "Trump Goes on Offense to Defend Campaign Manager Charged with Battery." *Washington Times*, March 30. http://www.washingtontimes.com/news/2016/mar/30/donald-trump-defends-corey-lewandowski/.

Newport, Frank. 2016. "Eight Things We Learned in This Election." *Gallup Poll*, November 10. http://www.gallup.com/opinion/polling-matters/197357/eight-things-learned-election.aspx?g_source=comey&g_medium=search&g_campaign=tiles.

Newton-Small, Jay. 2016. "Is Hillary Clinton 'Likable Enough?'" *Time*, May 25. https://www.yahoo.com/news/hillary-clinton-likable-enough-193304181.html.

O'Connor, Patrick. 2013. "Hillary Clinton Exits with 69% Approval Rating. *The Wall Street Journal*, January 17. http://blogs.wsj.com/washwire/2013/01/17/wsjnbc-poll-hillary-clinton-exits-with-69-approval-rating/.

Page, Susan. 2016. "'Why Are You Yelling?' Women Still Face a Political Double Standard." *USA Today*, June 6.

Page, Susan, and Paulina Firozi. 2015. "Poll By 2-1. Funding for Planned Parenthood Supported." *USA Today*, September 29. http://www.usatoday.com/story/news/politics/2015/09/29/poll-2-1-funding-planned-parenthood-supported/73016440/.

Paquette, Danielle. 2015. "Carly Fiorina and the Problem of Smiling while Woman." *Washington Post*, October 29. https://www.washingtonpost.com/news/wonk/wp/2015/10/29/carly-fiorina-and-the-problem-of-smiling-while-woman/?utm_term=.9dba2cb134fa.

Petri, Alexandra. 2016. "The Hideous, Diabolical Truth about Hillary Clinton." *Washington Post*, October 14.

Pew Research Center. 2015. "Hillary Clinton Favorability Timeline." *Pew Research Center*. May 19. http://www.people-press.org/2015/05/19/hillary-clinton-approval-timeline/.

Politico. 2016. "Hillary Clinton's Major Endorsements." March 7. http://www.politico.com/story/2016/03/hillary-clinton-endorsement-list-219796.

Poloni-Staudinger, Lori, J. Cherie Strachan, and Brian Schaffner. 2016. "In 6 Graphs, Here's Why Young Women Don't Support Hillary Clinton as Much as Older Women Do." *Washington Post*, April 11. https://www.washingtonpost.com/news/monkey-cage/wp/2016/04/11/in-6-graphs-heres-why-young-women-dont-support-hillary-clinton-as-much-as-older-women-do/?utm_term=.b3c719d31f01.

Rappeport, Alan. 2016. "Gloria Steinem and Madeleine Albright Rebuke Young Women Backing Bernie Sanders." *New York Times*, February 7. https://www.nytimes.com/2016/02/08/us/politics/gloria-steinem-madeleine-albright-hillary-clinton-bernie-sanders.html?_r=1.

Richardson, Bradford. 2015. "Fiorina Slams 'The View'." *The Hill*, November 11. http://thehill.com/blogs/ballot-box/gop-primaries/258775-fiorina-slams-the-view-for-remarks-about-her-face.

Roberts. Dan. 2015. "Bernie Sanders' Democratic Debate Challenge: Turning Down the Volume." *The Guardian*, October 12. https://www.theguardian.com/us-news/2015/oct/12/bernie-sanders-hillary-clinton-democratic-debate-preview.

Rosenwasser, Shirley M., and Jana Seale. 1988. "Attitudes toward a Hypothetical Male or Female Presidential Candidate." *Political Psychology* 9(4): 591–598.

Sanbonmatsu, Kira. 2002. "Gender Stereotypes and Vote Choice." *American Journal of Political Science* 46(1): 20–34.

Schmidt, Kiersten, and Wilson Andrews. 2016. "A Historic Number of Electors Defected." *The New York Times*, December 19.

Sharockman, Aaron. 2016. "The Truth about the 2016 Presidential Campaign." *PolitiFact*, September 26.

Shepard, Steven. 2016. "Donald Trump's Rock-Bottom Ratings with Women." *Politico*, March 31. http://www.politico.com/story/2016/03/donald-trump-women-unfavorable-ratings-221433.

Shorenstein Center on Media, Politics, and Public Policy. 2016. *News Coverage of the 2016 General Election: How the Press Failed the Voters*. Boston: Harvard Kennedy School.

Stein, Jeff. 2016. "Let's Clear Up Some Confusion about the Superdelegates and Bernie Sanders." *Vox*, May 6. http://www.vox.com/2016/5/6/11597550/superdelegates-bernie-sanders-clinton.

Summers, Juana. 2016. "Gloria Steinem: Young Women Back Bernie Sanders Because 'the Boys Are with Bernie.'" *Mashable*, February 6. http://mashable .com/2016/02/06/gloria-steinem-bernie-sanders/#KeDTQF2VbSq9.

Tani, Maxwell. 2016. "Donald Trump Mocks Jeb Bush for Asking His 'Mommy' to Campaign." *Business Insider*, February 7. http://www.businessinsider.com/ donald-trump-jeb-barbara-bush-mommy-2016-2.

Waldman, Paul. 2016. "Trump's History of Corruption Is Mind-Boggling." *Washington Post*, September 5.

Walsh, Joan. 2016. "Why I'm Supporting Hillary Clinton, with Joy and without Apologies." *The Nation*, January 27. https://www.thenation.com/article/ why-im-supporting-hillary-clinton-with-joy-and-without-apologies/.

Wattles, Jackie, and Brian Stelter. 2015. "Megyn Kelly: I Didn't 'Attack' Trump at the GOP Debate." CNN, August 9. http://money.cnn.com/2015/08/09/media/ megyn-kelly-donald-trump/.

Weigel, David. 2016. "Five Lessons about Millennial Voters from a Philadelphia Focus Group." *Washington Post*, October 6. https://www.washingtonpost.com/ news/post-politics/wp/2016/10/06/five-lessons-about-millennial-voters-from-a -philadelphia-focus-group/?utm_term=.c30cb0bdcc93.

Zeller, Shawn. 2016. "Clinton Has an Inherent Advantage, But It's Not as a Woman." Roll Call, September 26. http://www.rollcall.com/news/politics/ clinton-inherent-advantage-not-woman.

Zitner, Aaron, Dante Chinni, and Brian McGill. 2016. "How Clinton Won." *Wall Street Journal*, June 7. http://graphics.wsj.com/elections/2016/how-clinton-won/.

# Acknowledgments

We have many people to thank for their support and assistance. We owe a tremendous debt of gratitude to the extraordinary community of women and politics scholars. In fact, the idea for this book was born over the period of a few years at the Midwest Political Science Association's annual conference, where, for many years, the women and politics panels have been both inspiring and excellent. Without the incredible community of women and politics scholars presenting papers at the Midwest and other political science conferences or writing books and articles, and otherwise advancing the state of knowledge in the field, this book simply would not have been possible. The study of women and politics has grown terrifically in the last two decades and we are grateful to be part of the discussion.

Further, there are a number of individuals who have gone above and beyond to help us along the way. We would especially like to thank three senior scholars and pioneers in the field: Peggy Conway, Karen O'Connor, and Marian Lief Palley. All three of these women have written extensively about women and politics, and each of us has used their texts in preparing and teaching our own women and politics courses. We admire them as scholars, mentors, and teachers. We have all benefited from their guidance, advice, support, and friendship along the way. In fact, we owe special thanks to Karen O'Connor for bringing the three of us together and for introducing us to Peggy and Marian. We cannot express how grateful we are to be able to work with such extraordinary women.

We would also like to thank Barbara Palmer for sharing her cutting-edge research, advice, and sense of humor with us over the years. We thank Alana Jeydel, who provided much appreciated advice at the start of the project. The authors are grateful to the principal co-investigators of the American

Municipal Officeholder Survey, Daniel Butler of Washington University and Adam Dynes of Yale University, for sharing their data to be used in this third edition of the book. Political Parity, a nonpartisan organization working to increase women's political representation across the country, also shared important data with us, data that would have taken us ages to compile on our own. We also thank Irin Carmon and Shana Knizhnik for allowing us to reprint the fabulous cover of their forthcoming book on Ruth Bader Ginsburg, *Notorious RBG*. Evelina Moulder, Director of Survey Research for the International City/County Management Association, graciously provided us updated data on the number of women serving in local councils, which we feature in chapter 6.

The three of us would also like to thank the students in our women and politics courses, who have served as our inspiration and sounding board for years. In particular, Julie Dolan would like to thank her Spring 2015 Women and Politics students at Macalester College, including Annie Gurvis, Eleanor Fuqua, Darwin Forsyth, Jake Greenberg, Gabriella Gillespie, Isabella Soparkar, and Mariah Sitler. Several individuals also served as excellent research assistants over the last year or two in helping to revise this third edition, including Roxanne Fisher, Rose Allen, Patrick Blomgren, Isabella Soparkar, Lucas Smith, and Ashley Dunn from Macalester College, Kelli Baker from Georgetown, and Caitlin Steele and Victoria Venable from Washington College. In previous editions, we benefited from the assistance of a number of highly talented, dedicated, and capable research assistants, including Alix Heard, Kate Henningsen, Laura Dziorny, Erin O'Connor, Waffiyah Mian, Michele Parvinsky, Carin Larson, and Shauna Shames at Georgetown University; Jonathan Kropf, Elizabeth Durney, Kara Bovee, Kellan Anfinson, Egle Tamosaityte, Andy Haug, Patrick McGarrity, and Ben Garnett at Macalester College; and Christy Rowan, Tracey Stewart, Becky Binns, and Martin Dunphy at Washington College.

Each of us would also like to extend the warmest thanks to a number of people at our respective institutions. We would like to thank our colleagues in the Departments of Political Science at Macalester College and Washington College and in the Department of Government at Georgetown University. We are very grateful for the supportive and collegial environments they provide. We continue to be excited to work with Rowman & Littlefield on this Updated Third Edition and have found the enthusiasm and support for the project from Traci Crowell, our editor, and Mary Malley, assistant editor, to be remarkable. We would also like to thank the anonymous reviewers who provided comments and gave us feedback on the third edition of the textbook and helped to guide our revisions in this current edition.

Finally, we all three have amazing families to thank for their love and support. Each one of us is blessed with a wonderful husband (Bill Lee, Sean Fallon, and Andrew Todd Swers) and two amazing children (Oliver Lake

Lee, Easton Sylvester Lee, Mason Wesley Fallon, Gavin Christopher Fallon, Alexander Evan Swers, and Lisa Danielle Swers), and we cannot thank them enough for the constant joy and meaning they bring to our lives. Likewise, our extended families have provided years of support and love and we want to let them know how much we appreciate all they do for us: Dennis, Glenys, and Scott Dolan, Mildred Beltre, Sara and Phil Sanchez, TC, Lily and Ruby Lee, Lucy Wang, Jeff and Cathy Winter, Jack and Rose Cavanaugh, Lloyd and Diann Deckman, Andrew and Lesley Fallon, Fatma Jenkins, Theodore and Belle Probst, Arlene and Marvin Birnbaum, Ronald Swers, Jeffrey and Amy Swers, and forever in our hearts, Gwen Swers and Shana Swers.

# 1

# Introduction and Theoretical Framework

As this revised edition goes to press, three months have elapsed since Hillary Clinton conceded the presidential election to Republican Donald Trump. Despite amassing nearly three million more votes than Trump, Clinton became the second Democratic presidential candidate since 2000 to win the popular vote but lose in the Electoral College. Eight years earlier, after her 2008 failed bid to win the Democratic nomination for the presidency, Clinton quipped that although her defeat was disappointing, women in the United States were closer than ever to the presidency, having made 18 million cracks in the "highest, hardest glass ceiling in American politics." In conceding defeat to Donald Trump in 2016, Clinton again returned to the glass ceiling metaphor, reminding her supporters that "we have still not shattered that highest and hardest glass ceiling, but some day someone will and hopefully sooner than we might think right now."

Hillary's failed candidacy for the US presidency raises many questions about American women's political participation. More than two hundred years after the nation's founding, why hasn't the United States elected a woman to the presidency or vice presidency? Why are women so badly outnumbered just about everywhere in our political system? Does it matter if women, who constitute a majority of the US population, rarely surpass the 25 percent threshold in elected or appointed offices? Will a female president lead or govern the nation differently than all of the men who have preceded her?

This book examines the ways in which women participate in politics and explores what it means for women to be fully incorporated into politics and governance in the United States. Throughout the book, we address three primary questions: First, what do we already know about women's

1

participation and impact in politics? Scholars have spent years detailing and describing the nature of women's contributions throughout the polity and we share the wealth of that accumulated knowledge.

Second, we question whether women's historical exclusion from politics has shaped the nature, extent, and efficacy of women's contemporary participation. After sitting on the sidelines for over 200 years, can women enter the political arena and expect to find it responsive to their concerns? Some feminist scholars argue that the very masculine nature of politics not only turns off many women, but also creates an atmosphere that makes it more difficult for women to succeed once they decide to try their hand at politics (King 1995; Hawkesworth 2003). For example, MaryAnne Borrelli (2002) argues that "gender role traditions systematically privilege masculinity and deprecate femininity" such that women are routinely placed in less powerful political positions and have fewer opportunities to access the levers of power even when they hold virtually the same positions as do men in politics in government. Does women's status as relative newcomers and outsiders constrain their actions or necessitate that they play the game of politics in slightly different ways than their male colleagues?

Third, does it matter if women participate in politics and political life more broadly? Does their presence signal that politics and government are legitimate and open to women, and ultimately encourage other women to become involved? When women are at the helm, do they prioritize, champion, and act on issues that matter to women? Do they change the representational process to ensure that a greater range of voices and perspectives are heard? Throughout Clinton's 2016 campaign, pundits and voters alike contrasted her emphasis on women's varied concerns with Trump's outright hostility toward women. Will the first female president behave differently than Donald Trump and his male predecessors on policy questions involving gender? Does it matter if she is a Democrat or a Republican? How might partisanship or ideology circumscribe or shape a female president's ability to speak on behalf of women more generally?

To begin tackling these questions, this chapter outlines our theoretical framework for the remainder of the book. The concept of political representation is central to the study of American politics, and we draw on classic as well as emerging discussions of political representation to explore and investigate how women participate in and influence American democracy. We begin with a discussion of women's interests and how scholars have understood them over time before delving more deeply into the multifaceted nature of political representation. Each chapter to follow investigates how questions of representation have shaped our understanding of women's paths to power, their contributions to politics and governance, and their influence. Most chapters begin with a short narrative that highlights contemporary issues and policy debates and gives the reader a sense of some of the key questions for discussion and debate raised in the chapters.

## HISTORY AND WOMEN'S POLITICAL INTERESTS

In a representative democracy, we expect that those who govern are responsive and accountable to the citizenry. Yet, before American women secured the right to vote in 1920, most individuals gave little thought to women as a distinct part of the citizenry needing their own representation. As political scientist Virginia Sapiro (1981) explains, "In the beginning there was no problem of political representation of women. The reason was not that everyone agreed that women should not be represented; rather, the argument was that women *were* represented" (701; emphasis in original). Most people assumed that women were already represented by the men in their families—their fathers, husbands, and brothers. The concept of separate spheres is instructive. Historically, men and women occupied different spheres in society. Men's primary contributions to society were in the public sphere, where they worked outside the home to provide for the family. Women's contributions were centered within the private sphere, where they were responsible for running the household, raising and educating children, and attending to the religious and moral health of the family. Of course, these "separate spheres" often applied disproportionately to white women of privilege, as slaves, free women of color, and working class women were often forced to work outside of the home to provide for themselves and their families.

As a unit, men and women could cover both spheres. But when it came to politics or policy matters, the domain was reserved for men who were presumed to be looking out for the best interests of the family and society. As one US senator explained during a congressional debate on female suffrage, "The women of America vote by faithful and true representatives, their husbands, their brothers, their sons; and no true man will go to the polls and deposit his ballot without remembering the true and loving constituency he has at home" (Langley and Fox 1994, 140). As such, there was no reason for women to engage in the public sphere: not only would their contributions be superfluous, but would detract from their responsibilities and obligations in the private sphere.

In addition, most women and men agreed that such a division of labor was proper and naturally ordained. In fact, it was fairly common in the nineteenth and early twentieth centuries to exclude women from the public sphere based on assumptions about their different "natures." One accomplished paleontologist from the nineteenth century was opposed to female suffrage for the reason that "woman is physically incapable of carrying into execution any law she may enact. . . . [As such] the sexes cannot take an equal share of governmental responsibilities even if they should desire to do so" (Cope 1888). Besides natural differences in physical strength, he also drew distinctions between what he perceived to be natural differences in the mental capacities of the sexes: "We find in man a greater *capacity* for rational processes. . . . In women we find that the deficiency of endurance of the rational faculty is associated with a general incapacity for mental strain, and, as her emotional nature is stronger, that strain is more severe than it is in man under similar circumstances" (emphasis in original, Cope 1888).

The United States Supreme Court employed a similar type of reasoning in 1908 in the case of *Muller v. Oregon*, arguing that women's special role in the family, combined with their dependence on men, provided a societal justification for limiting their role in the workplace. As the opinion stated,

> That women's physical structure and the performance of maternal functions place her at a disadvantage in the struggle for subsistence is obvious . . . her physical structure and a proper discharge of her maternal functions—having in view not merely her own health, but the well-being of the race—justify legislation to protect her from the greed as well as the passion of man. (*Muller v. Oregon*, 208 U.S. 421)

At issue was an Oregon state law that prohibited businesses from allowing women to work shifts greater than 10 hours long. Just three years earlier, the Supreme Court had invalidated a New York state law that placed similar limitations on men's working hours (*Lochner v. New York*, 198 U.S. 45). Whether women wanted such restrictions on their labor or not, the nine male members of the Supreme Court unanimously declared that women's interests in negotiating the terms of their employment were less important than their family and societal responsibilities.

But our notions of representation and whose interests should be included in public deliberations have changed over time. Many social movements have successfully challenged and expanded our notions of whose interests matter and should be included in public discourse. These social movements have persuasively demonstrated that the status quo has been unresponsive to their interests and argued that extending greater political rights to women, people of color, and lesbian, gay, bisexual, and transgender (LGBT) individuals is a necessary change.

Social movements' successes in bringing new issues to the fore, however, may inadvertently signal that all group members share the same interests. But as we know, there is great diversity of perspectives and priorities among different members of the same group. Since the suffrage movement, women have repeatedly lined up on different sides of the aisle, fighting for their own conception of the ideal world. Yet, much research on women and men in politics highlights the ways in which women differ from men, suggesting that political women have more in common with one another than they do with political men. Although the temptation is to think of women as a monolithic bloc, the reality is much more complex.

We pay special attention to the diversity of women's experiences and interests in the chapters that follow. Much of the existing scholarship assumes that heterosexual white women's experiences are the norm and in doing so marginalizes the voices and experiences of women of color as well as LGBT women (hooks 1981; Strolovitch 2007). To return to an earlier example, when the Supreme Court handed down its ruling in *Muller v. Oregon*, not all working women were covered by protective labor legislation. Women's occupational choices were relatively limited at the turn of the century, even more so for women of color. Many African American women living in the post-Civil War south continued to toil greater than 10 hours a day, working in the fields by day and serving as house servants or domestics in the evenings (Jones 1986). Sojourner Truth's famous "Ain't I a Woman?" speech pointed out the hypocrisy of treating some women as too delicate to work long hours while black women like herself were expected to demonstrate strength over and over again. Assembled before the 1851 Women's Convention in Ohio, Truth called on her sisters to recognize her as a woman, too:

> That man over there says that women need to be helped into carriages, and lifted over ditches, and to have the best place everywhere. Nobody ever helps me into carriages, or over mud-puddles, or gives me any best place! And ain't I a woman? Look at me! Look at my arm! I have ploughed and planted, and gathered into barns, and no man could head me! And ain't I a woman? I could work as much and eat as much as a man—when I could get it—and bear the lash as well! And ain't I a woman?

Over 100 years later, many contemporary feminist scholars argue that women of color and LGBT women continue to be marginalized outsiders, doubly or triply disadvantaged by their gender, race, and sexuality in a political system that was created by and for white, heterosexual men (hooks 1981; Hawkesworth 2003). Many of these authors draw on the concept of intersectionality to better understand and reflect the totality of women's perspectives, highlighting that where one stands on any particular issue is related to the various identities she embodies: race, sexual orientation, class, and religion, for example (Hardy-Fanta et al. 2006; Smooth 2011; Strolovitch 2007). While the common experience of being excluded from the polity may create a shared interest in greater gender equality, as Sojourner Truth's comments above suggest, any single woman's orientation to politics and the way in which she articulates her own interests is likely shaped by her multiple identities and the interactions among these identities. Again reflecting Truth's experience, Patricia Hill Collins (2008) argues that because white women have long been dominant, they have set the standard for femininity such that women of color are never recognized as fully feminine beings worthy of the same protections and privileges as white women.

As we demonstrate throughout the remainder of this book, "women's interests" are no longer entirely relegated to the private sphere and are rarely monolithic. But whether or not women share some of the same interests and perspectives is immaterial if nobody is listening to their voices and attempting to translate their diverse desires and policy preferences into action. We turn next to a discussion of the various types of representation to provide a backdrop for interpreting women's actions and participation in American politics today.

## WOMEN'S REPRESENTATION

Before the passage of the Nineteenth Amendment guaranteed women the right to vote in 1921, some women could legitimately resurrect the colonial cry of "no taxation without representation." Unmarried women owned property in many states and paid property taxes. With one foot placed in both the public and private spheres, the claim that their male brethren were looking out for their best interests rang hollow. Without the capacity to vote in their own interests, women had little recourse to change laws that governed their lives.

As we discuss in greater detail in chapter 2, many women began coming together in annual assemblies to discuss how best to improve their political, economic, and social status. The first of these meetings was held in Seneca Falls, New York, in 1848, where 100 attendees, mostly women, signed a "Declaration of Rights and Sentiments," modeled after the Declaration of Independence penned by colonists some 72 years earlier. The Declaration of Rights and Sentiments listed a number of women's grievances and produced a set of resolutions aimed at improving women's status in society. One, in particular, focused on women's limited political rights and lack of representation: "Having deprived her of this first right of a citizen, the elective franchise, thereby leaving her without representation in the halls of legislation, he has oppressed her on all sides" ("Declaration of Rights and Sentiments"; see appendix A). Seventy-three years later, women finally secured the right to vote.

But winning the right to vote did not make female citizens political equals in all respects. Many states and localities banned women from jury service until the Supreme Court ruled such laws unconstitutional in 1975

(*Taylor v. Louisiana*, 419 U.S. 522). The contemporary women's movement challenged many blatantly discriminatory policies that relegated women to second-class citizens, such as pay disparities in the workplace, unequal access to financial credit, and sex-segregated want ads for job postings. Such examples illuminate a central question for this text: Can we thus assume that women will advocate on behalf of other women, or does suggesting as much relegate women to a category of homogenized "special interests" rather than full-bodied citizens with a multitude of perspectives, experiences, and preferences, only some of which can be traced back to their gender? Can any one woman speak for all women any more than any one man can speak for all men?

To help consider these debates, scholars turn to theories of representation. As scholars have long agreed, representation can take on many different forms. In her classic treatise *The Concept of Representation*, Hanna Pitkin (1967) identifies four primary types of representation: formalistic, descriptive, symbolic, and substantive. A formal representative is someone who has simply been given the authority to act on behalf of others. Pitkin further clarifies that this type of representation gives a political actor "a right to act which he did not have before, while the represented has become responsible for the consequences of that action as if he had done it himself" (39). For example, members of Congress are formal representatives for their constituents because the Constitution provides formal authority to act on their behalf.

Descriptive representation, the second type of representation, is the act of standing in for those who are otherwise absent, with the emphasis on what the representative looks like rather than whatever actions she or he takes. According to Pitkin, descriptive representation "depends on the representative's characteristics, on what he or she *is* or is *like*, on being something rather than doing something" (61, emphasis in original). Proponents of descriptive representation argue that it is important to have elected or appointed government bodies that reflect the make-up of its citizenry. For instance, men are not descriptive representatives for women, whites are not descriptive representatives for people of color, and heterosexuals are not descriptive representatives for LGBT individuals: they do not share the relevant attributes or characteristics and, as a result, make poor descriptive reflections of those for whom they stand.

As mentioned earlier, women's descriptive representation has not yet come close to approaching parity as women are still vastly outnumbered in American politics today. For high-ranking political offices, such as the US Congress and state governorships, the vast majority of candidates are still male. Further, although women continue to make inroads into political office across all three branches of government, men still outnumber women by large margins. Men hold approximately eight out of ten congressional and state legislative seats, governor's positions, and judicial posts in both state and federal courts. Only four women have ever served on the Supreme Court of the United States. Advocates for electing or appointing more women to political office maintain that it is inherently unfair in an elected democracy to have women represented in such low numbers compared to their presence in the population. Or, as the organization Political Parity, which seeks to increase women's political representation nationally, argues, "A more representative government leads to politics that represent more Americans" (Political Parity n.d.).

The third type of representation, symbolic, involves the use of symbols for eliciting a particular attitude or emotion. As Pitkin explains, "To say that something symbolizes something else is to say it calls to mind, and even beyond that evokes emotion or attitudes appropriate to the absent thing" (96). Political symbols often serve as powerful reminders of underlying shared values and possibilities. For example, Barack Obama's election as the first African American president of the United States is often interpreted to symbolize the democratic values of justice, equality of opportunity, and liberty to pursue one's dreams. In a similar way, electing Hillary Clinton to the presidency would have symbolized the country's greater openness to women's full participation in politics as well as the waning importance of the doctrine of separate spheres.

Symbolic representation is often employed to legitimize American politics as democratic and accessible to all. For example, a black female judge from Texas explained the importance of symbolic representation on the bench: "When I walk into that court and see all of the pictures of judges, I think there should be someone there who looks like me. And I think for all the people who are visiting the court, there should be judges who look like them" (quoted in Frederick 2014). When Professor Anita Hill accused future Supreme Court Justice Clarence Thomas in 1991 of sexually harassing her when they worked together at the Equal Employment Opportunity Commission, she was brought before the all-male, all-white Senate Judiciary Committee to share her story. The symbolism of having an all-male, all-white Senate Judiciary Committee interrogate an African American woman about sexual harassment was not lost, and many women were inspired to run for office to remedy the gender and racial imbalance in the US Congress in 1992 (Green 2013).

Once elected, women are often reminded of their symbolic status as outsiders. Former Congresswoman Cynthia McKinney, an African American woman, was often asked to show her credentials when entering the US House of Representatives. She interpreted these routine stops from security guards as a comment on her position as an outsider, explaining that security guards "just don't think about people of color as members of Congress" (quoted in Hawkesworth 2003, 532). Stories like these suggest that symbolic representation can both enhance and call into question the legitimacy of government in the eyes of an increasingly diverse public.

Finally, substantive representation is defined by Pitkin as "acting in the interest of the represented, in a manner responsive to them" (209). For many scholars of politics, substantive representation is central to our notions of democratic accountability. Citizens and scholars alike are concerned not only with the appearance of representation in our political bodies, but also with the actual policies and actions taken by those in formal power. In her widely acclaimed best seller on women's leadership, *Lean In*, Sheryl Sandberg (2013) argues that having more women at the top of corporate and political America will be good for all women, that women's experiences in a gendered world will shape their perspectives and lead them to make decisions that are more inclusive and sensitive to issues of diversity.

Many feminist scholars agree with Sandberg, arguing that increasing the descriptive representation of women in politics is a necessary but not sufficient condition for achieving the substantive representation of women's interests. Adding minority representation to the list as well, political theorist Jane Mansbridge (1999) has outlined several reasons why the presence of minority and female group members will improve the representation of underrepresented groups' interests: minority and female representatives are more inclined to represent the views of their group at the policymaking table; they bring new issues to the agenda that have thus far been neglected by the majority; they pursue more vigorous advocacy of the issues that affect their group; and they are often viewed as speaking with more moral authority on issues that disproportionately affect women and minorities.

Mansbridge also emphasizes potential symbolic benefits of representation: the presence of racial minorities and women in political institutions builds trust and legitimacy, especially where a history of discrimination and distrust exists between the majority and minority groups, and women and racial minorities serve as role models encouraging more women and minorities to see themselves as candidates.

Throughout the text, we discuss and analyze the different faces of representation across the American political landscape. Most chapters begin with basic descriptive information, including the percentage of women who have served in different areas of government and for how long they have enjoyed a seat at the table. We also emphasize the symbolic effects of women's presence in political arenas: Are they treated as full-fledged participants in politics or marginalized by their outsider status? Does women's presence in government inspire young girls and women to become more politically engaged and active? Finally, we focus on the substantive component of representation: Does policy look different, or is it more likely to incorporate or consider women's perspectives when women are incorporated into formal and informal positions of policy making?

In the chapters ahead, we showcase a variety of political women, who are far from monolithic when it comes to which issues matter most to women or which public policies they believe will help women most. Women who identify as politically progressive often argue for a larger role for the state to play in providing social welfare programs for women and their families. Moreover, they often call on government to increase regulations on the private sector to ensure that women have equal opportunity in the work force or that such businesses provide benefits that make work/family balance easier for working parents. Liberal feminists insist that government allows for safe and legal access to abortion as well as marriage rights for all citizens, including LGBT individuals, as such rights are essential to women's full equality, they maintain. Socially conservative women, however, argue that government should restrict access to abortion and make access to marriage available only to heterosexual couples, as both policies, they believe, help reinforce traditional families and women's roles as mothers. Libertarian women, including many women active in the Tea Party, focus less on social issues and instead say government should dramatically reduce its scope and size on economic issues, as lower taxes and less business regulation, they insist, will unleash the free market, creating job growth and ensuring that individuals—both women and men—will be less reliant on government handouts. Like men, women engaged in politics bring with them no shortage of political ideas and policy prerogatives.

After reading this text, readers should have an excellent grasp of women's status as political actors in the United States, their paths to higher office, their behavior in office, the diversity of viewpoints and goals among political women, and the difference they make. We showcase diverse political women across the ideological spectrum and in all sorts of venues, not only because their stories are fascinating but also because we hope to inspire a new generation of women to become politically engaged. As we demonstrate throughout the book, women from all walks of life have stood up to make their voices heard. They did not start out as professional politicians but as women who thought they could make a difference and improve their communities by getting involved. The United States is a much richer place because of their efforts.

## REFERENCES

Borrelli, MaryAnne. 2002. *The President's Cabinet: Gender, Power, and Representation*. Boulder, CO: L. Rienner Publishers.

Collins, Patricia Hill. 2008. *Black Feminist Thought: Knowledge, Consciousness, and the Politics of Empowerment*. New York: Routledge.

Cope, Edward D. 1888. "The Relation of the Two Sexes to Government." In *Women's Rights in the United States: A Documentary History*, edited by Winston Langley and Vivian C. Fox, 166–69. Westport, CT: Praeger Publishers.

Frederick, Angela. 2014. "'Who Better to Do It Than Me!': Race, Gender & the Deciding to Run Accounts of Political Women in Texas." *Qualitative Sociology* 37(3): 301–21.

Green, Emma. 2013. "A Lot Has Changed in Congress Since 1992, the 'Year of the Woman.'" *The Atlantic*. http://www.theatlantic.com/politics/archive/2013/09/a-lot-has-changed-in-congress-since-1992-the-year-of-the-woman/280046/ (accessed June 24, 2015).

Hardy-Fanta, Carol, Pei-te Lien, Dianne M. Pinderhughes, and Christine Marie Sierra. 2006. "Gender, Race, and Descriptive Representation in the United States: Findings from the Gender and Multicultural Leadership Project." *Journal of Women, Politics & Policy* 28(3–4): 7–41.

Hawkesworth, Mary. 2003. "Congressional Enactments of Race-Gender: Toward a Theory of Raced-Gendered Institutions." *American Political Science Review* 97(4): 529–50.

hooks, bell. 1981. *Ain't I a Woman: Black Women and Feminism*. Boston, MA: South End Press.

Jones, Jacqueline. 1986. *Labor of Love, Labor of Sorrow: Black Women, Work, and the Family from Slavery to the Present*. New York: Vintage Books.

King, Cheryl Simrell. 1995. "Sex-Role Identity and Decision Styles: How Gender Helps Explain the Paucity of Women at the Top." In *Gender Power, Leadership and Governance*, edited by Georgia Duerst-Lahti and Rita Mae Kelly, 67–92. Ann Arbor: University of Michigan Press.

Langley, Winston, and Vivian C. Fox. 1994. *Women's Rights in the United States: A Documentary History*. Westport, CT: Greenwood Press.

Mansbridge, Jane. 1999. "Should Blacks Represent Blacks and Women Represent Women? A Contingent 'Yes.'" *The Journal of Politics* 61(3): 628–57.

Pitkin, Hanna Fenichel. 1967. *The Concept of Representation*. Berkeley: University of California Press.

Political Parity. n.d. "Why Women." http://www.politicalparity.org/why-women/

Sandberg, Sheryl. 2013. *Lean In: Women, Work, and the Will to Lead*. New York: Knopf.

Sapiro, Virginia. 1981. "Research Frontier Essay: When Are Interests Interesting? The Problem of Political Representation of Women." *The American Political Science Review* 75(3): 701–16.

Smooth, Wendy. 2011. "Standing for Women? Which Women? The Substantive Representation of Women's Interests and the Research Imperative of Intersectionality." *Politics & Gender* 7(3): 436–41.

Strolovitch, Dara Z. 2007. *Affirmative Advocacy: Race, Class, and Gender in Interest Group Politics*. Chicago: University of Chicago Press.

# I

## WOMEN'S PATHS TO POWER

# 2

# Women in Social Movements and Interest Groups

Angered by President-elect Donald Trump's misogynistic behavior during his campaign and fearful about a potential rollback of women's rights during his administration, progressive women called for a Women's March. The day after Trump's inauguration, more than 3.3 million joined Women's Marches in 500 cities across the United States and solidarity marches were held in over 100 international locations (Frostenson 2017; Silver 2017). Marchers rallied for a wide variety of causes including but not limited to equal pay, reproductive freedom, criminal justice reform, immigrant rights, opposition to sexual violence, LGBTQ rights, and a living wage for domestic workers, particularly women of color (Cauterucci 2017; Crockett 2017a).

One week later another group of women descended on Washington for the 44th annual March for Life to protest the *Roe v. Wade* decision. The conservative women who participated in the march were hopeful about the future, expecting the Trump administration and the Republican Congress to pass more restrictions on abortion and to appoint pro-life justices to the Supreme Court (Desanctis 2017; Green 2017).

These drastically different marches demonstrate that there is no monolithic political view about what government actions are best to ensure that America's women and families thrive. While women today are actively engaged in social movements and in political interest groups, which enhances their descriptive representation, women's engagement in causes across the political spectrum raises fascinating questions as to substantive representation. Can women even agree on which issues would best serve their interests and what policy solutions will promote women's well-being?

This chapter takes a closer look at the significant social movements that changed the landscape of women's rights. It also examines the efforts of contemporary women's organizations on the left and right as they compete to frame political debates and offer policy solutions that reflect "what women truly want." The chapter begins with the first major movement for women's rights, the 70-year struggle for women's suffrage. We then examine the "second wave" of feminism that developed several decades after women gained the right to vote, as men and women adjusted to larger societal shifts in women's roles in the 1960s, including the increasing number of women in the workforce, the expansion of women's access to higher education, and rising divorce rates. Women organized to fight against the discriminatory behavior they faced at the workplace, in state and federal legislation, and in society. This chapter closely examines these struggles and how such battles culminated in the failed bid for an Equal Rights Amendment (ERA) to the US Constitution.

The unsuccessful battle over the ERA similarly revealed that women were not monolithic in their political views, as it sparked an intense backlash among more socially conservative women and men. These individuals believed that the second-wave feminist movement challenged women's traditional place in the home and undermined the American social fabric. Today debate about women's role in society continues, and women (and men) are of diverse opinions regarding numerous political issues relevant to women such as reproductive rights, child care, and education. We consider how contemporary women's organizations on the left and right compete to frame political debates and offer policy solutions that address the challenges faced by women in today's workplace and at home.

## EARLY WOMEN ACTIVISTS AND THE FIGHT FOR SUFFRAGE

Today we take for granted women's political rights and responsibilities. But for much of American history, politics in the United States was a "man's world" from which women were excluded on legal, moral, and social grounds. During the nineteenth and early twentieth centuries, women lost most of their legal rights upon marriage and were considered the property of their husbands. Married women had no right to own property, no right to an education, no right to their children in cases of divorce, no access to most professions, and no right to the wages they earned. Gender relations were guided by the principle of separate spheres in which men were the breadwinners for their families and represented their households in the public sphere. Women were expected to take care of the home, raise and educate the children, and conduct themselves on a higher moral plane.

Despite being largely excluded from the political world, including being denied the right to vote, some women still managed to participate in, and shape, public life. One early example of such political activism is in the abolitionist movement, in which many women worked alongside men to stop slavery. Elizabeth Cady Stanton and Lucretia Mott were two such women. They met each other at the 1840 World Anti-Slavery Convention in London. Skilled organizers in their own right, both were infuriated when they were denied seats at the convention and relegated to the balcony because they were women. Many female abolitionists began to realize that their lot in life was little better than that of slaves in that they shared few legal rights. As a result, Stanton and Mott organized the first women's rights convention in Seneca Falls, New York, in 1848, which marks the beginning of the American feminist movement. Issuing the Declaration of Rights and Sentiments modeled on the Declaration of Independence, these women called for a complete overhaul of the laws and traditions guiding relationships between the sexes (see appendix A for the full text of the Declaration of Rights and Sentiments). The women who gathered at Seneca Falls passed resolutions seeking to overhaul laws and achieve a more equitable social and legal standing for women, including the right to vote (Baker 1984; Hartmann 1989; Flexner and Fitzpatrick 1996).

The organizers at Seneca Falls, however, were far ahead of their time in terms of their conceptions about women's rights and had little real chance in the mid-nineteenth century of changing either the discriminatory laws against women or social views about women's place in public affairs. The organizers, however, began to see that women's ability to participate in elections was crucial to any changes in their status. As a result, the first widespread movement involving women was the fight for women's suffrage. Moreover, the 72-year fight (1848–1920) for suffrage reflects the evolution of different types of feminism. The women who organized the convention at Seneca Falls were feminists who sought a more radical restructuring of women's place in society, and many suffragists, such as Susan B. Anthony, would follow this rationale for attaining women's right to vote. Later, other women joined the battle for women's suffrage who were less interested in changing women's status, but instead used their moral authority as mothers to justify their participation in the movement. These women, such as temperance women who were opposed to the sale of alcohol, believed that the female vote would allow for the passage of legislation that would "clean up" corrupt government regimes along with society at large. The battle for suffrage also illustrates the conflicts that emerged among women as they confronted issues of race, region, and class (Kraditor 1981; Flexner and Fitzpatrick 1996).

The early suffragists who forged their political consciousness in the abolitionist movement based their calls for the ballot on human rights, the equality of citizens, and the rights of all humans to achieve self-actualization. The Declaration of Rights and Sentiments adopted at the Seneca Falls convention included the first formal demand for women's suffrage based on the equality of humankind and the right to the pursuit of life, liberty, and happiness laid out by Thomas Jefferson in the Declaration of Independence. Men including Horace Greeley, Henry Blackwell, and Frederick Douglass and women leaders such as Elizabeth Cady Stanton, Susan B. Anthony, and Lucy Stone worked to abolish slavery and gave speeches, organized petition drives, and lobbied legislatures on behalf of rights for African Americans and women.

To aid their cause, abolitionist leaders formed the American Equal Rights Association. After a successful campaign for the Thirteenth Amendment to abolish slavery, ratified in 1865, many believed that full citizenship rights for African Americans and women would soon be a reality. However, the introduction of the Fourteenth Amendment, which protects the privileges and immunities of citizens from infringement by the states and guarantees due process for citizens, created a major split in the movement for equal rights because for the first time the word *male* was used in the Constitution. It appeared in Section 2, which dealt explicitly with voting rights (Kraditor 1981; Flexner and Fitzpatrick 1996). Supporters of the amendment argued that because the Civil War was fought to abolish slavery and there was no public outcry in support of women's rights commensurate to the call for redressing the wrongs against former slaves, this was the "Negro's Hour." They believed that voting reform must be achieved incrementally. Tying women's suffrage to this already controversial proposal—which was geared at establishing full citizenship for the freed slaves and other African Americans—could doom the amendment. Those suffragists who opposed the amendment, including Susan B. Anthony and Elizabeth Cady Stanton, feared that including the word male in the Constitution would undermine women's claims to citizenship and the accompanying rights and privileges. Moreover, they believed that passage of the Fourteenth Amendment as written would require an act of Congress or even a constitutional amendment to grant women the right to vote in federal elections. Indeed, more than ten years later, in *Minor v. Happersett* (1875), the Supreme Court ruled that by refusing to register Virgina Minor, the president of the Missouri Woman Suffrage Association, to vote, the state of Missouri was not denying her the privileges and immunities of citizenship because voting was not a right of citizenship but a privilege granted by the states. Additional attempts to win the ballot by illegally registering women to vote and pursuing a citizenship claim through the courts were equally unsuccessful (Kraditor 1981; Flexner and Fitzpatrick 1996; Cushman 2001).

As a result of the conflict over the Fourteenth Amendment and the exclusion of sex from the Fifteenth Amendment, which bars denial of the right to vote based on "race, color, or previous condition of servitude," two competing organizations arose to fight for women's suffrage in 1869. The more radical group, the National Woman's Suffrage Association (NWSA), led by

Anthony and Stanton, was dedicated to winning a federal amendment for women's suffrage. They restricted membership to women only and were active in a range of causes including working conditions for women, divorce reform, and elevating the position of women in the church. The more conservative organization, the American Woman Suffrage Association (AWSA), led by Lucy Stone and Henry Ward Beecher, both notable abolitionists, concentrated only on the right to vote and avoided other causes that could alienate important members of the political community. Rather than working for a federal amendment, they focused their energy on a state-by-state campaign for the ballot. After more than 20 years, with little to show for their efforts, the two organizations finally merged to form the National American Woman's Suffrage Association (NAWSA) in 1890, which would concentrate its efforts on obtaining the right to vote within individual states (Flexner and Fitzpatrick 1996; Kraditor 1981; McConnaughy 2013).

By 1890 the Progressive movement was in full swing, and many of the white middle-class women who adopted the fight for the vote subscribed to a vision of civic motherhood that required women as selfless, moral agents to emerge from the private sphere and engage in the public realm in order to properly fulfill their roles as mothers and wives. Rapid urbanization and

Woman Suffrage Headquarters in Cleveland, Ohio, in 1912. Pictured at far right is Miss Belle Sherwin, president of the National League of Women Voters.
*Source*: Library of Congress.

industrialization created problems of public sanitation, education of new immigrants, and a need for more public services that aligned with women's traditional roles within the family. These dramatic changes in society required women to practice civic housekeeping, expanding their involvement from the home to the school, the local community, the state, and the national government (Baker 1984). On the basis of a desire to achieve a myriad of social reforms, Aileen Kraditor (1981) notes that the arguments made by suffragists in these years moved away from calls for the ballot on the basis of simple justice toward expediency, including why women deserved the vote and what women would do with the ballot. As Rheta Childe Door, journalist and member of the General Federation of Women's Clubs (GFWC), explained:

> Woman's place is in the home. . . . But Home is not contained within the four walls of an individual home. Home is the community. The city full of people is the Family. The public school is the real Nursery. And badly do the Home and the Family and the Nursery need their mother. (Door 1910, 327)

The Women's Christian Temperance Union (WCTU) was one of the first reform groups to adopt the fight for suffrage. Under the leadership of Frances Willard, in 1881, the group called for the vote as a "Home Protection Ballot." Willard and other temperance leaders believed that women voters would pass local and state laws banning the manufacture and sale of liquor—an important goal that they argued would stop the impoverishment of families and the abuse of women and children who were harmed by husbands and fathers who succumbed to alcoholism. Thus, union literature disassociated itself from the natural rights arguments of suffragist organizations by pointing out that "The WCTU seeks the ballot for no selfish ends. Asking for it only in the interest of the home, which has been and is woman's divinely appointed province, there is no clamor for 'rights,' only a prayerful, persistent plea for the opportunities of Duty" (quoted in Bordin 1981, 119).

Through the WCTU, numerous conservative women who would eschew a rights-based movement that challenged traditional gender roles were drawn to the cause of suffrage. During many state initiative fights to grant women the vote, it was these temperance women who provided the majority of the activists in the campaigns. However, the prominence of the temperance movement in the suffrage cause also provoked the opposition of liquor manufacturers to suffrage and the industry utilized its considerable resources to finance campaigns against suffrage whenever states held a referendum on the question (Tyler 1949; Bordin 1981; Flexner and Fitzpatrick 1996).

Like the women of the WCTU, the white upper middle and middle-class club women of the GFWC also took up the cause of suffrage in the 1900s in order to achieve their reform goals. The GFWC grew out of the numerous local literary women's clubs established in urban areas in the late 1860s. Seeking to continue their education after marriage, club women studied literature, art, and music. They presented papers and critiqued each other's works. By 1890, many of these clubs were involving themselves in social reform. The largest and most publicly active clubs included Sorosis, a club of career women in New York City, and the New England Federation of Women's Clubs, a group of elite reformers in Boston. Seeking to have a wider impact on public affairs, Jane Cunningham Croly, a journalist and leader of Sorosis, invited 97 clubs to attend its twenty-first anniversary convention and to form a national organization. The GFWC grew to 500,000 members in 1910 and 1 million by 1914. These women viewed the ballot as a necessary tool to achieve their plethora of reform goals including the establishment of kindergartens and traveling libraries, improvement of the working conditions of women and children, public sanitation, and natural resource conservation (Wood 1912; Wells 1953; Blair 1980).

Although the incorporation of club women and temperance crusaders expanded the ranks of those fighting for suffrage and united women across regions, the need to maintain the support of such a wide-ranging constituency also led to the adoption of tactics and policies antithetical to the cause of equal rights that suffrage represented. Reacting to the expansion of immigration in northern cities and racial relations in the South, many suffragists began to argue that women needed the vote in order to counteract the influence of the "undesirable" elements of society: the uneducated immigrants in the North who sold their votes to the political machines and black men in the South. Thus, speakers at suffrage conventions provided statistics to demonstrate that if granted the vote, the nativist educated white women would far outnumber the population of immigrant and black men who they believed contributed to the corruption of public affairs. To support the goal of limiting the vote to the more "deserving" elements of society, many suffragists advocated the adoption of educational requirements for the vote (Kraditor 1981; Flexner and Fitzpatrick 1996). Thus, Elizabeth Cady Stanton advocated an educational qualification for voters because:

1. It would limit the foreign vote
2. It would decrease the ignorant native vote by stimulating the rising generation to learning . . .
3. It would dignify the right of suffrage in the eyes of our people to know that some preparation was necessary . . .

As Stanton concluded, "One of the most potent objections to woman suffrage is the added ignorant and depraved vote that would still further corrupt and embarrass the administration of our Government. . . . It is the interest of the educating working-men, as it is of the women, that this ignorant, worthless class of voters should be speedily diminished. With free schools and compulsory education, there is no excuse in this country for ignorance of the elements of learning" (quoted in Kraditor 1981, 133).

To win the suffrage referendum in the southern states, the movement needed the support of southern women. Therefore, the leaders of NAWSA adopted a state's rights position that allowed local suffrage groups to exclude black women from their organizations and did not repudiate the racist arguments used in favor of the suffrage cause. At the same time, the National Association of Colored Women's Clubs argued for the ballot for all women and fought against lynching and Jim Crow laws. Still the suffrage movement endured years of defeats before the adoption of the Nineteenth Amendment to the US Constitution that granted women the right to vote federally. In 1890, Wyoming became the first state to enter the union with full suffrage for women, and Colorado adopted female suffrage in 1893. A few states adopted laws allowing women to vote in school board or municipal elections. However, after the 1896 state referendum in which Utah and Idaho became the third and fourth states to adopt women's suffrage, no other state voted to give women full suffrage until Washington in 1910 (Kraditor 1981; Flexner and Fitzpatrick 1996; McConnaughy 2013).

In campaign after campaign, suffragists were stymied by poor organization and a lack of resources as they faced opponents backed by business interests, the liquor industry, and political machines. These party machines feared that armed with the vote, women would seek to ban child labor, reform working conditions for women, pass prohibition, and support civil service reform. These antisuffrage groups had the support of important political figures, ranging from state legislators, members of Congress, and former President Grover Cleveland, who pointed to the destabilizing impact women's suffrage would have on the home, the family, and the nation. Additionally, antisuffragist women who came from wealthy families (and were often politically well connected) spoke out against suffrage as an unnecessary burden on women who did not want or need it because their men represented them and cared for their interests (Flexner and Fitzpatrick 1996).

Frustrated by the continued slow expansion of suffrage at the state level, in 1916 NAWSA leader Carrie Chapman Catt formulated a "winning plan." The plan called for abandoning the state-by-state campaigns that had yielded limited success in favor of a single-minded focus on a federal constitutional amendment. The Congressional Union for Woman Suffrage also championed the crusade for a federal suffrage amendment. Led by Alice Paul, these women had left the NAWSA because they believed the tactics of NAWSA leaders were too timid. Moreover, they rejected NAWSA's non-partisan advocacy, and building on Paul's experience with the militants in the British suffrage movement, the Congressional Union women advocated a policy of holding the party in power responsible for the lack of suffrage. They also picketed the White House, as the then president, Woodrow Wilson—a Democrat—shared the same party affiliation as the majority party in Congress. Therefore, they actively worked to defeat Democratic congressional candidates and to hold the Wilson administration responsible for women's exclusion from the vote, particularly in those states where women had already been granted the right to vote and could be galvanized as a potential voting bloc to punish politicians who did not support suffrage.

Ultimately, Wilson changed his mind and supported the suffrage cause, and what became known as the Susan B. Anthony Amendment passed through Congress and was moved to the states for ratification. After 56 state referendum campaigns, 480 efforts to get state legislatures to allow state referenda, 47 campaigns for suffrage at state constitutional conventions, 277 attempts to include votes for women in state party platforms, and 19 campaigns to get a federal amendment through Congress and then ratified by three-quarters of state legislatures, this goal was finally achieved when Tennessee became the thirty-sixth state to adopt the women's suffrage amendment in 1920 (Kraditor 1981; Klein 1984; Flexner and Fitzpatrick 1996).

## FEMINISM, THE SECOND WAVE (1960s–PRESENT)

After achieving the goal of suffrage, the women's movement lost its grassroots base. The country was recovering from World War I and desired a "return to normalcy" under President Warren G. Harding. Individual women leaders gravitated to new causes and became active in organizations promoting the interests of working-class women, peace, birth control, and equal rights. The leaders of NAWSA formed the League of Women Voters, a nonpartisan group dedicated to educating women about issues and their new responsibilities as voters so that women could cast intelligent ballots and participate effectively in politics. The more radical members of the Congressional Union established the National Woman's Party and promoted a new Equal Rights Amendment (ERA), authored by Alice Paul, to eliminate sex discrimination in all areas of society. Other women began to move into the male-dominated major political parties. There were some efforts to coordinate the demands of women reformers, particularly through the Women's Joint Congressional Committee. Established in 1919, the group brought together women's groups including the League of Women Voters, the Business and Professional Women's Clubs, the American Association of University Women, the National Consumers League, the Women's Trade Union League, the National Association of Colored Women, and the National Council of Jewish Women to lobby the state and national governments for legislation dealing with education, child labor, peace, maternal health, and a range of other issues. However, after a few legislative victories, particularly the passage of the Sheppard-Towner Act providing federal funds for prenatal and maternal health care education, the failure to deliver a unified women's vote nationally and a dispute over the ERA quickly eviscerated the power of this union (Hartmann 1989; Andersen 1996).

## The Rebirth of the Feminist Movement

The 1960s provided the confluence of factors that initiated the rebirth of the feminist movement. With regard to social conditions, the participation of women in the job market grew to 35 percent of the national workforce, birthrates declined, the introduction of the birth control pill allowed more women to control their fertility, and more women were enrolled in college. Additionally, an increased divorce rate and the decision of many women to marry later in life led to an increase in the number of unmarried women.

However, women's increased presence in the job market and in higher education did not translate into a transformation of attitudes concerning women's proper place among most Americans. After World War II, American society sent "Rosie the Riveter" and her female counterparts who worked in the war industries back home, and the country celebrated the ideal of female domesticity, taking care of home and children. Working women were concentrated in low-paying jobs and many college-educated women felt stifled by the routine of domesticity.

In 1963, Betty Friedan published *The Feminine Mystique*. Interviewing members of her class of 1942 at Smith College, Friedan found that these women were deeply dissatisfied with their lives as housewives and could not reconcile the intellectual and social stimulation of their college years with the isolation and routine of housework and child care. The book ignored the plight of minority and working-class women; however, it raised the consciousness of educated middle-class housewives who now realized that their feelings of powerlessness were shared, and they could use the political process to make changes (Hartmann 1989; Costain 1992). While *The Feminine Mystique* raised the consciousness of older educated middle-class women, younger college-aged women were coming to the conclusion that gender discrimination was pervasive in society rather than a consequence of personal failings. Moreover, these younger activists believed that this discrimination should be attacked through political action. Many college-aged women participated in the civil rights, student, and antiwar movements. Within these movements women learned how to gain attention to a cause and organize and mobilize a grassroots base.

While history books focus on leaders like Martin Luther King, Jr. and Malcolm X as the face of the civil rights movement, many women served as leaders in the cause (Robnett 2000). Precipitated by Rosa Parks refusing to give up her seat on the bus, the Montgomery Bus Boycott was a key moment in the effort to end racial segregation. To achieve success, the bus boycott had to be maintained. Jo Ann Robinson, an English teacher at Alabama State College, played a key role in building support in the black community to sustain the boycott for almost a year. Robinson led the Women's Political Council (WPC), an organization founded by local professional black women in 1946, to register black women to vote. Robinson and the WPC promoted the bus boycott by organizing WPC members and recruiting students and faculty at Alabama State College to prepare information sheets and distribute them throughout the black community. She also helped found the Montgomery Improvement Association. With Martin Luther King, Jr. as president, Robinson served on its executive board and edited its newsletter. She was a member of the team that negotiated with local and state officials and helped organize alternative transportation (Hartmann 1989).

Ella Baker was another key civil rights leader who often goes unmentioned. Baker was a founder of the Southern Christian Leadership Conference (SCLC) led by Martin Luther King, Jr. A community organizer, she served as NAACP field secretary and director of branches in the early 1940s and successfully developed NAACP chapters throughout the country. At great risk to her own life, Baker traveled the South enrolling blacks in the NAACP and helped to identify ways local leaders could combat segregation despite the fact that the NAACP was an outlawed organization in the South and its members were routinely tortured, killed, or run out of town (Omolade 2004). Although male ministers controlled the SCLC, in the 1950s Baker set up its office in Atlanta, was its first associate director, and temporarily served as executive director. Baker helped organize student protests and sit-ins and, through her position at SCLC, she provided the leadership and organizational support that led to the formation of the Student Non-Violent Coordinating Committee (SNCC)—a group committed to decentralized leadership and local control (Omolade 2004). She was involved in SNCC's major projects and decisions throughout its lifetime despite being significantly older than its membership. SNCC leader and current member of Congress, John Lewis (D-GA), proclaimed, "In terms of ideas and philosophy and commitment, she was one of the youngest persons in the movement" (Hartmann 1989).

While participation in the social movements of the 1960s provided women with important political and organizing skills, women also found that their contributions were not equally valued, and they were inhibited from advancing to leadership roles in their respective movements. When the civil rights movement increasingly turned toward "black power," white activists were pushed out of the movement as new, more radical leaders like Stokely Carmichael had begun to emphasize that black men needed to regain their manhood. In the antiwar movement, women found themselves in supporting roles as only men could burn their draft cards. Women who participated in the student movement and organizations such as Students for a Democratic Society were shut out of leadership roles and their concerns for women's rights were largely dismissed. In 1967 the National Conference for a New Politics gathered 200 civil rights, antiwar, and radical organizations. When women tried to raise their concerns about sex discrimination, the conference rejected these demands as trivial compared to the needs of other oppressed groups. This led women activists to start their own women's groups in cities across the country (Freeman 1975; Hartmann 1989).

### The Emergence of the Older and Younger Branches of the Feminist Movement

Although feminism has been defined in many ways over the years, most would agree that feminism embraces a view of women's place in society that emphasizes equality, the social construction of gender, and group identity. Feminists believe that women and men are inherently of equal worth. While sex is a biological category, feminists view gender as a social construct. Historical social practices have elevated men, leading to the devaluation of women, their talents, and their role in society. In response, feminists devote themselves to eliminating sex discrimination by raising women's consciousness so that the personal becomes political and women embrace a group identity that sees their individual struggles through a politicized lens. Since the subjugation of women stems from an accumulation of private and public actions and traditions, government action is required to level the playing field and encourage social change (Cott 1987; Lorber 1994; Friedman 2002).

The development of group consciousness and the harnessing of women's political power required an active social movement. Organizationally, scholars note that the feminist movement developed along two tracks, each of which embraced different strands of feminism. These two branches of the movement have been referred to as the older and younger branches or the liberal and radical feminist movements. Liberal feminists utilized political action to effect social and political changes that would eliminate sex discrimination and allow women to achieve equal rights whereas radical feminists eschewed traditional methods of politics and attacked the ingrained sexism of society in order to raise feminist consciousness and achieve women's liberation (Freeman 1975; Hartmann 1989; Costain 1992; Ferree and Hess 1994). Both branches of the women's movement were mobilized at a time when the political system was open to the influ-ence of new groups.

The younger branch focused its efforts on local activism and community building. Utilizing skills built in the protest politics of the civil rights, anti-war, and New Left movements, the activists in the younger branch devoted themselves to consciousness raising, which involved getting women to rec-ognize that what they believed were personal problems actually stemmed from inherent sex discrimination in the institutions of society and through socialization processes. The consciousness-raising sessions and writings that came out of participation in the movement advanced the theoretical and ideological foundations of feminism. These women formed groups that emphasized equality and participatory democracy in both action and structure. Therefore, they did not have hierarchical structures with recognized leaders. Instead, they rotated leadership positions and made decisions based on consensus. One group, the Redstockings Collective, cre-ated a Manifesto modeled on the Communist Manifesto that characterized women as an oppressed social class that must rise up in revolution against its oppressors (Freeman 1975; Shanley 1988) (see appendix B for the full text of the NOW Bill of Rights and the Redstockings Manifesto).

These younger branch feminists also sought to create new institu-tions devoted to women's needs. They established women's health clin-ics, feminist bookstores, child care centers, and rape crisis centers. Their consciousness-raising groups allowed women to share their experiences, provide mutual support, and explore the societal and political foundations of discrimination. Many younger branch groups also gained notoriety for employing radical shock protest techniques. Group names like SCUM (the Society to Cut Up Men) and WITCH (Women's International Conspiracy from Hell) were designed to shock mainstream America. WITCH staged hexing events such as the hexing of the New York Stock Exchange and Mrs. Pat Nixon during the first lady's trip to Portland, Oregon, in 1968. Other younger branch feminists staged a protest at the 1968 Miss America Contest in which they threw underwear, cosmetics, and false eyelashes into a "freedom trashcan" and crowned a sheep Miss America. The groups also held protests at bridal fairs and staged hairy legs demonstrations. These techniques often embarrassed the older branch of the movement, which preferred to focus on traditional lobbying methods, and feared the impact of these protests on public support for the larger movement (Freeman 1975; Hartmann 1989; Costain 1992; Ryan 1992).

In contrast, the older branch grew out of women's involvement with President Kennedy's Commission on the Status of Women (CSW) and focused most of their efforts on dismantling discrimination through legal change. Victorious in the extremely close presidential election of 1960, President Kennedy recognized that the New Deal coalition of voters forged by President Roosevelt was declining and both Republicans and Democrats were looking for ways to mobilize new groups of voters to create a governing majority. Viewing women as a potentially emerging voting force, Kennedy agreed with a suggestion from Esther Peterson, Assistant Secretary of Labor and the director of the Women's Bureau of the Department of Labor, that he appoint a CSW to recommend proposals to combat sex discrimination in government and the private sector. The CSW would have the added benefit of deflecting attention away from the demand for an ERA to the Constitution put forth by women's groups such as the National Woman's Party, the National Association of Colored Women, and the Business and Professional Women's Clubs. The ERA could potentially split the Democratic Party since organized labor vehemently opposed its adoption, fearing that it would lead to the elimination of the protective labor legislation that Progressive era reformers had fought for in order to improve the working conditions of women (Freeman 1975; Hartmann 1989; Costain 1992; Ryan 1992; Ferree and Hess 1994).

Chaired by Eleanor Roosevelt, the report issued by the CSW in 1963 documented social, economic, and legal discrimination against women across the country and led to the creation of a Citizen's Advisory Council on the Status of Women and an Interdepartmental Committee on the Status of Women. In response to the findings of the CSW and the pressure of women's groups, governors across the country created state-level Commissions on the Status of Women. These state commissions continued the work of documenting discrimination against women and met together in annual conferences to share their findings. Thus, the work of the federal and state commissions helped create the organizational capacity for a renewed feminist movement. With the support of the federal and state governments, commission members developed the data necessary to demonstrate pervasive discrimination against women. The national conferences brought women together from across the country to share their findings, network with fellow commission members, and develop contacts inside the federal government (Freeman 1975; Hartmann 1989; Costain 1992; Ryan 1992; Ferree and Hess 1994).

In addition to the creation of the State Commissions on the Status of Women, Congress passed two important pieces of legislation to advance women's rights. In response to the lobbying efforts of labor unions and women's groups organized by Esther Peterson, Congress passed the Equal Pay Act in 1963. Although the act would not address the fact that a sex-segregated workforce in which occupations predominantly composed of women pay less than occupations of similar skill levels that are predominantly composed of men, the act did mandate that employers could no longer pay women less than men who perform the same job and established a precedent of government action on behalf of economic equity for women (Hartmann 1989; Costain 1992).

The inclusion of sex in Title VII of the Civil Rights Act of 1964 constituted the second important legislative advancement for women. The act prohibits discrimination based on race, color, religion, sex, or national origin in public accommodations and employment. The law also created an Equal Employment Opportunity Commission (EEOC) to investigate job discrimination complaints. One of the crowning achievements of the civil rights movement, the inclusion of sex in Title VII was a contentious proposition (Freeman 1975; Hartmann 1989; Costain 1992; Ferree and Hess 1994; Gelb and Palley 1996). Although sincerely supported by some legislators, particularly Martha Griffiths (D-MI), who originally intended to introduce the addition of sex as her own amendment, other liberal members of Congress including Edith Green (D-OR), who sponsored the Equal Pay Act, opposed the addition of sex to the act for fear that it would doom the bill and its efforts to curtail racial discrimination. In fact, the incorporation of sex was added as an amendment in the House Judiciary Committee by an ardent opponent of the Civil Rights Act, Representative Howard Smith (D-VA), the chair of the House Rules Committee—who hoped to doom the entire bill. Numerous southern legislators voted in favor of the addition of sex and against the entire bill. During the House floor debate over the amendment, some liberal male members treated it as a joke. In response, Martha Griffiths (D-MI) scolded her colleagues asserting that "if there had been any necessity to have pointed out that women were a second-class sex, the laughter would have proved it" (quoted in Hartmann 1989, 55; Costain 1992, 38). Representative Edith Green (D-OR), who opposed the amendment, nonetheless sought to reinforce the legitimacy of claims of sex discrimination by stating, "Any woman who wants to have a career, who wants to go into the professions, who wants to work, I feel, cannot possibly reach maturity without being very keenly and very painfully made aware of all the discrimination placed against her because of her sex" (quoted in Costain 1992, 39). Despite its inauspicious start, the Civil Rights Act of 1964 with the incorporation of sex into Title VII ultimately passed.

The controversy surrounding the inclusion of sex in Title VII impacted the calculations of the EEOC concerning how heavily to focus on enforcement of the sex provision. With limited resources and a belief that race was the major focus of their mission, EEOC commissioners did not devote much attention to the task of rooting out sex discrimination in employment. Two of the EEOC commissioners, Richard Graham and Sonia Pressman, as well as other women serving inside the government, encouraged Betty Friedan to form an interest group outside of government—an NAACP for women—to put pressure on the EEOC. When the EEOC refused to address the problem of sex-segregated want ads in which newspapers listed positions by sex, the delegates to the national conference of the State Commissions on the Status of Women drafted resolutions urging the EEOC to enforce the Title VII provisions concerning sex discrimination. However, the delegates were barred from introducing these resolutions, as they would be construed as a criticism of the Johnson administration.

Recognizing the need for a pressure group that was independent of the government, Betty Friedan and others formed the National Organization for Women (NOW) in 1966. Among the group's 126 charter members were former EEOC commissioners Richard Graham and Aileen Hernandez and seven former and current members of State Commissions on the Status of Women. Thus, the group began as an elite Washington-based network that later developed a grassroots base of chapters throughout the nation (Freeman 1975; Hartmann 1989; Costain 1992).

In contrast to the younger branch of the feminist movement, which emphasized consciousness raising to change societal norms, NOW and other older branch organizations worked to achieve equality through legal reform. They believed that changes in law and adoption of public policies such as expansion of education and child care services and enforcement of antidiscrimination laws would allow women to achieve equality in society and the workplace. Therefore, the newly created NOW devoted itself to attacking sex discrimination by adopting a strategy that combined direct executive and legislative lobbying with mass protest and the litigation of test cases that had been perfected by the civil rights movement. Utilizing these multiple political tools, NOW convinced President Lyndon Johnson to expand the executive order that is the basis for federal affirmative action programs to include sex. They also forced newspapers to eliminate sex-segregated want ads after intensive lobbying and a protest campaign that included picketing the headquarters of the *New York Times* and a national day of demonstrations in five cities targeted at the EEOC. In addition to reversing its earlier ruling on sex-segregated job ads, NOW activities also contributed to the decision of the EEOC to withdraw its support for state protective laws that restricted women's access to employment (Freeman 1975; Hartmann 1989; Costain 1992; Ryan 1992; Carabillo, Meuli, and Csida 1993; Ferree and Hess 1994).

The litigation activities of NOW's Legal Defense and Education Fund (LDEF) also helped break down discriminatory barriers in all areas of society. For example, *Weeks v. Southern Bell* established the precedent that an employer must open all jobs to women who wish to apply by ruling that barring women from jobs that involve lifting more than 30 pounds constitutes a violation of Title VII of the Civil Rights Act of 1964. By 1974, NOW's LDEF had participated in more than 50 major legal cases concerning issues including family law, property rights, civil rights, and employment discrimination. Mass marches brought media attention to the movement and new members and supporters. For example, the 1970 "Women's Strike for Equality" held on the fiftieth anniversary of suffrage in favor of legalized abortion, government-sponsored child care, and equal educational and employment opportunities attracted 500,000 women in New York City and 20,000 women in 90 cities across 42 states to demonstrations and rallies. These mass protests often brought together women from the older and younger branches of the movement (Freeman 1975; Hartmann 1989; Costain 1992; Ryan 1992; Carabillo, Meuli, and Csida 1993; Ferree and Hess 1994).

Although NOW enjoyed numerous successes, it also experienced internal and external conflicts concerning its goals, tactics, and methods of organization. Soon after its formation, Betty Friedan drafted a NOW Bill of Rights to present to the parties and candidates in the 1968 election and to create a plan for political action (see appendix B). The inclusion of demands for an ERA and support for abortion rights drove some activists out of the organization. In particular, support for the ERA drove away women associated with organized labor whose unions opposed the elimination of protective legislation for women, such as laws regulating women's working hours (e.g., preventing businesses from making women work night shifts) and the types of jobs they could perform. Other women objected to the inclusion of abortion rights. Some of these women formed the Women's Equity Action League, which devoted itself solely to issues regarding employment, education, and taxes. Other activists objected to the hierarchical decision-making structure of NOW that limited opportunities for local initiatives and sharing of power (Freeman 1975; Hartmann 1989; Ryan 1992). Women like Ti-Grace Atkinson of the New York chapter of NOW left the group to form the Feminists, which adopted an organizational structure conducive to equal participation of all members. Over time, NOW and other feminist groups have also received criticism as being organizations of middle-class white women that neglect the interests of working-class and minority women (Hartmann 1989; Costain 1992; Barakso 2004; Strolovitch 2007).

In addition to these internal movement struggles, the women's movement began to face new barriers in the political system. The election of President Nixon in 1968 as an advocate for the conservative "Silent Majority" that was upset by the turmoil of the civil rights, New Left, antiwar, and women's rights movements closed the executive branch to women's influence. However, Congress was increasingly open to their demands. The civil rights movement—and the passage of the Civil Rights Act of 1964 and the Voting Rights Act of 1965—created a coalition of members of Congress that was responsive to initiatives framed as demands for equal rights. Between 1972 and 1974, Congress passed Title IX to the Educational Amendments Act barring gender discrimination in education, the Women's Educational

Equity Act, the Equal Credit Opportunity Act, and the ERA (Hartmann 1989; Costain 1992).

Although members of Congress embraced these initiatives that were designed to achieve what Gelb and Palley call "role equity" for women, they would not address legislation that embraced "role change" (Gelb and Palley 1996). In fact, movement historian Anne Costain (1992) claims that the agenda of the women's movement was co-opted by Congress as the groups focused on the equal rights agenda and set aside the special needs demands such as maternity leave rights in employment, establishment of government-funded child care centers, and tax deductions for home and child care expenses for working parents that were all included in the 1968 NOW Bill of Rights (see appendix B). Such treatment by Congress convinced many women's groups that true equality under the law would require a new constitutional amendment that guaranteed women equal rights.

## THE EQUAL RIGHTS AMENDMENT (ERA)

Section 1. Equality of rights under the law shall not be denied or abridged by the United States or by any state on account of sex.

Section 2. The Congress shall have the power to enforce, by appropriate legislation, the provisions of this article.

Section 3. This amendment shall take effect two years after the date of ratification.

After women won the vote, Alice Paul, leader of the National Woman's Party, believed that women needed an amendment to ban all discrimination based on sex, so that they could achieve full equality. To achieve this end, she drafted an ERA. First introduced in Congress in 1923, the amendment was reintroduced in various forms every year through 1971. Both major parties adopted platforms proclaiming their support, Republicans in 1940 and Democrats in 1944, despite facing strong opposition from labor unions that feared its impact on protective legislation for women workers. It would be another 30 years before Congress passed the ERA. Women's groups, including NOW and Business and Professional Women's Clubs, coordinated their actions with sympathetic members of Congress, who forced the ERA out of committee in order to achieve hearings on the issue and moved the amendment toward a vote by the full House and Senate. In 1972, the ERA was finally granted a floor vote and passed the House and Senate by wide margins: 354 to 23 in the House and 84 to 8 in the Senate. During the House and Senate debates, women's groups and their allies defeated unfriendly amendments, such as exceptions for state protective labor legislation for women workers (such as laws regulating the types of jobs they could perform) and the exclusion of women in combat that sought to weaken the ERA. Thirty states had ratified the amendment by early 1973 (Mansbridge 1986; Hartmann 1989).

However, the controversial 1973 Supreme Court decision *Roe v. Wade* activated a strong antifeminist movement that opposed the goals of feminists who supported abortion rights and the ERA. Led by conservative women like Phyllis Schlafly, founder of STOP ERA and Eagle Forum, and Beverly LaHaye, founder of Concerned Women for America, the women who participated in the anti-ERA effort and the larger New Right movement were often socially conservative Christians. Many of these women were from the middle and lower-middle classes, and a large proportion were homemakers (Conover and Gray 1983; Klatch 1987; Schreiber 2008). Often mobilized through activism in their churches, the opposition forces excelled at grass-roots organization and lobbying at the state level. The women involved in the anti-ERA movement wrote notes by hand to their state legislators and engaged in daily lobbying of individual state legislators in key states. Just as the pro-ERA forces utilized mass marches and protest techniques to highlight the connection between the ERA and American ideals of equality and the women's suffrage movement, anti-ERA activists engaged in their own symbolic politics as they sought to play on the American public's attachment to the ideals of motherhood, home, and family. Thus, STOP ERA activists handed out apple pies to state legislators with poems that read, "My heart and my hand went into this dough. For the sake of my family please vote no" (Mansbridge 1986; Ryan 1992; Ferree and Hess 1994).

Feminist groups countered with national economic boycotts against states that had not ratified the ERA, hundreds of letters mailed to legislators, and protest marches on state capitols. However, women's groups did not have grassroots organizations in specific states that had not ratified the amendment, particularly the conservative strongholds in the South. Additionally, it was difficult for the pro-ERA forces to point to concrete policy changes impacting gender roles that would result from the passage of the ERA. For example, many ERA activists used 59 cents, the wage gap between men and women, as an argument in favor of the ERA. However, since the ERA had passed Congress in 1972, several Supreme Court decisions and the actions of the EEOC had eliminated some of the most egregious examples of sex discrimination, such as the protective labor laws that prevented women from being hired for jobs in specific fields and regulated their hours. As an amendment to the federal constitution, the ERA's language was vague and would only apply to actions of the federal government. Therefore, it would provide limited authority to act on issues of sex discrimination by states or private employers. Although the impact of the ERA on sex discrimination in the workplace was a source of conflict, the one substantive impact that was not disputed by either the pro- or anti-ERA forces was that the ERA would

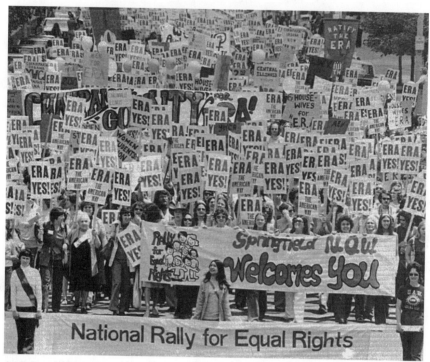

National Rally for Equal Rights

An estimated 10,000 marchers demonstrate in favor of passing the ERA at the state capitol in Springfield, Illinois, May 16, 1976. The Illinois state legislature ultimately voted against ratification.
*Source:* AP Photo.

require women to be drafted into the military if the country was to institute another draft during wartime. Drafting women was widely unpopular. In fact, one of the most effective strategies of anti-ERA activists in battleground states involved bringing baby girls wearing signs saying "Please don't draft me" to rallies at state capitols (Mansbridge 1986).

Although most Americans support the concept of equal rights, there is less agreement regarding appropriate gender roles in the realms of employment, family, and the military. Indeed, public opinion polls spanning from congressional passage in 1972 to its failure in 1982 indicated that a majority of the public supported the amendment (Mansbridge 1986). However, as shown in Table 2.1, while Americans' attitudes regarding gender roles have changed dramatically in the last 40 years, many Americans both support the idea of equality for women in the workplace and yet continue to value the ideal of women as mothers and primary caregivers of children. This ambivalence about the role of women creates conflict over policies that potentially impact the structure of family life, from public funding of child

Activist Phyllis Schlafly leads a demonstration in front of the White House against the ERA February 4, 1977.
*Source*: Library of Congress / Warren K. Leffler.

care to contraception and abortion. Opponents of the ERA capitalized on fears concerning the impact of the ERA and the larger feminist movement on the status of homemakers, the welfare of the nuclear family, the obligation of the husband to support his wife and children in marriage and in cases of divorce, and the moral fabric of society. Such fears contributed to the mobilization of a strong antifeminist backlash (Mansbridge 1986; Gelb and Palley 1996).

Despite the activism of the opposition groups, the national lobbying efforts by pro-ERA women's groups, which sponsored a large mass march on Washington to renew efforts to pass the amendment, convinced Congress to pass an extension of the original seven-year deadline that had been set when the ERA initially passed Congress in 1972. However, only five more states had ratified by 1977 and anti-ERA forces successfully persuaded some states that ratified the amendment to vote to rescind their ratification. Although these votes were nonbinding, they had a detrimental impact on the movement. The amendment went down to defeat in June 1982, falling three states short of ratification. This represents a much stronger performance than other recent popular amendments that have failed to make it out of Congress, including amendments requiring a balanced budget and amendments banning flag burning and abortion (Mansbridge 1986). The

**Table 2.1. Public Opinion and Gender Roles**

*It is much better for everyone involved if the man is the achiever outside the home and the woman takes care of the home and family.*

|          | 1972–1982 | 1998 | 2002 | 2006 | 2010 | 2014 |
|----------|-----------|------|------|------|------|------|
| Agree    | 65%       | 34%  | 38%  | 35%  | 36%  | 31%  |
| Disagree | 34%       | 63%  | 61%  | 63%  | 64%  | 68%  |

*A working mother can establish just as warm and secure a relationship with her children as a mother who does not work.*

|          | 1972–1982 | 1998 | 2002 | 2006 | 2010 | 2014 |
|----------|-----------|------|------|------|------|------|
| Agree    | 48%       | 67%  | 63%  | 67%  | 75%  | 76%  |
| Disagree | 50%       | 32%  | 36%  | 33%  | 24%  | 24%  |

*A preschool child is likely to suffer if his or her mother works.*

|          | 1972–1982 | 1998 | 2002 | 2006 | 2010 | 2014 |
|----------|-----------|------|------|------|------|------|
| Agree    | 66%       | 41%  | 45%  | 40%  | 35%  | 30%  |
| Disagree | 32%       | 56%  | 54%  | 59%  | 64%  | 69%  |

*Source*: General Social Surveys 1972–2014.

ERA has been reintroduced in every congressional session since its defeat. In subsequent years, many states added ERAs to their state constitutions. Most recently, in the 2014 elections, Oregon voters passed a ballot initiative to add the ERA to their state constitution (Phillips 2014). The map in Figure 2.1 indicates which states passed the federal ERA, which states adopted an ERA in their state constitutions, and which states have neither passed the federal ERA nor included the ERA in their state constitutions.

The fight for the ERA mobilized a new generation of activists on both the feminist and antifeminist sides and the political landscape became increasingly polarized regarding issues concerning the place of women in American society. With the election of Ronald Reagan in 1980, social conservatives gained a strong ally in the executive branch. Reagan openly opposed the ERA and the Republican Party eliminated support for the amendment from its party platform. Reagan used his executive authority to curtail affirmative action programs geared at hiring more women and minorities in government and to scale back the investigation and enforcement activities of the EEOC concerning racial and sex discrimination claims. He also used his nomination power to appoint conservative justices to the federal courts. Antifeminist groups utilized their increased access to the presidential administration to push for policy initiatives that would reinforce traditional family values and limit access to abortion and the expansion of sex discrimination laws (Mansbridge 1986; Costain 1992; Conway et al. 1999; Schreiber 2008). Meanwhile, feminist organizations aligned themselves with the Democratic Party and focused on electoral

**Figure 2.1. ERA in the States.**
*Source*: Adapted from the *Wall Street Journal* and Alice Paul Institute.

politics. Recognizing that more female than male state legislators voted for the ERA, feminist groups worked to increase the number of women elected to political office by recruiting, training, and raising funds for women candidates. In 1984, feminist activists were able to convince the Democratic presidential nominee Walter Mondale to choose the first female vice presidential candidate, Geraldine Ferraro (Mansbridge 1986; Costain 1992).

The conservative movement and social conservatives continued to gain power throughout the 1980s and 1990s. In 1994, Republicans gained the majority in Congress for the first time in 40 years and feminists no longer had access to the congressional agenda. The 2000 election and 2004 reelection of President George W. Bush meant that feminists had no allies among the ruling party in either the executive or the legislative branches of the national government. Although feminist groups helped elect more women to public office and continued to lobby Congress for legislation addressing reproductive rights, family leave, and sexual harassment,

Outraged at the election of Donald Trump, millions of women took to the streets in Washington, DC, and around the world on January 21, 2017, one day after his inauguration, to express their support for reproductive, civil, and human rights and other progressive causes that they believe may be threatened by the Trump administration.
*Source*: AP Photo / Mary Altaffer.

feminist groups found themselves on the defensive trying to prevent the passage of policy changes that would restrict women's rights, particularly in the area of reproductive freedom.

The Democratic takeover of Congress in 2006, which included the selection of the first female Speaker of the House of Representatives, Nancy Pelosi (D-CA), and the election of a Democratic president, Barack Obama, in the 2008 election reinvigorated feminists as they again gained access to policymakers. The Lilly Ledbetter Fair Pay Act, a bill to combat pay discrimination by making it easier for women to bring lawsuits, was the first bill signed by President Barack Obama. Obama's comprehensive health reform bill tried to expand access to health insurance and included coverage of women's health services such as contraception and other preventive care as services insurers must provide without charge (Swers 2013; Deckman and McTague 2015). However, the 2010 elections ushered in a Republican wave that returned Republicans to the House majority and opened the way for a new round of efforts to cut government spending on social welfare programs and increase restrictions on abortion.

After the 2016 election of Donald Trump, conservatives are ascendant. Pro-life groups and other social conservative organizations have the ear of the administration. Upon taking office, Congress and the president began implementing plans to restrict abortion and defund Planned Parenthood (Crockett 2017b; Haberkorn 2017). Whereas the Obama administration focused heavily on enforcement of civil rights laws, the Justice Department under Trump turned its attention to restricting immigration (Calamur 2017). Without allies in the major institutions of the federal government, anger over these actions has reinvigorated the feminist movement and spawned large protests such as the Women's March, which we discuss below.

## WOMEN AND INTEREST GROUPS

As a social movement, the first and second waves of the feminist movement sought to dramatically change American society by altering the accepted view of women's proper role in the public and private spheres. Social movements are both a cause and consequence of dramatic social upheaval. By contrast, interest groups are more enduring factors of the American political landscape. Their narrower purpose seeks to effect policy change on a specific issue or set of issues (McAdam 1982; Costain 1992; Gelb and Palley 1996). Often, political interest groups emerge as a result of social movement protests, when the most committed protestors and activists formalize their involvement in actual groups. Thus, the feminist movement sought to change public perceptions as a social movement while also forming groups geared at enacting specific political and policy goals. Even before women won the right to vote, they had joined and formed groups to persuade local, state, and national officeholders to change the law on issues ranging from abolition to temperance. Women's groups including the National Congress of Mothers, the Women's Christian Temperance Union (WCTU), the National Consumers League, the National Association of Colored Women, and the General Federation of Women's Clubs (GFWC) contributed greatly to the development of government responsibility for social welfare programs in the Progressive era (Skocpol 1992; Andersen 1996).

Advocating the philosophy of civic motherhood in which political activism was not a violation of the principle of separate spheres but a natural extension of women's duty to protect children and the home, these women lobbied the state and national governments for laws and programs addressing a wide range of issues, including maximum-hour laws for women and children, abolition of child labor, forestry and natural resource conservation, mothers' pensions (the precursor to modern-day welfare), public sanitation, civil service reform, and the creation of juvenile courts. These women's groups gained legitimacy by claiming to represent the interests and views of women, and they utilized their exclusion from traditional politics and the doctrine of separate spheres to claim authority as they sought reforms for moral and not political ends. Lacking the ability to vote politicians out of office, these groups were still able to sway officeholders because they had strong grassroots organizations in which local and state groups were connected to a national organization and could be mobilized to publicize issues and lobby government officials.

In her detailed study of the GFWC's involvement in the development of mothers' pensions, Theda Skocpol (1992) noted that for each issue engaged, club women consulted experts, undertook detailed investigations of current state practices, and studied the laws of other states. The clubs designed public education campaigns to gain support through moral exhortation and created model programs. Local and state legislatures were then lobbied to pass laws, establish regulatory commissions, and appoint women to these commissions. As a result of the activism of women's groups, women were appointed as factory inspectors, members of labor bureaus, truancy officers, police matrons, school board members, library commissioners, and members of social welfare agencies (Baker 1984; Skocpol 1992). Upon reviewing the efforts of the Harrisburg (PA) Women's Civic Club, a member reported:

> It is no longer necessary for us to continue at our own cost, the practical experiment we began in street cleaning . . . nor is it necessary longer to strive for a pure water supply, a healthier sewage system, or the construction of playgrounds. This work is now being done by the City Council, by the Department of Public Works, and by the Park Commission. (quoted in Door 1910, 37)

As a demonstration of the power of the activism of Progressive Era women's groups, surveying the development of state labor laws regarding women's working conditions, Skocpol found that state federations of women's clubs were active in lobbying for 13 of the 19 women's-hour laws that were passed from 1909 to 1917. Additionally, state federations actively lobbied for mothers' pensions to provide a source of financial support to widowed women with children in 24 states between 1912 and 1920. In those states where federations did not endorse pensions, the state legislature either failed to adopt pensions at all or adopted them much later than other states (Skocpol 1992). At the national level, the GFWC and other women's groups lobbied heavily for the Pure Food and Drug Act and the Sheppard-Towner Infancy and Maternity Protection Act.[1] They also worked for the establishment of the Children's Bureau and the reorganization of the Women's Division of the Bureau of Labor Statistics into a separate Women's Bureau to investigate the conditions of women workers and advocate for their welfare (Baker 1984; Skocpol 1992).

---

[1]The Sheppard-Towner Act was officially known as the Federal Act for the Promotion of the Welfare and Hygiene of Maternity and Infancy.

Like their Progressive Era counterparts, modern-day women's interest groups gain legitimacy by proclaiming to represent women's interests. However, groups have different and often opposing definitions of what constitutes women's interests and what women want. Many of the contemporary women's interest groups grew out of the feminist movement and the antifeminist countermovement. Additionally, there was an explosion in the number of national-oriented interest groups in the late 1960s and early 1970s. This interest group expansion stemmed from important changes that made the political system more open to interest group influence and from technological innovations that made it easier to contact and mobilize supporters (Berry 1997; Davidson et al. 2015). The increasing activism of the federal government during Lyndon Johnson's Great Society increased the number of government programs resulting in the creation of groups devoted to protecting and expanding their benefits and groups advocating for (or against) increased regulations on business and the environment, for example. In response to the Watergate scandal in the Nixon administration, Congress passed "sunshine laws" designed to open government activities to public scrutiny. As congressional hearings, committee meetings, and floor debates became open to the public, and information on the activities of the president and bureaucracy could be obtained through requests under the Freedom of Information Act, groups gained easier access to information impacting their interests.

Interest groups involved in elections also flourished as a result of the decline in the power of the political parties. Parties became weaker because of the expansion of direct primary laws (state parties had less control over nominees to represent them in the general campaign), candidate-centered campaigns (in which parties became less important in terms of running campaign organizations), and campaign finance reform laws in the 1970s that decreased the power of the party to raise campaign money. Following passage of the Federal Election Campaign Act (FECA) in 1971 and its amendments in 1974, interest groups began establishing political action committees (PACs) to donate money to candidates, which in turn expanded their access to policymakers.[2] Finally, the advancement of technology, particularly the recent development of the internet, has reduced the costs associated with establishing a group and mobilizing activists (Hall and Wayman 1990; Berry 1997).

---

[2]Political action committees or PACs were established by the federal government as part of the 1974 Federal Election Campaign Act in order to monitor and limit campaign spending by businesses and interest groups. Any corporation, union, or other interest group can form a PAC and register it with the Federal Election Commission, which monitors its spending on federal candidates. PACs are allowed to spend up to $5,000 on a federal campaign per election for each election cycle (meaning they can spend $10,000 if a candidate runs in a primary and in the general election).

NOW remains the most widely known women's group. As mentioned earlier, the group grew out of the President's Commission on the Status of Women and was created in 1966 with the intention of establishing an "NAACP for women" to eliminate discrimination against women (Carabillo, Meuli, and Csida 1993). Today NOW claims to be the largest grassroots-based feminist organization in the United States with chapters in all 50 states (National Organization for Women 2017a). The group has a broad-based agenda advocating for policies to eliminate discrimination against women in the workplace, schools, the justice system, and all other sectors of society. Reproductive rights and other women's health issues, violence against women, the ERA, pay equity, family-friendly workplaces, and eliminating discrimination based on race and sexual orientation are also among the group's top priorities (National Organization for Women 2017b).

From the early years, NOW committed itself to being an action-oriented group dedicated to the mobilization of women at the grassroots level and to the pursuit of fundamental social change rather than to the more limited goal of legal equality with men. To that end, NOW combines traditional lobbying and education activities with more radical forms of political engagement such as mass marches and protests (Freeman 1975; Barakso 2004). In recent years, the group has held mass protests to support abortion rights, promote gay marriage, and rally against domestic violence (Barr and Williamson 2004; NOW 2017c). Former NOW President Patricia Ireland describes the benefits of marches and other mass actions:

> We use them to organize and to inspire. A mass action builds our strength and our momentum—and shows that strength to politicians and to ourselves. Successful mass actions also have positive "hangover effects": the tremendous individual and group efforts needed to organize a big march expands our lists of contributors and supporters and provides an opportunity to develop skills and activism at the grass roots. These new community organizers can continue to expand that network and use it to turn out the vote or bring constituent pressure for an issue. (Ireland 1996, 249)

In addition to grassroots demonstrations and lobbying, NOW Foundation, the educational and legal arm of NOW, often uses the courts to pursue legal cases. With the courts playing such a key role in defining the parameters of women's rights, NOW Foundation has filed amicus (friend of the court) briefs seeking to expand or maintain women's rights in several recent high-profile cases including *Young v. United Parcel Services* regarding pregnancy discrimination, *King v. Burwell* concerning subsidies to help people pay for health plans under Obamacare, and multiple cases regarding gay marriage (National Organization for Women 2015a). The group works to mobilize younger generations of women through Campus Action Networks for women in college and NOW clubs for high school age teens. Finally,

Abortion rights supporters demonstrate at a rally marking the anniversary of *Roe v. Wade*, January 2014.
*Source*: National Organization for Women / NOW.org.

NOW, like many other organizations, has consistently been involved in presidential and congressional elections, conducting voter registration drives, endorsing candidates, and seeking to publicize its issues with the public and the major candidates. The group was an early and strong supporter of Senator Hillary Clinton (D-NY) in her race against Barack Obama for the 2008 presidential nomination. The group actively campaigned for Clinton in 2016 (National Organization for Women 2007, 2015b).

Although NOW continues to be the most widely known feminist organization, there are numerous other active feminist women's groups. These groups vary in the breadth of their agendas and the range of activities in which they participate. Founded in 2006 by Kristin Rowe-Finkbeiner and Joan Blades (who is also a co-founder of the liberal group MoveOn.Org), MomsRising is an online social media network that also has grassroots affiliates engaged in multiple levels of politics. MomsRising coordinates local activists to lobby their state legislators, calls on members to petition members of Congress through their web portal, and provides a forum for more than 1,000 bloggers to provide information about issues and policies important to their members. The activists with MomsRising employ motherhood rhetoric to build support for numerous progressive policies that call for more government assistance and regulation to help American families. For example, MomsRising promotes government-mandated sick days for American workers, arguing on its site that "no mother should have to choose between her job and taking care of a sick child. We are working to make earned paid sick days a right for all" (MomsRising.org n.d.a). Among other issues, MomsRising supports expanded maternity leave, more flexible work schedules, universal pre-kindergarten, environmental initiatives, and immigration reform—all in the name of making American families stronger (MomsRising.org n.d.b.).

Groups like the Feminist Majority Foundation and the American Association of University Women are similar to NOW and MomsRising in their devotion to a broad range of issues and their focus on political activism utilizing a wide range of techniques from lobbying to litigation, issue research, and mass protest. There is also an increasing trend toward specialization in the feminist community in which groups concentrate their activism and research on one specific issue such as abortion, gay rights, domestic violence, or pacifism. The National Abortion Rights Action League (NARAL), Planned Parenthood, the National Coalition Against Domestic Violence, and CODEPINK: Women for Peace are all groups that participate in grassroots activism for a particular cause. Still other organizations are brought together by a shared identity based on professional status or demographics such as age or race. Examples of these organizations include the Older Women's League, the Black Women's Health Imperative, The National Latina Institute for Reproductive Health, and Business and Professional Women.

Finally, there are numerous women's think tanks, which conduct public policy research on issues that impact women and families, and legal advocacy groups, which focus their energy on activities such as providing legal representation for women in discrimination cases. For example, the Institute for Women's Policy Research publishes annual reports on the Status of Women in the States that rank each state based on women's status in political participation, employment and earnings, social and economic autonomy, reproductive rights, and women's health and well-being (Institute for Women's Policy Research n.d.). These reports are used to garner attention to these issues and spur legislation and policy change to address women's concerns. Similarly, the National Women's Law Center and the Center for Women's Policy Studies also focus on legal aid and public policy research rather than grassroots activism.

Women's organizations achieved some progress toward their goals in the Obama years. The Lilly Ledbetter Fair Pay Act and various executive orders regarding equal pay moved the ball forward on pay equity. Obamacare, the president's health reform, expanded women's access to health care and provided important protections for women's health, including requiring coverage for prenatal care and contraception in basic health plans (Swers 2013). Feminist women's groups actively supported Hillary Clinton's run for the presidency and anticipated a renewed focus on women's rights. Clinton promised paid family leave, affordable child care, and greater protections for women's reproductive rights (Paquette 2016; Sussman and Meckler 2016).

Donald Trump's unexpected victory alarmed progressive women and galvanized them to action. A desire to protect gains made during the Obama years and to prevent a return to a more conservative vision of women's place in society may reinvigorate the feminist movement. The day after Trump's inauguration, thousands of women took to the streets in Washington, DC, and cities across the United States and around the world to protest for women's rights. Women's groups like Planned Parenthood and EMILY's List helped sponsor the marches (https://www.womensmarch.com/sponsors/).

Still, the march also received criticism from various quarters, including pro-life feminist women who were excluded from the march (Deckman 2017). Others urged march leaders to pay more attention to intersectionality, the problems faced by women of color and other groups outside of the white middle-class women that have dominated the feminist movement (Bates 2017; Desmond-Harris 2017). It remains to be seen whether feminist women's organizations can harness this energy to influence the direction of public policy.

**Conservative Women Fight Back**

While there is great diversity in the activities and goals of organizations associated with the feminist movement, there is also a burgeoning conservative women's movement. In her book, *Women of the New Right*, Rebecca Klatch (1987) describes two archetypes of conservative women: the socially conservative woman and the laissez-faire conservative. The political activism of the social conservative woman is strongly influenced by her religious beliefs and a desire to protect the traditional family, particularly regarding women's role in the home and in the care of children. Whereas the social conservative is motivated to activism by her moral code, the laissez-faire conservative is devoted to the ideals of individual rights, free market principles, and limited government. Thus, these women tend to eschew debates on social issues such as abortion and focus their efforts on economic concerns such as workplace issues. For example, laissez-faire conservative women oppose programs such as affirmative action as an unconstitutional preference and government intrusion that violates free market principles without improving the position of women and minorities (Klatch 1987; Schreiber 2002b, 2008).

Concerned Women for America is the largest group representing socially conservative women. Just as the awakening of a feminist consciousness in the early 1960s spurred the formation of NOW, Concerned Women for America grew out of the antifeminist countermovement. These women were mobilized in response to their opposition to the ERA, the *Roe v. Wade* decision on abortion, and the International Women's Year conferences and celebrations that elevated feminist principles concerning women's rights. Founded in 1979 in San Diego, California, by Beverly LaHaye, the group reaches out to Christian women as wives and mothers in an effort to protect the traditional family and reassert biblical principles as a foundation of public policy. LaHaye was at the center of the New Right movement in the 1970s and 1980s, traveling the country and giving speeches on family values and the moral decay of the nation, writing books, and conducting her own radio show. Her husband, the Reverend Tim LaHaye, was a founding member of Jerry Falwell's Moral Majority, one of the leading organizations in the mobilization of the New Right in the 1980s (Marshall 1995; Schreiber 2002a, 2002b, 2008). According to the group's mission statement, "CWA protects and promotes Biblical values and Constitutional principles through prayer, education, and advocacy" (Concerned Women for America 2017a).

In her memoir *Who But a Woman?* Beverly LaHaye maintains that she founded CWA to "combat the goals of the feminist movement" after witnessing what she and other Christian women viewed as an attack on traditional families that occurred at the National Women's Convention in Houston, Texas, in 1977 to celebrate International Women's Year. LaHaye opposed the adoption of resolutions by the convention including "the ratification of the Equal Rights Amendment; the 'right' of homosexuals and lesbians to teach in public schools and to have custody of children; federally funded abortion on demand; approval of abortion for teenagers without parental knowledge or consent; federal government involvement in twenty-four-hour-a-day child care centers, and more" (LaHaye 1984, 27). The group built its membership through church networks, attracting the support of ministers, distributing literature to recruit evangelical Protestant women, and holding coffees with like-minded women.

Today CWA represents a national network of prayer/action chapters connected to a professional staff at the national headquarters, which opened in 1985 (Concerned Women for America 2017b). The prayer/action chapters mobilize grassroots women by meeting to learn and pray about issues and then take action on them, such as writing letters to Congress or newspaper editorial boards. In order to promote the return to biblical values, the group focuses on issues such as opposition to abortion, homosexuality, and pornography. It also opposes the United Nations as undermining American sovereignty, advocates for the expansion of religious liberty, meaning the ability to bring religion back into the public square, and seeks to restore Judeo-Christian values and parental authority in the public school system (Concerned Women for America 2017c).

Like its feminist counterparts such as NOW and AAUW, CWA conducts lobbying efforts and prepares voter guides to draw the attention of its members and legislators to its key issues. The group is also particularly aggressive in exposing what it considers the excesses of the feminist movement in order to demonstrate that it is the "true" representative of mainstream women's opinion (Schreiber 2002a, 2002b, 2008). For example, in the early 1990s, CWA's magazine, *Family Voice,* ran a monthly series of "Feminist Follies" featuring radical quotes by feminist leaders as they appeared in their group's own publications and a cartoon of a disheveled woman wearing a large NOW button, with her fist in the air (Marshall 1995, 324–26).

In contrast to the social issue focus of Concerned Women for America, the Independent Women's Forum (IWF) concentrates on the economic and limited government issues that concern laissez-faire conservatives. Angered by the media coverage of the Clarence Thomas–Anita Hill hearings,[3] in which the feminist view was equated with the perspective of all women, a group of women who worked for the George H. W. Bush administration founded this organization in 1992. They decided to create an organization to counter the feminist establishment by providing a voice for conservative women who believe in individual freedom, self-government, and personal responsibility. IWF eschews moral debates and does not take a position on abortion. Instead, it focuses on economic issues and on reducing government regulation (Schreiber 2002a, 2002b, 2008).

The group believes that government programs designed to help women, in fact, disrespect women and limit their choices. For example, IWF opposes the Title IX program as it applies to athletics. Title IX is federal legislation that mandates that public schools that receive federal funds, both at the secondary and collegiate levels, must ensure that women's sports programs receive equal treatment and the same funding as men's programs. The IWF views Title IX as a quota system that demeans the legitimate athletic accomplishments of women and denies opportunities to men by requiring a strict measure of proportionality in participation in college athletics when women are relatively less interested in athletics than men (Schreiber 2002a, 2008). IWF leaders are well connected to, or are themselves, key policy and

---

[3]The hearings involved the confirmation of Clarence Thomas to be an Associate Justice on the United States Supreme Court in 1991. The all-male Senate Judiciary Committee heard testimony from Anita Hill, who had accused Thomas of sexual harassment when she worked for him at the Equal Employment Opportunity Commission. Liberal women's organizations believed that Hill was mistreated and her allegations were not taken seriously by many of the senators during questioning. Thomas, who denied the charges, was eventually appointed to the bench.

Rep. Michele Bachmann, R-Minn, speaking at a Tea Party Rally to oppose the constitution-ality of Barack Obama's health care overhaul on March 28, 2012, the day the Supreme Court heard oral arguments about the Affordable Care Act. Bachmann is flanked by Tea Party women activists, including Tea Party Patriots co-founder Jenny Beth Martin (left). *Source*: AP Photo / Carolyn Kaster.

opinion makers. Many of the women associated with IWF held positions in the administration of George W. Bush and advise Republican congressional and presidential campaigns. Thus, IWF leaders focus their efforts on providing research and gaining media attention to a conservative viewpoint on women's issues.

The economic turmoil of the Great Recession in 2007 and the government's response, including the bailout of the giant financial institutions that helped cause the economic collapse, angered conservatives. The policies of the Obama administration from the economic stimulus bill to Obamacare, the president's large scale health reform plan, further alarmed conservatives and sparked the Tea Party movement. Many conservative women joined Tea Party groups and became active on social media to spread their views. Indeed, case studies suggest that there may have been more women than men in leadership positions at the local level (Lo 2012). Interviewing Tea Party women across the country, Melissa Deckman (2016a) found that these women felt an obligation as mothers to get involved in politics to protect their children against reckless government spending and rising debt.

Several women also emerged as national Tea Party leaders. Sarah Palin, the 2008 Republican vice presidential nominee, galvanized conservative women by appealing to "Mama Grizzlies who would rise up to protect their young against the oppressive hand of government" (Deckman 2016a). Jenny Beth Martin co-founded and became the president of the Tea Party Patriots, arguably the nation's largest Tea Party organization. She helped organize and lead the September 2012 Taxpayer's March on Washington to protest Obama administration policies on government spending, health reform, and abortion (Altman 2010). Michele Bachmann (R-MN) also catapulted to the forefront of the national movement espousing Tea Party principles during her time as a representative in Congress and briefly running for the Republican presidential nomination in 2012.

Many Tea Party women also strongly supported Donald Trump. Trump spoke to these women's fears that the country is moving in the wrong direction both culturally and economically. They responded to his proposals to crack down on illegal immigration and bring back jobs to the U.S. Some Tea Party women took leadership roles in his campaign, including Katrina Pierson, the founder of a Texas Tea Party organization who became Trump's national spokesperson, and Amy Kremer, the former chair of the Tea Party Express's PAC, who co-founded the pro-Trump Super PAC known as The Great America PAC (Deckman 2016a, 2016b).

## WHAT DO WOMEN WANT?

Since the recession, economic inequality and the place of women in the economy have become a central focus of political debate. Since 1975, the percentage of women in the workforce has grown from 46.3 to 56.7 percent in 2015 (Women's Bureau United States Department of Labor n.d.a, b). Among women with children, less than half worked in 1975. By 2015, 69.9 percent of mothers with children under 18 worked and 61.4 percent of mothers with a child under three years of age were in the labor force (Women's Bureau Department of Labor n.d.b). Moreover, today's women are working longer into their pregnancies and going back to work earlier, creating pressures on families regarding work-family balance and the provision of child care and on employers to provide more family-friendly workplaces (Boushey 2014; Ingraham 2015). In the face of such a rapidly changing American workforce, both feminist and conservative women's groups compete to demonstrate that they are the true representatives of women's interests and to shape the policy debate regarding women and the economy.

Feminist groups from NOW to MomsRising argue for a higher minimum wage since women, particularly single mothers, are more likely to hold low-paying service sector jobs such as food service or home health workers. Feminist groups also focus on efforts to eliminate the pay gap and combat employment discrimination. Every April, feminist groups and their Democratic Party allies in government highlight Equal Pay Day, the date at which a woman's salary finally catches up to what a man made the previous year. In 2015, women earned 79.6 percent of a man's median annual earnings (Institute for Women's Policy Research 2016). Feminist advocates argue that to close the gender wage gap, the government should adopt policies that make it easier for employees to share salary information and engage in litigation to combat employment discrimination. They also advocate for changes in society that undervalue positions that are predominantly held by women compared to male-dominated fields. Thus, feminists ask why home health care and child care workers make less than truck drivers and security guards. Finally, feminist groups strongly advocate for policy changes that would make it easier for women to balance their work and family responsibilities such as paid family leave, paid sick days, and leave policies that encourage men as well as women to take leave (O'Leary and Kornbluh 2009; Boushey 2014).

While feminists look to public policy to expand opportunities for women in the workforce, conservative women strongly oppose these policies because they interfere with the private market and take away women's choices. Conservative women's groups such as IWF and Smart Girl Politics argue that the pay gap is a myth and, instead, reflects women's choices. For example, women are more likely than men to reduce their hours or to leave the workforce to take care of their children. Among college-educated workers, women are more likely to major in fields that emphasize caring and pay less. Thus more men major in various fields of engineering while more women major in early childhood education, social work, and psychology, which explains why women's average pay is lower nationally then men's (Sommers 2014). Conservative women also maintain that policies that mandate benefits like parental leave and seek to micromanage wages actually reduce women's choices, making it harder for them to negotiate flexible work schedules and pay, and reducing incentives for employers to hire more workers and more women (Lukas 2014). Similarly, conservative women's advocates argue for using the tax code through expansion of the Earned Income Tax Credit, a tax rebate for low-income workers, rather than expanding the minimum wage, a policy that would burden employers in sectors that hire more low-wage workers, forcing them to hire fewer employees (Currie 2014). As women's participation in the workforce continues to grow and change, both conservative and feminist women's advocates will compete to demonstrate that they understand women's needs and are promoting solutions that will help women meet their expanding range of responsibilities.

# CONCLUSION

Our discussion of women's participation in social movements and interest groups highlights a long, rich tradition of political activism among women. This activist tradition is marked by a great deal of diversity in the causes advocated by women, the ideological viewpoints of female activists, and the organizational tactics employed. Thus, during the fight for women's suffrage, women were active as both opponents and proponents of votes for women. Among the suffragists, women supported the movement for different reasons and they varied in the extent to which they sought to challenge traditional gender roles. Some women advocated for women's rights based on principles of human rights and individual freedom whereas others viewed the ballot as a means to achieve other social reforms by allowing women to act as civic mothers, viewing politics as a natural extension of women's private sphere responsibilities. Still other women sought the vote for more nefarious reasons, seeking to counteract the influence of minorities and immigrants in an effort to preserve white supremacy.

During the second wave of feminism, activists sought to expand women's rights in society and government. Through lobbying and legal reform, older branch groups like NOW sought to eliminate discriminatory employment practices and expand women's access to reproductive health services from abortion to contraception. Meanwhile, younger branch groups worked to raise women's group consciousness and to achieve women's liberation through profound changes in societal gender relations. Although the movement to pass an ERA to the Constitution failed, feminist groups continue to advocate for policy changes that will expand women's rights and improve women's lives.

In contemporary politics, women's organizations represent a wide range of issues and ideological perspectives. Thus, feminist groups such as NOW promote equal rights for women and the elimination of barriers to women's full participation in society whereas conservative women's organizations like Concerned Women for America promote the values of the traditional family and the primacy of motherhood. Economic conservatives, such as IWF, seek to reduce government barriers to women's exercise of their free choice and pursuit of their goals in the free market. As women's place in society continues to evolve, women's organizations on the left and right will continue to promote their vision of "what women want."

# REFERENCES

Altman, Alex. 2010. "Jenny Beth Martin." *Time*, April 29.
Andersen, Kristi. 1996. *After Suffrage: Women in Partisan and Electoral Politics before the New Deal*. Chicago: University of Chicago Press.

Baker, Paula. 1984. "The Domestication of Politics: Women and American Political Society, 1780–1920." *American Historical Review* 89(3): 620–47.

Barakso, Maryann. 2004. *Governing NOW: Grassroots Activism in the National Organization for Women.* Ithaca, NY: Cornell University Press.

Barr, Cameron W., and Elizabeth Williamson. 2004. "Women's Rally Draws Vast Crowd: Marchers Champion Reproductive Rights, Opposition to Bush." *Washington Post*, April 26.

Bates, Karen Grigsby. 2017. "Race and Feminism: Women's March Recalls the Touchy History." NPR, January 21.

Berry, Jeffrey M. 1997. *The Interest Group Society.* New York: Longman.

Blair, Karen. 1980. *The Clubwoman as Feminist.* New York: Holmes and Meier Publishers.

Bordin, Ruth. 1981. *Woman and Temperance.* Philadelphia: Temple University Press.

Boushey, Heather. 2014. "A Woman's Place Is in the Middle Class." From *The Shriver Report: A Woman's Nation Pushes Back From the Brink.* A Study by Maria Shriver and the Center for American Progress.

Calamur, Krishnadev. 2017. "What Trump's Executive Order on Immigration Does—And Doesn't Do." *The Atlantic*, January 29.

Cauterruci, Christina. 2017. "The Women's March on Washington Has Released an Unapologetically Progressive Platform." *Slate*, January 12.

Carabillo, Toni, Judith Meuli, and June Bundy Csida. 1993. *Feminist Chronicles 1953–1993.* Los Angeles: Women's Graphics.

Concerned Women for America. 2017a. "Our Mission." http://www.cwfa.org/about/vision-mission/ (accessed January 28, 2017).

———. 2017b. "Our History." http://www.cwfa.org/about/our-history/(accessed January 28, 2017).

———. 2017c. "Issues." http://www.cwfa.org/about/issues/(accessed January 28, 2017).

Conover, Pamela Johnston, and Virginia Gray. 1983. *Feminism and the New Right: Conflict Over the American Family.* New York: Praeger Publishers.

Conway, M. Margaret, David W. Ahern, and Gertrude Steuernagel. 1999. *Women and Public Policy: A Revolution in Progress*, 2nd ed. Washington, DC: Congressional Quarterly Press.

Costain, Anne N. 1992. *Inviting Women's Rebellion.* Baltimore: Johns Hopkins University Press.

Cott, Nancy F. 1987. *The Grounding of Modern Feminism.* New Haven: Yale University Press.

Crockett, Emily. 2017a. "The 'Women's March on Washington' Explained." *Vox*, January 21.

———. 2017b. "The House Just Passed a Sweeping Abortion Funding Ban: Here's What It Does." *Vox*, January 24.

Currie, Rachel DiCarlo. 2014. "Why the Earned Income Tax Credit Beats the Minimum Wage." *Policy Focus*. Washington, DC: Independent Women's Forum, Vol. 4, No. 4, April. http://c1355372.cdn.cloudfiles.rackspacecloud.com/83be67ce-7aab-4c5d-a0f9-f9b358246d47/PolicyFocus14_April_p2.pdf

Cushman, Clare, ed. 2001. *Supreme Court Decisions and Women's Rights: Milestones to Equality.* Washington, DC: Congressional Quarterly, Inc.

Deckman, Melissa. 2016a. *Mama Grizzlies and Politics: Motherhood, Feminism, and the Tea Party in America.* New York: NYU Press.

———. 2016b. "Some Women Actually Do Support Donald Trump. Here's Why." *Washington Post*, April 7.

———. 2017. "Can Pro-Choice and Pro-Life Women Find Common Ground? It's Complicated." *Washington Post*, January 20.

Deckman, Melissa, and John McTague. 2015. "Did the 'War on Women' Work? Women, Men, and the Birth Control Mandate in the 2012 Presidential Election." *American Politics Research* 43(1): 3–26.

Desanctis, Alexandra. 2017. "Huge Diverse Crowd Marches for Life in the Nation's Capitol." *National Review*, January 27.

Desmond-Harris, Jennee. 2017. "To Understand the Women's March on Washington You Need to Understand Intersectional Feminism." *Vox*, January 21.

Dorr, Rheta Childe. 1910. *What Eight Million Women Want.* Boston: Small, Maynard & Company.

Ferree, Myra Marx, and Beth B. Hess. 1994. *Controversy and Coalition: The New Feminist Movement*, rev. ed. New York: Twayne Publishers.

Flexner, Eleanor, and Ellen Fitzpatrick. 1996. *Century of Struggle: The Women's Rights Movement in the United States.* Cambridge, MA: Belknap Press of Harvard University.

Freeman, Jo. 1975. *The Politics of Women's Liberation.* New York: Longman Inc.

———. 2000. *A Room at a Time: How Women Entered Party Politics.* New York: Rowman & Littlefield Publishers, Inc.

Friedman, Estelle B. 2002. *No Turning Back: The History of Feminism and the Future of Women.* New York: Ballantine.

Frostenson, Sarah. 2017. "The Women's Marches May Have Been the Largest Demonstration in US History." *Vox*, January 22.

Gelb, Joyce, and Marian Lief Palley. 1996. *Women and Public Policies: Reassessing Gender Politics.* Charlottesville, VA: University Press of Virginia.

Green. Emma. 2017. "Will the Pro-Life Movement Split with Trump on Issues Other Than Abortion." *The Atlantic*, January 27.

Haberkorn, Jennifer. 2017. "Trump Revises Funding Ban to Groups Providing Abortion Overseas." *Politico*, January 23.

Hall, Richard, and Frank Wayman. 1990. "Buying Time: Moneyed Interests and the Mobilization of Bias in Congressional Committees." *American Political Science Review* 84: 797–820.

Hartmann, Susan M. 1989. *From Margin to Mainstream: American Women and Politics Since 1960.* Philadelphia: Temple University Press.

Harvey, Anna L. 1998. *Votes Without Leverage: Women in American Electoral Politics, 1920–1970.* New York: Cambridge University Press.

Ingraham, Christopher. 2015. "Today's Moms Are Working Later into Their Pregnancies—And Going Back to Work Earlier Too." *Washington Post*, April 1.

Institute for Women's Policy Research. n.d. *The Status of Women in the States.* Washington, DC: Institute for Women's Policy Research. http://statusofwomendata.org/

———. 2016. "The Gender Wage Gap: 2015 Annual Earnings Differences by Gender, Race, and Ethnicity." Washington, DC: Institute for Women's Policy Research. September.

Ireland, Patricia. 1996. *What Women Want.* New York: Dutton.

Klatch, Rebecca E. 1987. *Women of the New Right.* Philadelphia: Temple University Press.

Klein, Ethel. 1984. *Gender Politics: From Consciousness to Mass Politics.* Cambridge, MA: Harvard University Press.

Kraditor, Aileen S. 1981. *The Ideas of the Woman Suffrage Movement: 1890–1920.* New York: W.W. Norton & Company.

LaHaye, Beverly. 1984. *Who But a Woman? Concerned Women Can Make a Difference.* Nashville: Thomas Nelson Publishers.

Lo, Clarence. 2012. "AstroTurf Versus Grass Roots: Scenes from Early Tea Party Mobilization." In *Steep: The Precipitous Rise of the Tea Party,* edited by Lawrence Rosenthal and Christine Trost, 98–129. Berkeley: University of California Press.

Lorber, Judith. 1994. *Paradoxes of Gender.* New Haven: Yale University Press.

Lukas, Carrie. 2014. "The Family Act." *Policy Focus* Washington, DC: Independent Women's Forum, Vol. 4, No. 1, January. http://c1355372.cdn.cloudfiles.rack spacecloud.com/167e75a7-d65b-4c41-8b1a-14570e2268b1/PolicyFocus14_Jan _p1.pdf

Mansbridge, Jane. 1986. *Why We Lost the ERA.* Chicago: University of Chicago Press.

Marshall, Susan. 1995. "Confrontation and Co-optation in Antifeminist Organizations." In *Feminist Organizations, Harvest of the New Women's Movement,* edited by Myra Marx Ferree and Patricia Yancey Martin, 323–35. Philadelphia: Temple University Press.

McAdam, Doug. 1982. *Political Process and the Development of Black Insurgency, 1930–1970.* Chicago: University of Chicago Press.

McConnaughy, Corrine. 2013. *The Woman Suffrage Movement in America: A Reassessment.* New York: Cambridge University Press.

Momsrising.org. n.d.a. "Paid Sick Days" https://www.momsrising.org/issues_and _resources/paid-sick-days-all. Accessed January 28, 2017.

Momsrising.org. n.d.b. "Our Issues." https://www.momsrising.org/page/moms/our -issues. Accessed January 28, 2017.

Mott, Stacy. 2013. Personal interview with Melissa Deckman. February 27.

National Organization for Women. 2007. "NOW Political Action Committee Proudly Endorses Senator Hillary Rodham Clinton for President of the United States in 2008." Accessed online at http://www.now.org/press/03-07/03-28.html

———. 2015a. "NOW Foundation Joins Amicus Briefs in Supreme Court Cases." Accessed online at http://now.org/update/now-foundation-joins-amicus-briefs-in -supreme-court-cases/

———. 2015b. "NOW is a Proud Supporter of Women for Hillary." September 4. http://now.org/media-center/press-release/now-is-a-proud-supporter-of-women -for-hillary/

———. 2017a. "Frequently Asked Questions." Accessed online at http://now.org/ about/faqs/

———. 2017b. "Issues." Accessed online at http://now.org/issues/

———. 2017c. "History of Marches and Mass Actions." Accessed online at http://now.org/about/history/history-of-marches-and-mass-actions/

O'Leary, Ann, and Karen Kornbluh. 2009. "Family Friendly for All Families." From *The Shriver Report: A Woman's Nation Changes Everything*, edited by Heather Boushey and Ann O'Leary. A Study by Maria Shriver and the Center for American Progress.

Omolade, Barbara. 2004. "Ella's Daughters." In *Women's Lives: Multicultural Perspectives*, 3rd ed., edited by Gwyn Kirk and Margo Okazawa-Rey. New York: McGraw-Hill.

Paquette, Danielle. 2016. "The Enormous Ambition of Hillary Clinton's Child-Care Plan," *Washington Post*, May 12.

Phillips, Erica E. 2014. "Sex Equality Backers Seek Impetus in Oregon Measure." *Wall Street Journal*, October 29.

Robnett, Belinda. 2000. *How Long? How Long? African-American Women in the Struggle for Civil Rights*. Oxford: Oxford University Press.

Ryan, Barbara. 1992. *Feminism and the Women's Movement: Dynamics of Change in Social Movement Ideology and Activism*. New York: Routledge.

Schreiber, Ronnee. 2002a. "Injecting a Woman's Voice: Conservative Women's Organizations, Gender Consciousness, and the Expression of Women's Policy Preferences." *Sex Roles* 47: 331–42.

———. 2002b. "Playing 'Femball': Conservative Women's Organizations and Political Representation in the United States." In *Right-Wing Women: From Conservatives to Extremists Around the World*, edited by Paola Bacchetta and Margaret Power. New York: Routledge.

———. 2008. *Righting Feminism: Conservative Women and American Politics*. New York: Oxford University Press.

Shanley, Mary Lyndon. 1988. *Women's Rights, Feminism, and Politics in the United States*. Washington, DC: American Political Science Association.

Silver, Nate. 2017. "The Long March Ahead for Democrats." *FiveThirtyEight*, January 23.

Skocpol, Theda. 1992. *Protecting Soldiers and Mothers*. Cambridge, MA: The Belknap Press of Harvard University Press.

Sommers, Christina Hoff. 2014. "No, Women Don't Make Less Money Than Men." *Daily Beast*, February 1.

Strolovitch, Dara. 2007. *Affirmative Advocacy: Race, Class, and Gender in Interest Group Politics*. Chicago: University of Chicago Press.

Sussman, Anna Louise and Laura Meckler. 2016. "Clinton Offers New Details About Paid Family Leave Plan." *The Wall Street Journal*, January 7.

Swers, Michele L. 2013. *Women in the Club: Gender and Policy Making in the Senate*. Chicago: The University of Chicago Press.

Tyler, Helen. 1949. *Where Prayer and Purpose Meet: 1874–1949, The WCTU Story*. Evanston: The Signal Press National Woman's Christian Temperance Union Inc.

Wells, Mildred White. 1953. *The History of the General Federation of Women's Clubs*. Washington, DC: General Federation of Women's Clubs.

Wilcox, Clyde, and Barbara Norrander. 2005. "Change and Continuity in the Geography of Women Legislators." In *Women and Elective Office*, 2nd ed., edited by Sue Thomas and Clyde Wilcox. New York: Oxford University Press.

Women's Bureau U.S. Department of Labor. n.d.a. "Labor Force Participation Rate by Sex, Race, and Hispanic Ethnicity 1948-2015 Annual Averages." https://www.dol.gov/wb/stats/facts_over_time.htm#labor (accessed January 29, 2017).

———. n.d.b. "Labor Force Participation Rate of Mothers by Age of the Youngest Child March 1975-2015." https://www.dol.gov/wb/stats/facts_over_time.htm#labor (accessed January 29, 2017).

Wood, Mary I. 1912. *The History of the General Federation of Women's Clubs for the First Twenty-Two Years of Its Organization*. New York: History Department, General Federation of Women's Clubs.

# 3

# The Gender Gap in Elections and Public Opinion

Hillary Clinton launched her 2016 presidential campaign promising to put a focus on the needs of women and their families. According to Clinton and her Democratic supporters, women want equal pay, an increase in the minimum wage, access to paid leave, and affordable high quality child care (Allen 2015). Her opponent Donald Trump focused his campaign on blue-collar voters who had been hurt by trade deals and were uneasy about immigration. Trump was also heavily criticized for his long history of inappropriate comments toward and about women, which he insisted was merely "locker room talk." In an effort to appeal to suburban women voters, Hillary Clinton tried to capitalize on Trump's misogynistic statements by running advertisements showing young girls looking into a mirror while they listened to a litany of insulting comments Trump had made about women (Merica 2016). While Trump's campaign largely portrayed him as a strong, decisive leader who would "Make America Great Again," Trump also recognized the importance of outreach to women voters and tried to mobilize them with a plan developed by his daughter Ivanka to provide paid maternity leave and increase the affordability of child care through expanded tax credits for working mothers (Rucker 2016).

The contest between the first female presidential candidate and a candidate who continually highlighted his masculinity meant women voters were central to the 2016 campaign. Similarly, in recent elections, candidates, parties, and their interest group allies have typically crafted messages that will mobilize particular groups of women. In recent years, Democrats such as Barack Obama and Hillary Clinton have focused on equal pay, reproductive rights, child care affordability, and other policies targeted at women (Roarty 2012; Thompson 2012; Allen 2015).

Meanwhile, Republicans like George W. Bush and Mitt Romney have focused on women as entrepreneurs who will benefit from Republican tax policies and as mothers who are looking to protect the security of their families (Martinez and Carey 2004; Reinhard 2012). Such approaches by these campaigns raise an important set of questions: What do women voters want? Do women and men actually have distinct views about politics and divergent patterns in their voting behavior? How do other factors such as race, class, education, and marital status influence the worldviews of men and women?

In this chapter we examine differences in the voting behavior and political attitudes of men and women. The chapter traces the emergence of the gender gap in voting and explores the causes of this much talked about phenomena of American politics. We explore the efforts of the political parties to attract the votes of different demographic subgroups of women and examine whether women's position as a potential swing-voting group translates into political power and women-friendly policy. Finally, the chapter examines whether women voters constitute a key group of supporters for women candidates and we take a closer look at the 2008 and 2016 presidential campaigns of Hillary Clinton and her support amongst various groups of male and female voters.

## COURTING THE WOMEN'S VOTE: THE EARLY YEARS

As chapter 2 recounts, the struggle to achieve the right to vote for women spanned over 70 years of American history (1848–1920). (See Table 3.1 for a list of countries and when they granted women the right to vote.) During the campaign female reformers promised that when given the right to vote, women would "clean up" government and elect politicians committed to reforms that would help women and children, often involving enhanced regulation of industry. Wanting to court this new group of potential voters and facing pressure from women's organizations such as the General Federation of Women's Clubs and the National Congress of Mothers (today known as the PTA), members of Congress passed several important bills to help women and their families. These laws included the Sheppard-Towner Act (1921), the first government-supported program for educating mothers about infant and prenatal care, the Packers and Stockyard Bill (1921), requiring meat inspections to protect consumers, and the Child Labor Act (1924), an effort to pass a constitutional amendment limiting child labor (Klein 1984; Skocpol 1992; Flexner and Fitzpatrick 1996).

While reform-minded politicians eagerly anticipated a women's vote, others marshaled their resources against suffrage out of fear that women's

**Table 3.1. Women's Suffrage in Select Democratic Countries**

| Year | Country |
| --- | --- |
| 1893 | New Zealand |
| 1902 | Australia* |
| 1906 | Finland |
| 1913 | Norway |
| 1915 | Denmark |
| 1918 | Germany, United Kingdom |
| 1919 | Netherlands, Sweden* |
| 1920 | United States |
| 1944 | France |
| 1945 | Italy |
| 1952 | Greece |
| 1971 | Switzerland |

*Note*: In 1971, Switzerland became the last democratic country to adopt women's suffrage. In contrast to the United States where the Nineteenth Amendment to the Constitution mandated full suffrage for women, in Switzerland, the constitutional amendment passed allowed local cantons (the equivalent of states in the United States) to adopt their own laws concerning suffrage in local elections and for one house of the Swiss Parliament. As a result, two Swiss cantons did not adopt full suffrage for women until 1989 and 1990 (Banaszak 1996).
*Indicates that the right to vote was subject to conditions or restrictions.
*Source*: Inter-Parliamentary Union: 2005. "A World Chronology of the Recognition of Women's Rights to Vote and to Stand for Election." www.ipu.org/wmn-e/suffrage.htm.

votes would yield a flood of progressive legislation. Thus, business interests, including railroad, oil, meatpacking, and general manufacturing groups, opposed women's suffrage because they feared that women would vote to outlaw child labor and demand improved conditions for working women. The political machines opposed voting rights for women because they doubted their ability to control women's votes and feared their reform proposals for clean government. The liquor manufacturers were among the most ardently opposed to suffrage because of the leadership of women in the temperance movement (Flexner and Fitzpatrick 1996). Speaking at the 1912 convention of the National Retail Dealer's Association, association president, Neil Bonner, declared: "We do not fear the churches, the men are voting the old tickets; . . . we need not fear the YMCA, for it does no aggressive work; but, gentlemen, we need to fear the Woman's Christian Temperance Union and the ballot in the hands of women; therefore, gentleman, fight woman suffrage" (quoted in Tyler 1949, 159).

Yet proponents and opponents of women's suffrage, who foresaw the potential of having women vote en masse, were wrong. In the years immediately following the adoption of the Nineteenth Amendment, women did not vote in large numbers and a women's bloc of votes loyal to a specific set of issues or a particular party did not emerge. A generation of women who were raised to believe that politics was a male domain did not cast a ballot. Instead, like other new groups of voters, women had to develop the habit of voting (Corder and Wolbrecht 2016). In the 1920 election, only one-third of eligible women voted, and among those women, party affiliation, class, religion, and ethnicity, rather than sex, influenced their voting decisions. The greatest differences in turnout among women occurred among groups where sex role differences were most entrenched. Immigrant, rural, Southern, and poor women voted in much smaller numbers than their male counterparts, whereas the turnout rates of native-born, middle-class women were closer to that of men (Klein 1984; Andersen 1996).

During the Great Depression, New Deal Democrats courted women voters based on Roosevelt's social welfare policies. Thus, in 1936, First Lady Eleanor Roosevelt and Mary Dewson, the head of the Women's Division of the Democratic Party from 1932 to 1937, organized 60,000 women to canvass door-to-door for the Democrats (Klein 1984). Still, in presidential elections from 1920–1936 Corder and Wolbrecht (2016) find that women voters did not consistently favor any particular party's candidates more than men did. As new voters, in comparison to men, women's turnout levels varied more as a result of the competitiveness of the parties in their state and the restrictiveness of their state's electoral laws, such as registration requirements. Women's voting participation first exceeded 50 percent of eligible women in the hotly contested presidential race of 1948 in which Harry Truman survived a split of his party that led Strom Thurmond to run on a Dixiecrat ticket and Henry Wallace to run under the Progressive banner (Klein 1984). The race was so close that the *Chicago Tribune* mistakenly declared Republican Thomas Dewey the winner in its early morning edition (Norton et al. 1986).

By 1968 women's voting rates had largely caught up to the participation rates of men. Signaling the complete political integration of women in the realm of voting, since the 1984 election, women's participation rates in presidential elections have exceeded the rates of men across racial categories with the largest differences among African Americans (see Figures 3.1 and 3.2).[1] While the US Census has not yet released turnout figures for the 2016 election, between 1984 and 2004 white women were the most likely voters across all racial and gender groups. However, reflecting their enthusiasm for the election of the first African American President, Barack Obama, in 2008 and 2012 African American women exhibited the highest turnout (Center for American Women and Politics 2014).

---

[1]According to the Center for American Women and Politics (2014) in 2000, the first year for which data are available, Asian Pacific Islander men voted at a higher rate than Asian Pacific Islander women at 42.5 percent for women and 44.3 percent for men. Since 2000, voter turnout of Asian American women has equaled or exceeded the turnout rates among Asian American men.

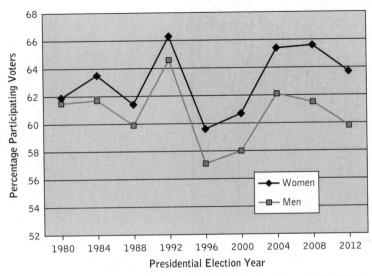

**Figure 3.1. Voter Turnout by Gender in Presidential Election Years 1980–2012.**
*Note*: Numbers are based on eligible voters as reported by the United States Census rather than the voting age population.
*Source*: "Gender Differences in Voter Turnout." Center for the American Woman and Politics (2014).

## THE EMERGENCE OF THE MODERN GENDER GAP

When most people think of the gender gap, they assume that it refers to the tendency of women to favor the Democratic Party. The media began paying attention to the gender gap in 1980 when Ronald Reagan's strong conservative politics, particularly his stances on the military and social welfare issues, gave him stronger support among men than women (Gilens 1988; Burrell 2005). However, this has not always been the case. Figure 3.3 identifies the gender gap in voting for the Democratic presidential candidates since 1952, measured as the difference between the percentage of men and women who support the Democratic candidate. The trends in presidential voting shown in Figure 3.3 and surveys of party identification since the 1950s demonstrate that women were aligned more closely with the Republican Party until 1964. This partially stems from the fact that in the 1950s and early 1960s, the majority of women were homemakers, whereas the majority of men were employed in blue-collar jobs. Homemakers and those in professional/managerial and clerical/sales jobs tend to vote Republican, whereas employees in blue-collar/service jobs who are often unionized are more likely to vote Democratic. Thus, the fact that in 1956, 64.5 percent of women were homemakers and only 16.9 percent held blue-collar jobs,

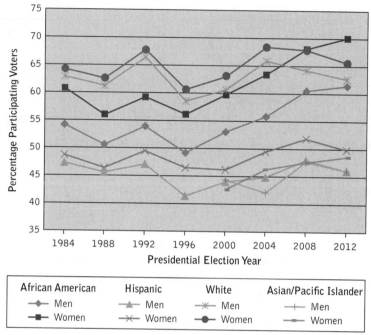

**Figure 3.2. Voter Turnout by Race and Gender in Presidential Elections 1984–2012.**
*Note*: Numbers are based on eligible voters as reported by the United States Census rather than the voting age population.
*Source*: "Gender Differences in Voter Turnout." Center for the American Woman and Politics (2014).

whereas less than 1 percent of men were homemakers and 64.8 percent were blue-collar workers, helps explain the gender gap in partisanship and voting during this period (Seltzer, Newman, and Leighton 1997; Norrander 2008).

Other scholars point out that the gender gap resulted more from men leaving the Democratic Party than women realigning toward it (Kaufmann and Petrocick 1999; Norrander 1999, 2008; Kanthak and Norrander 2004). Beginning in the 1960s, men, particularly white Southern men, increasingly became more Republican because of their opposition to the ascendancy of liberal views on civil rights and social welfare issues in the Democratic Party. At the same time, white Southern women also became more Republican but at half the rate of white Southern men. Outside the South, white men also affiliated more with the Republican Party but at a rate slightly lower than Southern white women. However, white women's partisan preferences outside the South showed no change over time (Norrander 1999, 2008; Kanthak and Norrander 2004). In the 1990s, there is some evidence

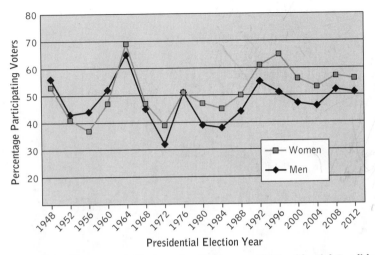

**Figure 3.3. The Gender Gap in the Vote for the Democratic Presidential Candidate.** *Source*: National Election Study.

that white women began to turn toward the Democratic Party because of the Democrats' more liberal positions on cultural issues (Kaufmann 2002).

Reflecting the slow but steady movement of white men, particularly white Southern men away from the Democratic Party, in 1960 men were 5 points more likely than women to vote for Democratic presidential candidate John F. Kennedy. However, by 1964, at the height of the civil rights movement, men were 4 points less likely than women to vote for Democratic President Lyndon Johnson and Democrats Hubert Humphrey and George McGovern in 1968 and 1972, respectively, drew slightly more women voters than men. In 1976, Jimmy Carter, a Southern moderate governor of Georgia running in the aftermath of the Watergate scandal, was able to win enough votes from men to eliminate the gap (Seltzer, Newman, and Leighton 1997; Norrander 1999, 2008). However, the gap reemerged and began to gain media attention when strong conservative Ronald Reagan was elected in 1980. Since the Reagan years, the gender gap is a consistent feature of American politics, averaging around 7 points. The gap peaked at 14 points with women voters strongly supporting President Bill Clinton's reelection over Republican Bob Dole in 1996. NES has not released its 2016 data. However, a comparison of exit poll data since 1992 in Figure 3.4 demonstrates that Democrats' reliance on women voters continued in 2016. Hillary Clinton's gender gap was in line with recent Democratic presidential candidates. In fact, Clinton's gender gap was most similar to the other contemporary Democratic candidate who won the popular vote but lost the Electoral College, Al Gore in 2000. Exit polls show a 13-point gender gap for Clinton, in

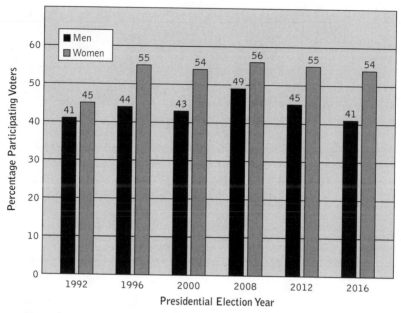

**Figure 3.4. The Gender Gap in the Vote for the Democratic Presidential Candidate 1992–2016.**
*Source*: Exit Polls Compiled by Center for American Women and Politics 2017. "The Gender Gap," http://www.cawp.rutgers.edu/sites/default/files/resources/ggpresvote.pdf.

which she won the support of 41 percent of men and 54 percent of women. Similarly, Al Gore won the support of 43 percent of men and 54 percent of women (Center for American Women and Politics 2017).

The persistence of the contemporary gender gap in which Democratic presidential candidates increasingly rely on women voters may reflect larger trends in the polarization of the political parties. The ideological polarization of the parties in which Republicans became more consistently conservative and Democrats increasingly liberal began at the elite level among officeholders and activists. The election of Ronald Reagan in 1980 and his delineation of strong conservative policies in combination with a more strongly partisan Congress, particularly after the 1994 Republican Revolution, sent strong signals to voters about what the parties stand for and precipitated an ideological realignment in the partisan preferences of voters (Abramowitz and Saunders 1998; Norrander 1999). There is also evidence that over time, the gender gap expands when the country becomes more ideologically conservative, when the economy declines, and when there is an increase in the number of single women (a group that is more likely to need the social welfare services provided by the government) (Box-Steffensmeier, De Boef, and Lin 2004).

While the gender gap is an important feature of contemporary electoral politics, it is smaller than other significant voting gaps in American politics. The greatest differences in American voting behavior are based on race. White voters are more likely to vote for Republican candidates while minority voters, including African Americans, Hispanics, and Asian Americans, lean toward Democrats. African Americans in particular vote overwhelmingly for Democrats. According to exit polls, in 2016, Hillary Clinton won 89 percent of African American voters, a proportion similar to the 88 percent of black voters won by John Kerry in 2004. Barack Obama, the first African American candidate and president, earned even more minority votes, winning 95 percent of African American votes in 2008 and 93 percent of these voters in 2012. Meanwhile, Democratic support among white voters has steadily declined. From 1992 through 2008, Democratic presidential candidates garnered between 41 and 43 percent of the white vote. By 2012 only 39 percent of white voters supported Barack Obama and Hillary Clinton garnered only 37 percent of the white vote in 2016 (Cilliza and Cohen 2012; CNN 2004, 2016a).

While the gap between African American and white voters remains both large and stable, the gap between white voters and other minority groups is expanding, particularly among Hispanics and Asian Americans. Thus, in 2004, 53 percent of Hispanic voters supported the Democratic presidential candidate, John Kerry, in his bid to unseat incumbent president George W. Bush. By 2012, 71 percent of Hispanic voters chose Democratic President Barack Obama. Similarly, Asian American support for the Democratic presidential candidate grew from 56 percent in 2004 to 73 percent in 2012. Hillary Clinton had less support from these minority voters than President Obama. Still, nearly two-thirds of Hispanic and Asian American voters supported Clinton, indicating that the Democratic Party is increasingly reliant on the support of minority voters as it continues to lose ground among white voters (Luhby 2016; Ramakrishnan 2016; Tyson and Maniam 2016).

Like the race gap, religious observance is a larger divide in American politics than the gender gap. Since 1992, those who attend weekly religious services are much more likely to vote for Republican presidential candidates than less observant voters. Thus, in 2016 62 percent of secular voters who never attend religious services supported Hillary Clinton while only 41 percent of voters who attend services weekly supported Clinton, a 21-point gap. The religiosity gap stems from the increased association of social conservatives with the Republican Party and a countermovement of secular voters to the Democratic Party (Fiorina 2011; CNN 2016a). The smaller size of the gender gap in comparison to other voting gaps in American politics may come as a surprise, given the level of attention devoted to the gender gap by the media and political candidates. However, women constitute a larger potential pool of voters than the voters in other categories, women have higher turnout rates than men, and women are often perceived as swing voters by both the Republican and Democratic Parties (Burrell 2005; Norrander 2008).

## THE GENDER GAPS: VOTING TRENDS ACROSS DIFFERENT GROUPS OF WOMEN

Since voting is influenced by a variety of demographic factors from race to education and marital status, it is important to examine trends in the voting behavior of different groups of women. While Hillary Clinton won more votes from women overall, she lost white women. Fifty-two percent of white women voted for Donald Trump while only 43 percent of these women supported Clinton (CNN 2016a). Media commentators decried the lack of female solidarity. "Clinton Couldn't Win Over White Women," "Why Hillary Clinton Couldn't Win Over Female Voters," and "White Women Sold Out the Sisterhood and the Whole World by Voting for Trump" were just some of the shocked headlines after the election (Anderson 2016; Malone 2016; Newton-Small 2016). Given Trump's salacious comments directed toward numerous women during the campaign, as well as the outcry after the leaked audiotape in October 2016, which heard him brag about his ability to sexually assault women because of his fame, many commentators assumed that women would abandon Trump in November. Comedienne Samantha Bee fumed "a majority of white women, faced with the choice between the first female president and a vial of weaponized testosterone, said, 'I'll take Option B. I just don't like her.' Hope you got your sticker, ladies. Way to lean out" (Bradley 2016). Yet in contemporary politics, white women consistently lean Republican, and the 2016 results were very similar to white women's voting behavior in the past several election cycles. While fewer white women vote Republican than white men, in the 2012 election 56 percent of white women voted for Republican Mitt Romney, while only 42 percent of white women (compared to 35 percent of white men) supported Barack Obama (CNN 2012; Dittmar 2016a).

Reflecting the fact that race is such a fundamental divide in American politics, African American and Hispanic women are much more likely to support Democratic candidates than white women. These women overwhelmingly voted for Hillary Clinton with 94 percent of black women, compared to 82 percent of black men, and 69 percent of Latino women, compared to 63 percent of Latino men, supporting Clinton. As the first African American president, Barack Obama received even more support from minority voters. In 2012, 96 percent of African American women and 87 percent of African American men voted for President Obama, and 76 percent of Latina women, compared to 65 percent of Latino men, favored

Barack Obama (Center for American Women and Politics 2012; Junn and Garcia Bedolla 2013; CNN 2016a).

The gender gap is also more pronounced at higher education and professional levels and between single men and women in comparison to married men and women. Some scholars argue that we should expect a larger gender gap among highly educated professionals because labor force participation exposes women to gender inequalities they would not see as homemakers and gives these women a means of economic independence that shapes their political behavior. Thus, the expectation is that professional women will be attracted to Democratic Party proposals related to equal pay and employment discrimination (Carroll 1988; Box-Steffensmeier, De Boef, and Lin 2004; Huddy, Cassese, and Lizotte 2008). Alternatively, other scholars maintain that the professional advancement of highly educated women leads to more shared experiences with men and will lead to a convergence of the political views of educated, professional men and women (Box-Steffensmeier, De Boef, and Lin 2004).

The education divide was a major factor in 2016. Clinton won college-educated white women by 7 points (51 to 44 percent), the only group of white women that favored Clinton. In 2012, these women had supported Mitt Romney. However, the dramatic shift of non-college-educated voters to Donald Trump propelled him to victory, particularly in key swing states, including Ohio, Pennsylvania, and Wisconsin. White voters without a college degree favored Trump by 39 points, a margin larger than Ronald Reagan's 1984 landslide against Walter Mondale (Brownstein 2016). By contrast, in 2012 non-college-educated whites voted for Romney 61–36, a healthy 25-point margin but 14 points less than Trump's support from these voters. Clinton did particularly poorly with white men without a college degree, losing them by 48 points (23–71 percent) but white women without a college degree also favored Trump by 27 points (34–61 percent) (Brownstein 2016; Dittmar 2016a; Tyson and Maniam 2016).

Finally, marital status is also an important influence on voting behavior. Single women are the strongest supporters of Democratic candidates, while married women are more likely to favor Republicans. Indeed, in 2016 63 percent of single women supported Hillary Clinton. While Clinton won unmarried women by 31 points (63–32), she only won married women by 2 points (49–47), and 57 percent of married men supported Trump (CNN 2016a). This small victory with married women represents the first time a Democratic presidential candidate had won married women in the last 20 years (Dittmar 2016a). For example, 53 percent of married women favored Mitt Romney in 2012 (CNN 2012). While there are currently more married than single voters, larger social trends indicate that marriage rates are declining. For example, the percentage of voters that were married dropped from 66 percent in 2008 to 60 percent in 2012 (Deckman 2012). The preference of single women for the Democratic Party is attributed to the fact that these women are the most economically vulnerable and thus the most likely to need the social welfare programs supported by the Democratic Party. Meanwhile married women are more likely to be older, white, more religious, and financially secure—all groups that lean Republican (Box-Steffensmeier, De Boef, and Lin 2004; Huddy, Cassese, and Lizotte 2008; Norrander 2008).

In sum, it is too simple to say that women as a group favor Democrats while men vote Republican. Instead, the gender gap varies across all types of men and women. Minority women heavily favor Democrats, while white women lean to the Republicans. College-educated women are increasingly moving to the Democratic Party, but women who did not attend college swing Republican. Unmarried women strongly support Democrats, while married women generally favor Republicans. In the competition for votes, the parties try to create policy platforms that will appeal to particular subgroups of men and women as they work to create a coalition that will propel them to victory.

## ISSUES THAT EXPLAIN THE GENDER GAP

To understand the nature of the gender gap and how likely it is that this gap will continue to manifest itself in electoral politics, one needs to examine the underlying causes of the gender gap in men and women's political attitudes and concerns. Beginning in the 1970s, survey research has demonstrated that women evince greater support for social welfare spending and a more activist government role in assisting the poor, in guaranteeing jobs, and in guaranteeing a standard of living (see Figure 3.5). In addition to differences in attitudes on social welfare issues, women are more likely to express feelings of insecurity and pessimism about the general economy and their own personal finances (Shapiro and Mahajan 1986; Seltzer, Newman, and Leighton 1997; Chaney, Alvarez, and Nagler 1998; Kaufman and Petrocik 1999; Norrander 1999, 2008; Box-Steffensmeier, De Boef, and Lin 2004). There are also some gender differences on environmental issues. Because women are more risk averse than men, a gender gap emerges on environmental regulations related to reducing risks such as health risks. However, there is no gender gap on issues where environmental protection is weighed against taxes or job growth (Norrander 2008).

Women's greater support for social welfare spending and government intervention in the economy may stem from the fact that, on average, women are more economically vulnerable than men. Women earn less than men, are more likely to receive welfare benefits, and are more likely to be

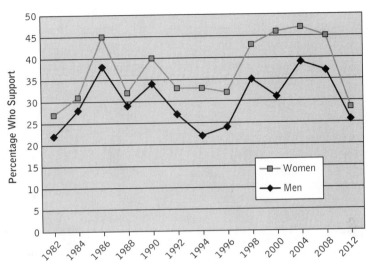

**Figure 3.5. The Gender Gap in Support for Increased Government Services and Spending.**
*Source*: National Election Study.

employed in social welfare occupations that rely on government funding (Norrander 1999, 2008). Among women, the minority women, particularly African American and Latina women, who most strongly support Democratic candidates, are more likely than white women to be single mothers with children under age 17 at home and are more likely to be low-income. Thus, these women have a stronger need for social safety net programs (O'Leary and Kornbluh 2009; Junn and Garcia Bedolla 2013). Additionally, there is some evidence that men are more likely to be pocketbook voters, basing their vote on their personal economic situation, whereas women are more likely to be sociotropic voters who weigh societal conditions more heavily. Therefore, women's greater empathy for the poor may drive their support for increased social welfare spending (Huddy, Cassese, and Lizotte 2008). Since social welfare issues and government spending have constituted a major fault line between the Republican and Democratic Parties since the New Deal, the gender gap will likely continue to be a feature of American politics for the foreseeable future.

Sex differences in support for the use of force constitute another important component of the gender gap. Over time, women have been less supportive of military intervention than men and less supportive of increased defense spending (see Figure 3.6). These issues played a particularly important role in determining the gender gap in the 1980s when women were less supportive of Ronald Reagan's defense buildup and more in favor of a freeze on nuclear weapons development than were men (Smith 1984;

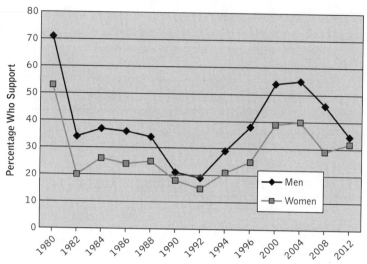

**Figure 3.6.  The Gender Gap in Support for Increased Defense Spending.**
*Source*: National Election Study.

Shapiro and Mahajan 1986; Seltzer, Newman, and Leighton 1997; Norrander 1999, 2008). Looking specifically at the issue of war, Figure 3.7 brings together public opinion polls from World War II through current debates about whether to send ground troops to defeat the Islamic terror group known as ISIS. Although the question wording differs slightly in each case, depending on the source and year, there are some clear patterns. While a majority of women have often supported the deployment of troops, in every case women are less inclined to support war than men are. Interestingly, in the most recent conflicts, the Iraq War and the campaign against ISIS, only a bare majority of women, 51 percent, supported going to war against Iraq in 2003, while men (67 percent) were strongly supportive of the war. Once the war became unpopular as a result of mounting casualties and costs to the economy, women were still more likely to oppose the war than men. Similarly, while a bare majority of men, 52 percent, would support sending troops to combat the terror group ISIS, only 41 percent of women favor sending ground troops to defeat ISIS as of May 2015.

Delving into opinions about terrorism, research on torture and the war on terrorism demonstrates that women are more likely than men to oppose the use of harsh interrogation techniques. Because women are more conscious of sexual violence than men, gender differences were largest regarding techniques that make the detainee feel the most personally vulnerable, such as sexually humiliating a detainee, forcing a detainee to go naked, or holding a detainee's head under water (Haider-Markel and Vieux 2008).

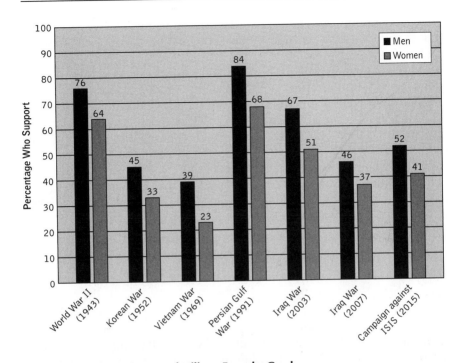

**Figure 3.7. Support for Use of Military Force by Gender.**
*Source*: World War II (Gallup, October 1943); Korean War (Roper Organization, October 1952); Vietnam War (Gallup, October 1969); Persian Gulf War (CBS/New York Times 1991); Iraq War 2003 (ABC News/Washington Post 2003); Iraq War 2007 (Gallup 2007); Campaign against ISIS (Pew Research Center 2015). In most cases, the surveys asked respondents about the use of force, but in the case of the Vietnam War question, Gallup asked respondents to describe themselves as hawkish or dovish when it came to Vietnam. Respondents who described themselves as hawkish are listed above.

With regard to use of force issues on the home front, women are more likely to oppose capital punishment and to support gun control measures (Seltzer, Newman, and Leighton 1997; Norrander 1999, 2008).

In contrast to conventional wisdom, feminist or women's issues are not an important component of the gender gap. Men and women express similar attitudes on gender roles, equality for women, and abortion. Although the media attributed the emergence of the gender gap in 1980 to Ronald Reagan's opposition to the ERA and his conservative position on abortion, research has shown that men and women were equally supportive of the ERA and equally likely to utilize it as a determinant of their vote (Mansbridge 1986). More recently, a study of support for the Obamacare mandate requiring that insurers provide contraceptive coverage found that greater female support for the birth control mandate stemmed from women's stronger commitment to the social safety net and government's role in providing social services and not to their attitudes about abortion (Deckman and McTague 2015).

However, there is some evidence that women do feel more intensely about their abortion position, particularly pro-life women. Moreover, women are more likely to hold positions at the extremes, either supporting abortion in all cases or prohibiting it in all circumstances (Seltzer, Newman, and Leighton 1997; Norrander 1999, 2008; Kaufmann 2002; Jelen and Wilcox 2005). Perhaps related, there is also evidence that women are more religious and they express slightly more conservative attitudes on some additional social issues, including school prayer, sexual mores (such as pornography), and civil liberties (Seltzer, Newman, and Leighton 1997; Norrander 1999, 2008).

## COURTING THE WOMEN'S VOTE IN A COMPETITIVE POLITICAL CLIMATE

Throughout the 1990s and 2000s, political competition between Republicans and Democrats intensified at all levels of government, aided in part by the realignment of many white Southerners to the Republican Party. Since 1994, when the Republican Revolution election gave Republicans control of both houses of Congress for the first time in more than 40 years, party control of the House and Senate has rested on a handful of seats, and control of each chamber has shifted multiple times. At the presidential level, races have been so tight that twice in the new millennium the winner of the popular vote did not win the Electoral College and the presidency. In 2000, the contest between Al Gore and George W. Bush was decided by such a small number of votes that the recounting of votes in Florida and the dispute over how to count those votes kept the outcome from being decided long after Election Day. Like 2000, in 2016 the Democratic candidate Hillary Clinton won the popular vote but lost the Electoral College. President Trump secured victory in the Electoral College by winning three states, Michigan, Wisconsin, and Ohio, by less than 1 percent of the vote—0.2, 0.7, and 0.8 percent, respectively. Thus, Trump won these states by less than 80,000 votes in an election where Clinton won the popular vote by almost 2.9 million (Bump 2016).

In such a volatile and competitive electoral climate, both parties scramble for ways to motivate their base and attract the elusive swing voter to expand their voting coalition in order to achieve a governing majority. Consequently, each election cycle, the parties target specific groups of women voters. Women are particularly courted because they routinely vote at higher rates than men, are less likely than men to be strong partisans, and are

Governor Sarah Palin, the Republican candidate for vice president, campaigns in Colorado Springs, Colorado, November 3, 2008.
*Source*: AP Photo / David Zalubowski.

more likely to decide on their vote later in the election cycle (Burrell 2005; Norrander 2008).

The Republican Party focuses the most attention on white, married, suburban women with children. Married voters lean Republican more than single voters, and married voters are more likely to turn out to vote than single voters. Married women are also more religious than singles, making them more open to the traditional family values message of the Republican Party (Brownstein 2008; Elder 2008; Norrander 2008). Indeed, religiosity is now a better predictor of voting behavior than religious affiliation, meaning, for example, that an observant Catholic or Protestant is more likely to vote Republican than a Catholic or Protestant voter who rarely attends services (Brownstein 2013). Thus, married, suburban, white women were the "soccer moms" that Bill Clinton and Bob Dole competed over in 1996. They were the voters that George W. Bush tried to appeal to in 2000 with his message of "compassionate conservatism." In 2004, these married, white, suburban women became "security moms" who were concerned about the threat of terrorism and the security of their families (Kanthak and

Norrander 2004; Martinez and Carey 2004; Norrander 2008). Similarly, in 2016 Trump's tough talk on immigration and terrorism appealed to Republican women's concerns about their children's safety (Deckman 2016).

Responding to the economic recession, Republicans focused even more attention on non-college-educated white women in 2008 and 2012. The media described these voters as "waitress moms" or "Wal-Mart moms" who "shop at Wal-Mart at least once a week, earn less than $60,000 a year, [and] have less than a college education" (Zerinke 2008; Trotta 2012). John McCain's selection of Alaska Governor Sarah Palin as his running mate was an important part of his effort to reach working-class women voters and evangelical women. Palin frequently described herself and her female supporters as "hockey moms" or "mama grizzlies" seeking to protect their families from government overreach and trying to put the government's fiscal house in order (Healy 2008; Kaufman 2008). While non-college-educated women are less likely to turn out than college-educated voters, married women without college degrees voted strongly Republican in 2012. Donald Trump was particularly successful with non-college-educated voters. These voters powered his destruction of the traditional "blue wall" as he won Rust Belt states, including Michigan, Pennsylvania, and Wisconsin, that had voted for Democratic presidential candidates in five or more of the previous presidential contests (Brownstein 2016; Collingswood 2016).

As an anti-establishment candidate stirring up populist anger, Trump focused very little attention on courting women voters compared to previous Republican nominees. Instead, his "Make America Great Again" slogan was aimed at mobilizing male voters, particularly those rural and working-class voters displaced by the loss of manufacturing jobs. Emphasizing a protectionist message on trade and a crackdown on illegal immigration, Trump appealed to these voters' feelings of economic anxiety and racial resentment (Collingswood 2016; Cramer 2016; Guo 2016).

Throughout the campaign, Trump portrayed himself as the strong alpha male who would never back down from a fight. During the primary, he belittled his opponents by portraying them as too feminine and weak to exercise leadership. He ridiculed Jeb Bush as low energy and characterized Marco Rubio as "Little Marco" (Chavez and Stracqualursi 2016). He dismissed Carly Fiorina, declaring, "Look at that face, would anyone vote for that?," and he took aim at Ted Cruz by posting an unflattering picture of Cruz's wife Heidi next to a picture of his model wife Melania (Estepa 2015; Green 2016). Trump even touted the size of his manhood in a presidential primary debate when he pushed back on Marco Rebio's campaign rally taunt that Trump had "small hands" (Flores 2016).

Trump's appeal to male vigor was reflected in his primary numbers. Throughout the primaries, Trump earned a plurality of male and female voters in a majority of states. However, Trump consistently earned stronger support from men. Looking at the states where exit polls were conducted, Trump earned an average of 7 percent more votes from male than female primary voters, winning an average of 46 percent of men and 39 percent of women. By contrast, Ted Cruz and John Kasich ran relatively evenly with men and women, with women favoring both candidates by only one point. Before he dropped out of the race, Marco Rubio did an average of 4 points better with women than men (author analysis of CNN 2016b; Dittmar 2016b). This strong support from men helped propel Trump to victory since more men than women vote in Republican primaries (Norrander 2003; Dittmar 2016b).

In the general election campaign, Trump continued his appeal to masculinity. He claimed Hillary was playing the woman card and repeatedly questioned her stamina (Ball 2016; Deckman 2016). Clinton responded by selling a woman card on her campaign website and declaring "if fighting for women's health care, paid family leave, and equal pay is playing the woman card, then deal me in" (Bellstrom 2016). Trump campaign rallies featured T-shirts emblazoned with macho and sexist messaging, including "Trump: Finally Someone with Balls" and "Trump That Bitch" (Ball 2016). After a video tape emerged where Trump described grabbing women by the genitals against their wishes, he and his campaign surrogates dismissed it as locker room talk (Reily 2016).

While Trump largely focused his efforts on mobilizing men, particularly non-college-educated white men, he did try to appeal to subgroups of women that traditionally support Republicans. Like previous Republican candidates, Trump sent female surrogates to court women voters. Trump's campaign manager Kellyanne Conway made a career of advising male Republican candidates on how to speak to women voters (Rubin 2016). Sarah Palin was an early supporter of Donald Trump, endorsing him right before the Iowa caucuses, the first contest in the Republican nomination battle. Other high profile and conservative Tea Party women also campaigned for Trump, including Ann Coulter and Phyllis Schlafly, the head of Eagle Forum and champion of the STOP ERA movement (Deckman 2016). In September, his campaign kicked off a Women's Empowerment tour headlined by his daughter-in-law Lara Trump and featuring female supporters, including his national spokeswoman Katrina Pierson and a pair of African American women, Diamond and Silk, who had a popular YouTube channel supporting Trump (Glueck 2016). His strongest surrogate to women voters, particularly white, suburban women, was his daughter Ivanka Trump, an accomplished businesswoman and mother. Speaking at the Republican National Convention, Ivanka Trump called for paid family leave and tax credits for child care, policy positions that have not been embraced by contemporary Republican presidential candidates. She helped Trump craft a policy plan to make child care more affordable and provide women, but not men, with six weeks of paid maternity leave (Drabold 2016; Sullivan and Costa 2016).

While Republicans work to increase turnout among subgroups of married, white women, Democratic strategists target single women, college-educated women, minority women, and millennials. Single heads of households are more economically insecure and, therefore, expected to be more inclined to support Democratic social policy initiatives. Single women under 40 and older women with grown children are particular targets of the get-out-the-vote efforts of the Democrats (Brownstein 2008, 2013; Norrander 2008). The group Women's Voices, Women's Votes was created to register and mobilize single women, as these women are less likely to vote than their married counterparts (http://www.wvwvaf.org/). To appeal to single women, Democrats emphasize issues such as abortion rights, access to emergency contraception for young single women, affordable health care, equal pay, and, for senior women, improvements to Medicare and Social Security (Martinez and Carey 2004; Roarty 2012; Tumulty 2012).

Throughout the Obama years, Democrats increasingly focused on courting these groups of minority, college-educated, single, young millennial, and minority women. This coalition is often referred to as the "Rising American Electorate" because these demographic groups constitute a growing proportion of the American electorate. For example, between 2000 and 2012 racial minorities grew from 19 percent to 26 percent of the electorate (Frey, Teixeira, and Griffin 2016). According to exit polls, nonwhite voters constituted 29 percent of the electorate in 2016 (CNN 2016a). These voters are projected to make up 40 percent of voters by 2032 because of immigration trends and the fact that younger generations coming up are more racially mixed (Frey, Teixeira, and Griffin 2016).

In 2008 and 2012, Barack Obama heavily courted the minority, single, college-educated, and millennial women that are a part of the Rising American Electorate. To mobilize these voters, Obama highlighted women's issues, including health care, equal pay, and reproductive rights. In 2008, he touted his support for equal pay by campaigning with Lilly Ledbetter, the woman who unsuccessfully sued the Goodyear Tire Company for years of being paid less than her male colleagues and who was ultimately denied redress by the Supreme Court (Zerinke 2008). The Lilly Ledbetter Equal Pay Act was the first bill that Obama signed as president (Murray 2009). In 2012 and the 2014 congressional midterm elections, Obama and congressional Democrats accused Republicans of waging a "war on women" in which they opposed efforts to achieve equal pay for women and wanted to deny women access to the contraceptive services that were guaranteed under the preventive health provisions of Obama's Affordable Care Act (Reinhard 2012; Roarty 2012; Thompson 2012).

President Barack Obama appears with Lilly Ledbetter, left, and Vice President Joe Biden, right, before signing the Lilly Ledbetter Bill for equal pay for equal work Thursday, Jan. 29, 2009. The pay discrimination Ledbetter experienced at Goodyear Tire and Rubber Co. became a rallying cry for women across the country. Ledbetter campaigned heavily for President Obama in 2008.
*Source*: AP Photo / Pablo Martinez Monsivais.

Furthermore, in his campaign speeches, Obama frequently paid tribute to his mother, who was a single mother, and to his grandmother, who helped raise him. He celebrated his wife's strength and accomplishments and spoke of his hopes for his two daughters (Levey 2008). Prominent celebrities like Oprah Winfrey and female officeholders from Democratic leader Nancy Pelosi to Obama's former primary opponent and future Secretary of State Hillary Clinton worked to mobilize women voters during his first race for the presidency (Healy 2008; Vedantam 2008).

As the first female presidential nominee of a major party, in 2016 Hillary Clinton openly embraced her gender. Outreach to the Democratic leaning groups of women who constitute the Rising American Electorate was central to her campaign strategy. Clinton drafted detailed policy proposals to reduce child care costs, raise the minimum wage, tackle student loan debt, and safeguard reproductive rights (Ehrenfreund and Tankersley 2016; Paquette 2016a; Siddiqui and Gambino 2016). She touted a plan for 12 weeks of paid family leave and promised to appoint a cabinet that was half women (Sussman and Meckler 2016; Crockett 2016). The video introducing Clinton at the Democratic National Convention included a montage of the

Protestors hold a sign, "Stop the War on Women," during the "Walk in My Shoes, Hear Our Voice" protest Monday, March 12, 2012, at the state capitol in Atlanta. The rally was held to protest against legislation passed by the Georgia State Senate banning abortion coverage under state employees' health care plans and exempting religious health care providers from having to cover birth control.
*Source*: AP Photo / *Atlanta Journal-Constitution*, Jason Getz.

previous male presidents and ended with Clinton shattering a virtual glass ceiling (Fang 2016). When she accepted the nomination, Clinton came out in a white pantsuit to evoke the white dresses suffragettes wore when they marched for women's voting rights (Jamieson 2016).

In her campaign appearances and her television advertising, Clinton spoke of her long career fighting for women and children, including her work for the Children's Defense Fund and her focus on education and health care as first lady (Baird 2016). She also touted her commitment to women's rights across the world, including her speech as first lady at the UN World Conference on Women in Beijing where Clinton declared women's rights are human rights and her work to empower women in the developing world during her time as Secretary of State (Newton-Small 2015). Clinton appeared frequently with prominent women leaders, including Senator Elizabeth Warren (D-MA), former Secretary of State Madeleine Albright, and first lady Michelle Obama, as well as female celebrities from Katy Perry to Beyoncé (Gass 2016; Phillip 2016). Pushing back against Donald Trump's sexist rhetoric, Clinton denounced Trump's attacks on her and other women. She ran commercials showing young girls looking at themselves in the mirror and listening to insulting Trump remarks about women's looks (Merica 2016; Siddiqui and Gambino 2016).

Ultimately, college-educated, minority, single, and millennial women strongly supported Hillary Clinton, helping her win the popular vote by nearly three million votes (Walsh 2016). However, Clinton's support from these women was offset by Trump's gains among non-college-educated white men and women in the Rust Belt states, propelling Trump to victory in the electoral college (Brownstein 2016).

Post-election, there were numerous analyses that showed that elements of the Rising American Electorate had not turned out as strongly for Clinton as they did for Barack Obama. In the key states of Wisconsin, Michigan, and Pennsylvania, African American turnout fell from 2012 levels (Jackson 2016). Similarly, in 2016, millennials, voters between age 18 and 35, were now as large a share of eligible voters as the baby boomers (age 52–70) (Fry 2016). However, younger voters turn out at lower rates (Fry 2016). Thus, in 2016 voters between 18 and 44 made up 44 percent of the electorate, while voters over 45 constituted 56 percent of the electorate (CNN 2016a). As the establishment candidate in a change election year, Clinton had trouble building enthusiasm and mobilizing some of the voters in her coalition (Blake 2016; Brownstein 2016).

Mobilization of single, minority, and young voters is a continuing challenge for Democrats. While these voters pushed Barack Obama over the finish line in 2008 and 2012, they are less likely to vote than older, married, and white voters. Indeed, in midterm elections, when congressional candidates are up for reelection but the president is not on the ballot, voter turnout falls from an average of 60 percent to about 40 percent (Kernell et al. 2014). Compared to presidential years, the voters in midterm elections are generally older, whiter, and wealthier, a profile that favors Republican candidates (Brownstein 2013). Thus, between Obama's 2012 presidential election and the 2014 midterm elections, turnout among young voters (18–29) dropped 6 points from 19 percent to 13 percent of the electorate, and turnout among single women dropped from 23 percent to 21 percent of the electorate (CNN 2012, 2014). A two-point decline might seem small, but these differences represent millions of voters (PBS Newshour 2014).

For Republicans, their challenge is that their most reliable voters constitute a shrinking proportion of the electorate, particularly in presidential years. With increasing racial diversity, Republicans must win a greater share of white voters to prevail. Yet the population of white voters continues to decline. When Ronald Reagan won the presidency in 1980, white voters made up 88 percent of the electorate (Brownstein 2013). By 2016, only 71 percent of the electorate was white (CNN 2016a). Looking to the future, Democrats hold an advantage with the fastest growing groups in the electorate (minorities, youth, single women), but they need to work harder to mobilize their voters. Meanwhile, Republicans need to grow their coalition to capture some of the expanding groups in the electorate, including racial minorities, college-educated women, and single women. As a result, we should expect both parties to continue targeting subgroups of women that might favor their candidates.

## DOES THE GENDER GAP BRING WOMEN POLITICAL POWER?

In the early 1980s, feminists and women's organizations, particularly the National Organization for Women (NOW), coined the term *gender gap* and worked to draw the attention of the media and party leadership to the potential importance of women as a voting bloc. Sending a monthly "Gender Gap Update" to several thousand reporters, Ellie Smeal (president of NOW) and other women leaders sought to parlay the gender gap into stronger support for the ERA and, in 1984, to pressure Walter Mondale, the Democratic nominee for president, to select a woman as his running mate. Although the campaign for the ERA ultimately fell three states short of ratification, women's groups and concerns about the gender gap did play a key role in Walter Mondale's decision to tap Congresswoman Geraldine Ferraro to be his vice presidential candidate (Bonk 1988; Frankovic 1988). Similarly, Ronald Reagan's concerns about his lack of support among women voters in 1980 led him to promise to appoint the first woman to the Supreme Court, a promise that he fulfilled with the appointment of Sandra Day O'Connor (Burrell 2005). Does the gender gap empower women and pressure politicians to adopt policies that benefit specific groups of women? Or do politicians pay lip service to the needs of particular subgroups of women in an effort to win elections and then ignore the needs of women when governing?

At the presidential level, Burrell (2005) argues that incumbent presidents running for reelection will use the power of their office to create initiatives that will appeal to women voters. Thus, in an effort to mobilize women voters for the 1996 election, President Clinton increased the number of grants to combat violence against women, convened an Early Child Development and Learning Conference and a White House Conference on Child Care, held a roundtable on pay equity, and created a White House Office for Women's Initiatives and Outreach that held roundtables across the country on women's issues. He also proposed new legislation on pay equity and an expansion of family and medical leave (Burrell 2005). Underscoring the effort to reach female voters, the Family and Medical Leave Act was the first bill President Clinton signed into law.

Similarly, Barack Obama used his executive authority to pursue policies for women. Upon winning office in 2008, the first piece of legislation

Obama signed into law was the Lilly Ledbetter Fair Pay Act (Murray 2009). He supported inclusion of a broad mandate for contraception in the Affordable Care Act. Obama used executive orders to provide some paid leave for federal workers and to further equal pay by requiring government contractors to disclose more details about what their employees earn and to let their employees share salary information to reduce pay secrecy (Eilperin 2014; Wheeler 2015).

While these initiatives are meant to help women and their families, Susan Carroll argues that the courting of ephemeral swing voting groups like soccer moms actually disempowers women. Examining the 1996 reelection bid of Bill Clinton, Susan Carroll (1999) argued that the competition for the votes of "soccer moms" between Bill Clinton and Bob Dole in 1996 did not lay a foundation for significant policy changes to benefit women and left out broad segments of women voters. During the campaign, Clinton appealed to "soccer moms" by touting his support for policies, including v-chips in televisions, school uniforms, and an expansion of the Family and Medical Leave Act to allow parents to attend parent–teacher meetings. Bob Dole campaigned with soccer moms at his side and promoted the ways in which his tax cuts would help these women and their families. According to Carroll, the focus on the soccer mom and policy proposals related to children essentialized women as mothers and deflected attention away from the concerns of other subgroups of women (including older women, women on welfare, women of color, and professional women). This focus on soccer moms gave the campaigns the appearance of being responsive to the concerns of women while ignoring the majority of women. Therefore, despite the largest gender gap in presidential voting history—one that was not caused by the votes of soccer moms—activists representing various women's groups could point to no specific campaign promises that gave them a mandate to demand action on behalf of women on issues such as health care, abortion, welfare, employment, or child care (Carroll 1999).

By contrast, in her research on gender differences in the policy activities of members of the House of Representatives and Senate, Swers (2002, 2013) found that concern about the gender gap among the leadership of the Democratic and Republican Parties raises the profile of women members of Congress, facilitates their efforts to gain positions of power in the party and committee structures, and enhances their ability to pursue policy initiatives related to women.

Due to their traditional advantage with women voters and the identification of many social welfare and feminist issues with the Democratic Party, Democrats are particularly eager to highlight issues and themes that will reinforce voters' perception of Democrats as the party advancing women's rights. To solidify this image, the party seeks out women members to speak on the House floor and in the media on women's issues, ranging from reproductive health to family and medical leave. Accepting these roles enables female Democrats to raise their public profile and enhance their standing with the party leadership. These Democratic women can then use their political capital to persuade party leadership to advance legislative proposals related to women's issues, sometimes even pushing leadership to take a stronger position in favor of women's rights (Swers 2002, 2013). In recent years, female Democratic senators acting individually and as a group pressured the Obama administration and Democratic leaders to include broad provision of contraceptive services among the preventive services covered by insurance companies under the Affordable Care Act, and they pressured the administration to narrowly limit the types of employers that could gain a religious exemption from providing contraceptive services (Swers 2013).

In sum, the question of whether the gender gap brings women political power is a complicated one. Women's groups have long tried to harness the power of the gender gap to lobby politicians to champion proposals that advance women's rights. As women increase their presence in Congress, some female members have utilized the gender gap to push their parties to support policies that will help women and their families. Still, parties are electoral coalitions working to solidify their base and expand their outreach to swing voters. Subgroups of women that don't fall into these categories of coveted voters can find their needs ignored.

## DO WOMEN VOTE FOR WOMEN?

It is often assumed that women provide a natural constituency of voters for women candidates. However, this is not necessarily the case, and current research provides conflicting evidence. The most important predictor of an individual's vote is party identification. Voters who identify as Democrats tend to vote for Democratic candidates. Similarly, voters who identify as Republicans are more likely to vote for Republican candidates. In 2016, there were many articles suggesting that Republican women would turn away from Trump, but in the end, women largely voted their party, and Clinton's support among women largely followed the trajectory of previous Democratic candidates. Indeed, Trump won 88 percent of self-identified Republican voters even though four of the last five Republican presidential nominees refused to endorse him and Trump took policy positions that conflict with the conservative ideology espoused by traditional Republican elites and officeholders, particularly his stance against trade deals and his advocacy of a large infrastructure spending program (CNN 2016a; Enten 2016).

At the congressional level, voters are increasingly voting a straight party ticket, aligning their votes for the House and Senate with their presidential votes. In 2016, for the first time there were no split tickets, meaning that every state that voted for the Democratic presidential candidate, Hillary Clinton, also supported the Democratic Senate candidate and states that voted for the Republican, Donald Trump, also sent a Republican to the Senate (Enten 2016; Phillips 2016). Beyond party, incumbency plays a powerful role in vote choice as incumbents, particularly House incumbents, are routinely reelected at rates above 90 percent. Incumbent members of Congress, who are largely men, enjoy significant advantages over their male and female challengers, including superior fundraising, higher name recognition, and a large staff assisting them in helping constituents and building a policy record to run on (Herrnson 2012; Jacobson 2013).

Given the overwhelming importance of party identification and incumbency, is there any room for a voter's sex to impact his or her candidate choice? Some research suggests an affinity effect does exist in which voters are more likely to support a candidate of the same sex. For example, Sanbonmatsu (2002) finds that voters have a standing baseline gender preference to vote for a male or a female candidate and women are more likely than men to express a gender preference and to prefer a female candidate. Alternatively, women may vote for women because they trust them more on "group salient" issues that have a larger impact on women such as sexual harassment, child care, or abortion, especially when an election emphasizes these group salient issues (Paolino 1995; Dolan 2008b).

Others claim that women may be more likely to vote for women because of a shared gender consciousness that recognizes that women are underrepresented in government and that women's political futures are tied together (Rinehart 1992; Rosenthal 1995; Lewis 1999). However, race consciousness among blacks is more widespread than gender consciousness among women, as African Americans are more likely to express a sense of linked fate. The social organization of race is based on separation between whites and blacks, whereas the social organization of gender incorporates intimacy among men and women. Moreover, as a majority in the population women are divided by race, class, education, and other identities, creating a large array of opinions among women (Huddy, Cassese, and Lizotte 2008; Burns and Kinder 2011; Tesler 2016). Yet much of the research on gender and candidate evaluations is based on experiments in which voters are asked about hypothetical candidates rather than real world elections where the ratio of female to male candidates is smaller. Examining election results, scholars find that women may be more inclined to vote for women candidates when gender issues are primed and highly salient to the campaign, most notably during the 1992 Year of the Woman elections (Sapiro and Conover 1997; Dolan 2004, 2008a). Women might also be more inclined to vote for women candidates in low-information elections where less is known about the positions of the candidates (McDermott 1997). In a comprehensive analysis of the 1990–2000 elections, Dolan (2004) found a limited impact for sex, as women were more likely to vote for women in House races but not in Senate races. However, in a more recent analysis of the 2010 elections Dolan (2014) found that after accounting for partisanship and incumbency, women were no more likely to support female candidates in House, Senate, or governors races.

Additionally, the ability to determine whether women vote for women is complicated by the fact that the gender gap in women's voting patterns favors Democrats, and more women candidates run as Democrats. For example, in the 2016 election, among the 167 women running for the House of Representatives, 120 candidates were Democrats while only 47 candidates were Republicans (Center for American Women and Politics 2016). Therefore, it is possible that women are not voting for women but are simply more likely to vote for Democrats (Norrander 1999, 2008). Indeed, analyses of voter opinions about the parties demonstrate that voters trust Democrats to handle issues that align with stereotypes about the issue expertise of female candidates, including health care, education, and family issues, while preferring Republicans to handle the male issues of national security and tax policy (Dolan 2004, 2014; Winter 2010). This alignment of partisan and issue stereotypes has led to characterization of the Democratic Party as the "mommy party" and the Republican Party as the "daddy party" (Winter 2010). Moreover, Palmer and Simon find that certain districts are more likely to elect women candidates to Congress and these districts are more urban, more diverse, and have higher median household incomes. In the current political climate, these are also more likely to be Democratic districts (Palmer and Simon 2012). Just as particular subgroups of women are more likely to vote for Democratic presidential candidates, research indicates that certain groups of women are more likely to support female candidates, including feminists, liberals, African Americans, and well-educated women (Rosenthal 1995; Smith and Fox 2001; Lynch and Dolan 2014).

## HILLARY CLINTON AND THE WOMEN'S VOTE

Hillary Clinton's historic run for the presidency provides the first opportunity to test whether women are more likely to support female candidates at the presidential level. As noted earlier in the chapter, Clinton's 13-point gender gap was on the higher end but in line with previous Democratic candidates. She had strong support from the minority, single, and college-educated women that have tilted toward the Democrats in recent elections. Clinton did better than previous candidates with college-educated white women and married women. Indeed, her 2-point advantage with married women marks the first time a Democratic presidential candidate had won married white women in the last 20 years (CNN 2016a; Dittmar 2016a). Clearly there was not a large gender affinity affect that helped Clinton in the general election.

However, there was a male backlash. Compared to President Obama who won men by 1 point (49–48) in 2008 and lost men by 7 points (45–52) in 2012, Donald Trump beat Hillary Clinton among male voters by 11 points (52–41). It seems that more men voted for third party candidates in 2016, as 7 percent of men supported a third party candidate compared to only 3 percent in 2012 (CNN 2008a, 2012, 2016a). However, Al Gore and John Kerry also lost men by 11 points, as Bush beat Gore among men 54–43 and Kerry by 55–44 (Center for American Women and Politics 2017).

Clinton's biggest problems were with white men. While Clinton lost white women to Trump by 9 points (52–43), she lost white men by a gaping 31 points (62–31). Yet in 2012, Obama also lost white men by 27 points (35–62) and white women by 14 points (42–56). Non-college-educated white men most vehemently opposed Clinton. She lost them by 48 points (23–71), but she also lost non-college-educated white women by 27 points (34–61). The education gap among white voters was a major shift in 2016 as there was not a large education gap in 2012 (CNN 2012, 2016a). It is not clear how much of Clinton's problems with white men are based on gender bias against a female candidate or responsiveness to the heightened masculinity in Trump's campaign. However, group solidarity based on a shared gender consciousness was clearly not a strong factor in the general election (Tesler 2016).

There is some evidence of women voting for women in the Democratic primary. Since the Reagan years, feminists and women's groups are an increasingly important part of the Democratic Party (Freeman 1986; Grossmann and Hopkins 2015). Furthermore, more women than men vote in the Democratic primary (Norrander 2016a). In both 2008 and 2016, Hillary Clinton's strongest support came from women voters. Table 3.2 reports the average proportion of the vote Hillary Clinton, Barack Obama, and Bernie Sanders won from various subgroups of men and women across the states. For example, across 37 states that conducted exit polls in the 2008 Democratic primary, Hillary Clinton won an average of 51 percent of women's votes and 42 percent of men's votes, a 9-point gender gap. In 2016, across 27 states that utilized exit polls, Clinton won an average of 60 percent of women's votes and 49 percent of men's votes, an 11-point gender gap (author analysis CNN 2008b, 2016b).

Comparing Democratic primaries from 1980 to 2000, Norrander finds that a gender gap emerged in one quarter of these primaries. The largest gap was in 2000 when in half of the primaries, women voters favored Al

**Table 3.2.  The Gender Gap in the 2008 and 2016 Democratic Primaries**

| | 2008 Average Gender Gap Across States | | | | | | 2016 Average Gender Gap Across States | | | | | |
| | Clinton | | | Obama | | | Clinton | | | Sanders | | |
| | Women | Men | Diff. | Women | Men | Diff. | Women | Men | Diff. | Women | Men | Diff. |
|---|---|---|---|---|---|---|---|---|---|---|---|---|
| All | 51 | 42 | +9 | 45 | 52 | –7 | 60 | 49 | +11 | 38 | 49 | –11 |
| *Race* | | | | | | | | | | | | |
| White | 60 | 49 | +11 | 35 | 44 | –9 | 58 | 44 | +14 | 41 | 55 | –14 |
| Black | 18 | 13 | +5 | 81 | 86 | –5 | 80 | 80 | 0 | 19 | 19 | 0 |
| Latino | 69 | 59 | +10 | 31 | 40 | –9 | 72 | 63 | +9 | 28 | 36 | –8 |
| *Marital Status* | | | | | | | | | | | | |
| Married | 50 | 41 | +9 | 45 | 53 | –8 | 68 | 61 | +7 | 38 | 46 | –8 |
| Single | 48 | 37 | +11 | 48 | 57 | –9 | 53 | 34 | +19 | 45 | 65 | –20 |

*Notes:* Numbers are average % support from each group across states that held exit polls in the 2008 and 2016 Democratic primaries. 37 states conducted exit polls in 2008 and 27 states held exit polls in 2016.
*Source:* CNN Primary Exit Polls 2008 and 2016.

Gore by a margin of 5 percent (Norrander 2003, 2016a). Clearly Clinton had robust support from Democratic women in both her primary runs. The larger gender gap in the 2016 primary likely reflects the fact that in 2008 Clinton downplayed her gender while in 2016 Clinton decided to emphasize women's issues and the historic nature of her candidacy (Lawrence and Rose 2010; Traister 2016). This more overt discussion of gender and women's issues may have garnered the support of more Democratic women while also driving away some Democratic men. Indeed, Clinton struggled the most with unmarried men losing them to Obama by 20 points (37–57) in 2008 and to Sanders by a wider 31-point margin (34–65) (CNN 2016b; CNN 2008b) (see Table 3.2).

Among groups of women, Clinton's support varied across the two primary campaigns depending on how voters responded to her opponent. Thus, in 2008 when Clinton ran against Barack Obama, black voters enthusiastically supported the first African American president as he earned the votes of an average of 81 percent of black women and 86 percent of black men. In 2016, when Obama was not on the ballot and Hillary Clinton was running as the former Secretary of State from the Obama administration, on average 80 percent of black voters supported Clinton. Black voters were particularly important to Clinton's 2016 victories in Southern states. For example, in Mississippi black women constituted 47 percent of the Democratic primary electorate and Clinton won 90 percent of their votes compared to 86 percent of black men and 71 percent of white women (CNN 2016c; Norrander 2016b). Meanwhile, in both 2008 and 2016 more Latino voters chose Hillary Clinton over her opponent. Thus, Clinton garnered an average of 69 percent of Latina women's votes in 2008 and 72 percent of these women's votes in 2016. Her gender gap among Latinos was 10 points in 2008 and 9 points in 2016, but on average, she still earned the majority of Latino men's support, 59 percent in 2008 and 63 percent in 2016 (CNN 2008b, 2016b) (see Table 3.2).

As the establishment candidate touting her experience and extensive policy knowledge, in both 2008 and 2016 Clinton earned the most support from older voters while she had more trouble connecting with younger voters who were looking for a change. Indeed, in 2008 Clinton lost 18–29-year-olds to Obama by an average of 26 points (35–61). In 2016, the gap widened as younger voters favored the septuagenarian Sanders by an average of 43 points (71–28) and Sanders won younger women by an average of 37 points (CNN 2008b, 2016b; Reston and Ramirez 2016). While Clinton earned more support from women than men in all age categories, media commentators frequently noted the contrast between older women who strongly supported Clinton and their younger counterparts who embraced the message of change promised by Obama in 2008 and Sanders in 2016 (Kantor 2008a, 2008b; Steiger 2016).

Older women most closely identified with Clinton's struggles as a woman competing in the male-dominated political world. These women witnessed the feminist movement and are more likely to have faced employment discrimination and the challenges of balancing work and child care responsibilities (Kantor 2008a, 2008b; Huddy and Carey 2009; Steiger 2016). Growing up in a society changed by the feminist movement and just starting out in their careers, younger women did not feel as much of a sense of urgency to elect a female president. In 2016, facing a tough job market after the Great Recession and high rates of student loan debt, many young women were more drawn to Sanders's broadly progressive economic message of raising the minimum wage, reducing student debt, and health care for all (Bruenig 2016). Interestingly, one study found that younger women who had already experienced workplace discrimination and/or having child care responsibilities limit their employment prospects were more likely to support Clinton than other young female voters (Poloni-Staudinger, Strachan, and Schaffner 2016).

Presidential nominee Hillary Clinton appears with pop star Katy Perry to court younger women voters; while younger Democratic women tended to side with Bernie Sanders in the primary election, Clinton's strong support among older women ensured that she won the women's vote during the Democratic primaries. Clinton also extended the gender gap in the presidential race, although her margin with women voters was not enough to win the presidential election.
*Source*: REUTERS / Alamy Stock Photo.

Moving beyond 2016, it remains to be seen how much of Clinton's experience with male and female voters related to her gender and how much related to her status as a Clinton and her long career in the public eye. Will a future female presidential candidate who runs on a message of change attract more young voters? How will stereotypes that associate the presidency with male leadership affect the issue and style emphases of the next female presidential candidate and their ability to appeal to different subgroups of primary and general election voters?

## CONCLUSION

Since the 70-year-long struggle for the right to vote, candidates, political parties, and the media have tried to identify and attract the women's vote. Scholarly evidence indicates that the modern gender gap, in which women are prone to favor Democratic candidates, stems from men leaving the Democratic Party—not from women flocking to it. Social welfare issues and an increased support for government spending on these programs constitute a major source of the gender gap. Women's lower levels of support for defense spending and military action have also played a role in explaining the gender gap over time.

Although smaller than other voting gaps, particularly race, the gender gap expanded in the 1990s and became a major focus of presidential candidates during this period of close party competition as campaigns tried to mobilize their base and lure swing-voting groups of women from white, middle-class "soccer moms" to blue-collar "Wal-Mart women" and single mothers. It is an open question whether the aggressive courting of subgroups of women leads to policy changes to benefit women in society. Still, given that more women vote than men and women are more likely than men to be undecided voters, it is likely that the gender gap will continue to play a role in future elections and political parties will work to target different groups of women voters.

## REFERENCES

Abramowitz, Alan I., and Kyle L. Saunders. 1998. "Ideological Realignment in the U.S. Electorate." *Journal of Politics* 60: 634–652.

Allen, Jonathan. 2015. "What Losing in 2008 Taught Hillary About How to Win in 2016." *Vox*, April 10.

Andersen, Kristi. 1996. *After Suffrage: Women in Partisan and Electoral Politics Before the New Deal*. Chicago: University of Chicago Press.

Anderson, L.V. 2016. "White Women Sold Out the Sisterhood and the World by Voting for Trump." *Slate*, November 9.

Baird, Samira. 2016. "Hillary Clinton has been Fighting for Women, Children, and Families Since She Began Her Career." *hillaryclinton.com*, June 20. https://www .hillaryclinton.com/post/om-hillary-clinton-has-been-fighting-women-children -and-families-she-began-her-career/.

Ball, Molly. 2016. "What Kind of Man Is Donald Trump." *The Atlantic*, October 8.

Banaszak, Lee Ann. 1996. *Why Movements Succeed or Fail: Opportunity, Culture, and the Struggle for Woman Suffrage.* Princeton: Princeton University Press.

Bellstrom, Kristen. 2016. "Hillary Clinton's Campaign Is Issuing Actual 'Woman Cards.'" *Fortune*, April 29.

Blake, Aaron. 2016. "Yes You Can Blame Millennials for Hillary Clinton's Loss." *Washington Post*, December 2.

Bonk, Kathy. 1988. "The Selling of the Gender Gap." In *Politics of the Gender Gap: The Social Construction of Political Influence*, ed. Carol Mueller. Newbury Park, CA: Sage.

Box-Steffensmeier, Janet, Suzanna De Boef, and Tse-Min Lin. 2004. "The Dynamics of the Partisan Gender Gap." *American Political Science Review* 98: 515–528.

Bradley, Laura. 2016. "Samantha Bee Slams White Women After Trump's Win." *Vanity Fair*, November 10.

Brownstein, Ronald. 2008. "The Hidden History of the American Electorate." *National Journal*, October 18.

———. 2013. "Bad Bet: Why Republicans Can't Win With Whites Alone." *National Journal*, September 5.

———. 2016. "How the Rustbelt Paved Trump's Road to Victory." *The Atlantic*, November 10.

Bruenig, Elizabeth. 2016. "Why Are Millennial Women Gravitating to Bernie Sanders?" *New Republic*, February 9.

Bump, Phil. 2016. "Donald Trump Will Be President Thanks to 80,000 People in Three States." *Washington Post*, December 1.

Burns, Nancy, and Donald Kinder. 2011. "Categorical Politics: Gender, Race, and Public Opinion." In Adam Berinsky, ed. *New Directions in Public Opinion*. New York: Routledge.

Burrell, Barbara C. 2005. "Gender, Presidential Elections and Public Policy: Making Women's Votes Matter." *Journal of Women, Politics, & Policy* 27: 31–50.

Carroll, Susan J. 1999. "The Disempowerment of the Gender Gap: Soccer Moms and the 1996 Elections." *PS: Political Science and Politics* 32: 7–11.

———. 1988. "Women's Autonomy and the Gender Gap: 1980 and 1982." In *The Politics of the Gender Gap: The Social Construction of Political Influence*, ed. Carol Mueller. Newbury Park, CA: Sage.

Center for American Women and Politics. 2008. "Proportions of Men and Women Who Voted for Hillary Clinton in the Super Tuesday Races of February 5, 2008." New Brunswick: Center for American Women and Politics, Rutgers, State University of New Jersey.

———. 2012. "Women's Votes Decisive in 2012 Presidential Race." New Brunswick: Center for American Women and Politics, Rutgers, State University of New Jersey.

————. 2014. "Fact Sheet: Gender Differences in Voter Turnout." New Brunswick: Center for American Women and Politics, Rutgers, State University of New Jersey.

————. 2016. "Women Candidates 2016." New Brunswick: Center for American Women and Politics, Rutgers, State University of New Jersey.

————. 2017. "The Gender Gap: Voting Choices in Presidential Elections." New Brunswick: Center for American Women and Politics, Rutgers, State University of New Jersey.

Chaney, Carole K., R. Michael Alvarez, and Jonathan Nagler. 1998. "Explaining the Gender Gap in the U.S. Presidential Elections, 1980–1992." *Political Research Quarterly* 51: 311–340.

Chavez, Paola, and Veronica Stracqualursi. 2016. "From 'Crooked Hillary' to 'Little Marco,' Donald Trump's Many Nicknames." ABC News, May 11.

Cilliza, Chris, and Jon Cohen. 2012. "President Obama and the White Vote? No Problem." *Washington Post*, November 8.

CNN. 2004. "U.S. President/National/Exit Poll." http://www.cnn.com/ELECTION/2004/pages/results/states/US/P/00/epolls.0.html. Accessed January 10, 2017.

————. 2008a. "Election Center 2008 Exit Polls." www.cnn.com/ELECTION/2008/results/polls/#USP00p1. Accessed March 25, 2009.

————. 2008b. "Election Center Primaries." http://www.cnn.com/ELECTION/2008/primaries/results/candidates/#1746. Accessed January 10, 2017.

————. 2012. "Election Center President: Full Results." http://www.cnn.com/election/2012/results/race/president/. Accessed January 10, 2017.

————. 2014. "House Full Results Exit Polls" http://www.cnn.com/election/2014/results/race/house#exit-polls. Accessed May 7, 2015.

————. 2016a. "Exit Polls" http://edition.cnn.com/election/results/exit-polls/national/president. Accessed January 10, 2017.

————. 2016b. "Democratic and Republican Exit Polls." http://www.cnn.com/election/primaries/polls. Accessed January 24, 2017.

————. 2016c. "Mississippi Exit Polls" http://www.cnn.com/election/primaries/polls/MS/Dem. Accessed January 24, 2017.

Collingswood, Loren. 2016. "The County by County Data on Trump Voters Shows Why He Won." *Washington Post*, November 19.

Corder, J. Kevin, and Christinan Wolbrecht. 2016. *Counting Women's Ballots: Female Voters from Suffrage through the New Deal*. New York: Cambridge University Press.

Cramer, Katherine. 2016. "How Rural Resentment Helps Explain the Surprising Victory of Donald Trump. *Washington Post*, November 13.

Crockett, Emily. 2016. "Hillary Clinton Plans to Fill Half Her Cabinet with Women, Here's Why That Matters. *Vox*, July 6.

Deckman, Melissa. 2012. ""The GOP's Marriage Problem." *Public Religion Research Institute*, November 16. http://publicreligion.org/2012/11/the-gops-marriage-problem/#.VYhVjqaPqUd.

————. 2016. "Some Women Actually Do Support Donald Trump. Here's Why." *Washington Post*, April 7.

Deckman, Melissa, and John McTague. 2015. "Did the 'War on Women' Work? Women, Men, and the Birth Control Mandate in the 2012 Presidential Election." *American Politics Research* 43: 3–26.

Dittmar, Kelly. 2016a. "No, Women Didn't Abandon Clinton, Nor Did She Fail to Win Their Support." *Presidential Gender Watch*, November 11.

———. 2016b. "Gender Matters: A Status Check on the Gender Gap in Presidential Primaries." *Presidential Gender Watch*, March 17.

Dolan, Kathleen. 2004. *Voting for Women: How the Public Evaluates Women Candidates.* Boulder: Westview Press.

———. 2008a. "Women Voters, Women Candidates: Is There a Gender Gap in Support for Women Candidates?" In *Voting the Gender Gap.* ed. Lois Duke Whitaker. Urbana and Chicago: University of Illinois Press.

———. 2008b. "Is There a 'Gender Affinity Effect' in American Politics?: Information, Affect, and Candidate Sex in U.S. House Elections." *Political Research Quarterly* 61: 79–89.

———. 2014. *When Does Gender Matter? Women Candidates & Gender Stereotypes in American Elections.* New York: Oxford University Press.

Drabold, Will. 2016. "Read Ivanka Trump's Speech at the Republican Convention." *Time*, July 21.

Ehrenfreund, Max, and Jim Tankersley. 2016. "What Hillary Clinton Would Do to America." *Washington Post*, June 7.

Eilperin, Juliet. 2014. "Obama Takes Executive Action to Lift the Veil of Pay Secrecy." *Washington Post*, April 8.

Elder, Laurel. 2008. "Whither Republican Women: The Growing Partisan Gap Among Women in Congress." *The Forum* 6: Issue 1, Article 13.

Enten, Harry. 2016. "'Demographics Aren't Destiny' and Four Other Things This Election Taught Me." *FiveThirtyEight*, November 14.

Estepa. Jessica. 2015. "Donald Trump on Carly Fiorina: 'Look at that Face!'" *USA Today*, September 10.

Fang, Marina. 2016. "Watch Hillary Clinton Break the Glass Ceiling." *Huffington Post*, July 27.

Fiorina, Morris P., with Samuel J. Abrams and Jeremy C. Pope. 2011. *Culture War? The Myth of a Polarized America*, 3rd Edition. New York: Longman.

Flexner, Eleanor, and Ellen Fitzpatrick. 1996. *Century of Struggle: The Woman's Rights Movement in the United States.* Cambridge: The Belknap Press of Harvard University Press.

Flores, Reena. 2016. "Republican Debate: Donald Trump Defends the Size of His Hands, and More." CBS News, March 3.

Frankovic, Kathleen. 1988. "The Ferraro Factor, the Women's Movement, the Polls, and the Press." In *Politics of the Gender Gap: The Social Construction of Political Influence*, ed. Carol Mueller. Newbury Park, CA: Sage.

Freeman, Jo. 1986. "The Political Culture of the Democratic and Republican Parties." *Political Science Quarterly* 101: 327–356.

Frey, William H., Ruy Teixeira and Robert Griffin. 2016. "America's Electoral Future: How Changing Demographics Could Impact Presidential Elections from 2016 to 2032." *Center for American Progress*, February.

Fry, Richard. 2016. "This May Be the Last Election Dominated by Boomers and Prior Generations." *Pew Research Center*, August 29.

Gass, Nick. 2016. "Michelle Obama, Warrant to Campaign for Clinton." *Politico*, September 6.

Gilens, Martin. 1988. "Gender and Support for Ronald Reagan: A Comprehensive Model of Presidential Approval." *American Journal of Political Science* 32: 19–49.

Glueck, Katie. 2016. "Trump Takes Aim at Clinton's Lead Among Women." *Politico*, September 10.

Green, Emma. 2016. "The Weaponization of Heidi Cruz and Melania Trump." *The Atlantic*, March 24.

Grossmann, Matt, and David A. Hopkins. 2015. "Ideological Republicans and Group Interest Democrats: The Asymmetry of American Party Politics." *Perspectives on Politics* 13: 119–139.

Guo, Jeff. 2016. "Yes, Working Class Whites Really Did Make Trump Win. No, It Wasn't Simply Economic Anxiety." *Washington Post*, November 11.

Haider-Markel, Donald P., and Andrea Vieux. 2008. "Gender and Conditional Support for Torture in the War on Terror." *Politics & Gender* 4: 5–33.

Hains, Tim. 2016. "Hillary Clinton Campaigns with Beyoncé, Jay-Z, Bon Jovi, LeBron James, Katy Perry." *Real Clear Politics*, November 6.

Healy, Patrick. 2008. "With Elbows in Check, Making a Pitch to Women." *New York Times*, September 21.

Herrnson, Paul. 2012. *Congressional Elections: Campaigning at Home and in Washington*, 6th ed. Washington, D.C.: CQ Press.

Huddy, Leonie, Erin Cassese, and Mary-Kate Lizotte. 2008. "Sources of Political Unity and Disunity Among Women: Placing the Gender Gap in Perspective?" In *Voting the Gender Gap*, ed. Lois Duke Whitaker. Urbana and Chicago: University of Illinois Press.

Huddy, Leonie, and Tony E. Carey, Jr. 2009. "Group Politics Redux: Race and Gender in the 2008 Democratic Presidential Primaries?" *Politics & Gender* 5: 81–95.

Inter-Parliamentary Union. 2005. "Women's Suffrage: A World Chronology of the Recognition of Women's Rights to Vote and to Stand for Election." www.ipu.org/wmn-e/suffrage.htm. Accessed May 28, 2009.

Jackson, Natalie. 2016. "Trump's Win Isn't All About White People: Clinton Lost Black and Brown Votes in Key States." *Huffington Post*, November 15.

Jacobson, Gary. 2013. *The Politics of Congressional Elections*, 8th ed. Boston: Pearson.

Jamieson, Amber. 2016. "Why She Wore White: Deconstructing Hillary Clinton's Convention Pantsuit." *The Guardian*, July 29.

Jelen, Ted G., and Clyde Wilcox. 2005. "Attitudes Toward Abortion in Poland and the U.S." *Politics & Gender* 1: 297–317.

Junn, Jane, and Lisa Garcia Bedolla. 2013. "Redefining the Gender Gap: An Intersectional Analysis of Vote Choice." Prepared for Presentation at the Annual Meeting of the Midwest Political Science Association, Chicago.

Kanthak, Kristin, and Barbara Norrander. 2004. "The Enduring Gender Gap?" In *Models of Voting in Presidential Elections: The 2000 Election*, ed. Herbert Weisberg and Clyde Wilcox. Stanford: Stanford University Press.

Kantor, Jodi. 2008a. "Clintons Bloc Becomes the Prize for Election Day." *New York Times*, June 7.

———. 2008b. "Gender Issue Lives on as Clinton's Bid Wanes." *New York Times*, May 19.

Kaufman, Jonathan. 2008. "Crossing Over: As the U.S. Economy Sputters, Working-Class Women Shift to Obama." *Wall Street Journal*, October 11.

Kaufmann, Karen M. 2002. "Culture Wars, Secular Realignment, and the Gender Gap in Party Identification." *Political Behavior* 24: 283–307.

Kaufmann, Karen M., and John R. Petrocik. 1999. "The Changing Politics of American Men: Understanding the Sources of the Gender Gap." *American Journal of Political Science* 43: 864–887.

Kernell, Samuel, Gary C. Jacobson, Thad Kousser, and Lynn Vavreck. 2014. *The Logic of American Politics*, Sixth Edition. Washington, D.C.: CQ Press.

Klein, Ethel. 1984. *Gender Politics*. Cambridge: Harvard University Press.

Ladd, Everett Carll. 1997. "Media Framing of the Gender Gap." In *Women, Media, and Politics*, ed. Pippa Norris. New York: Oxford University Press.

Lawrence, Regina G., and Melody Rose. 2010. *Hillary Clinton's Race for the White House: Gender Politics & The Media on the Campaign Trail*. Colorado: Lynne Rienner.

Levey, Noam M. 2008. "Obama Courts Female Vote with His Family Stories." *Los Angeles*, September 4.

Lewis, Carolyn. 1999. "Are Women for Women? Feminist and Traditional Values in the Female Electorate." *Women and Politics* 20: 1–28.

Luhby, Tami. 2016. "How Hillary Clinton Lost." CNN, November 9.

Lynch, Timothy R., and Kathleen Dolan. 2014. "Voter Attitudes, Behaviors, and Women Candidates." In *Women and Elective Office: Past, Present, and Future*, eds. Sue Thomas and Clyde Wilcox. New York: Oxford University Press. pp. 46–66.

Malone, Clare. 2016. "Clinton Couldn't Win Over White Women." *Fivethirtyeight*, November 9.

Mansbridge, Jane. 1986. *Why We Lost the ERA*. Chicago: University of Chicago Press.

Martinez, Gebe, and Mary Agnes Carey. 2004. "Erasing the Gender Gap Tops Republican Playbook." *CQ Weekly* (6 March): 564–570.

McDermott, Monika L. 1997. "Voting Cues in Low-Information Elections: Candidate Gender as a Social Information Variable in Contemporary U.S. Elections." *American Journal of Political Science* 41: 270–283.

Merica, Dan. 2016. "New Clinton Ad Shows Girls Looking in Mirror as Trump Insults Women." CNN, September 23.

Murray, Shailagh. 2009. "Fair-Wage Bill Clears the Senate." *Washington Post*, January 23.

National Election Study. Guide to Public Opinion and Behavior. www.umich.edu/~nes/nesguide/nesguide.htm. Accessed May 1, 2015.

Newport, Frank. 2008. "Hillary Maintains Loyalty of Democratic Women Up to End." Gallup, June 3.

Newton-Small, Jay. 2015. "Inside Hillary Clinton's Beijing Speech." *Time*, November 23.

———. 2016. "Why So Many Women Abandoned Hillary Clinton." *Time*, November 10.

Norrander, Barbara. 1999. "Is the Gender Gap Growing?" In *Reelection 1996: How Americans Voted*, ed. Herbert F. Weisberg and Janet M. Box-Steffensmeier. New York: Chatham House Publishers.

———. 2003. "The Intraparty Gender Gap: Differences Between Male and Female Voters in the 1980–2000 Presidential Primaries." *PS: Political Science and Politics* 36: 181–186.

———. 2008. "The History of the Gender Gaps." In *Voting the Gender Gap*. ed. Lois Duke Whitaker. Urbana and Chicago: University of Illinois Press.

———. 2016a. "Women Vote at Higher Rates Than Men. That Might Help Clinton in November." *Washington Post*, June 27.

———. 2016b. "Is Hillary Losing the Women's Vote? Nope. Here's How the Gender Gap Really Works." *Washington Post*, February 26.

Norton, Mary Beth, David M. Katzman, Paul D. Escott, Howard P. Chudacoff, Thomas G. Paterson, and William M. Tuttle, Jr. 1986. *A People and a Nation: A History of the United States*. 2nd ed., Volume II: Since 1865. Boston: Houghton Mifflin Company.

O'Leary, Ann, and Karen Kornbluh. 2009. "Family Friendly for All Families." In *The Shriver Report: A Woman's Nation Changes Everything*, eds. Heather Boushey and Ann O'Leary. A Study by Maria Shriver and the Center for American Progress.

Palmer, Barbara, and Dennis Simon. 2012. *Women & Congressional Elections: A Century of Change*. Boulder: Lynne Rienner Publishers.

Paolino, Phillip. 1995. "Group-Salient Issues and Group Representation: Support for Women Candidates in the 1992 Senate Elections." *American Journal of Political Science* 39: 294–313.

Paquette, Danielle. 2016a. "The Enormous Ambition of Hillary Clinton's Child-Care Plan." *Washington Post*, May.

———. 2016b. "The Unexpected Voters Behind the Widest Gender Gap in Recorded Election History." *Washington Post*, November 9.

PBS Newshour. 2014. "Election 2014 Briefing Book."

Phillip, Abby. 2016. "Clinton Pitches to Minority Millennials with the Help of Beyoncé, Jay Z." *Washington Post*, November 4.

Phillips, Amber. 2016. "Is Split-Ticket Voting Officially Dead?" *Washington Post*, November 17.

Poloni-Staudinger, Lori, J. Cherie Strachan, and Brian Schaffner. 2016. "In 6 Graphs, Here's Why Young Women Don't Support Hillary Clinton as Much as Older Women Do." *Washington Post*, April 11.

Ramakrishnan, Karthick. 2016. "Trump Got More Votes from People of Color than Romney Did. Here's the Data." *Washington Post*, November 11.

Reily, Katie. 2016. "Donald Trump Again Dismissed His Lewd Comments as 'Locker Room Talk.'" *Fortune*, October 9.

Reinhard, Beth. 2012. "Caught in the Cross Fire: The So-Called War on Women is More About Playing to Their Fears." *National Journal*, August 30.

Reston, Maeve, and Gabe Ramirez. 2016. "Hillary Clinton Splits Younger, Older Democratic Women." CNN, June 10.

Rinehart, Sue Tolleson. 1992. *Gender Consciousness and Politics*. New York: Routledge.

Roarty, Alex. 2012. "Debate Triggers War Over Women on TV, Twitter, Trail and Phone." *National Journal*, October 17.

Rosenthal, Cindy Simon. 1995. "The Role of Gender in Descriptive Representation." *Political Research Quarterly* 48: 599–611.

Rubin, Jennifer. 2016. "Conway Loses Her Integrity and Eviscerates GOP's Appeal to Women." *Washington Post*, October 11.

Rucker, Philip. 2016. "Ivanka Trump Stars in New Campaign Ad to Help Her Father Appeal to Women." *Washington Post*, September 30.

Sanbonmatsu, Kira. 2002. "Gender Stereotypes and Vote Choice." *American Journal of Political Science* 46(1): 20–34.

Sapiro, Virginia, and Pamela Johnston Conover. 1997. "The Variable Gender Basis of Electoral Politics: Gender and Context in the 1992 U.S. Election." *British Journal of Political Science* 27: 523.

Seelye, Katherine Q. 2008. "In Clinton vs. Obama, Age Is One of the Greatest Predictors." *New York Times*, 22 April.

Seltzer, Richard, Jody Newman, and Melissa Voorhees Leighton. 1997. *Sex as a Political Variable: Women as Candidates and Voters in American Elections.* Boulder: Lynne Rienner Publishers.

Shapiro, Robert, and Harpreet Mahajan. 1986. "Gender Differences in Policy Preferences: A Summary of Trends from the 1960s to the 1980s." *Public Opinion Quarterly* 50: 42–61.

Sherman, Jake, and John Bresnahan. 2013. "GOP Pollster: Stop Talking About Rape." *Politico*, January 17.

Siddiqui, Sabrina, and Lauren Gambino. 2016. "How Women Could Vote Hillary Clinton into the White House." *The Guardian*, November 3.

Skocpol, Theda. 1992. *Protecting Soldiers and Mothers.* Cambridge: The Belknap Press of Harvard University Press.

Smith, Eric R. A. N., and Richard Fox. 2001. "The Electoral Fortunes of Women Candidates for Congress." *Political Research Quarterly* 54: 205–221.

Smith, Tom. 1984. "The Polls: Gender and Attitudes Toward Violence." *Public Opinion Quarterly* 48: 384–396.

Steiger, Kay. 2016. "Why Younger Women Love Bernie Sanders and Why It Drives Older Women Crazy." *Vox*, February 11.

Sullivan, Sean, and Robert Costa. 2016. "Donald Trump Unveils Child-Care Policy Influenced by Ivanka Trump." *Washington Post*, September 13.

Sussman, Anna Louise, and Laura Meckler. 2016. "Clinton Offers New Details About Paid Family Leave Plan." *The Wall Street Journal*, January 7.

Swers, Michele L. 2002. *The Difference Women Make: The Policy Impact of Women in Congress.* Chicago: University of Chicago Press.

———. 2013. *Women in the Club: Gender and Policy Making in the Senate.* Chicago: University of Chicago Press.

Tesler, Michael. 2016. "Why the Gender Gap Doomed Hillary Clinton." *Washington Post*, November 9.

Thompson, Krissah. 2012. "Obama Campaign Steps Up Appeals to Women Voters." *Washington Post*, August 24.

Traister, Rebecca. 2016. "Hillary Clinton vs. Herself." *New York Magazine*, May 30.

Trotta, Daniel. 2012. "Who's the Undecided Voter? It May be the 'Walmart Mom.'" *Reuters*, October 3.

Tumulty, Karen. 2012. "To Claim Virginia, Obama's Hopes Rest on Women." *Washington Post*, September 19.

Tyler, Helen. 1949. *Where Prayer and Purpose Meet 1874–1949: The WCTU Story.* Evanston: The Signal Press National Woman's Christian Temperance Union Inc.

Tyson, Alec, and Shiva Maniam. 2016. "Behind Trump's Victory: Divisions by Race, Gender, and Education." *Pew Research*, November 9.

Vedantam, Shankar. 2008. "The Oprah Effect." *Washington Post*, September 1.

Walsh, Kenneth. 2016. "Clinton Wins Popular Vote by Nearly 3 Million Ballots." *US News and World Report*, December 21.

Wheeler, Lydia. 2015. "Obama to Push for Mandatory Paid Leave." *The Hill*, January 14.

Winter, Nicholas J. G. 2010. "Masculine Republicans and Feminine Democrats: Gender and Americans' Explicit and Implicit Images of the Political Parties." *Political Behavior* 32: 587–618.

Zerinke, Kate. 2008. "Both Sides Seeking to Be What Women Want." *New York Times*, September 15.

# 4

# Gender and the Decision to Run for Office

When she was elected to represent the 4th congressional district of Utah in 2014, Mia Love made history on at least two counts: she became the first African American elected to Congress from Utah and the first black Republican woman ever elected to the United States Congress. While African American women have held congressional seats going back to 1968, not a single one of these other 36 women have been members of the Republican party ("Women of Color in Congress | US House of Representatives: History, Art & Archives" n.d.). Born in Brooklyn, New York, to Haitian immigrant parents, Love moved to Utah after college, married, and started a family. Active in her community of Saratoga Springs, she was approached by neighbors and encouraged to run for an open city council seat, which she did. After serving on the city council for six years, she ran for mayor and was elected with 60 percent of the vote. A few years later, she launched an unsuccessful bid to unseat Democratic incumbent Congressman Jim Matheson in 2012, losing narrowly. Love was the Republican favorite when Matheson announced he was retiring in 2013. She promptly entered the race and easily won the Republican nomination before going on to defeat her Democratic opponent in the general election (Siegelbaum 2012; Running Start 2013).

Besides the historic nature of her candidacy and election, Love's election to Congress is noteworthy because it illustrates a number of truisms about women's experiences as political candidates. First, neighbors prompted Love's initial foray into politics by encouraging her to run for a city council seat. For women, receiving encouragement from colleagues, friends, and party members is often a necessity. Far fewer women than men imagine themselves as candidates or think of politics as a viable career, perhaps

Republican Mia Love celebrates with her family, her father wrapping her in a big hug, after winning the 2014 race for Utah's 4th Congressional District. Love is the first black female Republican elected to Congress.
*Source*: AP Photo / Rick Bowmer.

understandably when the vast majority of elected officials in the United States are men. Not only do women need encouragement more than men, but they are also significantly less likely to receive it (Fox and Lawless 2004). Second, Love's political experience as a small town mayor and a member of her town's city council are fairly typical for female candidates, who tend to begin their careers in local offices. For most women, especially those with small children, like Love, local office is easier to balance with their household and family responsibilities than higher office. Finally, Love received a fair bit of media coverage highlighting her symbolic story as the first African American congresswoman elected from the state of Utah as well as within the Republican Party, also typical for many trailblazing women like herself.

Love's election is even more remarkable considering that she had the guts to put herself forward as a candidate. Women in politics today suffer from what might be termed a confidence gap: even when they are qualified by all objective measures, women are far more likely than men to lack the confidence to put themselves forward or to conjure up reasons why they should not run. For many women, losing one election is so devastating that many decide to opt out of politics altogether rather than run again. The fact that Mia Love ran again after her narrow defeat in 2012 is noteworthy because women are less likely than men to run for election after suffering defeat.

The end result is that while many men run for office, very few women do so. American women are far outnumbered in the ranks of political candidates for just about all elected offices. While women have increased their numbers over time, men still lead the numbers game by substantial margins. The numbers at the top of the ticket are especially telling. Out of a field of 22 Democratic and Republican presidential hopefuls in 2016, each party fielded exactly one female candidate: Hillary Clinton and Carly Fiorina, respectively. In the 2012 presidential elections, Congresswoman Michele Bachmann was the only female candidate on either side of the aisle. Her Republican male colleagues outnumbered her by a margin of 8:1. In the 2014 congressional elections, the vast majority of House and Senate races pitted two men against each other, with women contesting roughly one-third of the available seats (Center for American Women and Politics 2014). These numbers persist despite the fact that scholars long ago determined that when women run, women win (Darcy, Welch, and Clark 1994).

Nearly 100 years after women won the right to vote, why are women so much more reluctant than men to try their hand at politics? Does it matter if women, who constitute more than 50 percent of the US population, typically make up such a small proportion of the candidate pool? What explains the persistent gender gap in political candidacies? What does it suggest about the nature of our democracy when women are so much more likely than men to hold themselves back from running?

This chapter takes up these questions, focusing on three explanations that increasingly dominate the scholarly discussions: women don't run because they underestimate their own qualifications; they are less likely than men to be recruited by parties and other political players; and their greater family responsibilities discourage them from undertaking the demanding and erratic hours necessary for political candidacy and subsequent office-holding. In addition, we pay special attention to questions of symbolic representation. When Love was elected in 2014, a *Christian Science Monitor* article made explicit her symbolic appeal, claiming that Love "is poised to become an important symbol for the GOP as the party seeks to broaden its appeal among blacks and other minorities" (Bruinius 2014). Yet, in her bid for Congress, Love downplayed her role as a symbolic representative, noting that "Saratoga Springs didn't elect me with 60% of the vote because I'm black and female," but rather, because she brought the necessary abilities and leadership to get the job done (Siegelbaum 2012). However, emerging political science scholarship suggests that women's candidacies and presence in elected offices inspire and engage other women and signal that politics is no longer a man's domain, but open to women. Will Love inspire women to follow in her footsteps? Can we expect to see more Republican women, particularly women of color, throwing their hat into the ring, given that currently far more women run as Democrats? Will the boys' club finally become more open and appealing to women only when there are substantially more women in office?

## A CONFIDENCE GAP: WOMEN UNDERESTIMATE THEIR POLITICAL ABILITIES

*Filling the pipe at one end does not, it turns out, guarantee a robust result at the other end.*

—Melody Rose (2012)

Throughout the 1970s and 1980s, female candidates began making steady, incremental progress into elected office, winning their elections as frequently as their male counterparts and leading scholars to conclude that "when women run, women win" (Darcy, Welch, and Clark 1994). Women certainly lagged behind men, but their numbers in lower level positions were especially encouraging and suggested that once they developed the requisite skills and experience in lower level offices, they would continue to progress through the political pipeline and reach the highest ranks of the political hierarchy. Of course, far fewer women were running compared to men, a point many scholars attributed to the different occupational and professional career paths of men and women. But increasing numbers of women were also breaking into and building experience in springboard occupations, such as law and business, again fueling speculation that we would see accompanying increases in the numbers of women running for (and winning) office. The presumption was that these women would begin their candidacies with lower level offices, such as school boards and city councils, and gradually work their way into higher and higher offices. Thus, it would be just a matter of time before women reached parity in elected offices.

But as the quotation above suggests, the pipeline theory has not panned out the way scholars expected. Before women can begin to traverse the pipeline to set their careers in motion, they must first decide they are ready to run for office. And women appear to have much greater apprehensions about their own qualifications for office than do men. As political consultant Cathy Allen puts it, "Men decide to run in two hours after someone in the law firm says, 'You've got to run.' . . . The average woman takes two years to decide. She'll wait until she has the perfect campaign manager, the right 17 endorsements, until she's gotten down to a perfect size 10 and the kids are out of school" (Collins 1998).

In their path-breaking analyses of thousands of women and men in the eligibility pool, Richard Fox and Jennifer Lawless uncover persuasive corroborating evidence: women are significantly less likely than men to plan a run for political office sometime in the future. Even when these women are highly qualified by all objective standards, they are still more likely than men to cite their own qualifications as a reason not to run, convincing themselves they are not worthy candidates (Fox and Lawless 2004, 2011). As told by many politically active women, part of this reluctance stems from the fear of being summarily dismissed by voters. When former South Carolina state legislator Harriet Keyserling was considering her first run for office, for a seat on the local county council, she doubted her own qualifications, explaining, "I conjured up so many reasons not to run—I was shy, I was afraid of speaking in public, I didn't know enough about government or the men who ran it. These are pretty typical reasons most women give for not running for office. They would rather work for candidates, stuffing envelopes and making phone calls, than be candidates" (Keyserling 1998, 47). Lack of confidence afflicts all sorts of women: Democrats and Republicans, old and young, and those with and without children (Fox and Lawless 2014).

Journalists Katty Kay and Claire Shipman (2014), in their interviews with many highly influential women in politics and other fields, noticed a similar pattern. Simply put, they deduced that many professional women suffer from an "acute lack of confidence." In study after study, they find that women generally underestimate their own abilities and are more risk averse when it comes to putting themselves forward for promotions or for risky ventures like running for political office. As the quotation above suggests, women typically wait until they are 100 percent qualified before undertaking a new venture while men hold themselves to a much lower threshold. Building on Facebook COO Sheryl Sandberg's exhortation to women to lean in to their careers, Kay and Shipman (2014) posit that "underqualified and unprepared men don't think twice about leaning in. Overqualified and overprepared, too many women still hold back. Women feel confident only when they are perfect." And if female candidates wait until they are perfect and men do not, we will continue to see far fewer women running for office: far fewer women than men will populate the pipeline.

But why do women hold themselves to such impossible standards? In part, Kay and Shipman (2014) suggest that it is because women and men experience and process failure and success in different ways. They argue that women are more likely to internalize failure and externalize success whereas men are inclined to do the opposite. So when things go poorly, women tend to blame themselves and conclude that their own personal shortcomings are responsible. Yet, when women are successful, they tend to downplay their own efforts and suggest that their positive outcomes are due to luck or to factors and forces outside of their control. For men, the reverse is often true: they often shrug off failure as the result of circumstances outside of their control and take full credit for their own successes.

As such, they are more likely to engage in risky behavior like running for office because failure is less costly to their psyches—if they fail, it's not because they weren't good enough, but because other mitigating circumstances caused the failure. If they win, they gain the confidence that comes with successfully managing a risky venture.

It's a troubling combination, according to Kay and Shipman (2014), because it means that women are less likely to undertake risks and thus have fewer opportunities to deal constructively with failure. In contrast with men, women will avoid taking risks like running for office for fear that losing will signal that they are out of their league and have no business running in the first place. If they win, they derive few confidence-boost benefits because they downplay their own agency in creating the victory.

As such, it's not particularly surprising that even once women have gotten elected, the confidence gap persists. Female officeholders exhibit less desire to run for higher office and pick much more modest lower level offices when they express a desire to move ahead in politics. Whereas men aspire to the presidency and Congress, women set their sights much lower, such as city council or state legislative seats (Kirkpatrick 1976; Sapiro and Farah 1980). Political women also generally spend more years serving in lower level offices or gaining other relevant political experience before pursuing higher offices. Scholars theorize that they do so in order to build up their confidence, develop new skills, and master their current environment before pursuing new and risky challenges.

Featured at the beginning of this chapter, Congresswoman Mia Love amassed 11 years of political expertise before running for Congress: seven years on the Saratoga Springs City Council and four more as mayor. In contrast, her male predecessor in office, Jim Matheson, ran for Congress without any previous experience in elected office. His father had served as governor of Utah, but Jim's experience was in the business sector where he owned his own energy consulting firm. The end result is that women running for high-ranking office like the United States House of Representatives are *more* qualified than their male colleagues: they have amassed greater experience in other elected offices before staging a congressional run (Pearson and McGhee 2013).

How can women overcome the confidence barrier? Many women, like Congresswoman Love, are persuaded when friends, family, advocacy groups, and party officials show faith in their abilities and encourage them to run. Indeed, Fox and Lawless (2004) find that women need more encouragement to overcome the confidence barrier, yet are less likely than men to be recruited by the parties or by other political actors. Many women's organizations recognize this gap and host training seminars and schools to provide skills and know-how for women considering a run for office. Running Start is one of these organizations. Founded in 2007, the

Graduates from the 2015 class of Running Start's Young Women's Public Leadership Program, a week-long leadership training program that provides high school girls with the tools necessary to become the political leaders of tomorrow.
*Source*: Photo by Sara Blanco, courtesy of Running Start.

nonpartisan organization hosts a variety of programs to provide "young women and girls with the skills and confidence they need to become the political leaders of tomorrow" (Running Start 2015). They also demonstrate their faith in many aspiring women by giving out annual awards to women whom they have identified as "Women to Watch." Mia Love received one of these awards while she served as the mayor of Saratoga Springs and before winning election to Congress in 2014.

Yet, we know that these schools cannot possibly reach all potential female candidates or draw reluctant women out of the woodwork. In the United States, parties play an essential role in developing and recruiting candidates for elected office. We turn next to examine the parties' checkered past in terms of incorporating and supporting women over time.

## POLITICAL PARTIES' EFFORTS TO INCORPORATE WOMEN

Today, much research confirms that the confidence gap can be overcome when women are actively recruited to run for office. Potential female candidates begin with less confidence in their abilities to wage a successful campaign, but this confidence gap can be overcome when women are actively recruited and supported by power brokers, especially party leaders. Yet, the parties are more likely to recruit men than women, a longstanding pattern in the United States. Why is this so?

As Kira Sanbonmatsu (2010, 36) argues, "Too often, political parties have been an obstacle that women must overcome." Political parties have historically stood in the way of women's candidacies, using a number of mechanisms to keep women on the outside. First, parties kept women marginalized to the party apparatus itself by assigning them volunteer roles rather than candidate-grooming roles. Second, after realizing that women were not likely to form a voting bloc following passage of the Nineteenth Amendment, parties disbanded their women's divisions and placed little emphasis on developing female leaders. Third, once women became active in the party, often through volunteer roles, they were often offered up as sacrificial lambs, or candidates who had little chance to win. Fourth, party leaders selected individuals like themselves to stand for office. Because women are outsiders, they are less likely to be perceived as candidate material than men.

We provide a brief history of women's involvement in the political parties below, also emphasizing the ways in which the Republican and Democratic parties have diverged over time. As we discuss in more detail in chapter 7, Democratic women have enjoyed much greater gains than Republican women in securing elective office over the last few decades. More Democratic women run for office and more of them win their elections, with the result that Democratic women continue to make incremental gains in state legislatures and the United States Congress while Republican women's numbers are declining (Crowder-Meyer and Lauderdale 2014; Shames 2015). However, this was not always the case. We discuss the parties' historical efforts to attract and support women before moving on to contemporary times.

The major political parties have only reluctantly shared the levers of power with women, whether as party workers, delegates to national conventions, or candidates for elected office. In fact, women first gained meaningful influence in third parties. Associated with reform movements such as temperance, cleaning up government, and social welfare reform, third parties including the Prohibition Party, the Populists, and the Progressives gave women leadership positions on party committees, allowed them to serve as delegates to party conventions, and even supported their candidacies for office on their tickets. Women gained support from these parties both because of their devotion to the party's reform causes and because of the parties' hope that the mobilization of women as a new voting bloc could help them build the majority coalition that would lead them to become a major force in American politics (Andersen 1996; Freeman 2002).

The major political parties, in contrast, were bastions of male power that more often dismissed women's political ambitions and kept them out of leadership positions. Political parties were historically part of the male/public sphere and women struggled to gain entry into these organizations in the same way that women had to fight for the right to vote. Throughout the 1800s and early 1900s, party politics was also a major part of male social life. According to Paula Baker (1984), parties united all white men across the social classes by providing entertainment, a definition of manhood, and the basis for male ritual. Men advertised their partisanship by taking part in rallies, joining local organizations, reading party newspapers, and wearing campaign paraphernalia. In the cities, men participated in military-style parades in support of their candidates and in rural areas, the parties sponsored picnics. In an effort to combat the idea that women were too emotional to participate in politics, speaking in the late 1890s, the suffragist Anna Howard Shaw described male partisan gatherings this way:

> Women are supposed to be unfit to vote because they are hysterical and emotional . . . I had heard so much about our emotionalism that I went to the last Democratic National Convention held at Baltimore, to observe the repose of the male contingent. I saw some men take a picture of one gentleman whom they wanted elected, and it was so big they had to walk sideways as they carried it forward; they were followed by hundreds of other men yelling, shouting, and singing the "Hown Dawg" song; then, when there was a lull, another set of men would start forward under another man's picture, not to be outdone by the "Hown Dawg" melody, screaming, yelling, and shouting at their people. I saw men jump upon the seats and throw their hats in the air and shout: "What's the matter with Champ Clark?" Then, when those hats came down, other men would kick them back into the air, shouting at the top of their voices: "He's all right!!!" Then I heard others screaming and shouting and yelling for "Underwood!! Underwood, first last and all the time!!!" No hysteria about it—just patriotic loyalty, splendid manly devotion to principle. And so they went on and went on until 5 o'clock in the morning—the whole night long, I saw men jump in their seats, and jump down again, and run around in a ring . . .
>
> I have been to a lot of women's conventions in my day, but I never saw a woman knock another woman's bonnet off her head as she shouted: "She's all right!" (Quoted in Kraditor 1981, 108–9)

Given the centrality of political parties in the life of the male citizen, it is not surprising that the major parties, the Democrats and the Republicans, opposed suffrage and any role for women in the parties beyond the supporting role of helping to canvass for candidates and mobilize voters. But during the 1916 presidential election, in an appeal to the 4 million women voters living in states where female suffrage was permitted under state law, both the Republican and Democratic parties reversed course and endorsed suffrage. However, neither party included support for a federal amendment in its platform (Freeman 2002).

After women won the right to vote in 1919, the parties initially made aggressive efforts to mobilize the thousands of newly enfranchised female voters but remained reluctant to open the levers of power and influence within the party to women. The parties created women's divisions, bureaus, and committees and slowly began to expand women's representation on national and state party committees, in some cases adopting 50-50 rules for women's and men's representation (Burrell 2009; Freeman 2002). But once it became clear that no women's vote would materialize, the parties scaled back their efforts to woo women.

By the late 1960s, presidential primaries took the presidential nomination process out of the hands of party leaders and gave the voters the power to select the nominee. The party faithful continued to press for a role at the national conventions and previously marginalized groups like women and African Americans also pressed for a greater voice in the delegate selection process. After the tumultuous 1968 Democratic National Convention that included riots in the streets of Chicago over civil rights and the Vietnam War, the Democrats appointed the McGovern-Fraser Commission to recommend reforms. The commission's recommendations included a directive that women, African Americans, and youth should be represented at Democratic Party conventions in proportion to their numbers in the electorate. These recommendations became a permanent part of the Democratic National Committee's charter in 1980. Similarly, in the early 1970s, the Republican Delegates and Organizations Committee recommended to the states, but did not require, equal representation for women at its conventions (Freeman 2002; Sanbonmatsu 2002a; Burrell 2014a).

As a result of these changes, the number of women attending both conventions increased significantly in 1972 (see Figure 4.1). However, since 1972, women have constituted a greater percentage of the delegates at the Democratic than at the Republican conventions. Ironically, the expansion of women's representation at party conventions coincided with the decline of the party convention as a pivotal player in the nomination of presidential candidates as control over the nomination shifted from party elites to primary election voters (Sanbonmatsu 2002a; Burrell 2014b).

Nevertheless, many of these women gained important experience through involvement with the parties and began putting themselves forward as candidates. In these early years, both parties frequently ran women as sacrificial lambs (that is, had them oppose strong incumbents from the other party in a futile campaign rather than let the incumbent run unopposed in elections) or widows who were chosen to succeed their husbands in office in order to keep the seat in party hands and prevent an internal party struggle until a male frontrunner emerged (Burrell 1994; Gertzog

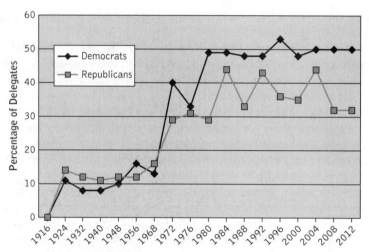

**Figure 4.1. Women as Delegates to the Major Party Conventions, in percent.**
*Source*: 1916–1956 data, Andersen, Kristi. 1996. *After Suffrage: Women in Partisan and Electoral Politics before the New Deal*. Chicago: University of Chicago Press, p. 83; 1968–2000 data, Sanbonmatsu, Kira. 2002. *Democrats, Republicans and the Politics of Women's Place*. Ann Arbor: University of Michigan Press, p. 43; 2004 data for Democrats from CNN (www.cnn.com/ELECTION/2004/special/president/convention/dnc/delegate) and Republican data from www.2004nycgop.org/; 2008 data for Democrats from Democratic National Convention Committee (www.demconvention.com/assets/downloads/Delegate-Diversity-1984-2008.pdf) and Republican data from CBS News (http://cbs2.com/politics/gop.poll.bush.2.807390.html); 2012 data, Mauriello, Tracie. 2012. "Delegates Cherish Diversity That McGovern Began." *Pittsburgh Post-Gazette*. September 5th. Local Section.

1995; Sanbonmatsu 2002a). For example, before she ran for the United States Congress, Republican Susan Molinari got her start in city politics in New York City. With a city council entirely controlled by Democrats, Molinari was approached and encouraged to run by Staten Island political leaders for a seat she had no realistic chance of winning. She was challenging a Democratic incumbent in a district that was more heavily Democratic than Republican, she was only 26 years old and had never held political office before, and she was running as a conservative Republican in a liberal Democratic city. On the plus side, her father was a long-serving and well-respected member of Congress, giving her excellent name recognition in her district. She ended up winning the seat and served for four years before eventually running for and winning her father's old congressional seat (Molinari and Burkett 1998).

Other women tell stories about approaching their party to seek support, only to be told that the timing was not right or that the party had someone else in mind for the position. As US Senator Tammy Baldwin, elected in

1998 as the first female congresswoman from the state of Wisconsin and the first openly lesbian woman in the United States Congress, puts it,

> I was projected to lose every competitive race I entered. People told me that I wouldn't be able to win, that I should get out of the race to ensure a clean primary, or that I should step aside to ensure that a candidate who "could win in the general election" would win our primary. Well, I proved them all wrong, having won every race I was supposed to lose. ("No Limits for Women" 2002, 12)

Why would the parties be reluctant to support female candidates? Some argue that in their recruiting efforts, state party chairs have discriminated against women either because they are more likely to recruit candidates like themselves—other men—or because they do not believe that voters will elect women (Niven 1998; Sanbonmatsu 2002b, 2006; Carroll and Sanbonmatsu 2013). David Niven (1998) suggests that unconscious discrimination on the part of party elites is to blame. As he argues, party leaders have a tendency to select candidates who look and behave like themselves. Because women traditionally enter politics through community service or activism in local organizations, their qualities and credentials are often discounted by male party elites, who more often rise through the ranks of the party leadership or enter politics through business connections.

Furthermore, women have traditionally played supporting rather than leadership roles within the party ranks (Fowlkes, Perkins, and Rinehart 1979; Carroll 1994), making them relatively invisible to party elites when it comes to seeking out prospective candidates. If women are largely seen but not heard in party organization ranks, they have fewer chances of coming to the forefront as viable candidates. However, female party elites appear more supportive of and open to the possibility of women as candidates, so greater gender balance in party leadership ranks may increase women's chances in the future (Niven 1998; Carroll and Sanbonmatsu 2013).

In addition, Kira Sanbonmatsu (2006) finds that party leaders recruit fewer women because they do not think all districts are equally winnable by female candidates. If this is the case, we can assume that women are not recruited to run across the board, but only for a limited number of legislative seats. This finding echoes the work of Barbara Palmer and Dennis Simon (2008) on women's candidacies for the United States House going back to 1956. In their research, they uncover what they term "women friendly districts." According to Palmer and Simon, certain types of congressional districts elect a disproportionate share of women. These districts are typically urban, wealthier than average, and racially diverse. Thus, if only a fraction of the total legislative seats are open to women's candidacies, it will be a long time, indeed, before women reach anything approaching parity in elected offices.

Finally, the two parties have adopted different strategies for recruiting and supporting women over time. For most of the twentieth century, the Republican Party was more open to the women's rights agenda than the Democratic Party. The Republicans endorsed suffrage before the Democrats and they were the first to support the Equal Rights Amendment (ERA) as labor unions, an important Democratic constituency, opposed the amendment throughout the 1960s. Early legislation for women, including the Equal Pay Act of 1963, the addition of sex to Title VII of the Civil Rights Act, and congressional passage of the ERA in 1972, was passed with bipartisan support. However, neither party made women's rights a central part of its agenda.

The national Democratic and Republican parties began creating programs to recruit women candidates in the 1970s. For example, in 1974, the Democratic Party sponsored a Campaign Conference for Democratic women to help train women to run for office. In 1976, the National Federation of Republican Women began publishing a booklet, *Consider Yourself for Public Office: Guidelines for Women Candidates.* Since the 1992 "Year of the Woman" elections highlighted the underrepresentation of women in office and the potential benefit of women as outsider candidates, both parties have created various programs to recruit and train more women to run for elective office. The Republican Party's Excellence in Public Service Series is a political leadership development program led by groups of Republican women in several states. The typical program includes eight monthly sessions and a three-day leadership seminar in Washington, DC. The first program, the Richard Lugar Series, was founded in 1989 and the series continues to spread, with more states adopting these programs every year (Burrell 2014a).

Elected women in both parties have also done their part to support other female candidates and have been selected to chair key congressional campaign committees, such as the Democratic and Republican House and Senatorial Campaign Committees. These committees recruit and fund candidates for the House and Senate and have increased their outreach efforts to potential women candidates over the years. Under congressional women's watch, both parties have launched programs to raise funds specifically for female candidates. On the Democratic side, Women Lead targets female donors and encourages them to contribute to women candidates running in the House and the Women's Senate Network raises money for female Senate candidates. The Republican Party debuted VIEW (Value in Electing Women) in 1997, a leadership PAC devoted to raising money for Republican female candidates (Burrell 2009).

In 2014 Republicans created Project Grow (Growing Republican Opportunities for Women) to recruit more women to run for office and to help Republican candidates appeal to female voters (Zremski 2014). In recent years, women have risen to chair the major party fundraising committees; for example, Debbie Wasserman-Schultz served as chair of the Democratic

National Committee from 2011 to 2016, raising money for Democratic candidates at all levels of office. Representative Nita Lowey (D-NY), Senator Patty Murray (D-WA), and former Senator Elizabeth Dole (R-NC) have all served as chairs of their party's congressional campaign committees. Most recently, Patty Murray (D-WA) led the Democratic Senatorial Campaign Committee during the 2012 cycle. Under her leadership, Murray emphasized recruitment of female candidates and she pushed a Democratic message focused on women's issues, particularly pay equity and reproductive rights. Through her efforts, four new women were elected to the Senate including Tammy Baldwin (D-WI), Mazie Hirono (D-HI), Heidi Heitkamp (D-ND), and Elizabeth Warren (D-MA) (Burrell 2014a, 2014b). Other female senators have launched their own projects to get women more involved in politics. For example, Kirsten Gillibrand's Off the Sidelines Political Action Committee (PAC) recruits, and raises money for, female candidates while promoting a larger empowerment agenda for women in politics and society (http://offthesidelines.org/).

Yet, such progress in both parties belies the way in which the parties began to diverge in terms of their support for women and women's issues. By the 1970s, the second wave of the feminist movement and the antifeminist countermovement led to a realignment within the voting bases of the two parties with feminists aligning themselves with the Democratic Party and social conservatives moving to the Republican Party. By 1980, the Republican Party platform no longer supported the ERA and as conservatives in the mold of Ronald Reagan came to dominate over more moderate Republicans, the party embraced a strongly pro-life stance. During this time frame, women's groups became key players in the Democratic coalition and less central to the Republican coalition. In her analysis of the two major parties, Jo Freeman argues that by 1992, it was clear that the Democratic Party embraced feminism and expanded roles for women while the Republican Party valued family values and more traditional gender roles (Freeman 1993). As she explains, distinct cultures define the political parties: the Democrats are much more inclined to make gender equality a core component of the party platform and consider women an important constituency while the Republican Party is more likely to downplay gender equality and eschew identity politics in their efforts to field candidates and secure votes among their base.

Reflecting these distinct party cultures, the coalitions of interest groups that have grown up to support party candidates also differ in the extent to which they prioritize the election of women. One of the most important factors in a race is the ability to raise money. To successfully campaign for a House seat, candidates must raise at least $1 million and Senate races typically require multiple millions (Jacobson 2013). A network of outside groups has arisen to help candidates raise money. The most successful of these organizations is EMILY's List. Established in 1984 to elect more pro-choice Democratic women to office, the group has a PAC that bundles money to donate to candidates and a Super PAC called Women Vote that is allowed to raise unlimited donations to use on independent expenditures such as advertisements to support or oppose a specific candidate. EMILY's List stands for Early Money is Like Yeast (it makes the dough rise), and is one of the most influential groups in Democratic politics. Their influence comes from their ability to recruit and endorse strong female candidates and support them with a large fundraising network. Women's PACs supporting Republicans such as She PAC and Maggie's List are newer to the scene. These groups have more difficulty raising money than EMILY's List because they are not as widely known and because Republican donors are not as responsive to calls to elect more women, rejecting the idea of identity politics (Burrell 2014a, 2014b).

Women's electoral fortunes reflect such differences between the parties. The 1992 elections, widely referred to as the "Year of the Woman," are a case in point. Perceiving that voters were fed up with politics as usual and looking for change, both parties courted female candidates. A record number of women won their party nominations, and 47 emerged victorious in November (Center for American Women and Politics 2014). The vast majority of these newly elected women were Democrats (20 out of 24),

EMILY's List backs pro-choice Democratic women running for federal, state, and local office. They provided support to Los Angeles mayoral candidate Wendy Greuel in 2013 and then again when she ran for Congress in 2014.
*Source*: © WENN Ltd / Alamy Stock Photo.

leading many to argue that 1992 was more appropriately titled the year of the Democratic Woman. As an important component of the Democratic Party base, women typically do well when their party does well.

For Republican women, the picture is more complex. Perhaps reflecting the Republican Party's less diverse base and its move away from prioritizing gender issues when compared to the Democratic Party (see also chapter 3), Republican women constitute a much smaller share of their party's candidates in any given year and their fortunes do not appear to be as closely linked to those of their party as they are for their Democratic sisters. The 2010 elections are illustrative. Republicans took control of both the House and Senate in 2010, gaining a total of 63 new House and 6 new Senate seats. Yet, Republican women won a paltry share of these seats, less than 20 percent of the newly acquired seats. As Figure 4.2 shows, the Republican Party fields far fewer female candidates in any given election year than does the Democratic Party. Republican women have not always lagged behind, as the graph shows. Yet, without some changes, the partisan gap will likely continue to grow. After developing a creative measure to estimate the potential supply of female candidates in each party's base, two scholars find that

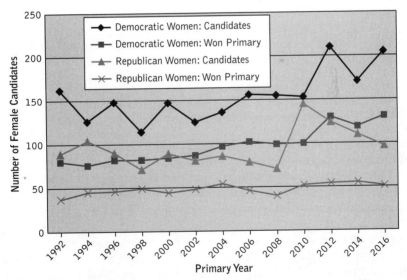

**Figure 4.2. Democratic and Republican Women Congressional Candidates and Primary Winners Over Time.**
*Source*: Data generously provided by Political Parity, from Political Parity. 2015. Primary Hurdles Report. Available at https://www.politicalparity.org/wp-content/uploads/2015/01/primary-hurdles-full-report.pdf. 2016 data available from Center for American Women and Politics, Women Candidates 2016. Available at http://cawp.rutgers.edu/sites/default/files/library/cansum16.pdf.

women constitute more than half of the potential candidate pool for Democrats and only about one-quarter of the pool among Republicans (Crowder-Meyer and Lauderdale 2014). The nonprofit organization Political Parity is particularly attuned to this partisan gap and is working to identify remedies and strategies for encouraging more Republican women to run.

One encouraging piece of evidence suggests that the parties do not need to entirely revamp their recruitment efforts or develop and fund new training schools to support women's candidacies. In fact, one study focusing on Republican Party recruitment efforts found that simply having local party officials vocalize their support for female candidates at party caucus meetings was sufficient to significantly increase the numbers of women running for spots as party delegates. So while good ol' fashioned one-on-one recruitment will continue to be effective in persuading reluctant women to run for office, smaller gestures that signal that the Republican Party is open to women are seemingly effective, and much less costly, for increasing the numbers of Republican women in the pipeline (Karpowitz, Monson, and Preece 2015).

## FAMILY CONSTRAINTS

Finally, scholars argue that situational constraints effectively diminish women's likelihood of putting themselves forward as candidates. As Ruth Mandel (1981) explains,

> The political world does not work on the steady, weekly routine of an office, factory, or retail business schedule. Mothering requires predictable scheduling, whereas politicking requires availability for erratic scheduling. (86)

Holding public office is notoriously time consuming, often demanding long and irregular hours and trips away from the home district to conduct legislative business in the state or national capital. Because American women continue to bear a disproportionate share of childrearing and housekeeping responsibilities, many women simply postpone their political careers until their children are grown and have left the household. Although men certainly face family constraints in their pursuit of public office, they do not appear to weigh as heavily on men's decisions to run as women's (Carroll and Strimling 1983; Elder 2004). For men considering a run for public office, having small children at home is not all that atypical. For women, however, it is fairly atypical. Political women are far less likely than political men to have small children at home (Carroll and Strimling 1983).

Former Congresswoman Patricia Schroeder campaigned for her United States House seat and subsequently served in office while raising small children. Besides voters' persistent questions about her motives and ability to serve while simultaneously fulfilling her role as mother, other political women were not always so enthusiastic about her choice. When she first met Bella Abzug, an outspoken feminist and sitting congresswoman from New York City, Abzug said to her, "I hear you have little kids. . . . You won't be able to do this job" (Schroeder 1998, 24). More recently, Representative Mary Bono's mother-in-law publicly lamented that her grandchildren "would essentially become orphans open to abuse by strangers" if Ms. Bono was successful in her bid to fill the seat vacated by her late husband Sonny Bono (Henneberger 1998). Not surprisingly, then, women are usually older than men when they first become candidates for office (Burrell 2014a).

The family constraints theory may help explain why women run far more often for seats on school boards and city councils than for state legislative or congressional seats. Local offices are closer to home and are often part-time positions with more flexible hours. Many city councils meet once a week or less, and school boards typically meet even less frequently. As such, women considering a run for public office may decide to begin locally so as to more easily balance their work and family responsibilities. New research confirms that potential female candidates find local offices more compatible with their presumed family and household responsibilities. In an experimental design that asks male and female undergraduates to indicate their likelihood of running for political offices, Rachel Silberman (2014) finds that female undergraduates are twice as likely as male undergraduates to say they would run for state legislature if the legislature were close by (less than 15 minutes away), and concludes that young women are already figuring out ways to balance work and family in ways that men are not. In addition, she finds that districts that are further away from state capitals are significantly less likely to have female candidates running for office than are those that are less distant. Silberman concludes that professional women tend to avoid inflexible careers, such as politics, because their expectations about family responsibilities weigh heavily on their career ambitions.

On the other hand, other research finds that family responsibilities are less of an impediment to women's political ambitions than they once were. It is certainly more common for political women today to run for and serve in office while having small children at home, which suggests that times are changing. Fox and Lawless (2014) argue that family responsibilities no longer constrain political women's ambitions more so than men's ambitions, suggesting that professional women are accustomed to navigating the "double burden" at home. Women continue to bear a disproportionate burden of household and child care responsibilities, but these responsibilities do not appear to dampen their electoral ambitions in the ways in which previous research suggested.

## SYMBOLIC REPRESENTATION: DOES IT MATTER IF WOMEN RUN FOR OFFICE?

Recognizing the confidence gap, scholars have begun to question whether women's lack of confidence in pursuing elected office may be a function of their poor descriptive representation among candidates and officeholders. That is, since political women remain the exception rather than the rule, perhaps seeing so few women like themselves running for or serving in office signals to women and girls that politics is men's business and that they are not welcome. Some political theorists argue that previously excluded groups like women and racial minorities will find politics and governance more legitimate when they see more people that look like themselves standing for and serving in office, so termed the "role model effect." According to Jane Mansbridge (1999), improved descriptive representation serves a number of symbolic purposes: it helps to lower distrust among previously excluded groups and increase the legitimacy of the state, it demonstrates that once marginalized groups are fit to rule, and it gives these groups faith that someone is looking out for them. As Barbara Burrell (1988, 51) offers,

> Women in public office stand as symbols for other women, both enhancing their identification with the system and their ability to have influence within it. This subjective sense of being involved and heard for women, in general, alone makes the election of women to public office important because, for so many years, they were excluded from power.

Until 2008, very few women had been highly visible in US politics at any one given time. But in 2008, Hillary Clinton made her historic bid for the Democratic nomination for the US presidency, Sarah Palin ran as the first female vice presidential candidate on the Republican ticket, Congresswoman Nancy Pelosi served as Speaker of the House of Representatives, and Condoleezza Rice served as Secretary of State. All of these women appeared regularly on television and in the print media and were highly visible to even the most casual observer of US politics. Did their presence increase political interest and engagement among women and girls?

The research is mixed, depending on how political interest and ambition are measured as well as whether the analyses focus on officeholders or candidates. National surveys consistently show that men are more politically engaged than women: they report greater interest and pay closer attention to politics. Since 1960, 12 percent more men than women, on average, indicate that they pay attention to public affairs most of the time. With so many high-profile women in the public eye in 2008, were female citizens particularly attuned to politics and energized by women's historic gains? Not exactly. Only 20 percent of women in 2008 indicated that they followed public affairs most of the time, down from 21 percent in 2004. In contrast, men were slightly more interested in 2008 compared to 2004 (33 and 31 percent) (electionstudies.org). Preliminary analysis of the 2016 election data suggests that Clinton's presence at the top of the ticket may have piqued more women's political interest than ever before. For example, the gap between women's and men's participation narrowed substantially in 2016, with women actually outpacing men. The percentage of women indicating they planned to vote was higher in 2016 than 2012 and eclipsed the percentage of men planning to vote, suggesting women were particularly attuned to this election in a way that men were not (Matthews 2016). But whether such interest translates into a desire to run for public office at some point is a different question altogether.

Scholars have also looked beyond simple levels of interest to determine whether or not highly visible female candidates shape girls' and women's likelihood of becoming more politically active and perhaps running for office in the future. On this score, the results are mostly encouraging. Anecdotally, many women credit other pioneering women with influencing their decision to become active in politics. Nikki Haley, the first female governor of South Carolina and current Ambassador to the United Nations, credits Hillary Clinton with inspiring her own entrance to politics. As she explains, Clinton gave a speech at a local conference she attended and encouraged women to run. As Haley retold it, Clinton emphasized, "There will be all of these reasons that people tell you you can't do it. She said that there's only one reason for you to do it, and it's because you know it's the right thing. I walked out of there thinking, I've got to do this" (Cox 2012).

Focusing on high school students, David Campbell and Christina Wolbrecht (2006) hypothesize that the presence of highly visible female role models in politics will make young girls more likely to express an intention to engage in politics as adults. While they do not ask specifically about girls' likelihood of running for office, they find a clear relationship between the presence of high-profile political women and girls' intentions to be politically active in the future. After Geraldine Ferraro made history as the first major party vice presidential candidate in 1984 and again after the historic 1992 "Year of the [Democratic] Woman," girls were significantly more likely to indicate that they intended to become politically active in the future. Not only did their political interest levels spike upward compared to previous years, but they also became significantly more interested than boys in these same years. The same effect occurs when girls see high-profile women running for political office in their home states, suggesting the efficacy of a role model effect. When no viable women are running, girls and boys give similar answers when asked about their future political involvement. But when one or more viable women runs for office, girls envision themselves as being much more politically active in the future when compared to boys.

Focusing on adult women we find similar results. Women demonstrate much greater interest and engagement in politics when they live in states in which elections pit a competitive woman against a man (Atkeson 2003). Among other things, women in these states discuss politics more often and are more likely to try to influence someone else's vote compared to women in states where no competitive women are running for office. These effects are even stronger when a woman in their own party is running, suggesting that women are most engaged and interested in politics when a viable woman from their own party is on the ballot (Reingold and Harrell 2010).

As such, to answer one of the questions posed at the beginning of this chapter, we can expect to find women in Utah more politically engaged as a result of their Congresswoman Love's 2012 and 2014 candidacies, and Republican women will likely be even more engaged than Democratic women. Whether or not Love will inspire black women, who overwhelmingly identify as Democrats, is uncertain. Because she is the first black Republican woman in Congress, there is little scholarship to inform the question. When Sarah Palin and Barack Obama were on the presidential ticket in 2008, black women exhibited considerable gains in their feelings of political efficacy, or beliefs that government was responsive to them and that they could understand politics. These gains were much larger for black women than for black men and women of other races, leading the authors to conclude that "as double minorities, Black women may respond more enthusiastically to bids by numerically underrepresented groups. They may see more meaning in the advancement of the politicians from socially disadvantaged groups" (Stout and Tate 2013). If so, Congresswoman Love may inspire many additional women, black as well as from other racial backgrounds, to become politically involved.

There is additional evidence that women's descriptive representation has symbolic effects: women represented by women in Congress tend to offer more positive evaluations of their members of Congress than do women represented by men (Lawless 2004), women are more likely to be active in politics when represented by a female senator in Congress (Fridkin and Kenney 2014), and women are more likely to correctly identify their female senators compared to the male voters in their state (Dolan 2011).

## CONCLUSION

As this chapter makes clear, there is no single explanation why women continue to lag significantly behind men as candidates. Rather, it is likely a mix of factors that inhibits women from becoming candidates: a lack of confidence that leads women to doubt their own qualifications and competency, party leaders who consciously or unconsciously discriminate against women in their recruitment efforts, and women's desire to put family first and forgo political careers until their children have grown.

But we contend that greater representation of women as candidates in American politics is crucial for democracy. Women have long expressed less interest in politics than men, but promising new evidence suggests that women's interest levels and their likelihood of considering politics as a career will grow as the number of viable women running for office continues to increase. That is, we tend to agree that "political engagement among the American electorate is gendered, in part because political representation is gendered" (Reingold and Harrell 2010). As young girls and women see more and more women like Mia Love running for office, they will begin to receive the message that politics is open to them, that women are fit to rule, and that their contributions to the polity are valued.

## REFERENCES

Andersen, Kristi. 1996. *After Suffrage: Women in Partisan and Electoral Politics before the New Deal*. Chicago: University of Chicago Press.

Atkeson, Lonna Rae. 2003. "Not All Cues Are Created Equal: The Conditional Impact of Female Candidates on Political Engagement." *Journal of Politics* 65(4): 1040–61.

Baker, Paula. 1984. "The Domestication of Politics: Women and American Political Society, 1780–1920." *The American Historical Review* 89(3): 620–47.

Bruinius, Harry. 2014. "Mia Love, First Black Republican Woman in Congress, Is 'Solid Gold' for GOP." *The Christian Science Monitor* 17.

Burrell, Barbara. 1988. "The Political Opportunity of Women Candidates for the U.S. House of Representatives in 1984." *Women & Politics* 8(1): 51–68.

———. 1994. *A Woman's Place Is in the House: Campaigning for Congress in the Feminist Era*. Ann Arbor: University of Michigan Press.

———. 2009. "Political Parties and Women's Organizations: Bringing Women into the Electoral Arena." In *Gender and Elections: Shaping the Future of American Politics*, edited by Susan J. Carroll and Richard L. Fox, 210–38. New York: Cambridge University Press.

———. 2014a. *Gender in Campaigns for the U.S. House of Representatives*. Ann Arbor: University of Michigan Press.

———. 2014b. "Political Parties and Women's Organizations: Bringing Women into the Electoral Arena." In *Gender & Elections: Shaping the Future of American Politics*, edited by Susan J. Carroll and Richard L. Fox, 211–40. New York: Cambridge University Press.

Campbell, David E., and Christina Wolbrecht. 2006. "See Jane Run: Women Politicians as Role Models for Adolescents." *Journal of Politics* 68(2): 233–47.

Carroll, Susan J. 1994. *Women as Candidates in American Politics*. Bloomington: Indiana University Press.

Carroll, Susan J., and Kira Sanbonmatsu. 2013. *More Women Can Run: Gender and Pathways to the State Legislatures*. New York: Oxford University Press.

Carroll, Susan J., and Wendy S. Strimling. 1983. *Women's Routes to Elective Office: A Comparison with Men's: Report*. New Brunswick, NJ: Center for American Women and Politics.

Center for American Women and Politics. 2014. *Election 2014: Women Candidates for United States Congress and Statewide Executive Office*. New Brunswick, NJ: Eagleton Institute of Politics.

———. 2016. *Election Watch: Women Candidates 2016*. New Brunswick, NJ: Eagleton Institute of Politics.

Collins, Gail. 1998. "Why the Women Are Fading Away." *New York Times Magazine*: 6, 54:1.

Cox, Christopher. 2012. "Governor Nikki Haley: New Horizons." *Vogue*. http://www.vogue.com/865354/governor-nikki-haley-new-horizons/(accessed May 21, 2015).

Crowder-Meyer, Melody, and Benjamin E. Lauderdale. 2014. "A Partisan Gap in the Supply of Female Potential Candidates in the United States." *Research & Politics* 1(1): 1–7.

Darcy, R., Susan Welch, and Janet Clark. 1994. *Women, Elections & Representation*. Lincoln: University of Nebraska Press.

Dolan, Kathleen. 2011. "Do Women and Men Know Different Things? Measuring Gender Differences in Political Knowledge." *The Journal of Politics* 73(1): 97–107.

Elder, Laurel. 2004. "Why Women Don't Run: Explaining Women's Under-Representation in America's Political Institutions." *Women & Politics* 26(2): 27–56.

Fowlkes, Diane L., Jerry Perkins, and Sue Tolleson Rinehart. 1979. "Gender Roles and Party Roles." *The American Political Science Review* 73(3): 772–80.

Fox, Richard L., and Jennifer L. Lawless. 2004. "Entering the Arena? Gender and the Decision to Run for Office." *American Journal of Political Science* 48(2): 264–80.

———. 2011. "Gendered Perceptions and Political Candidacies: A Central Barrier to Women's Equality in Electoral Politics." *American Journal of Political Science* 55(1): 59–73.

———. 2014. "Reconciling Family Roles with Political Ambition: The New Normal for Women in Twenty-First Century U.S. Politics." *The Journal of Politics* 76(2): 398–414.

Freeman, Jo. 1993. "Feminism vs. Family Values: Women at the 1992 Democratic and Republican Conventions." *PS: Political Science and Politics* 26(1): 21–28.

———. 2002. *A Room at a Time: How Women Entered Party Politics*. Lanham, MD: Rowman & Littlefield.

Fridkin, Kim L., and Patrick J. Kenney. 2014. "How the Gender of U.S. Senators Influences People's Understanding and Engagement in Politics." *The Journal of Politics* 76(4): 1017–31.

Gertzog, Irwin N. 1995. *Congressional Women: Their Recruitment, Treatment, and Behavior*. Westport, CT: Praeger.

Henneberger, Melinda. 1998. "No Escaping Motherhood on Campaign Trail. (National Desk)." *The New York Times*: A1.

Jacobson, Gary. 2013. *The Politics of Congressional Elections*. 8th ed. New York: Pearson.

Karpowitz, Christopher F., J. Quin Monson, and Jessica Robinson Preece. 2015. "How to Elect More Women: Gender and Candidate Success in a Field

Experiment." Paper presented at the Annual Meeting of the Midwest Political Science Association, Chicago, IL. April 2015.

Kay, Katty, and Claire Shipman. 2014. "The Confidence Gap." *The Atlantic*. http://www.theatlantic.com/features/archive/2014/04/the-confidence-gap/359815/ (accessed January 29, 2015).

Keyserling, Harriet. 1998. *Against the Tide: One Woman's Political Struggle*. Columbia, SC: University of South Carolina Press.

Kirkpatrick, Jeane J. 1976. *The New Presidential Elite: Men and Women in National Politics*. New York: Russell Sage Foundation [Distributed by Basic Books].

Kraditor, Aileen S. 1981. *The Ideas of the Woman Suffrage Movement, 1890-1920*. New York: Norton.

Lawless, Jennifer L. 2004. "Politics of Presence? Congresswomen and Symbolic Representation." *Political Research Quarterly* 57(1): 81.

Mandel, Ruth B. 1981. *In the Running: The New Woman Candidate*. New Haven: Ticknor & Fields.

Mansbridge, Jane. 1999. "Should Blacks Represent Blacks and Women Represent Women? A Contingent 'Yes.'" *The Journal of Politics* 61(3): 628–57.

Matthews, Morgan C. 2016. "When Women Roar: Women's Political Participation in the 2016 General Election." *The Society Pages*, November 2. https://thesocietypages.org/feminist/2016/11/02/when-women-roar-womens-political-participation-in-the-2016-general-election/

Molinari, Susan, and Elinor Burkett. 1998. *Representative Mom: Balancing Budgets, Bill, and Baby in the U.S. Congress*. New York: Doubleday.

Niven, David. 1998. *The Missing Majority: The Recruitment of Women as State Legislative Candidates*. Westport, CT: Praeger.

"No Limits for Women: The Official Word." 2002. *In These Times* (22 July): 12.

Palmer, Barbara, and Dennis Michael Simon. 2008. *Breaking the Political Glass Ceiling: Women and Congressional Elections*. New York: Routledge.

Pearson, Kathryn, and Eric McGhee. 2013. "What It Takes to Win: Questioning 'Gender Neutral' Outcomes in U.S. House Elections." *Politics & Gender* 9(4): 439–62.

Reingold, Beth, and Jessica Harrell. 2010. "The Impact of Descriptive Representation on Women's Political Engagement: Does Party Matter?" *Political Research Quarterly* 63(2): 280–94.

Rose, Melody. 2012. *Women and Executive Office: Pathways and Performance*. Boulder: Lynne Rienner Publishers.

Running Start. 2013. "2013 Women to Watch Awards." http://runningstartonline.org/program/2013-women-to-watch-awards (accessed June 17, 2015).

Running Start. 2015. "About Us." http://runningstartonline.org/about-us/history mission (accessed June 25, 2015).

Sanbonmatsu, Kira. 2002a. *Democrats, Republicans, and the Politics of Women's Place*. Ann Arbor: University of Michigan Press.

———. 2002b. "Political Parties and the Recruitment of Women to State Legislatures." *Journal of Politics* 64(3): 791–809.

———. 2006. "Do Parties Know That 'Women Win'? Party Leader Beliefs about Women's Electoral Chances." *Politics & Gender* 2(4): 431–50.

———. 2010. "Life's a Party." *Harvard International Review* 32(1): 36–39.

Sapiro, Virginia, and Barbara Farah. 1980. "New Pride and Old Prejudice: Political Ambition and Role Orientations among Female Partisan Elites." *Journal of Women, Politics & Policy* 1(1): 13–36.

Schroeder, Pat. 1998. *24 Years of Housework . . . and the Place Is Still a Mess: My Life in Politics*. Kansas City, MO: Andrews Mcmeel Pub.

Shames, Shauna. 2015. *3:1 Republican Women Are Outnumbered in Congress: Right the Ratio*. Cambridge, MA: Political Parity. Hunt Alternatives.

Siegelbaum, Debbie. 2012. "Love at First Sight: Utah Mayor Mia Love Blazing GOP Trail in Bid for House Seat.(CAPITAL LIVING)(Grand Old Party)." *The Hill* 19(87): 18.

Silbermann, Rachel. 2014. "Gender Roles, Work-Life Balance, and Running for Office." http://csap.yale.edu/sites/default/files/files/silbermann.pdf (accessed May 26, 2015).

Stout, Christopher, and Katherine Tate. 2013. "The 2008 Presidential Election, Political Efficacy, and Group Empowerment." *Politics, Groups and Identities* 1(2): 143–63.

"Women of Color in Congress | United States House of Representatives: History, Art & Archives." n.d. http://history.house.gov/Exhibitions-and-Publications/WIC/Historical-Data/Women-of-Color-in-Congress/(accessed June 11, 2015).

Zremski, Jerry. 2014. "GOP Wages War on 'War on Women'—The Buffalo News." *www.buffaloNews.com*. http://www.buffalonews.com/city-region/washington-politics/gop-wages-war-on-war-on-women-20140531 (accessed June 25, 2015).

# 5

# Women on the Campaign Trail

Republican Senator Joni Ernst became the first woman to represent Iowa in federal office and the first female combat veteran in the United States Senate when she was elected during the 2014 mid-term elections. She campaigned using the motto "Mother, Soldier, Conservative," promising to cut federal spending in a controversial campaign advertisement that equated her experience castrating pigs on an Iowa farm with her ability to create change in Washington. The ad went viral, boosting Ernst's profile, fundraising receipts, and support among male voters across the state (Do 2014). True to her campaign theme, Ernst's campaign communications touted her status as a mother of three, her service as a member of the US Army Reserves during the Iraq War, and as a conservative prepared to cut spending in Washington. But despite hailing from a state that had never before elected a woman to Congress or its state governorship, Ernst refused to make gender an issue during her campaign, insisting, "I'm not running on my gender" (Stolberg 2014). Former State Senator Staci Appel, another Iowan running for a United States House seat in the same election year, took a different tack in her campaign, explicitly encouraging Iowans to elect her as their first female member of Congress. Like Ernst, Appel emphasized her status as a mother during the campaign, but unlike Ernst, decided to draw attention to the historic nature of her candidacy (Stolberg 2014). Why the difference?

The growing academic scholarship suggests that Republican women face a slightly different set of gender-based constraints on the campaign trail than do Democratic women (Sanbonmatsu and Dolan 2009; Lawrence and Rose 2012). Indeed, before she became Donald Trump's campaign manager in 2016 Republican pollster Kellyanne Conway advised Republican women like Ernst to avoid running "overtly as a woman" (Stolberg 2014). Because

As shown here, Iowa Republican senatorial candidate Joni Ernst emphasized her status as mother, soldier, and conservative in many of her 2014 campaign materials.
*Source*: AP Photo / Charlie Neibergall.

Democratic and Republican women must appeal to different bases of voters, Democratic women typically get more mileage out of gender-based appeals than do Republican women.

But women in both parties must negotiate the "double bind" to convince voters that they can successfully navigate the masculine world of politics. Instead of discussing gender explicitly, many female Republican candidates draw on powerful symbols like motherhood to signal their femininity while simultaneously highlighting their outsider status to voters. To make sure that voters do not dismiss them as too feminine for the job, these same women often play up their masculine qualities. For example, another Ernst campaign ad featured her driving a Harley-Davidson motorcycle to a shooting range, where she demonstrated her mastery at target shooting, symbolically taking aim at Obamacare. Other ads reminded voters that Ernst was a combat veteran with 20 years' experience in the Army, who had spent a yearlong deployment commanding troops in Kuwait during the Iraq War. Ernst's campaign thus gives us clues about how female candidates navigate the double bind, but also about the ways her Republican party affiliation shaped her strategy.

This chapter examines women who have made the decision to run for office, investigating the ways in which female candidates across the spectrum navigate challenges on the campaign trail (see also the book preface for analysis of Hillary Clinton's and Carly Fiorina's 2016 presidential campaigns). We focus especially on women's attempts to manage the often gendered expectations of voters and media by drawing on Kathleen Hall Jamieson's (1995) concept of the double bind. Yet, we also pay attention to new scholarship that suggests that the tide is turning for women running for office, with voters and the media perhaps more accepting of female candidacies than before. Conventional wisdom has long held that female politicians are judged by different standards than their male colleagues, but new research suggests that such stereotypes may not function in the way in which we have long presumed they do (Brooks 2013; Dolan 2014). The fact that women like Ernst continue to make historic inroads into offices previously reserved for men suggests on the one hand that the playing field is beginning to level. On the other hand, it may also signal that female candidates are more astute and adept campaigners than ever before, preemptively fashioning strategies for counteracting voter misgivings about their abilities to succeed in a man's world.

The research in this area is still growing, and scholars will undoubtedly study Hillary Clinton's 2016 presidential campaign in depth for years to come. But only a few short months after her defeat, the preliminary evidence suggests that the double bind is alive and well: many voters disliked both Trump and Clinton, but the media hyped Clinton's likability problem more than Trump's, despite the fact that more voters found Trump unlikable than they did Clinton (see the preface).

We also provide brief case studies of Hillary Clinton's and Sarah Palin's 2008 political bids for the presidency and vice presidency in this chapter. Our book preface examines the 2016 presidential race, with analysis of both Hillary Clinton's general and primary election campaigns as well as the primary campaign of Carly Fiorina to illustrate the unique challenges women still face in seeking the nation's most powerful political position.

## CHALLENGES ON THE CAMPAIGN TRAIL AND STRATEGIES FOR SUCCESS

Even though women are more reluctant than men to contest office, women's success rates at the polls are encouraging. Scholars argue that voter discrimination worked against women in the 1960s and 1970s, but most public polls today demonstrate that very few voters flat-out refuse to vote for female candidates. The result is that most scholars today conclude that "when women run, women win." Whether in primary or general election contests, female candidates now compare very favorably to their male counterparts (Darcy, Welch, and Clark 1994; Burrell 2014).

If women tend to win about as often as men, why are so few women sitting in elected office? First, as detailed in chapter 4, women are significantly less likely than men to run. Until female candidates reach parity with men in the candidate pool, their progress into elected office will continue to be slow and incremental. Second, incumbency is a major factor. The majority of incumbents are still men, and it is very difficult to unseat incumbents in the United States (Jacobson 2013). Combined with the fact that the vast majority of incumbents seek reelection year after year, quality electoral opportunities arise relatively rarely for women and other underrepresented groups. Third, a limited number of congressional districts have sent a disproportionate share of women to Congress (Palmer and Simon 2006). If women are electable in some, but not all, districts, we may reach a plateau where women continue to replace other women in office, but fail to increase their numbers overall as they cannot make inroads into less friendly districts. At the state legislative level, this may already be occurring. Over a time span of nearly 20 years, women's representation in state legislatures has remained fairly stagnant (going from 21.8 percent in 1998 to 24.8 percent in 2017). Women have continued to make incremental progress in the United States Congress, increasing their numbers by nearly 5 percentage points over the last 10 years, going from 15 to 19 percent (Center for American Women and Politics 2017a, b). Thus, even if women begin running and winning in similar numbers, the power of incumbency, combined with a limited number of "women friendly districts," virtually ensures that it will take many years to significantly alter the existing gender imbalance in elected positions.

Relatively similar success rates at the polls do not necessarily mean that women and men face the same challenges and constraints on the campaign trail. Rather, the historical evidence indicates that voters perceive female and male candidates through different lenses and that the press treats their candidacies differently. Emerging research suggests that voter stereotypes and gendered press coverage may no longer be as detrimental to women's candidacies as we once thought, but that the playing field is not yet entirely equal. In addition, scholars are beginning to better understand the way in which race and gender intersect on the campaign trail, suggesting that voters and the media use different frames for evaluating and reporting upon female candidates depending on their racial background. Finally, in an era of great party polarization, we are uncovering evidence that Republican and Democratic women are confronted with slightly different challenges on the campaign trail.

## Voter Stereotypes about Female Candidates: A Double Bind

All political candidates must figure out a way to appeal to a general public that pays relatively little attention to politics and election campaigns. Most citizens devote very little time to informing themselves about candidates, relying instead on cues like party identification and incumbency when casting their ballots. Especially true in local, low-stimulus elections such as city council or school board elections, voters tend to take shortcuts when deciding for whom to vote. That is, most people simply do not have the time or interest to research all of the candidates running, compare and contrast their policy positions and experiences, and select the candidate who most closely approximates their own ideals. It is far easier to rely on a few shortcuts, such as party identification and/or incumbency. If the incumbent has performed relatively well in office, or has avoided scandal or controversy during his or her tenure, voters more often than not decide to return him or her to office (Jacobson 2013). Voters also rely on partisan identification to simplify their voting decisions. Thus, if all else is equal, voters tend to pick the candidate who shares their own partisan identification.

Gender likewise serves as a voting cue, but in a more complicated way than party identification and incumbency. For voters, the generic male and female candidates simply stand for different things. In assessing candidates, especially those for lower level offices where information is scarce, voters tend to use gender stereotypes and apply them to the particular candidates running for office, regardless of whether or not the individual candidates fit the stereotypes. As Kim Fridkin Kahn (1996) explains the process,

> When developing impressions of others, people routinely give priority to judgments based on stereotypes rather than judgments based on new information. People prefer to limit their cognitive efforts by drawing stereotypical impressions rather than processing new information that may alter their initial assumptions. (4)

As such, voters presume that female candidates possess certain feminine personality traits whereas men possess certain masculine traits. Female candidates are seen as more compassionate, moral, honest, and ethical than men. Voters perceive men as tougher, better able to handle crises, more qualified, and more decisive than women (Alexander and Andersen 1993). If both sets of personality characteristics were equally valued, female candidates would be on relatively equal footing with male candidates. But voters value masculine traits over feminine traits (Rosenwasser and Dean 1989; Huddy and Terkildsen 1993). As such, we can expect that voter stereotypes will hurt women more often than they will help them. In the widely acclaimed "Year of the Woman" in 1992, voters were said to be in the mood for change and eager to throw out incumbents who were guilty of overdrawing their official checking accounts in the House of Representatives. Believing that women were more honest, moral, and ethical, the political climate was favorable for women in that year and 24 new women were elected to the United States House. Ten years later, in the aftermath of September 11, 2001, and with war against Iraq on the horizon, voters were presumably looking for tough, masculine candidates. Only seven new women were elected to the House of Representatives.

Second, voters presume that women are more competent in dealing with issues such as health care, social security, and education whereas men are better at dealing with the economy and taxes, the military, and crime (Rosenwasser and Dean 1989; Alexander and Andersen 1993; Sanbonmatsu 2002). Accordingly, women's electoral fortunes can be expected to rise and fall depending on the issues deemed most salient immediately preceding an election. If voters are particularly concerned about the economy, terrorism, or military crises, they tend to assume that male candidates are more capable for the job. On the other hand, women can be expected to do better in election years in which education, health care, or other social issues are on the forefront of citizens' minds.

Third, voters tend to overestimate female candidates' liberalism (McDermott 1997; Koch 2000). For certain women, such as Republican women running in moderate to liberal districts or Democratic women running in liberal or very liberal districts, such perceptions may work to their advantage. For women running in more conservative districts, however, the public's overestimation of female candidates' liberalism may work against them at the polls. Featured at the beginning of this chapter, Joni Ernst's prominent inclusion of the word "conservative" in many of her campaign communications may have been undertaken specifically to squelch such a misperception of her own ideological leanings.

Voter assumptions about female candidates' ideology, combined with increasing party polarization, may also help to explain why fewer Republican women than Democratic women have been running for Congress over the last decade. Although the percentage of Republican and Democratic female congressional candidates was relatively equal until 1988, Democratic women now lead the way. More Democratic women seek their party's nomination in the primary, and more Democratic women win their party's nomination to go on to the general election (Palmer and Simon 2001; Lawless and Pearson 2008). If the public assumes that Republican women are more liberal than they are, contesting a Republican Party primary may prove quite difficult for these women because primary voters are typically more ideologically extreme than are those who vote in the general election. Even if female Republican candidates are sufficiently conservative, primary elections are often low-information races, the type of races in which voters are most likely to rely on voter stereotypes.

What can female candidates do, if anything, to counteract such damaging voter stereotypes about their capabilities and ideological leanings? As communications scholar Kathleen Hall Jamieson (1995) contends, female political candidates run up against what she terms a "double bind," a Catch-22 situation that expects women, but not men, to simultaneously exhibit stereotypical feminine and masculine traits. A woman that comes across as very masculine invariably invokes criticism for being too harsh, aggressive, and unladylike (read "bitchy"), whereas a woman who is too feminine will be dismissed for lacking the skills necessary to compete and survive in the rough-and-tumble world of politics. Thus, the challenge for political women is to convince the public that they are sufficiently aggressive and tough without being tagged as an "Iron Lady," a woman who has lost touch with her feminine side. As former Congresswoman Pat Schroeder put it, "The electorate seems to be looking for representatives that are half-Marine, half-legislator. That's tough for a woman to pull off" (Mashek 1986).

Female candidates deal with the double bind in a variety of ways. Profiled at the beginning of this chapter, Joni Ernst's campaign materials advertised her status as a mother, a soldier, and a conservative. The first two words communicated to voters that she was tough enough to govern, yet feminine enough to take care of her family. Perhaps responding to voter presumptions that female candidates are more liberal than their male co-partisans, featuring the word "conservative" on her campaign materials served to remind voters that she was ideologically in step with her party's base. Other campaigns have adopted similar strategies. Mary Beth Rogers, a campaign manager for the late Texas Governor Ann Richards, explained that their campaign made a concerted attempt to present Richards as both a tough, savvy politician and a caring, compassionate family woman. They emphasized her experience in a traditionally masculine domain, as state treasurer responsible for the fiscal health of the state. After a particularly nasty primary battle involving a great deal of negative advertising, Richards softened her image for the general election by airing commercials that showed her in maternal roles, with both her grandchildren and ailing father (Morris 1992; Tolleson-Rinehart and Stanley 1994). Other female candidates have done the same—while leveling negative attacks against their opponents, they remind voters of their feminine side by airing positive ads showing themselves in loving relations with family members, in stereotypically feminine situations (homemaker, mother), or speaking to stereotypically feminine issues (Sheckels 1994).

Thus, many female candidates take proactive steps to present themselves as both masculine and feminine and to communicate their ideological dispositions so that voters need not resort to stereotypes. And according to new research, these strategies appear to be working. In her analysis of the impact of gendered stereotypes on voters' decisions regarding for whom to vote, Kathleen Dolan (2014) finds that voters are savvier than we previously thought. She surveyed voters across the country before and after the 2010 elections, gauging their thoughts about generic male and female candidates. She finds, like many before her, that when asked about hypothetical candidates, voters typically give stereotyped responses: women are more compassionate and bring policy expertise in domestic policy issues like health care, while men are more decisive and competent in dealing with defense issues. But when they are presented with an opportunity to vote for an actual male or female candidate, these stereotypes matter very little. As Dolan and Lynch (2014) explain, in actual elections, voters "don't treat . . . candidates as abstractions but instead draw on traditional political criteria in making vote-choice decisions." Partisan affiliation is chief among these criteria in predicting a citizen's vote: Democrats vote for Democrats and Republicans vote for Republicans, almost regardless of their attitudes about the strengths and weaknesses of generic female candidates.

Yet, the relationship is a bit more complex for Republican women: some stereotypes help and others hurt their election chances. Republican voters who think that female candidates are more compassionate and honest than male candidates are more likely to vote for a female Republican than those who hold no such attitudes. When it comes to their policy expertise, the reverse is true: Republican voters are *less* likely to vote for female Republican candidates on the ballot when they assume that women are better suited than men in dealing with stereotypically feminine policy issues like health care and education. Interpreted in this light, perhaps Ernst's decision to feature her status as a soldier and a conservative worked to shore up her support from Republican voters who might otherwise assume that her strengths lay elsewhere. Additional research corroborates Dolan's (2014) findings: Republican voters consider Republican women less conservative than Republican men, have greater misgivings about their presumed policy strengths, and are less likely to vote for them in primary elections (King and Matland 2003; Sanbonmatsu and Dolan 2009).

However, additional research suggests that voter stereotypes are waning as voters are being exposed to more and more female candidates. As Deborah Brooks (2013) characterizes the early research, most studies found that female candidates were held to a double standard: they were expected to act like ladies as well as leaders, control their emotions, especially crying and displays of anger, and had to work twice as hard to get half as far as male candidates. If they did not successfully traverse this tightrope of gendered expectations, voters would punish them, but would not hold male candidates to the same expectations. In a nutshell, Brooks argues that in the absence of many high-profile women running for office, voters perceived female candidates as women first, politicians second. But in today's world, she finds evidence that voters evaluate women as leaders first and ladies second. In what she terms the leaders-not-ladies theory, she uncovers preliminary evidence that voters no longer apply double standards when evaluating female candidates. For example, she finds gender stereotypes are virtually nonexistent when voters are evaluating candidates with a great deal of political experience.

Yet as our analysis of Hillary Clinton's campaign reveals (see preface), Brooks's research likely underestimates the role played by the media and political opponents in caricaturing female politicians, including those with a great deal of experience. If these women already have been tagged as unsuitable for office, voters will have more difficulty in honestly evaluating their generic leadership qualities and may choose instead to base their assessments on whether or not the woman in question possesses gender appropriate, or ladylike, traits. In addition, Brooks's analysis is based solely on congressional candidates. For women seeking the highest office in the land, an office never held by a woman, voters may not be so gender neutral in their assessments of female candidates and their leadership capacities.

Finally, scholars have long speculated that women of color face a double disadvantage, with voters likely to punish them for their status as women and racial minorities (Beal 2008). Yet, because most of the existing scholarship focuses primarily on white women, there is little empirical evidence on the matter. In addition, numerous scholars have pointed out that women of color constitute a larger share of elected officeholders within their racial group than do white women. For example, Latina, African American, and Asian women made up nearly one-third of their racial group's membership in the 113th Congress, while white women constituted just 18 percent of the white membership (Garcia Bedolla, Tate, and Wong 2014). Thus, women of color's better representation, at least compared to white women, seems inconsistent with the supposition that they are facing more discrimination than their male colleagues. In a new study, Christina Bejarano (2013) argues that Latinas are actually less electorally disadvantaged than Latino men. Her evidence suggests that two dynamics are at work. First, white women are more likely than white men to hold positive attitudes about minority women's candidacies, making them more inclined to vote for Latina women compared to white male voters. Second, she argues that racial minority voters are much more likely to vote for someone who looks like them, an aspect of descriptive representation. As such, Bejarano argues that "minority females encounter a positive interaction of their gender and race/ethnicity that results in fewer electoral disadvantages" (2). They benefit from "their multiple community identifications" (Smooth 2006) in a way that white women do not. As more women of color continue to run for office, we can expect additional scholarship to investigate the combined impacts of race and gender on women's candidacies.

As much as candidates can control their own messaging and the ways in which they communicate their strengths to voters, in this day and age of 24-hour news cycles and social media, they must also take careful aim to generate positive and deflect negative media coverage. When it comes to media, how do female candidates fare? Does the press hold them to different standards than their male colleagues? Focus on style over substance?

## Media Coverage of Female Candidates

Depending on the level of office sought, most candidates need to interact with the media. Local races for mayor, city council, or school board often receive coverage in local newspapers and radio programs. As one moves up the hierarchy of elected offices, candidates generally rely more heavily on media coverage to communicate with voters. Some state legislative candidates and virtually all congressional and gubernatorial candidates attempt to secure some sort of television coverage. What types of media coverage do male and female candidates report? Do they receive similar amounts of coverage by media outlets? Are more stories devoted to men's or women's candidacies? Does the press take seriously women's policy positions? Do they focus disproportionately on their status as outsiders?

Communications scholars Diana Carlin and Kelly Winfrey (2009) argue that much media coverage of female politicians is problematic because journalists interpret and report on women's campaigns using a narrow set of gendered frames. Journalists use frames in order to "guide the selection, presentation, and evaluation of information. . . by slotting the novel into familiar categories" (Norris 1997, 2). For example, a frame frequently employed by journalists covering elections is the "horse race," in which stories are pegged around which candidate leads or lags in the polls. Journalists could, instead, choose to focus on different components of the campaign, such as the candidates' backgrounds or policy positions, but they rely on the competitive nature of the campaign as a convenient and conventional frame for structuring their stories. For women, whose candidacies are typically more novel than men's, journalists resort to familiar and gendered frames such as the mother, the pet or child, the seductress, or the iron maiden in covering their campaigns (Carlin and Winfrey 2009).

None of these frames are particularly flattering or helpful for women seeking the trust of the voting public. The mother frame implies a candidate who is nurturing and compassionate, but who will have trouble balancing her public leadership and maternal responsibilities. For example, reporters often relied on this frame in covering Sarah Palin's 2008 vice presidential candidacy. Typical was this front-page story in the *New York Times*, which ran during the Republican National Convention entitled "A New Twist on the Debate on Mothers," in which two female reporters interviewed dozens of women as to their opinions about Sarah Palin's candidacy: "With five children, including an infant with Down syndrome and . . . a pregnant 17-year-old, Ms. Palin has set off a fierce argument among women about whether there are enough hours in the day for her to take on the vice presidency, and whether she is right to try" (Kantor and Swarns 2008). Another exchange between CNN journalists John Roberts and Dana Bash illustrates the double standard inherent in the mother frame. Roberts called into question Palin's fitness for office by wondering how she would have time for both family and the vice presidency, noting that "children with Down syndrome require an awful lot of attention. The role of vice president . . . would take up an awful lot of time, and it raises the issue of how much time will she have to dedicate to her newborn child?" Dana Bash responded, "If it were a man being picked who also had a baby . . . born with Down syndrome, would you ask the same question?"

Other women report similar treatment, suggesting that the media could not see past their maternal roles and responsibilities in evaluating their candidacies. When Joan Growe was running for a United States Senate seat from the state of Minnesota, she lamented that reporters would steer conversations toward questions about her children when she was in the midst of discussing arms control policy (Watkins and Rothchild 1996). Additional research confirms that the press pays less attention to female candidates' policy positions than they do for men, even when female candidates devote greater attention to policy issues in their own political communications (Kahn 1996). An unfortunate implication of such slanted coverage is that voters may come away with the impression that female candidates are light on policy details, incapable of balancing their maternal responsibilities with the rigors of public office.

A second frame, the sex object or seductress, draws attention to the physical appearance, attributes, and feminine characteristics or mannerisms of the subject. During the 2008 presidential election season, the media paid a great deal of attention to Sarah Palin's appearance. Early profile stories almost always mentioned her background as a beauty pageant contestant and *New York Times* columnist Maureen Dowd referred to her as Caribou Barbie in at least one column (Carlin and Winfrey 2009). Other members of the media frequently used sexist terms to describe her physical appearance. For example, Rush Limbaugh referred to her as a "babe" (Limbaugh 2008) while talk show radio host Chris Baker referred to her as "a smoking-hot chick from Alaska" (Media Matters 2008). While campaigning to be governor of Michigan in the early 2000s, Democratic candidate Jennifer Granholm received similar treatment, being described in one article as "slim and about five feet seven inches, [with] blue eyes, meticulously coiffed short blond hair, and chiseled facial features straight out of a Barbie doll catalog" (Cohn 2002). According to Jane Danowitz, former director of the Women's Campaign Fund, such coverage "knock[s] women down a peg or two on the credibility ladder. . . . News stories focusing on appearance detract from and dilute a candidate's message" (Jahnke 1992). If a woman is too attractive, the implication is that she cannot be taken seriously as a political candidate.

The third frame, the iron maiden or iron lady, suggests that a woman is so masculine that she has lost touch with her feminine side. Former British Prime Minister Margaret Thatcher is often used as the classic prototype for this frame. As the first female Prime Minister of the United Kingdom, Thatcher was given credit for her toughness and command, especially surrounding her decision to wage war against Argentina in the Falkland Islands, but was less often portrayed as having a compassionate or sympathetic side. When Congresswoman Michele Bachmann was campaigning for the Republican presidential nomination in 2012, she embraced the iron lady moniker. Leading up to the Iowa caucuses, she referred to herself as "America's Iron Lady" and encouraged Iowa voters to send a strong woman to the White House ("Michele Bachmann Plays Gender Card as Iowa GOP Vote Nears" 2012). Despite having made history as the first woman to win the Ames Straw Poll a few months earlier, Bachmann ultimately bowed out of the race after finishing a distant sixth in the Iowa caucuses (Cillizza 2011; "Michele Bachmann Drops out of GOP Race after Iowa Caucuses" 2012).

Some of Hillary Clinton's media coverage in the 2008 and 2016 campaigns similarly played into the iron lady frame by focusing on her toughness and suggesting that her masculine traits had overwhelmed her feminine ones. For example, the top positive character narratives in media stories about Clinton concerned her qualifications and preparedness to lead the country, but questions about her likability, trustworthiness, and whether or not she represented the "status quo" also appeared frequently in media narratives (Pew Research Center's Project for Excellence in Journalism 2008; Shorenstein Center 2016b). Conservative talk show host Rush Limbaugh likened Hillary's power within the Democratic Party to a "testicle lockbox," saying that "her testicle lockbox can handle everybody in the Democratic hierarchy." He later claimed that "Clinton reminds men of the worse characteristics of women they've encountered over their life: totally controlling, not soft and cuddly. Not sympathetic. Not understanding" (Smith 2008).

Finally, the pet or child frame suggests that the subject lacks agency as well as the ability to make things happen. A child must rely on the good graces of others to help her navigate her way in unfamiliar territory; she has neither the experience nor the knowledge to lead on her own. For example, when Elizabeth Dole ran for the Republican presidential nomination in 2000, reporters frequently drew connections to Robert Dole, her spouse, a former senator and presidential candidate himself. An analysis of editorial cartoons found Dole disproportionately portrayed in domestic settings with her husband and relatively mute on political issues. In contrast, her male colleagues were almost always portrayed in public settings and engaging the political issues of the day, the contrast implying "that Dole is unfamiliar with or has no opinions on issues of vital importance to the office of president, and is, therefore, unqualified for the post" (Gilmartin 2001).

Hillary Clinton was likewise discussed in relation to her husband, former President Bill Clinton, but reporters rarely employed the pet or child frame in these stories, perhaps because the iron lady frame more appropriately characterized her candidacy. The McCain campaign was guilty of employing the child frame from time to time in its portrayal of Sarah Palin (Carlin and Winfrey 2009). When reporters started pressing Palin on her lack of foreign policy experience, the campaign tried to deflect attention away from her inexperience by emphasizing that McCain was at the top of the ticket, not her, or they emphasized that she was part of a team, a quick study who would learn much as vice president. When CNN anchor Campbell Brown asked campaign spokesman Tucker Bounds why he thought Sarah Palin was ready to be commander-in-chief, he responded, "Governor Palin has the good fortune of being on the ticket with John McCain, who . . . is the most experienced and has shown proven judgment on the international stage" ("Brown: Tucker Bounds Interview Becomes Lightning Rod" 2008). Whether it was poor planning on the part of the campaign or an honest reflection of their concerns about Palin's abilities, such treatment did not convince the public that Palin was cut out for the job.

Black women are framed in even more narrow terms—as mammies, jezebels, or sapphires (West 2008). The mammy frame is similar to the mother frame in emphasizing black women's nurturing and caretaking roles; mammies are self-sacrificing women, but are also portrayed as content taking on multiple responsibilities, happily living under discrimination and crushing workloads. The jezebel is comparable to the sex object frame, with the added characteristics of promiscuity and immorality, suggesting that sexual violence against black women is not problematic or even unwelcome. The sapphire image is comparable to the iron lady frame, an overbearing masculine woman who emasculates men with her aggressive and dominating behavior. The angry, black woman frame is a variation of the sapphire frame. Some conservative commentators used this frame to depict Michelle Obama during the 2008 presidential campaign, taking issue with the comment she uttered during a campaign event that "for the first time in my adult life, I am proud of my country because it feels like hope is finally making a comeback" (Merida 2008). While these frames are, no doubt, damaging and insulting to black women across the board, there is little scholarship that examines their impact on black women's candidacies or their ability to wage successful campaigns.

Early scholarship consistently found that in addition to being subjected to a narrow and usually unflattering set of frames to tell their stories, female candidates for high-ranking offices received less but more negative media coverage than similarly situated men, making it more difficult for them to communicate their message to voters (Kahn 1996; Aday et al. 2000). Emerging research analyzing female candidates for the US House finds a more gender-neutral balance in terms of both quantity and tone of news reporting (Lavery 2013; Hayes and Lawless 2015), but presidential candidate Hillary Clinton enjoyed no such balance. She received more news coverage than primary opponent Bernie Sanders, but it was significantly more negative. Looking solely at news covering her policy positions as reported in eight national media outlets, one study found 84 percent of Clinton's issue coverage negative in tone, four times the amount of negative coverage Bernie Sanders received (Shorenstein Center 2016b). Facing off against Donald Trump in the general election, Clinton received less media coverage but the coverage she received was slightly more positive than was Trump's. Perhaps this is not particularly surprising considering that Trump railed against the mainstream media, often labeling their coverage as phony or dishonest, and revoked press credentials for numerous journalists covering his campaign (Farhi 2016). What is perhaps more surprising is that there was not a greater discrepancy between the two candidates in the tone of their coverage. Even on the issue of their overall fitness for office, the vast majority of Trump's as well as Clinton's media coverage was negative in tone (87 percent for both) (Shorenstein Center 2016a), despite the fact that the public judged Clinton much more favorably on this dimension.

Does the double bind continue to shape women's candidacies? Joni Ernst's story at the beginning of this chapter suggests that successful female candidates proactively attempt to counter damaging stereotypes by simultaneously portraying themselves as both masculine and feminine. In addition, Republican women have the added challenge of convincing their party faithful that they are conservative enough for the job. But Hillary Clinton's 2016 and 2008 presidential bids, as well as Sarah Palin's 2008 campaign for vice president, suggest the double bind remains an issue for women pursuing the presidency. Before we explore these historic candidacies in more detail, we provide a brief history of women running for the presidency and vice presidency.

## FEMALE PRESIDENTIAL AND VICE PRESIDENTIAL CANDIDATES

In April 2015, Hillary Clinton announced her second bid for the US presidency. Her status as the favorite for the Democratic nomination is noteworthy, but not historic. Until 2007, Elizabeth Dole had been the most viable woman to contest her party's nomination for the presidency. Leading up to her 1999 run, Dole had amassed substantial executive experience in and outside of government. She was a member of both President Reagan's and George H. W. Bush's cabinets, had served as a White House aide for two additional presidents (Watson and Gordon 2003), and had led the American Red Cross as president for eight years before announcing her own candidacy. Future president George W. Bush was clearly the hands-down favorite among Republican voters in 1999, but public opinion polls regularly showed Dole in second place. Until she dropped out of the race in October of 1999, Dole was running ahead of all the other Republican candidates, including Senator John McCain, businessman Steve Forbes, and former Vice President Dan Quayle, her closest competitors. Dole performed similarly well in the presidential trial heats. When likely voters were asked for whom they would vote if the presidential election pitted Elizabeth Dole against Vice President Al Gore, Dole routinely received more support than did Gore (Polling Report 2000). Dole withdrew from the race in October of 1999, citing her difficulties in raising money.

Clinton's 2008 candidacy demonstrated that women can be serious contenders for the presidency, and likely opened the door a little bit wider for future female presidential candidates. By the time her second presidential campaign got underway, Clinton had already racked up a number of historic accomplishments. First, when she announced her first candidacy in 2007, she immediately became the most viable female candidate ever to run for the US presidency. Not only did Democratic voters prefer her by a margin of nearly 2–1 over Barack Obama, her closest competitor for the nomination, but she also matched up very well in the general election against Republican hopefuls such as John McCain, Mitt Romney, and Rudy Guiliani (Polling Report 2008b; Gallup 2007). In fact, it seemed to many that she was the inevitable Democratic nominee.

Second, Clinton became the only former first lady to run for the US presidency. While spousal succession is common in many other countries, the United States relies upon the sitting vice president to assume the office if the president is removed or becomes unable to carry out his or her duties and responsibilities. Thus, first ladies have no line of succession to the office of the presidency in the United States but must campaign for the office like anyone else. Hillary Clinton had positioned herself well for a presidential candidacy, campaigning for and winning a US Senate seat in New York state while simultaneously serving as the nation's first lady. Never before had a first lady done such a thing.

Third, Clinton broke previous records by competing in all 50 state primaries and caucuses, amassing more votes (nearly 18 million) and delegates (1,896) than any other female presidential candidate in history. Her victory in the New Hampshire primary, edging out Barack Obama by two points, made her the first woman to win a major party's presidential primary for the purpose of delegate selection (Center for American Women and Politics 2008). In contrast with Clinton, the vast majority of women who have run for the US presidency dropped out long before their party's nominating conventions and very few of them earned any delegates along the way. Republican Senator Margaret Chase Smith held the previous record for most votes in the presidential primaries. Competing in five states in

1964, Smith received over 200,000 votes before eventually dropping out of the race. Shirley Chisholm, a sitting congresswoman from New York, became the first Democratic and African American woman to run for the office when she competed for the 1972 Democratic presidential nomination. She ran in state primaries in 12 states, and secured 151 delegates at the Democratic National Convention before dropping out of the race (Center for American Women and Politics 2012).

Finally, Clinton's candidacy called into question a great deal of scholarship that suggests female candidates have a difficult time convincing the public that they are tough enough for the job and that they have what it takes to be the commander-in-chief of the United States. Even with the wars in Iraq and Afghanistan topping the list of many voters' concerns in 2008, Hillary Clinton did not appear to suffer any gender-based assumptions about her foreign policy capacities. Democratic voters gave her higher marks than all of her male primary opponents for her ability to be commander-in-chief, for her toughness, and for her overall strength and leadership (Washington Post-ABC News Poll 2008).

## Vice Presidential Candidates

On August 29, 2008, Republican presidential candidate John McCain made history by announcing Alaska Governor Sarah Palin as his vice presidential pick, the first Republican woman selected for the position. Palin was following in the footsteps of Geraldine Ferraro, Democratic presidential candidate Walter Mondale's choice some 24 years earlier to become the first female vice presidential candidate on a major party ticket. After McCain announced Palin at a campaign rally in Ohio, she made reference to both Ferraro and Clinton in her comments, noting, "I can't begin this great effort without honoring the achievements of Geraldine Ferraro in 1984, and, of course, Senator Hillary Clinton, who showed such determination and grace in her presidential campaign. It was rightly noted . . . that Hillary left 18 million cracks in the highest, hardest glass ceiling in America. But it turns out the women of America aren't finished yet, and we can shatter that glass ceiling once and for all" (Barnes and Shear 2008).

Palin's addition to the campaign appeared to pay immediate dividends. In the few days following her announcement, the McCain campaign received a boost of $7 million in campaign contributions ("McCain Pick . . ." 2008). White women, in particular, were buoyed by Palin's candidacy. Before Palin, some polls estimated that John McCain led Barack Obama among white women by 5 points (44 to 39 percent). McCain received a 9 percent bounce with white female voters that he retained until Election Day, but Obama captured the overall women's vote due to his greater margin of support among women of color (CNN 2008).

The McCain campaign selected Palin, in part, to energize the Republican base of socially conservative voters, many of whom had serious misgivings about McCain's credentials as a social conservative. On this score, Palin proved enormously successful as her appearances on the campaign trail resulted in McCain receiving audiences far larger than usual. One campaign advisor estimated that audiences were about 12 times larger after Palin joined the ticket (Baird 2008). Palin clearly struck a chord with many conservative voters, who were ecstatic that she was selected to join McCain on the Republican ticket. Not surprisingly, Republican voters evinced much greater enthusiasm about voting for McCain after Palin joined the ticket (Gallup Poll 2008).

The campaign also hoped to attract female voters who were disappointed with Hillary Clinton's loss (Baird 2008), and presented Palin as a working mom who understood the concerns and values of other women. In story after story, many women explained that they liked Palin because they found her relatable, because she was an average mom who just happened to be the governor of Alaska. As one female college student enthused, "I love that she is a mother, wife *and* a politician. That's very admirable. She's not a career politician who's been affected by the Washington games" (Merida 2008).

But while Palin clearly energized the base and appealed to many women, her star began to fade. After her rousing and well-received acceptance speech at the Republican convention, the McCain campaign refused media access to her for almost two weeks. Palin eventually made herself available through a series of lengthy and high-profile interviews with Charles Gibson of ABC News, Sean Hannity of FOX News, and Katie Couric of CBS. Her performance in these interviews, especially those with Gibson and Couric, fell short of the hype created by her convention speech. To many, she seemed unprepared and rehearsed, and polling data began to show declining voter confidence in her ability to handle the job. Between late September and early November, a CNN poll of likely voters recorded a 10-point drop in the percentage of people who thought Palin had the personality and leadership qualities a president should have (47 to 37 percent). For McCain, Obama, and Biden, these numbers all increased or remained the same over the same period of time. Similarly, the percentage of likely voters who said Palin's addition to the Republican ticket made them more likely to vote for McCain declined over time (Polling Report 2008a).

Less than a year after the election, Palin surprised many by resigning her position as governor of Alaska. In her farewell speech, Palin told the audience that she did not need the title of governor to work for them, and that she could spare them the lame-duck legislative session by leaving office in the midst of her term (Rucker and Saslow 2009). Her surprise resignation led many to speculate that she was positioning herself for a presidential run. Instead, she formed her own political action committee, SarahPAC, became the subject of the reality television series called "Sarah Palin's

Alaska," and became actively involved in the growing Tea Party movement, campaigning on behalf of many Republican candidates across the country.

## The Double Bind in the 2008 Elections: Hillary Clinton and Sarah Palin

Existing research tells us a great deal about how the media and voters evaluate women, but we know far less about how female candidates attempt to deal with the double bind, how they position themselves and sell their candidacies to a public more accustomed to evaluating male candidates and politicians. By focusing on their own communications, we examine Hillary Clinton and Sarah Palin's likely strategies for dealing with the double bind. Moreover, as scholars Regina Lawrence and Melody Rose (Lawrence and Rose 2010, 2012, 2014) note, any woman seeking the presidency must consider gendered strategies that also mesh with the culture of her own political party. Given that women candidates are often perceived as more liberal than their male counterparts, this perception may help Republican women in general elections, but hurt their chances in primary elections, in

Florida State Senator Lizbeth Benacquisto (left) and former Alaska Governor Sarah Palin joke with guests while they serve barbecue at a private fundraiser for Benacquisto's unsuccessful 2014 congressional campaign. Since running for Vice President in 2008, Palin has actively campaigned for numerous conservative Republican female candidates across the country.
*Source*: AP Photo / *Naples Daily News*, Scott McIntyre.

which they must appeal to their party's more conservative base of voters. Likewise, a female Democratic presidential candidate may be forced to consider a strategy that perhaps modifies perceptions of any liberal bias that may alienate centrist voters in the general election.

### Hillary Clinton and the Double Bind

When Hillary Clinton began her first presidential campaign in January of 2007, both she and her campaign advisors painted a picture of her as tough, strong, and experienced (Baker and Kornblut 2008). In the first campaign brochure Clinton distributed to Iowa voters in July of 2007, she featured "Ready to Lead" as a prominent campaign slogan and repeatedly emphasized her experience throughout the brochure (Kornblut 2007). Further, in numerous television advertisements, Clinton's tag line was a variation on her strength ("the strength to fight"), her experience ("the experience to lead"; "time for a president who is ready"), or both. Perhaps the most widely covered ad was her "3:00 a.m." spot, which touted her preparedness and resolve. Throughout the ad, a phone rings unanswered in the background while children sleep soundly in their beds. The male narrator asks:

> It's 3 A.M. and your children are safe and asleep. But there's a phone in the White House and it's ringing. Something is happening in the world. Your vote will decide who will answer that call, whether it's someone who already knows the world's leaders, knows the military, someone tested who is ready to lead in a dangerous world . . . who do you want answering the phone?

Clinton's campaign advisors rarely missed an opportunity to tout her toughness and experience. After an October 2007 debate in Philadelphia, in which her Democratic rivals repeatedly attacked Clinton, one Clinton advisor said, "Ultimately, it was six guys against her, and she came off as one strong woman" (Kornblut and Balz 2007a). Clinton also made remarks on the campaign trail to shore up any voter doubts about her ability to compete in the masculine world of politics. When asked what lessons she learned from John F. Kerry's failed 2004 presidential bid, Clinton responded, "When you're attacked, you have to deck your opponents. . . . You can count on me to stand my ground and fight back" (Kornblut and Balz 2007b).

Voters also thought Clinton brought stereotypically masculine character traits to the table. When asked who was the strongest leader and who was the candidate with the best experience to be president, Clinton consistently outpaced both Barack Obama and John Edwards—her main competitors, at least through February of 2008. Just a month before the Democratic primaries and caucuses got underway, 61 percent of Democratic-leaning voters identified Clinton as the strongest leader in the Democratic field, more than three times the number that thought either Obama or Edwards was the strongest leader. This gap narrowed over time, but Clinton enjoyed a 24-point lead over Obama on this measure going into Super Tuesday, February 5, 2008 (*Washington Post*-ABC News Poll 2008). Yet, while the polling numbers always demonstrated that the public found her strong, intelligent, and qualified for the job, she often lagged behind Barack Obama on measures of trustworthiness, honesty, and compassion, traits for which female candidates are usually given the edge. In numerous polls, Obama bested Clinton by nearly 20 points when voters were asked who was more honest and trustworthy. Clinton and Obama were closer in voters' minds when it came to their compassion and concern for others, but Obama again typically outpaced her by 10 or more points (NBC/Wall Street Journal 2008).

Political scientists Susan B. Hansen and Laura Wills Otero (2006) argue that voters typically prefer presidential candidates who are both strong and compassionate leaders. Combined with the aforementioned double bind, female candidates who are perceived to be strong leaders must also take steps to remind voters that they are not iron ladies, that they have not lost touch with their feminine side. Veteran political communications consultant Peter Fenn puts it this way: "The most personal vote a voter will cast is for the Presidency of the United States. Voters want to like the person they are voting for, to feel like this person is like them and understands what makes them tick" (Fenn 2008). For Clinton, the challenge was to convince voters that she could be tough but still compassionate, the most experienced candidate who also happened to understand their problems and concerns.

There is ample evidence that the Clinton campaign understood the challenges of presenting her as a warm and caring woman and took steps to show just how compassionate and likable she was throughout the campaign. They tried to soften her image by showing her as a loving mother, daughter, and friend. For example, when Clinton kicked off her campaign in January of 2007, she did so from the comfort of her home in Washington, DC, taking on what one journalist called "the demeanor of a kaffe-klatching neighbor" (Hornaday 2007). Many of her television ads likewise attempted to soften her image, presenting her as a caring, warm, and compassionate woman. The visual imagery of the ads was often vibrant and pleasing, with soothing or triumphant background music in the background. Clinton was routinely shown in close contact with individuals from all walks of life, including the elderly, children, families, women, African Americans, and blue-collar workers, and they all looked genuinely delighted to be with her. Clinton was often shown listening intently to voters, nodding in agreement with them, and sometimes gently touching them. While she definitely communicated her policy priorities in the ads, the unspoken message was that Clinton cared deeply about people, she listened to them, and she would always do what she could to help them.

The one incident that went the furthest toward softening her image was not likely planned by the campaign, however. After unexpectedly finishing third in the Iowa caucus—the first contest held in the 2008 primary election campaign—Clinton was behind Obama by roughly 10 points going into the New Hampshire primary, a short five days after the Iowa caucuses. In a coffee shop in Portsmouth, New Hampshire, a female supporter asked her, "How do you do it? How do you keep upbeat and so wonderful?" After taking a moment, Clinton responded that it wasn't easy, and went on to talk about the reasons she was running. But rather than a standard stump speech, her response was heartfelt and human, showing a vulnerable side rarely seen in public. As she said,

> You know, this is very personal for me. It's not just political, it's not just public. I see what's happening [in this country] and we have to reverse it. And some people think elections are a game, they think it's like who's up or who's down. It's about our country, it's about our kids' futures, and it's really about all of us, together.

Her voice began to break about halfway through, her eyes went moist, and she almost demurely rested her chin in her left hand for a few seconds while she spoke ("Clinton Wells Up" 2008). As one journalist noted, Clinton "had a jarring moment of vulnerability" (Givhan 2008). The episode received much media attention, and seemed to be just the thing many female voters needed—they were already convinced of her intelligence, experience, and toughness, but also wanted to know that she was a real woman, sometimes vulnerable and breakable. Clinton went on to eke out a victory in the New Hampshire primary, coming from well behind Obama to beating him by 2 percent of the vote, and many identified her rare display of emotion as partially responsible for her victory. In fact, among those who said that they made their vote choice on the basis of which candidate "cares about people like me," a standard measure of compassion, Clinton was the top vote getter. Edwards did best among this group in Iowa, but Clinton edged him out in New Hampshire and also beat Obama by a 2–1 margin among this group (Dionne 2008).

So why did Clinton ultimately lose the Democratic nomination to Barack Obama? Part of the reason is that the Obama campaign made a brilliant move by preparing for a longer, broader fight by contesting caucus states rather than focusing more money and resources for a Super Tuesday sweep of key primary states and by utilizing newer campaign technologies, including social media, more effectively than the Clinton campaign (Lawrence and Rose 2014). Moreover, Hillary's vote in favor of the Iraq War in 2003 as a United States Senator stood her apart from Barack Obama, who as a state legislator had publicly protested the war effort—a key difference that appealed to many Democratic party voters in the primaries and caucuses. As Lawrence and Rose (2014) note, too, Clinton ran a largely "gender neutral" campaign, which may have been a good general election strategy but also meant that she perhaps missed the opportunity to appeal to women voters within her own party, who often care deeply about women's rights and social welfare policies and likely would have responded to Clinton's historic candidacy as the first woman to be elected president. Indeed, it is telling that in her first major campaign kick-off event in June 2015, in her second bid to win the Democratic nomination for president, Clinton proudly declared that while she would not be the youngest candidate to win the presidency at the age of 67, she would be "the youngest woman president."

However, some placed the blame for Clinton's 2008 loss on her inability to convince enough voters that she was likable and compassionate. Although voters who met her in person often commented on how warm and funny she was, the grueling and compressed schedule of primaries and caucuses made it nearly impossible to sustain personal interactions with so many voters after the first contests wrapped up in Iowa and New Hampshire. With 22 states holding their primaries and caucuses on Super Tuesday, a mere four weeks after the New Hampshire primary, all the candidates were forced to rely more heavily on the mass media for communicating their message. And for Hillary Clinton, this may have been particularly challenging. Unfortunately for Clinton, voters seemed to have more misgivings about her as an individual than they did about the other candidates. No doubt, voters' impressions of her were influenced by her eight years in the White House and the intense media scrutiny she received as a politically involved and active first lady. She was widely blamed for the failure of her husband's health care plan in 1994 (Bernstein 2007), and was tarnished by her involvement in many other missteps of the Clinton administration. Few other candidates faced such a challenge in redefining themselves for the electorate.

When Clinton announced her 2016 candidacy, early polling numbers suggested that her years as Secretary of State had improved voters' perceptions of her. A Gallup Poll taken in March of 2015 demonstrated that not only did she have the highest favorability numbers among a field of 16 potential presidential candidates, Democrat and Republican, the gap between those who had favorable and unfavorable opinions about her was considerably more positive for her than for all other prominent candidates: 50 percent of adults surveyed indicated that they had a favorable opinion of Clinton and 39 percent had an unfavorable opinion, a difference of 11 points. In contrast, Vice President Biden had identical favorability and unfavorability ratings of 39 percent and slightly more individuals felt unfavorably than favorably toward New Jersey Governor Chris Christie (3 percent). Clinton's favorability numbers had fallen from a high point of 66 percent during her tenure as Secretary of State, but were comparable to her ratings at a similar point during her 2008 campaign. In addition, her unfavorable numbers were considerably lower than they were during the 2008 campaign, suggesting that her time as Secretary of State helped to improve her image among some of her previous detractors, at least for a while (Gallup News Services 2015).

Yet by July of 2016, Clinton's favorability numbers had sunk considerably: only 39 percent of Americans viewed her favorably (Gallup News Services 2016). On the eve of the election, her favorability numbers had rebounded to 43 percent and voters judged Clinton both as more qualified and likable than Trump (CNN 2016). Yet Trump won the election. Interpreted through the lens of the double bind, Clinton failed to strike the elusive balance between masculine and feminine: her impressive credentials were recognized by voters, but many harbored concerns about her lack of stereotypically feminine characteristics such as honesty and likability (see the preface). For her male opponent, whom voters deemed less trustworthy, less likable, and less qualified, no such double bind existed.

### Sarah Palin and the Double Bind

The challenges to overcome voter stereotypes were quite different for vice presidential candidate Sarah Palin. In contrast with Clinton's struggles to convince voters she was likable, Palin's toughest challenge was convincing voters that she was qualified for the job. Perhaps because she was a relative unknown when John McCain announced her as his running mate, a mere 39 percent of registered voters agreed that she was qualified to assume the presidency while almost an equal number (33 percent) said that she was not qualified. As the campaign progressed, however, voters did not change their minds about her qualifications for the job. She never did convince a majority of voters that she was qualified as a vice presidential candidate or potential president (*Newsweek* 2008).

Where Palin did well with voters was on stereotypical feminine traits like compassion, trustworthiness, and likability. Seventy percent of registered voters rated her as likable a few weeks before the election, and approximately 60 percent of voters agreed that she was honest, trustworthy, and cared about the problems of people like themselves throughout the campaign (ABC News 2008; *Newsweek* 2008; Polling Report 2008a).

So how did the McCain campaign address the double-bind problem for Sarah Palin? Their presentation of her suggests that the campaign was trying to present her as both masculine and feminine, showing her as both tough and compassionate, as a political executive with real experience who was also an outsider committed to reform. She talked tough, leveled negative attacks against Obama, and reminded voters that she was a hockey mom and a hunter. But she also stressed her feminine traits: a small town regular "gal" rather than a polished politician, a mother and wife, and someone who could finally shatter "the highest, hardest glass ceiling in America."

From the start, the campaign sought to portray her as a "caring mom who can be tough" (Shear and Murray 2008). When he announced her as his running mate, McCain touted her experience fighting against "oil companies and party bosses and do-nothing bureaucrats," and assured voters that she was tough enough to stand up for what's right, not letting "anyone tell her to sit down." Like many vice presidential candidates before her, she adopted the role of an attack dog on the campaign. Her convention acceptance speech not only criticized Democratic nominee Barack Obama for his policy stances but also called into question his character. She mocked his previous experience as a community organizer, suggesting her own experience as a small town mayor was better preparation for the presidency. As she quipped, "A small town mayor is sort of like a community organizer, except you have actual responsibilities." She also took a number of personal digs at Obama, suggesting he was more interested in self-promotion than serving his country and that his campaign was a self-indulgent "journey of personal discovery" that the country could hardly afford (Palin's Speech 2008).

The campaign was careful to showcase her feminine side, too. Lawrence and Rose (2012) note that to counter perceptions that women with political ambition—particularly those seeking the nation's highest elective office—can be unfeminine and distasteful, the McCain campaign drew a "traditional feminine veil" over Palin's ambition, noting that she dressed in overtly feminine clothes with long hair and high heels while embracing motherhood as a rationale for seeking political office. When she was first introduced by McCain, her seven-year-old daughter Piper stood close by her side while her husband and three of her other four children appeared in the background. As we soon learned, her eldest son was a soldier in the Army getting ready to ship off to Iraq. Palin described herself as "just your average 'hockey mom'" and "a mother of one of our troops" (CBS News 2008). Moreover, Palin routinely appeared with her young family, including her special needs infant son, at most of her campaign appearances, which no doubt held important symbolism for many Republican voters, many of whom are socially conservative. And the campaign made no secret of the fact that they thought she would be very appealing to many female voters who were disappointed that Clinton did not win the Democratic nomination (Baird 2008).

The campaign also highlighted her status as an outsider who would help McCain bring change to Washington. This strategy often works well for female candidates, as voters perceive women as more trustworthy and ethical than men. Indeed, part of the campaign's strategy was to present her as the campaign's antidote to Barack Obama. If he could bring change to Washington, so could she. McCain touted his own maverick status throughout the campaign in an attempt to distance himself from an unpopular president of his own party, and concluded many of his campaign ads with the slogan "Change is coming." But as a US Senator with more than 25 years of experience in Washington, his message of change was hard for many to swallow. Governor Palin, a relative unknown before she was selected as McCain's running mate, could more persuasively sell the message of change. Elected as governor of Alaska just two years before, she was not a career politician and had never lived in Washington, DC. In her own acceptance speech at the Republican convention, Palin reminded voters that she is not part of the "permanent political establishment." Further, as a 44-year-old woman, she looked a lot more like the face of change than did the 72-year-old McCain.

While the campaign was successful in presenting her as a tough but caring mother and an outsider, it was less successful in convincing voters that Palin had a sufficient grasp of foreign or domestic policy issues. Some began to question her command of the issues following high-profile televised interviews with Charlie Gibson (ABC News) and Katie Couric (CBS News) and following her debate performance with Democratic vice presidential candidate Joe Biden. While Palin did not commit any major gaffes in these appearances, she also did not come across as very well versed in the issues. Her poll numbers reflect as much. Following her convention speech in August, a high of 47 percent of voters thought Palin was prepared to be vice president. By late October, only 35 percent of likely voters thought she was prepared. When asked about whether or not she was well informed about the issues, Palin's numbers took a similar turn for the worse, going from 45 percent in late September to 35 percent in late October (CBS/New York Times 2008; *Newsweek* 2008).

What can we learn about Palin's candidacy? It is tempting to conclude that Palin is a personification of the female candidate too feminine to be taken seriously. As an attractive and stylish mother of five, described by some as the "Hottest Governor," Palin had to demonstrate that she was more than a pretty face, that she was knowledgeable and aggressive enough to play the part. In portraying her as a "caring mom who can be tough," the campaign was successful in convincing voters that she was tough enough and likable enough for the job. But by relying so heavily on selling her as an outsider and an agent of change, the campaign had a difficult time dispelling voter concerns about her qualifications and preparedness for office. That is, it proved difficult to sell her inexperience and outsider status as a plus on the one hand and then to turn around and argue that it should not be held against her when she lacked the knowledge and experience that voters sought. But in the end, the public was not convinced that she was qualified for the job. Despite the fact that the majority of voters thought Palin was likable and compassionate, the campaign could not convince them that she had what it takes to be president of the United States.

## CONCLUSION

As the discussions of both Hillary Clinton and Sarah Palin reveal, female candidates today cannot entirely dismiss the double bind. Even more revealing, this is true for women running at the highest levels where we might expect plentiful information about the candidates to drive out gendered stereotypes about their capabilities and character traits. Nor can female candidates expect media coverage that is entirely equitable. Reporters continue to rely on simplistic frames that suggest political women are novelties in the manly world of politics. Not only does such coverage give voters reason to call into question women's fitness for office, but it may also discourage other women from running in the future.

As this edition goes to press, scholarly analysis of Hillary Clinton's historic presidential campaign is still getting underway. But as we argue in the preface, voters' perceptions of Clinton in 2016 very much mirrored those from the 2008 campaign: they rated her as very qualified yet not sufficiently likable. Only time will tell whether the next female presidential candidate, Republican or Democrat, will face similar challenges, but the evidence from 2016 suggests that many voters and journalists continue to struggle in reconciling their notions of power and femininity.

## REFERENCES

ABC News. 2008. ABC News/Washington Post Poll. October 2nd. Accessed through Polling the Nations.

Aday, Sean, James Devitt, White House Project Education Fund, and Women's Leadership Fund. 2000. *Style over Substance: Newspaper Coverage of Female Candidates: Spotlight on Elizabeth Dole.* New York: Women's Leadership Fund.

Alexander, Deborah, and Kristi Andersen. 1993. "Gender as a Factor in the Attribution of Leadership Traits." *Political Research Quarterly* 46(3): 527–45.

Baird, Julia. 2008. "From Seneca Falls To—Sarah Palin?" *Newsweek* 152(12): 30–36.

Baker, Peter, and Anne E. Kornblut. 2008. "Turning It Around; Down in Polls after an Iowa Loss, Hillary Clinton Had No Victory Speech for New Hampshire. But Then an Unexpected Thing Happened: She Won." *The Washington Post*: A1.

Barnes, Robert, and Michael D. Shear. 2008. "McCain Picks Alaska Governor; Palin First Woman on GOP Ticket." *The Washington Post.* http://www.washingtonpost.com/wp-dyn/content/article/2008/08/29/AR2008082901112.html (accessed June 24, 2015).

Beal, Frances M. 2008. "Double Jeopardy: To Be Black and Female." *Meridians: feminism, race, transnationalism* 8(2): 166–76.

Bejarano, Christina E. 2013. *The Latina Advantage: Gender, Race, and Political Success.* Austin, TX: University of Texas Press.

Bernstein, Carl. 2007. *A Woman in Charge: The Life of Hillary Rodham Clinton*. New York: Alfred A. Knopf.

Brooks, Deborah Jordan. 2013. *He Runs, She Runs: Why Gender Stereotypes Do Not Harm Women Candidates*. Princeton, NJ: Princeton University Press.

"Brown: Tucker Bounds Interview Becomes Lightning Rod." 2008. http://www.cnn .com/2008/POLITICS/09/05/brown.bounds/#cnnSTCText

Burrell, Barbara. 2014. *Gender in Campaigns for the U.S. House of Representatives*. Ann Arbor: University of Michigan Press.

Carlin, Diana B., and Kelly L. Winfrey. 2009. "Have You Come a Long Way, Baby? Hillary Clinton, Sarah Palin, and Sexism in 2008 Campaign Coverage." *Communication Studies* 60(4): 326–43.

CBS News. 2008. "America: Meet Sarah Palin." (August 29). Accessed at www .youtube.com/watch?v=Gg0darQB7r4

CBS/New York Times. 2008. CBS/New York Times Poll. (October 30, September 8). Accessed through Polling the Nations.

Center for American Women and Politics. 2008. *The 2008 Presidential Campaign of Hillary Rodham Clinton*. Rutgers University, New Brunswick, NJ: Eagleton Institute of Politics.

———. 2012. *Women Presidential and Vice Presidential Candidates*. Rutgers University, New Brunswick, NJ: Eagleton Institute of Politics.

———. 2017a. *Women in State Legislatures 2017*. Rutgers University, New Brunswick, NJ: Eagleton Institute of Politics.

———. 2017b. *Women in the U.S. Congress 2017*. Rutgers University, New Brunswick, NJ: Eagleton Institute of Politics.

Cillizza, Chris. 2011. "Michele Bachmann Wins the Ames Straw Poll." *The Washington Post*. http://www.washingtonpost.com/blogs/the-fix/post/michele-bachmann -wins-the-ames-straw-poll/2011/08/13/gIQApgnoDJ_blog.html (accessed June 24, 2015).

"Clinton Wells Up: 'This is Very Personal.'" 2008. WMUR-TV, New Hampshire (January 7). Accessed online at https://www.youtube.com/watch?v=pl-W3IXRTHU

CNN. 2008. CNN Exit Polls. Accessed online at www.cnn.com/ELECTION/2008/ results/polls/

———. 2016. CNN Exit Polls. Accessed online at http://edition.cnn.com/election/ results/exit-polls/national/president.

Cohn, Jonathan. 2002. "Jennifer Granholm and the New Woman Candidate: Gender Bender." *The New Republic* 227(16): 16–20.

Darcy, R., Susan Welch, and Janet Clark. 1994. *Women, Elections & Representation*. Lincoln: University of Nebraska Press.

Dionne, E. J. 2008. "A Shocker, in Hindsight." *The Washington Post*: A.21.

Do, Quynhanh. 2014. "Going Viral and the Iowa Senate Race." *The New York Times*. http://www.nytimes.com/video/us/politics/100000003202077/going-viral-and -the-iowa-senate-race.html (accessed June 22, 2015).

Dolan, Kathleen. 2014. *When Does Gender Matter? Women Candidates and Gender Stereotypes in American Elections*. New York: Oxford University Press.

Dolan, Kathleen, and Timothy Lynch. 2014. "It Takes a Survey: Understanding Gender Stereotypes, Abstract Attitudes, and Voting for Women Candidates." *American Politics Research* 42(4): 656–76.

Farhi, Paul. 2016. "Trump Revokes Post Press Credentials, Calling the Paper 'Phony' and 'Dishonest.'" *Washington Post*, June 13.

Fenn, Peter. 2008. Personal interview conducted by Julie Dolan (May 16). St. Paul, MN.

Gallup News Services. 2007. "Update on 2008 General Election Preferences." June 20. http://www.gallup.com/poll/27940/Update-2008-General-Election-Preferences .aspx.

———. 2015. *Gallup News Service: Opinions of Potential 2016 Presidential Candidates*. Gallup News Service.

———. 2016. *Trump, Clinton Favorability Back to Pre-Convention Levels*. August 11. http://www.gallup.com/poll/194552/trump-clinton-favorability-back-pre -convention-levels.aspx?g_source=clinton%20favorability&g_medium=search&g _campaign=tiles

Gallup Poll. 2008. "Palin Unknown to Most Americans." (August 30th). Accessed online at www.gallup.com/poll/109951/Palin-Unknown-Most-Americans-aspx

Garcia Bedolla, Lisa, Katherine Tate, and Janelle Wong. 2014. "Indelible Effects: The Impact of Women of Color in the U.S. Congress." In *Women and Elective Office: Past, Present and Future*, edited by Sue Thomas and Clyde Wilcox, 235–52. New York: Oxford University Press.

Gilmartin, Patricia. 2001. "Still the Angel in the Household." *Women & Politics* 22(4): 51–67.

Givhan, Robin. 2008. "A Chink in the Steely Facade of Hillary Clinton." *The Washington Post*: C.1.

Hansen, Susan B., and Laura Wills Otero. 2006. "A Woman for U.S. President? Gender and Leadership Traits Before and After 9/11." *Journal of Women, Politics & Policy* 28(1): 35–60.

Hayes, Danny, and Jennifer L. Lawless. 2015. "A Non-Gendered Lens? Media, Voters, and Female Candidates in Contemporary Congressional Elections." *Perspectives on Politics* 13(01): 95–118.

Hornaday, Ann. 2007. "Throwing Her Hat on the Web." *The Washington Post*. http:// www.washingtonpost.com/wp-dyn/content/article/2007/01/20/AR2007012001430 .html (accessed June 25, 2015).

Huddy, Leonie, and Nayda Terkildsen. 1993. "The Consequences of Gender Stereotypes for Women Candidates at Different Levels and Types of Office." *Political Research Quarterly* 46(3): 503–25.

Jacobson, Gary C. 2013. *The Politics of Congressional Elections*. Boston: Pearson.

Jahnke, Christine K. 1992. "Beauty Pageant: How to Avoid Gender Issues in Your Campaign." *Campaigns & Elections* 12(5): 41–42.

Jamieson, Kathleen Hall. 1995. *Beyond the Double Bind: Women and Leadership*. New York: Oxford University Press.

Kahn, Kim Fridkin. 1996. *The Political Consequences of Being a Woman: How Stereotypes Influence the Conduct and Consequences of Political Campaigns*. New York: Columbia University Press.

Kantor, Jodi, and Rachel L. Swarns. 2008. "A New Twist in the Debate on Mothers." *The New York Times*. http://www.nytimes.com/2008/09/02/us/politics/02mother .html (accessed June 24, 2015).

King, David C., and Richard E. Matland. 2003. "Sex and the Grand Old Party: An Experimental Investigation of the Effect of Candidate Sex on Support for a Republican Candidate." *American Politics Research* 31(6): 595–612.

Koch, Jeffrey W. 2000. "Do Citizens Apply Gender Stereotypes to Infer Candidates' Ideological Orientations?" *The Journal of Politics* 62(2): 414–29.

Kornblut, Anne E. 2007. "In Iowa, Clinton Camp Scripts Bill's Role to Keep Focus on Hillary." *The Washington Post*. http://www.washingtonpost.com/wp-dyn/content/article/2007/06/30/AR2007063000774.html (accessed June 25, 2015).

Kornblut, Anne E., and Dan Balz. 2007a. "Clinton Regroups As Rivals Pounce: [FINAL Edition]." *The Washington Post*: A.1.

———. 2007b. "Clinton Begins Her Run in Earnest." *Washington Post* (January 28): A1.

Lavery, Lesley. 2013. "Gender Bias in the Media? An Examination of Local Television News Coverage of Male and Female House Candidates." *Politics & Policy* 41(6): 877–910.

Lawless, Jennifer L., and Kathryn Pearson. 2008. "The Primary Reason for Women's Underrepresentation? Reevaluating the Conventional Wisdom." *Journal of Politics* 70(1): 67–82.

Lawrence, Regina G., and Melody Rose. 2010. *Hillary Clinton's Race for the White House: Gender Politics and the Media on the Campaign Trail*. Boulder, CO: Lynne Rienner Publishers.

———. 2012. "The Real '08 Fight: Clinton vs. Palin." In *Women and Executive Office: Pathways and Performance*, edited by Melody Rose, 11–31. Boulder, CO: Lynne Rienner Publishers.

———. 2014. "The Race for the Presidency: Hillary Rodham Clinton." In *Women and Elective Office: Past, Present and Future*, edited by Sue Thomas and Clyde Wilcox, 67–79. New York: Oxford University Press.

Limbaugh, Rush. 2008. "Feminism and Sarah Palin—The Rush Limbaugh Show." *Rush Limbaugh*. http://www.rushlimbaugh.com/daily/2008/09/05/feminism_and_sarah_palin (accessed June 24, 2015).

Mashek, John W. 1986. "A Woman's Place Is on the Ballot in 86." *U.S. News & World Report* 101: 21.

"McCain Pick Appears to Bring in $7 Million." 2008. *Washington Post* (August 31): A13.

McDermott, Monika L. 1997. "Voting Cues in Low-information Elections: Candidate Gender as a Social Information Variable in Contemporary United States Elections." *American Journal of Political Science* 41(1): 270–83.

Media Matters. 2008. "Women, Minorities, Autistic Children: Conservative Radio's Vitriol Not Reserved for Obama." *Media Matters for America*. http://mediamatters.org/research/2008/11/13/women-minorities-autistic-children-conservative/146117 (accessed June 24, 2015).

Merida, Kevin. 2008. "She's the Star the GOP Hitched Its Bandwagon To." *Washington Post* (September 11): C1.

"Michele Bachmann Drops out of GOP Race after Iowa Caucuses." 2012. *The Washington Post*. http://www.washingtonpost.com/politics/michele-bachmann-drops-out-of-gop-race-after-iowa-caucuses/2012/01/04/gIQAP6L9aP_story.html (accessed June 24, 2015).

"Michele Bachmann Plays Gender Card as Iowa GOP Vote Nears." 2012. *Des Moines Register.* http://caucuses.desmoinesregister.com/2012/01/01/bachmann-plays -gender-card-as-iowa-gop-vote-nears/(accessed June 24, 2015).

Morris, Celia. 1992. *Storming the Statehouse: Running for Governor with Ann Richards and Dianne Feinstein.* New York: Scribner's Sons.

NBC/Wall Street Journal. 2008. "NBC News / Wall Street Journal Poll, Study #6080. March. Accessed online at http://online.wsj.com/public/resources/documents/ WSJ-20080312-poll.pdf

*Newsweek.* 2008. *Newsweek* Poll. October 10. Accessed through Polling the Nations.

Norris, Pippa. 1997. *Women, Media, and Politics.* New York: Oxford University Press.

Palmer, Barbara, and Dennis Michael Simon. 2001. "The Political Glass Ceiling: Gender, Strategy, and Incumbency in U.S. House Elections, 1978-1998." *Women & Politics* 23: 59–78.

———. 2006. *Breaking the Political Glass Ceiling: Women and Congressional Elections.* New York: Routledge.

Palin's Speech at the Republican National Convention. 2008. Transcript available at http://elections.nytimes.com/2008/president/conventions/videos/transcripts/ 20080903_PALIN_SPEECH.html

Pew Research Center's Project for Excellence in Journalism. 2008. *Character and the Primaries of 2008.* http://www.journalism.org/files/legacy/MASTER%20NARRA TIVES%20FINAL_NOEMBARGO.pdf

Polling Report. 2000. "White House 2000: Republicans." Accessed online at www .pollingreport.com/wh2rep.htm

———. 2008a. "Campaign 2008." Accessed online at www.pollingreport.com/ wh08.htm

———. 2008b. "White House 2008: Democratic Nomination." Accessed online at www.pollingreport.com/wh08dem.htm. Polling the Nations =

Rosenwasser, Shirley Miller, and Norma G. Dean. 1989. "Gender Role and Political Office." *Psychology of Women Quarterly* 13(1): 77–85.

Rucker, Philip, and Eli Saslow. 2009. "Sarah Palin to Resign as Alaska Governor, Citing Probes and Family Needs." *The Washington Post.* http://www.washingtonpost .com/wp-dyn/content/article/2009/07/03/AR2009070301738.html (accessed June 24, 2015).

Sanbonmatsu, Kira. 2002. "Gender Stereotypes and Vote Choice." *American Journal of Political Science* 46(1): 20–34.

Sanbonmatsu, Kira, and Kathleen Dolan. 2009. "Do Gender Stereotypes Transcend Party?" *Political Research Quarterly* 62(3): 485–94.

Shear, Michael D., and Shailagh Murray. 2008. "Back on the Stump, Candidates Attack Each Other on Economy." *Washington Post* (September 6): A1.

Sheckels, Theodore F. 1994. "Mikulski vs. Chavez for the Senate from Maryland in 1986 and the 'rules' for Attack Politics." *Communication Quarterly* 42(3): 311–26.

Shorenstein Center on Media, Politics and Public Policy. 2016a. *News Coverage of the 2016 General Election: How the Press Failed the Voters.* Boston: Harvard Kennedy School.

———. 2016b. *Pre-Primary News Coverage of the 2016 Presidential Race.* Boston: Harvard Kennedy School.

Smith, Anne. 2008. "Limbaugh Returned to 'Testicle Lockbox'; Claimed Clinton 'Reminds Men of the Worst Characteristics of Women.'" *Media Matters for America*. http://mediamatters.org/research/2008/02/15/limbaugh-returned-to-testicle -lockbox-claimed-c/142573 (accessed June 24, 2015).

Smooth, Wendy. 2006. "Intersectionality in Electoral Politics: A Mess Worth Making." *Politics & Gender* 2(3): 400–14.

Stolberg, Sheryl Gay. 2014. "Joni Ernst's Playbook, for Women to Win Men's Vote." *The New York Times*. http://www.nytimes.com/2014/10/29/us/iowans-playbook -for-women-to-win-mens-vote.html (accessed June 22, 2015).

Tolleson-Rinehart, Sue, and Jeanie Ricketts Stanley. 1994. *Claytie and the Lady: Ann Richards, Gender, and Politics in Texas*. Austin, TX: University of Texas Press.

Washington Post-ABC News Polls. 2008. (February 4). Accessed online at http:// www.washingtonpost.com/wp-srv/politics/polls/postpoll_020308.html

Watkins, Bonnie, and Nina Rothchild. 1996. *In the Company of Women: Voices from the Women's Movement*. St. Paul: Minnesota Historical Society Press.

Watson, Robert P., and Ann Gordon. 2003. *Anticipating Madam President*. Boulder, CO: Lynne Rienner.

West, Carolyn M. 2008. "Mammy, Jezebel, Sapphire, and Their Homegirls: Developing an 'Oppositional Gaze' Toward the Images of Black Women." In *Lectures on the Psychology of Women*, edited by J. Chrisler, C. Golden, and P. Rozee, 286–99. New York: McGraw-Hill.

# II

## WOMEN IN POWER

# 6

# Women in Local Politics and Government

While the actions of local governments often don't generate national headlines, a move by the Topeka City Council in Kansas did just that in October of 2011. The council voted, 7 to 3, to decriminalize domestic violence in response to the Shawnee County District Attorney's decision that he would no longer prosecute such cases under state law because of budget cuts. In order to avoid spending money on prosecuting these cases itself, the city of Topeka chose to decriminalize domestic violence as a city crime so that it would not have jurisdiction to prosecute such cases, arguing instead that domestic violence was a state matter in Kansas. As a result, 18 people arrested in Topeka on domestic assault charges in September 2011 were released because neither the county nor the city would press charges, each claiming the other had jurisdiction in the matter. While most council members claimed their vote was really about budget politics—and not a move to deny abuse victims protection from domestic violence—City Councilwoman Denise Everhart, who voted against the repeal, said to reporters, "I just ask everybody to consider the message we're sending" (quoted in Hanna 2011).

Although the Shawnee County District Attorney ultimately recanted his decision, announcing he would resume the prosecution of such cases given the massive public outcry against his actions (Goodmark 2011), the shocking move by the Topeka City Council to decriminalize domestic abuse serves as a reminder of how the work of local government can be of vital importance to women's well-being. While domestic violence is an issue that has prompted national legislation, most recently in the form of the Violence Against Women Act, renewed by Congress in 2012, much of the work of stopping domestic abuse happens at the local level of government. As we document later in this chapter, local women advocates at the grassroots level of politics have fought for decades against domestic violence, spear-heading the establishment of domestic shelters, raising awareness about intimate partner violence, and placing pressure on local lawmakers to pass legislation that takes such abuse seriously. Moreover, women lawmakers at the local level often express greater interest in and recognition of domestic violence as a political issue, along with a range of other issues that may be particularly germane to women. Studying women's involvement in local politics, both as elected officials and as activists, is important to fully under-stand how well government is meeting the needs of its women citizens.

Analyzing women in local politics is also important because women are more likely to serve at the local level of government than at the state or national level. One reason is obvious—there are many more opportunities to participate. The US Census Bureau (2012) reports that there are more than 89,000 government units in the United States, ranging from school boards, townships, counties, municipalities, and "special districts," which are independent government units designed for a specific special purpose, such as handling public transportation. Table 6.1 lists the numbers and types of local governments according to the US Census Bureau (data are reported for 2012, the last time such data were collected). Combined, these local governments allow for the election of almost 500,000 public officials nationwide. Women are also more likely to be elected at the local level than at other levels of government because such offices are often part-time, non-partisan, less costly to campaign for, and less high-profile. Thus, running for local political office involves fewer resources and less media scrutiny (Van Assendelft 2014). Serving in local elected offices means that women do not have to relocate or spend as much time away from their families. As Silbermann's (2014) research on state legislative districts shows, distance from the state capital correlates with women's representation in state poli-tics: the farther away the legislative district, the smaller the odds that the representative will be a woman and that candidates for that office will be women. However, Silbermann found no such correlation between the pro-portion of women serving in local government and distance from the state capital, leading her to speculate that geographical distance from where the work of government gets done can influence a woman's decision to run for office. Hence, women are likely to find local-level politics more appealing than state-level politics.

Not only are women more likely to be elected at the local level of gov-ernment, but enhanced opportunities to affect public policy also exist for women in local bureaucracies and in grassroots, nongovernmental organizations (Palley 2001). In many ways, the daily lives of women (and men) are deeply touched by local governments. Though local-level politics is less glamorous than national or state politics, local politicians grapple with issues that impact women and children disproportionately, such as

**Table 6.1. Type of Local Governments**

| Type of Government | Number |
| --- | --- |
| Federal Government | 1 |
| State Governments | 50 |
| Local Governments | |
| *General Purpose*: | |
| County | 3,033 |
| Municipal | 19,492 |
| Township | 16,519 |
| *Special Purpose*: | |
| School Districts | 13,051 |
| Special Districts | 37,381 |

*Source*: US Census Bureau. 2012. "Government Units in 2007." *US Census of Governments.*

education, social services, and as previously mentioned, domestic violence. In addition, local government is where public access to elected officials is greatest. Given that decentralization is a hallmark of American government and politics, examining the impact and activism of women in local politics is important.

This chapter takes a look at women in local politics in several areas that tap into the larger themes of representation that we consider in the book. First, we examine women in local elected office, both as elected executives and as part of local legislatures such as city councils and school boards. With an eye toward the question of descriptive representation, we consider how many women are elected to these positions and what factors may inhibit or help women achieve parity in such positions. We also consider whether these local offices actually serve as political steppingstones. Many advocates who desire seeing more women elected to state legislatures, Congress, or statewide executive office often look down the political pipeline at women serving in local politics as potential prospects for higher office, given that time spent in local government gives potential candidates vital political experience.

Second, turning to the issue of substantive representation, once women are elected to serve in local government, we consider whether their presence actually improves the status of women in their communities. Do women pursue different policies than men at the local level of government, or do they govern in a different manner?

Lastly, we also examine the role of women in grassroots activism and NGOs, recognizing that participation in these areas often results in demands for government to address a variety of concerns like environmental issues, labor disputes, and economic development. We also pay closer attention to the grassroots movement that led to the establishment of domestic violence clinics nationally. We profile several cases of local activism in which women made a unique contribution, showcasing how women have been involved in both progressive and conservative politics within their communities.

## DESCRIPTIVE REPRESENTATION: WOMEN SERVING IN LOCAL GOVERNMENT

### Women as Municipal Leaders

Most municipalities have mayors, although they vary with respect to their selection style and their formal powers. Mayors who are elected directly by the public and have independent executive powers, such as budget authority or the veto, are known as strong mayors. Weak mayors, by contrast, are largely ceremonial. Selected by the city council, weak mayors share an equal vote with the council and govern in what are known as council-manager systems. Often, the day-to-day job of running cities in such systems falls to a hired city manager. According to the National League of Cities, most cities (55 percent) use the council-manager system. More than one-third of municipalities, especially those in the Northeast and Mid-Atlantic states, use the mayor-council systems (National League of Cities n.d.); however, the nation's largest cities are more likely to have separately elected mayors. Smaller municipalities or townships sometimes have governments without a formal executive, such as commissions or town meetings.

The first woman elected mayor in the United States was Susanna Madora Salter, who in 1887 was elected mayor of Argonia, Kansas, as part of the Prohibition Party (Kansas Historical Society n.d.) (see Box 6.1). Salter, however, was the exception, and not the rule, for most of America's history. Although systematic data on the presence of women mayors in all cities are hard to

**Box 6.1.   Susanna Madora Salter, America's First Female Mayor**

In 1887, Susanna Madora Salter was elected mayor of Argonia, Kansas, well before women had gained the elective franchise nationally in the United States. Active in the Women's Christian Temperance Union, Salter ran for mayor as part of the Prohibition Party when several men in Argonia who opposed efforts to ban alcohol nominated her as a joke. Yet, she handily won the election and served one term with distinction before her family moved to Oklahoma (Kansas Historical Society n.d.). *Photo source*: Kansas Historical Society.

collect, the Center for American Women and Politics at Rutgers University has tracked the progress of women as mayors in cities with a population of 30,000 or more residents. In 1971, just 1 percent of such cities had female mayors. While women are currently better represented as mayors of larger cities than as governors, scholars who study women mayors note that their progress as the city's top official has largely stymied in the last two decades, and in some cases, has actually declined. For example, in the late 1990s and early 2000s, women crossed the 20 percent threshold as mayors in cities with more than 30,000 residents. Since 2003, however, the Center for American Women and Politics reports that fewer than 20 percent of such cities have had women mayors (Carroll and Sanbonmatsu 2010). Currently, women make up just 17.5 percent of mayors in cities with more than 30,000 residents.

Women are even less represented among mayors of the nation's most populous cities. Table 6.2 lists the 19 women serving as mayors among the 100 largest cities in America as of 2016 (Center for American Women and Politics 2016). Of those, four are African American (Ivy Taylor, Muriel Bowser, Stephanie Rawlings-Blake, and Paula Hicks-Hudson) and two are Latina (Nelda Martinez and Mary Casillas Salas). In January 2015, Muriel Bowser became the second woman of color to be sworn in as the mayor of Washington, DC, which is the nation's 23rd largest city. In America's fourth largest city, Houston, Annise Parker served as the first openly lesbian mayor of a major city in the United States (see Box 6.2). Parker grew up in Houston

**Table 6.2. Women Mayors of 100 Largest US Cities 2016**

| Mayor | City | Population | Rank |
|---|---|---|---|
| Ivy R. Taylor | San Antonio | 1,327,407 | 8 |
| Betsy Price | Fort Worth, TX | 792,727 | 16 |
| Jennifer W. Roberts | Charlotte, NC | 646,449 | 20 |
| Muriel Bowser | Washington, DC | 626,681 | 25 |
| Stephanie Rawlings-Blake | Baltimore, MD | 620,961 | 26 |
| Carolyn Goodman | Las Vegas, NV | 583,756 | 32 |
| Ashley Swearengin | Fresno, CA | 509,924 | 36 |
| Jean Stohert | Omaha, NE | 421,570 | 42 |
| Nancy McFarlane | Raleigh, NC | 403,892 | 45 |
| Libby Schaaf | Oakland, CA | 390,724 | 49 |
| Betsy Hodges | Minneapolis, MN | 382,578 | 50 |
| Angie M. Carpenter | Islip, NY | 335,543 | 57 |
| Nelda Martinez | Corpus Christi, TX | 305,215 | 62 |
| Paula Hicks-Hudson | Toledo, OH | 287,208 | 69 |
| Nancy Barakta Vaughan | Greensboro, NC | 269,666 | 73 |
| Mary Casillas Salas | Chula Vista, CA | 243,916 | 81 |
| Hillary Schieve | Reno, NV | 225,221 | 93 |
| Beth Van Duyne | Irving, TX | 216,290 | 97 |

*Data*: Center for American Women and Politics, Fact Sheet, 2016; Population sizes and ranks are drawn from US Census Bureau estimates.

**Box 6.2.  Annise Parker, Former Mayor of Houston**

Annise Parker made history in 2009 when she became the mayor of the city of Houston, the largest American city to elect an openly gay mayor. She was term-limited in 2016 and has indicated a desire to seek higher statewide office.

*Photo source:* The City of Houston, http://www.houstontx.gov/mayor.

and attended Rice University, becoming an economic analyst for the oil and gas industry. While working in the private sector, however, she was a very vocal lesbian activist within the city, becoming the city's first openly gay elected official when she was elected to the City Council in 1997. After two terms as the City Controller, Parker won her first term as mayor in a run-off but easily won reelection in 2011 and 2013 in part because of her deft handling of Houston's finances during the nationwide recession in 2010 (Dart 2014). She is also the first person in Houston to have served as a city council member, controller, and mayor. In Parker's final term—Houston mayors can only serve 3 two-year terms—she tried to win passage of the Houston Equal Rights Ordinance or HERO ordinance, which "bans discrimination against LBGT people in housing, in employment, and in public spaces" in the city of Houston (Kuruvilla 2014). However, when Parker chose to subpoena the sermons of several Houston pastors who opposed the ordinance to determine if they had used the pulpit for the purposes of organizing a ballot initiative to repeal HERO, the pastors and other religious activists charged Parker with violating their religious liberty rights. Parker dropped the subpoenas. The mother of four adopted minority children with her longtime partner and now wife Kathy Hubbard (Lawson 2015), Parker is now weighing her options for a statewide run, which could be challenging in Texas because of her sexual orientation, her advocacy for HERO, and the fact that she is a Democrat in a solidly red state (Thompson 2015).

To gain a better understanding of the type of women who serve as mayors, Susan Carroll and Kira Sanbonmatsu (2010) surveyed the entire universe of American women mayors in 2008 in cities with 30,000 or more residents as well as a random sample of male mayors for comparison purposes.[1] Their study finds that most mayors, both women (64.3 percent) and men (68.7 percent), come into office through direct election and that the vast majority of these offices are nonpartisan. By contrast, almost one-third of women mayors preside in council-manager systems, which means that they were selected by their fellow council members to be mayor after they were elected to serve on the council. Overwhelmingly non-Hispanic and white in terms of ethnicity, women mayors are both less likely to be married than their male counterparts and less likely to have children under the age of 18 (ibid.). Before being elected to office, most women mayors were very active in women's organizations such as the League of Women Voters and other civic groups such as religious organizations, local service organizations, and business/professional groups. Compared with their male counterparts, women were much more likely to be involved in organizations that focused on children's issues (ibid.). Politically, women mayors also engaged in more partisan and electoral activities than men prior to their time before serving as mayor, including holding previous elective or appointment positions before becoming mayor. In short, women mayors "have had as much or more experience than their male counterparts before becoming mayors" (11), echoing other findings about women and political office, which shows that women who become candidates are often *better* qualified than men before they decide to run for office. Consistent with studies that examine political ambition among women candidates for other offices, Carroll and Sanbonmatsu's work finds that women mayors are more likely to focus on public policy as a motivator to seek office compared with men, while men are more likely to express general political ambition. For instance, when asked to name the single most important reason for seeking the mayoralty, 41.2 percent of women compared with 26.8 percent of men selected "my concern about one or more specific public policy issues" as the most frequent response. By contrast, male mayors were more than twice as likely as female mayors to say that their "longstanding desire to be involved in politics" was the most important reason for their seeking mayoral office.

A more recent study to consider when it comes to women's descriptive representation in local politics as executives is the American Municipal Officials Survey (AMOS), a nonpartisan survey conducted jointly by scholars at Yale University and the Washington University of St. Louis in

---

[1]Carroll and Sanbonmatsu report that their overall response rate was 48.2 percent for a total sample size of 189. Women mayors were more likely to respond, and the authors express confidence with the generalizability of the results for the women mayors given that more than half of them (52.4 percent) responded to their survey request. They argue that the results for the male respondents should be viewed with more caution given that fewer than half—43.9 percent—of the men responded.

2012 and 2014.[2] Turning to women as elected or appointed executives, which included the position of mayor, commissioner, or deputy mayor, AMOS found that 18 percent of positions listed above are held by women, numbers that are remarkably comparable to the 17.5 percent of women serving as mayors in America's largest metropolitan cities (cities with more than 30,000 residents). While the dataset is not large enough to break down the sample by race, the data do allow for partisan, ideological, and regional analysis by gender. The AMOS study shows that there are no regional differences when it comes to the likelihood that a woman or a man will serve as a municipal executive—women are evenly represented in municipalities in the Northeast, South, Midwest, and West. Women executives in local government do differ when it comes to party and ideology from their male counterparts, however. Among women executives in municipalities, 41 percent identify as Democrats, 29 percent identify as Republicans, and 29 percent identify as Independents. By contrast, 48 percent of such men identify as Republicans, 26 percent as Democrats, and 26 percent as Independents.[3] Women also identify themselves as more politically liberal than their male counterparts. In this respect, women as elected executives in municipalities appear to be very similar to political women in state and congressional offices, disproportionately Democratic and liberal compared with political men (see chapter 7 on women in legislatures). For a look at another pathbreaking woman leader in American politics, see Box 6.3, which profiles Wilma Mankiller, the first woman elected as Tribal Chief of the Cherokee Nation. Native American tribes operate under their own system of government set apart from federal or state government.

While not elected, another important position to consider in city leadership is the position of professional city manager or chief administrative

---

[2]The results of the American Municipal Officials Survey should be viewed with some caution, as the survey is not a truly random sample of officeholders. As a first step, researchers selected a random sample of local, general-purpose governments known as municipalities from the 2011 United States Census of Governments, which included cities, towns, townships, boroughs, and villages. Researchers located e-mail contact information about locally elected officials from the municipalities' websites, which meant that localities that did not provide the e-mail contact information of their officeholders were excluded from the sample. Those elected officials with an e-mail address were contacted several times to complete an online survey. As a result, the elected officials who completed the surveys were drawn disproportionately from larger municipalities, which were often likely to have e-mail contact information for their elected officials. The total sample size in which data on gender were included was approximately 1,600 cases. For more information about the survey see http://municipalsurvey .commons.yale.edu. The authors are grateful to the principal co-investigators of the survey, Daniel Butler of Washington University and Adam Dynes of Yale University, for sharing their data to be used in our book.

[3]The authors calculated these data. Partisanship differences among women and men local executives are found to be statistically significant using a chi-square test ($p = 0.018$) and ideological differences were found to be statistically significant using an ANOVA test ($p = 0.001$). By contrast, a chi-square test that examined the relationship between gender of the local executive by region is not significant ($p = 0.916$).

**Box 6.3.  Wilma Mankiller, First Woman Chief of the Cherokee Nation**

Women have also begun to make their mark as tribal leaders, as Native American tribes represent another form of American government. Wilma Mankiller (1945–2010) was elected in 1987 as the first woman chief of the Cherokee Nation, the second largest tribe in the United States. In more recent years, women continue to make gains in tribal governments. In 2006, according to data from the National Congress of Indians, the number of women leaders of tribes was 133 among the more than 560 recognized tribes (Davey 2006).
*Photo source*: © Buddy Mays / Alamy Stock Photo.

officer (CAO), found in the council-manager form of government. The city manager is an appointed position first developed around the turn of the twentieth century as part of a larger movement to reform government, particularly in urban areas. Popular at this time was the idea that administration could be separate from politics, known among public administration scholars as the "politics–administration" dichotomy. There is a recognition that although managers often have a large hand in guiding policy implementation while working with the council, they typically try and stay above partisan politics, relying on the professional standards developed by groups such as the International City/County Management Association (Montjoy and Watson 1995). Women currently make up about 13 percent of city managers or CAOs—a number that has not changed in 30 years despite the fact that women are more likely to earn Master's of Public Administration degrees than men (Beaty and Davis 2012) and given that they are very well represented in other city management positions. For instance, the International City/County Management Association (ICMA) reports that in 2013, women represented 30 percent of department heads in city government, 34 percent of assistant CAOs, and 53 percent of assistants to the CAO—all positions that would naturally serve as a great stepping stone to city manager (Voorhies and Lange-Skaggs 2015).

Given women's educational and professional experience in city administration, why do so few women then become city managers? Voorhies and Lange-Skaggs (2015) found that women cite work/family balance issues as one factor that inhibits them from seeking a city's top administration position. Moreover, women are reluctant to apply for the position of city manager because they believe they have to have all the necessary experience before applying for their next positions, often downplaying their skills and abilities—a common tendency in women professionals according to Facebook COO Sheryl Sandberg in her book *Lean In*, who argues that women are more risk averse than men when it comes to seeking leadership roles (see also Kay and Shipman 2014). At the same time, Voorhies and Lange-Skaggs (2015) argue that supervisors, who make hiring decisions, may have misconceptions about women's leadership abilities. Women's stagnation at the level of city manager has prompted calls to make gender more visible within the leadership curriculum in MPA programs (Beaty and Davis 2012), and to promote mentorship programs and greater inclusion of women in professional city and county management events.

## Women in Local Legislatures

We next consider how many women serve on local legislatures such as city and county councils. Counties and cities are still viewed as arms of the states, which confer all formal powers to local governments through state constitutions or by acts of the state legislature (Ross and Levine 2001). Local legislatures at the county level are typically known as county councils, boards of supervisors, or boards of commissioners. In municipalities and cities, they are typically known as city councils. Traditionally, counties performed state-mandated duties such as record keeping, assessing property, maintaining and building local roads, administering local elections, law enforcement, and judicial functions—tasks that still make up the bulk of what county governments do. But counties have increasingly taken on more responsibilities in the wake of the "devolution revolution" that has been occurring in American politics since the late 1980s. Devolution involves shifting policy responsibilities from the federal government to the state and local levels. Local government power was probably most curtailed in the 1960s, with the federal government taking a more proactive role in trying to coordinate and fund public programs geared at tackling poverty, health care, economic development, and education in urban, suburban, and rural areas. However, as it became clear that a nationally mandated focus was making little headway in actually solving these intractable problems, and as both state and local governments began to chafe under the regulations that accompanied the grant money given to address these issues, calls came for greater freedom for such governments to handle social services and design policies that better suited their own localities. Of course, critics of devolution point out that this greater "freedom" has meant reduced spending on the part of the federal government, meaning that states and localities have either had to raise more money independently or cut back on social services. Although counties vary nationwide regarding the extent to which they provide such services, local shares of domestic expenditures on such programs grew dramatically from the 1970s to the 1990s, indicating that subnational governments such as counties have risen in importance as devolution has taken place (Weber and Brace 1999).

The US Census of Governments used to collect data on the gender of officeholders at all levels of government every ten years, but stopped doing so after its 1992 Census, so the most recent, systematic data available about the number of women serving on county councils are dated. In 1992, the Census of Governments reported that almost 13 percent of elected county council members were women, which was smaller than the percentage of women serving in state legislatures or city councils at that same time. There is little reason to suspect that this number has not increased, however, as women posted tremendous gains at this elected position from the 1970s. In 1987, 8.6 percent of county council members were women, more than triple the number of women serving at this position in 1975 (Manning 1988).

Data on women serving in city councils are more recent. Data from the International City/County Management Association report that women in 1991 held 18.7 percent of city council seats, a number that increased to 22.1 percent by 2001. Their survey from 2011 shows that women hold approximately two out of seven city council seats nationally, for an average of about 28 percent (Moulder 2015). However, the representation of women varies dramatically on city councils. Take the case of America's two largest cities—New York City and Los Angeles. In New York, women are fairly well represented on its large city council, holding 14 of its 51 elected positions (27 percent) as of 2015. Moreover, Melissa Mark-Viverito, the first Latina and Puerto Rican to be elected to citywide office in New York City, is the current leader of the council, known as the Council Speaker. However, the situation in Los Angeles, America's second largest city, is dismal. In 2017, just one woman, Nury Martinez, held a seat on the 15-member city council. By contrast, in 2002, women held 5 of those seats. Why are women practically non-existent on the Los Angeles City Council? Gloria Romero, who serves as the first female majority leader in the California State Senate, told *LA Weekly* that she believes it is because of the high costs of such seats: "I think it says a lot about the difficulties of women raising money. It's an old boys' network. The lobbyists are all male; they're all chummy with each other. You go hang out on the damn golf course" (quoted in Aron 2013). The situation for women with respect to descriptive representation in two other large California cities is equally bleak: both Fresno and Bakersfield have only one female city council member. Women do fare better on other city councils in the Golden State: one 2014 study found that 28 percent of California City Council members are women. However, while 12 percent of City Councils (61 out of 482) in California have a women's majority, 15 percent (71 out of 482) have no women serving on them (California Women Lead 2014).

The 2012 and 2014 AMOS also surveyed the men and women who serve on local legislative councils in addition to those who serve as mayors or local executives. In this survey, 27 percent of survey respondents were women—which, again, corresponds closely with other studies that track the number of legislators in local offices by gender. Similar to the AMOS data on local women executives, local women legislators are no more or less likely to serve in any one region of the country. Yet, they are more liberal than their male counterparts. Female legislators are also significantly more likely to identify as Democrats (50 percent) than male legislators (28 percent). Men serving on municipal councils, by contrast, are more likely to identify as Republicans (42 percent) than women (28 percent) and also as Independents than women (31 percent compared with 22 percent, respectively).[4]

Next, we consider the factors that help to explain why women are better represented on some city councils than others, including whether there is a relationship between women's representation, council size, and council electoral structure. Having a larger council improves the chances that at least one woman will serve on a city council (Alozie and Manganaro 1993; Trounstine and Valdini 2008). However, whether the electoral structure of city councils impacts the number of women serving on the councils is less clear. Racial and ethnic minorities have long argued that single-member districts are more beneficial to their groups because waging a campaign in a single district is less expensive than running at large, in which candidates have to compete citywide for the position as opposed to a smaller district. Minorities also maintain that it is easier to be elected in single-member

---

[4]The authors calculated these data. Partisanship differences among women and men serving on local councils are found to be statistically significant using a chi-square test ($p = 0.000$), as are ideological differences using an ANOVA test ($p = 0.000$). By contrast, a chi-square test that examined the relationship between gender of the local executive by region was not significant ($p = 0.124$).

districts because neighborhoods tend to be segregated racially; hence, the odds of electing a minority from a minority-majority district are likely higher than facing several opponents at large as most blacks vote for black candidates and most whites vote for white candidates (see, e.g., Browning, Marshall, and Tabb 1994). Most research shows that such districts have been beneficial to the descriptive representation of both African Americans and Latinos (for an excellent summary of this literature, see Trounstine and Valdini 2008).

By contrast, many feminists have long argued that at-large elections would provide more opportunities for women to serve on city councils than single-member districts. Unlike racial minorities, women are not geographically isolated in city neighborhoods. The thinking is that women would do better in citywide races because voters would not be faced with a zero-sum choice as they would in a single-district race that elected just one member, in which voting for a woman would mean not choosing a man. When voters can make several choices (as opposed to one choice in a single-member district), they are more likely to want to balance and diversify the ticket (Thomas 1998).

The data, however, do not always support these suppositions when it comes to women and the electoral structure of city councils. Most scholars conclude that women are not advantaged in at-large elections (Bullock and MacManus 1991; Alozie and Manganaro 1993; MacManus and Bullock 1993; Darcy, Welch, and Clark 1994). In the most definitive study to date of the effects of single-member versus at-large districts on the diversity of city councils, which analyzes electoral outcomes in more than 7,000 cities, Jessica Trounstine and Melody E. Valdini (2008) found that having a majority of council members elected by districts as opposed to at-large greatly improves the odds of electing any African American to the city council by more than 10 percent, but that those findings also hinged on the proportion of the city's population that is black. The impact of the electoral system for Latinos, however, is negligible. Turning to women, their work confirms previous research that women do better on larger city councils: the more council seats, the better the odds that women will be elected. Electoral structure impacts the odds of women serving on city councils, but only in a modest way: the odds of a woman elected in an at-large city council improve about two percent over a city council that has district elections. However, the impact of electoral structure does not affect all women the same. Trounstine and Valdini find that African American men get a significant boost from single-member district electoral structures but not African American women. For Latinos and Latinas, electoral structure has no effect on their odds of improving their representation on city councils. Lastly, white women appear to benefit slightly if they compete in at-large as opposed to single-member elections.

The proportion of the nonwhite population has also been linked to higher levels of representation of minorities at different levels of political office, including county, municipal, and school board offices. In one path-breaking study known as the Gender and Multicultural Leadership Project (GMLP), researchers found that African Americans, Asian Americans, and Hispanic Americans enjoyed more electoral success in districts that were racially diverse—although large percentages of minority groups in districts (or states) does not always result in equitable parity when it comes to office-holding for men or women of color (Hardy-Fanta et al. 2006). For female elected officials of color, the authors define equitable parity as "the extent to which women of color elected officials have reached a share of a given level of office proportionate to their share in the population" (ibid., 16). Indeed, they find that parity ratios differ with respect to race, level of office, and state. For example, women of color, especially Latina and Asian American women, often enjoy higher parity values in terms of elected representation than do (non-Hispanic) white women. That is, their presence in local political offices more closely approximates their share in the population. The findings are mixed for African American women, depending on the level of government.

Finally, we consider the number of women serving on elected school boards. In the late 1860s, several women were elected to school boards in Massachusetts (where they are known as school committees), marking the first elected political position held by women in the nation (Darcy, Welch, and Clark 1994). Moreover, many states granted women the limited right to vote in school board elections long before women gained universal suffrage in 1920. Historically, education has been viewed as a special prerogative of women, given many women's status as mothers. Even today, women devote more of their civic activism to education than to other political issues (Schlozman et al. 1995).

It should come as no surprise, then, that school boards represent the local political office to which women are most likely to be elected. In 2002, 39 percent of school board members were women (Hess 2002). Most recently, the National School Board Association in 2015 reports that 44 percent of board members are women (National School Board Association 2015). The ranks of women at the school board level have increased greatly from the early 1970s, when the National School Boards Association estimated that 12 percent of board members were women (Blanchard 1977).

Although some view school board elections as akin to community service, school boards decide many important political decisions. School board elections have become a hotly contested venue in the "culture wars" of American politics. As pitched battles over sex education, censorship, and school prayer demonstrate, the school district is one arena in which moral values often intersect with education (Deckman 2004). School boards help to establish the direction of local education policy by selecting and monitoring school administrators and they also establish district priorities through budgeting.

How do men and women compare as school board candidates? Data from a national 1998 survey of school board candidates show that 38 percent were women, corresponding closely to their ranks as elected school board members at the time (Deckman 2006).[5] These same data show that women and men win school board seats at roughly the same rates, as 65 percent of women candidates and 62 percent of men candidates succeeded in their elections. Gender remains an insignificant factor in terms of predicting school board success when controlling for other variables such as incumbency, campaign resources, and type of district. While female school board candidates are slightly more ideologically moderate than male school board candidates, more Republican women run at this level than at other levels of government and women school board candidates are more likely to describe themselves as moderate-to-conservative ideologically. More specifically, 42 percent of women school board candidates nationally identified as Republicans compared with 34 percent as Democrats, with the remainder identifying as politically Independent. While a plurality of women candidates—30 percent—describe themselves as "middle of the road" ideologically, 41 percent describe themselves as either slightly conservative or conservative, with just 24 percent describing themselves as either slightly liberal or liberal. In this respect, women who run for school boards look different as a whole than women running for other levels of political office as they are more conservative and more Republican.

## Summary: Women's Representation in Local Government and the Political Pipeline

While women have made great strides in terms of their representation in local government from the 1970s, and they are better represented at this level of government than in higher state offices or Congressional office, women still do not hold office in numbers that match their presence in the US population. Table 6.3 summarizes women's descriptive representation in various local offices with the most recent data available. The political office in which women come closest to parity with men is the school board level, with women serving on 44 percent of such seats, followed by city

---

[5]Data come from a survey conducted by Deckman in 1998, in which 300 school districts were randomly selected nationwide, stratified by size, and asked to provide lists of candidates who ran in the most recent school board elections. A total of 1,220 school board candidates were identified, and after two waves of mailing, 671 usable responses were received, for a response rate of 55 percent.

**Table 6.3. Percentage of Women as Local Government Officials: Estimates and Sources of Data**

| Position | Percentage | Year of Data Collection | Source |
|---|---|---|---|
| *Executives* | | | |
| Mayors of Cities with More Than 30,000 People | 18 | 2016 | CAWP |
| Mayors of Municipalities | 18 | 2012, 2014 | American Municipal Officials Survey |
| Elected County Executives | 8 | 2014 | NACO |
| Women as City Managers | 13 | 2015 | ICMA |
| *City Councils, County Councils, and School Boards* | 28 | 2011 | ICMA |
| City and Town Councils | 27 | 2012, 2014 | American Municipal Officials Survey |
| County Councils | 13 | 1992 | US Census of Governments |
| School Boards | 44 | 2015 | NSBA |

councils, in which women hold approximately 28 percent of such positions. Findings from the American Municipal Officials Survey also suggest that women make up about 28 percent of city and town councils as well. Compared with congressional or state legislative seats, women's representation as councilors is slightly better, but again does not come close to their numbers in the general population. As elected executives, particularly as mayors, women still have a way to go in terms of descriptive representation, as data from several sources suggest that women make up fewer than 20 percent of the nation's elected executives in municipalities of various sizes.

Given that women are best represented among officeholders at the local level of government, many argue that women will not go on to pursue higher political office until they have more experience at local offices such as school boards or city and county councils. While relatively few studies of progressive political ambition among local officeholders exist, the ones that do suggest that those who believe the local pipeline will generate much higher numbers of women candidates for higher office may be disappointed. For instance, Laura Van Assendelft's (2014) study of women mayors and city council members in rural Virginia shows that the vast majority of women—about 80 percent—holding these offices show little interest in pursuing higher office. Instead, these women worry that serving in higher office will negate the very features of serving locally that they enjoy, namely the ability to interact regularly with the people who live in their local communities and the nonpartisan nature of the work. One woman she interviewed commented that she enjoyed solving problems in her small town, working as a collaborative team. Susan Abram Beck's (2001) study of town council members also finds little progressive political ambition among individuals serving at this level of government—either women or men. At the school board level, Deckman's (2007) research shows that school board candidates, both male and female, are not likely to express much political ambition outside of this local elected office—and that they are more likely to consider their work as community service. The vast majority of candidates who run for school boards list community goals as the primary reason they ran for office. By contrast, just 10 percent of women candidates and 16 percent of men candidates said they ran for school board because they wanted political experience in case they might want to run for higher office one day.

The most recent data suggest that women's numbers might be leveling off at the local level of government in terms of descriptive representation. The good news is that for women who run for local office, electoral structure or discrimination on the part of voters does not appear to hinder their success. Women candidates win at the same rates as male candidates, even at the local level of government. The bad news is that women still show a reluctance to take the initial step to become candidates in the first place, for a variety of reasons that chapter 4 explores more fully. Few women in local government appear to express political ambition for higher office.

## SUBSTANTIVE REPRESENTATION: DOES HAVING WOMEN IN LOCAL GOVERNMENT MATTER?

As we document in our chapter on women in legislatures (see chapter 7), women officeholders at the state and congressional level do sometimes govern uniquely compared to men. Here, we consider whether women in local government govern differently than men, which is a key consideration when it comes to substantive representation. Having more women serving in local politics could be important if women bring with them different experiences, leadership styles, and policy concerns than men. Indeed, political theorists and women's interest groups have often argued that only when women achieve greater numbers of elected seats in government will they, as a group, have their concerns and preferences reflected in policy outcomes. First, we examine the substantive impact of women serving in municipalities and then turn our attention toward school board office.

Historically, women's presence as urban reformers during the Progressive Era shows that women have always played a part in pressuring local government to address issues of special concern to women and families, whether that meant improving city schools, pursuing labor reform, or spearheading hunger and homelessness efforts (see chapter 2 for more details). Women such as Jane Addams spearheaded the settlement house movement. Women volunteers in the early twentieth century largely ran settlement houses, which sought to address the underlying causes of poverty in inner cities (Blair 1980). Eventually, these settlement houses led to the establishment of the field of professional social work.

Given women's historical role in addressing numerous social issues in urban environments, and given studies of women lawmakers at other levels of government that show that women often prioritize concerns of special interest to women and families, it would stand to reason that women office-holders in municipalities and counties would perhaps champion different political causes than their male counterparts. Studies that examine women and men serving in local governments, however, find relatively few gender differences among such officeholders when it comes to identifying the most important issues facing their cities. Simply put, both men and women serving as mayors and on local councils spend most of their time dealing with economic development and service delivery (Mezey 1978; Crow 1997; Flammang 1987; Beck 2001; Boles 2001; Tolleson-Rinehart 2001; Weikart et al. 2006; Holman 2014). Urban scholars have long recognized that governing cities is particularly challenging given the outsized role that private actors often play in city politics. Cities tend to prioritize developmental policies, which include attracting businesses and new jobs to their cities, and basic service provision, as both are viewed as vital to maintaining higher-income residents who may otherwise flee to the suburbs and whose exit would create a downward spiral of lower tax revenues (Peterson 1981). Or, as Susan Abrams Beck (2001) put it in her comparative study of councilwomen and councilmen in suburban towns, all local officeholders are "hostage to the tax rate, persistently seeking ways to keep it down" (55). The many everyday responsibilities that are charged to localities, whether city or county government, such as making sure the garbage is picked up, potholes are filled, taxes are collected, and public parks are open and safe, are largely done in a gender-neutral fashion.

Although much of the substance of local government can be described as gender-neutral, and women and men who serve in them tend to prioritize the same issues when it comes to the day-to-day implementation of such policies, scholars do find some gender differences even at this level of government. While the actual ability of local government officials to address concerns about what are traditionally viewed as "women's issues," such as domestic violence, child care, sexual assault, or childbirth in public hospitals is often circumscribed by budget realities and development priorities, councilwomen and female mayors are more likely than their male counterparts to identify such issues as germane to the work of local government and to spend more time working on such issues than men (Flammang 1985; Boles 2001; Holman 2014). One early study by Schumaker and Burns

(1988) also identified numerous "gender cleavages" among the policy decisions in the city of Lawrence, Kansas.[6] They found that male councilors and policy elites were more supportive of economic growth policies whereas female officials and elites were more supportive of neighborhood preservation policies and increasing financial contributions to social services. However, similar to other studies, Schumaker and Burns discovered that the city prioritized economic policies at the expense of social welfare programs.

Studies of local women officeholders also suggest that women may have a different *style* of governing than men. For instance, women mayors are more likely to say that they value collaboration. In comparing how female and male mayors view the role of their staff, for instance, women are more likely to identify their staff as an important part of a government team, while male mayors are more likely to view their staff as sounding boards (Tolleson-Rinehart 2001). Studies also find that women in local government are more likely than their male counterparts to seek input from community actors, bring neglected groups into the decision making process, spend more time on their jobs than men, and believe that their constituents place greater trust in them than they would in men (Merritt 1980; Antolini 1984; Manning 1988; Beck 2001; Ulbig 2007). In Beck's (2001) work on municipal councils, both women and men council members agreed that women are more responsive to constituents, but many councilmen found this attribute to be negative, claiming that such responsiveness means women are more likely to make council decisions based on sentiment or—in the words of one councilman—"sympathy thoughts" (56). Yet, most councilwomen Beck interviewed believe that such an approach makes them better representatives than councilmen. As one councilwoman stated, the women's desire to seek more input from the community is about a willingness to "listen, not look for a quick solution. Men were looking for the management solution" (58). Laura Van Assendelft (2014) finds that the women mayors she studied in rural Virginia towns thought women bring a unique perspective. Said one mayor in the study, "Women are better communicators. They bring balance, they look at the whole issue and make better decisions in a more timely process" (quoted in Van Assendelft 2014, 206).

Mirya Holman's book *Women in Politics in the American City* (2014) offers the most comprehensive work to date on how men and women govern as mayors and as city councilors. Holman gathered data on how the gender of mayors and city councilors influences city politics by selecting 100 cities (all with more than 30,000 residents), matched so that 50 had women

---

[6]Moreover, Schumaker and Burns found that gender cleavages were more frequent than other types of cleavages based on factors such as socioeconomic status, race, and partisan identification. Cleavages predicated on neighborhoods and ideology, however, were more frequent than those based on gender.

mayors and 50 had male mayors. Like others, she finds that the ability of women in city politics to effect change when it comes to women's issues is circumscribed by budget realities and that in all cities, general government, development, and quality of life issues predominate at city council meetings over traditional women's concerns. Yet, she also finds that male officeholders felt a greater sense of duty to represent development groups than women and cultivated closer ties with such groups. Women, on the other hand, felt a greater obligation to represent racial groups, women, and the poor, and spent more time interacting with such constituencies. Moreover, women who expressed the strongest responsibility to represent women's issues, whom Holman describes as *preferable descriptive representatives*, are significantly more likely than men or other women to prioritize women's issues and to initiate discussion of women's issues in city council meetings.

In cities with female mayors, while development and general government discussions still predominate in city council meetings, Holman writes that "discussions of women's issues occurred at more than twice the rate, 26 percent of all discussions, than they did in cities with male mayors, where discussion of women's urban issues were 12 percent of discussions" (47). By women's issues, Holman means affordable housing, children's welfare, education, social welfare, and domestic violence. While she finds that discussion of women's issues increases in city council meetings as the percentage of women on the council grows, under female mayors especially, this relationship is even more significant. In other words, when cities have female mayors *and* women make up multiple members of such councils, women's issues get addressed more often than in other cities.

*Women in Politics in the American City* also confirms previous studies' findings that women's leadership in cities can have a transformative impact on the behavior and attitudes of constituents. For instance, the public tends to comment more in cities with female mayors than in cities run by men, which suggests that women mayors have a more inclusive style when they govern. It may also suggest that female leaders encourage broader participation by changing the substance of policy discussions. As one female leader in Holman's study put it, "We [women] tend to discuss topics more readily, find compromises, and share feelings, not just ideas of agenda. This helps get citizens out: they think we will listen to them" (76).

Women's more inclusive approach to governing in cities also spills over into the budgeting process. In their study of 120 US mayors, composed of 65 female and 55 male mayors, Weikart et al. (2006) find that women mayors were more likely than their male counterparts to change budgeting procedures to address policy goals and were more likely to view the budgetary process as a way to encourage more community participation in government. Mirya Holman (2014) finds that women leaders in cities are more likely to want to increase funding (81 percent) on women's issues than men (65 percent), while men are more likely to want to increase funding in development than women. Moreover, cities with female mayors are more likely to fund some programming (approximately 81 percent of cities) compared with cities with male mayors (61 percent) and those cities with female mayors spend more per resident on such programs. Funding for such programs also increases under female mayors when they have more women on the city council. Finally, cities that have women mayors are also more likely to hire women to work in city government, which enhances the opportunity for women's representation in local bureaucracies (Salzstein 1986; Holman 2014).

Yet, for all the progress that women mayors and councilors have made serving in local government, some women still report that they face obstacles based on their gender. Women mayors are far more likely to agree that they face particular obstacles because of their gender than do men (Weikart et al. 2006). These women mayors often cite the personal experience they face with respect to gaining credibility among many community and business leaders and being taken seriously, particularly when it comes to business-related decisions. Other studies of women leaders in localities find that women sometimes still face a double bind as elected officials, in which women are often judged by different criteria than are their male counterparts. The women Sue Tolleson-Rinehart interviewed in her comparative study of women and men mayors (2001) acknowledge that women often have to work harder to prove their qualifications and to overcome voter stereotypes about their toughness as leaders. One black woman mayor that she interviewed also noted the "double whammy" of being black and a woman. As she relates, "People's perceptions of me—on the one hand, expectations are more, because women have a reputation for being exhaustive workers, and constantly reaching out and giving of themselves. And on the other hand, there's some misunderstanding about your intellectual capacity and ability to be tough" (160). Despite the recognition that women leaders can face different standards, Tolleson-Rinehart's study still finds relatively few gender differences in how men and women manage the day-to-day work of running cities. Both the women and men she studies "used their cities' needs as the criterion for assessing political problems" (164), identifying the same issues as the ones that demanded the most city attention.

Though evidence suggests that women mayors view their jobs and relate with their constituents differently than do their male counterparts, the ability of women to make gains in terms of substantive representation is limited. This finding does not suggest that having greater numbers of women serving in city government is unimportant, however. Take, for instance, Stacy Ulbig's (2007) research, which examined the relationship between descriptive representation and levels of political trust among constituents in 70 different municipalities. Ulbig finds that levels of political trust among men and women differed as the number of women serving in city councils rose. Among citizens with a moderate awareness of politics and government, women exhibited higher levels of political trust as their city councils gained more women members, while the opposite happened for men, demonstrating that legitimacy in one's government can be related to the gender of who is serving in office and illustrates why having diversity in government is important.

## School Boards

Shifting our attention from women's substantive representation in municipalities, we now examine whether women and men govern differently at the school board level. First, women and men could have different policy prerogatives once elected to school boards that have important gender implications. We might find, for instance, that female school board members would be more proactive in supporting special education, racial equality, and vocational education. With respect to education policy that directly impacts girls, some research suggests that girls are more likely to face discrimination in the classroom by teachers in terms of time and attention, and girls are less likely to take science and math classes than boys (AAUW 1992, 1998). Moreover, the number of lawsuits filed concerning Title IX enforcement has grown tremendously at the secondary school level as parents seek to address the imbalance of funds and resources devoted to boys' sports at the expense of girls (Pennington 2004).

If so, one plausible hypothesis is that women school board members will be more likely to advocate for policies that help girls and disadvantaged youths. However, this is not necessarily true. Although Jesse Donahue's research of school board or committee members in Massachusetts finds that 79 percent of women board members agree that "public education needs to do more to foster equality for girls," compared with just 50 percent of male board members, very few women (8 percent) have ever worked on gender equity measures designed to help girls in their school districts, which is comparable to the findings for men (Donahue 1999). Donahue believes this discrepancy is due to a lack of women's interest groups to lobby on behalf of these issues at the school board level, the lack of formal powers that many school boards have to address such changes, and the substantial minority of board members who strongly disagree that girls need extra help in public schools. As Donahue notes, "At best, women [school board members] demonstrate an informed interest in the topic [of gender equality] but frequently fail to pursue measures that would help girls in their system. At worst a substantial minority of women committee members are openly hostile to the very idea that they should be representing girls in their school systems . . ." (Donahue 1999, 77). Instead, men and women board members spend more time discussing more "mainstream" agenda items such as budgeting, curriculum, staff, facilities, and class size (Donahue 1997).

Apart from policy advocacy, a second way that gender could impact school board service is related to *how* members approach their positions. In other words, do male and female board members perceive their roles as board members differently? One study from the early 1970s found that male superintendents viewed female board members as more difficult to interact with compared with male members, including this Boston superintendent: "By and large, women on school committees (boards) are nit-picking, emotional, use wiles to get what they want, demand to be treated as equals but have no hesitancy at all to put on the pearls and insist on 'respect' when the going gets rough—and they talk too much" (quoted in Mullins 1972, 27). This superintendent was speaking from limited experience with female board members in a different era and his perspective diverged from the findings of other scholars in the 1970s, who concluded that female and male board members were remarkably similar in how they approached their jobs. More recently, Donahue (1997) has found that women school board members actually talk on average *less* than men during board meetings, a finding based on the condition that men are more likely than women to chair school boards, and board chairs have a larger speaking role as facilitators of the meetings.

These findings beg the question—does it matter that women are underrepresented in school board politics? On the one hand, the most recent research suggests that gender does not matter when it comes to school board governance, both in terms of substantive representation in the form of helping advance gender equality in schools and in terms of doing the actual day-to-day work of school boards. Instead, school board members of both genders are likely to conform to the role of a school board member once elected. On the other hand, gender might still impact school board governance in ways that have not been quantified or documented. For instance, some speculate that because school boards are still predominantly male in most districts, it is harder for women to be appointed as school superintendents (Czubaj 2002). Thus, this important administrative position remains male dominated nationally. Also, research from almost three decades ago found that female board members were more likely than male board members to say that serving as a community liaison was a vital aspect of their jobs. This finding corresponds with findings about women serving in other legislative bodies and demonstrates that women might bring their own unique understanding to what the role of legislators should be even at this local level of government. More updated research is needed at the school board level to determine if women school board members still view this aspect of the position differently than their male counterparts.

# WOMEN AS POLITICAL ACTORS OUTSIDE OF GOVERNMENT

Women's involvement in local policy and politics is not limited to their roles as elected officials. In fact, women's activism is perhaps strongest in nongovernmental organizations and in grassroots politics, in which women often become involved in community issues through more informal networks of friends, kinship, and the neighborhood. Indeed, as chapter 2 notes, women led local social reform movements despite being formally disenfranchised from the political system. Often, such involvement stems from women's concerns as mothers and a need to improve their children's lives, whether that means seeking government assistance with poverty or job training or cleaning up polluted environments. Women's activism at the local level is sometimes geared toward the business community as well, with women leading the movement to unionize for greater rights and protections or to litigate against sexual discrimination and harassment in the workplace.

## Women at the Grassroots

Poor or working-class women engage in much local political activism in communities. Yet, too often, scholars who study the women's movement overlook poor women's efforts to gain a better life for themselves and their families, whether their efforts involve addressing environmental concerns, a lack of day care or good-paying jobs, or domestic violence, focusing instead on the efforts of middle-class or educated white women to affect public policy (Bookman and Morgen 1988; Boris 2002). But fighting for domestic rights such as welfare, as noted sociologists Frances Fox Piven and Richard Cloward have argued, means fighting for public rights (Piven and Cloward 1997). The efforts of poor, often minority, women in these struggles have important dimensions that broaden our understanding of politics as "an attempt to change the social and economic institutions that embody the basic power relations in our society" (Bookman and Morgen 1988, 4).

For African American women, the black church has long provided an opportunity for political involvement, including during the civil rights movement, when black women—although excluded from formal leadership positions as activists—often served as "bridge leaders" between social movements and local communities (Robnett 1998). But other women of color, such as Latinas, have not traditionally had organizations of their own from which to generate community activism. Latina women are not typically found in the normal channels of political and social activism at the community level, which is not meant to imply that Latinas do not enjoy a sense of political consciousness or that their ideas of politics are the same as those of Latino men. For example, Carol Hardy-Fanta (1993, 1997) studies Latina political activism in Boston. She finds that Latina women—like many women—have a blurred perception between the private and public dimensions, in which their roles as mothers play heavily. For these Latina women, politics consists of helping others and providing support, serving as "connectors" linking the Latino community to city hall informally. Yet, many Latinas continue to struggle with poverty issues, bilingual education, and achieving greater rights for undocumented Hispanic workers, and are often hesitant to enter the more traditional realms of politics because of language and other racial and cultural barriers (Benmayor and Torreullas 1997).

However, it is important to recognize that not all women activists root their community involvement in progressive causes. Julia Wrigley (1998) writes a fascinating case study of white working-class women engaged in the struggle against school busing in Boston, forced on Boston residents in the 1970s after federal Judge Arthur Garrity's decision to desegregate the public schools by busing black students into predominantly white schools and white students into predominantly black schools in two of Boston's poorest communities. Garrity believed that the Boston school board, composed of all white elected officials, had deliberately underfunded black schools in Boston. Upon litigation in the federal courts when the school board refused to increase its spending on such schools, Garrity ruled that forced busing was the only way to ensure equal protection for African American students. Garrity's decision, however, caused shock waves in the local communities, particularly in white neighborhoods. The antibusing forces organized ROAR—Restore Our Alienated Rights—that was led by white women who arranged school protests and boycotts, distributed flyers, made public statements, and put pressure on state and national politicians to stop busing. That women emerged as leaders of the movement was somewhat surprising in a city dominated by male involvement in politics. Yet, Wrigley argues that it was the "intense separation of women's and men's activities and daily lives in Boston that allowed women to take early command of the anti-busing movement" (253). In other words, education was viewed as a mother's domain, and activists, such as this one, linked their involvement directly to their maternal roles: "I always say it's like a lioness in her den. You know, these are my children. The father, I'm sure, feels that way, but the mother had a little more time. The fathers were out working . . ." (261). ROAR engaged in mass demonstrations called "Mother's Marches." These demonstrations—which were often raucous events and staged in illegal areas—allowed women to act outside the "appropriate" norms for femininity, and local police were hesitant to do much about them. Ultimately, Garrity's ruling held for more than two decades, and with ROAR unable to stop court-ordered busing, many white working-class parents fled to the suburbs or sent their students to parochial schools. As chapter 2 details, conservative women are also active in the Tea Party movement, using motherhood frames, again, to justify their political engagement.

Motherhood has also served as a political impetus in the environmental movement. As Temma Kaplan (1997) writes in *Crazy for Democracy: Women in Grassroots Movements*, "When toxic pollution or expulsion from their homes threatens their communities, certain women will take action according to female consciousness, confronting authorities to preserve life" (6). One of the most well-known grassroots campaigns dealing with the environment took place in Love Canal, a lower-middle-class neighborhood in Niagara Falls, New York. In 1956, low-cost housing was built for blue-collar workers in Love Canal—a canal that was filled in after the city had used the area for a landfill for more than 50 years. From 1947 to 1952, the Hooker Chemical Company, which was located in the area and produced pesticides and plastics, dumped more than 80 different chemicals into the canal, unbeknownst to homeowners (Kaplan 1997). In the 1970s, women who lived in Love Canal began to notice that women in the area were far more likely to suffer from frequent miscarriages and had higher rates of disabled children. For example, in 14 pregnancies that occurred during one year (1979–1980), only two resulted in able-bodied infants. Many homeowners also found black sludge filling in their basements and under swimming pools. Yet, local officials decried such evidence as anecdotal, referring to the women activists as "hysterical housewives" (Kaplan 1997, 20). This propelled the women to form Love Canal Homeowners Association, which pestered government officials at local and state meetings and even lobbied the Democratic National Convention in August 1980, raising national attention to their plight. The women activists deliberately chose a strategy that portrayed them as helpless mothers, all the while growing stronger. Eventually, the group persuaded the Carter administration in Washington to sign an agreement with the state of New York to allocate $15 million for the purchase of Local Canal homes, which at that point were uninhabitable (ibid.). Environmental causes continue to concern women activists at the grassroots. In recent years, local women have been at the vanguard of the environmental racism movement, which seeks to combat the placement of locally undesirable land uses (LULUs) in poor and economically depressed neighborhoods (Prindeville and Bretting 1998).

Not all women at the grassroots root their activism in motherhood appeals, however. While many women active in the Tea Party do, in fact, embrace motherhood as a primary rationale for their involvement in this conservative political movement, some women activists within the movement, including Keli Carendar, generally eschew motherhood appeals. While Carendar recognizes that motherhood rhetoric may be a powerful source of inspiration for some women, the reliance on such rhetoric by conservative leaders may be too limiting and hold little appeal for women without children, for example. She believes a better strategy is make larger appeals as to why their Tea Party message should apply to everyone at the grassroots, no matter their motherhood status or even gender. Carendar says, "We don't want to be a part of the balkanization of our society and to some extent if you really, really change your messaging for different groups of people, you are contributing to that. We'd rather teach people why our message is a unifying message and why everyone should support it and it doesn't matter who you are." (See Box 6.4 for more on Carendar.)

**Box 6.4. Keli Carendar, Millennial Tea Party Activist**

Millennial Keli Carendar is credited with organizing the first Tea Party rally. In February 2009, she held the first Porkulus Protest in her native Seattle in response to the stimulus bill passed by Congress that increased government spending on infrastructure and established programs geared at helping homeowners in danger of foreclosure on their mortgages. The bill, which increased the national deficit, outraged many conservatives. Carendar's role in leading the Porkulus Protest caught the attention of national conservative figures, which led to her becoming the National Grassroots Coordinator for the Tea Party Patriots, the nation's largest Tea Party organization.

*Photo source*: Douglas Graham / CQ Roll Call via AP Images.

## Women's Advocacy Against Domestic Violence

Women's activism in grassroots politics has been especially pronounced in the area of domestic violence. The first shelter for victims of domestic violence opened in California in 1964, which precipitated a movement to open such shelters nationwide and to recognize domestic violence as a serious problem during the next decade. By 1979, more than 250 shelters had opened their doors in local communities, in part as a response to the development of local Commissions on the Status of Women, which were formed by local governments to identify problems faced by women in their communities. Battered women and rape were issues that ranked high in importance for these commissions to tackle. There was a recognition that the traditional institutions of the community—the law, the church, and the medical profession—were not effective in dealing with the problems caused by spousal and partner abuse.

Researcher Anne Wurr documents one attempt by the women in Santa Clara County, California, to combat domestic violence through their formation of the Mid-Peninsula Support Network for Battered Women in 1978, which was a response to a finding by the county's Commission on the Status of Women that an urgent need existed for battered women's services in the area (Wurr 1984). In Santa Clara, women not only spearheaded the opening of several shelters, but they also worked to educate women's organizations such as local NOW chapters and child advocacy groups about their efforts. In addition, they lobbied members of the county council and placed pressure on local law enforcement agencies to institute new policies and training for police officers to deal with women who were victims of spousal abuse through the efforts of a subcommittee of the local bar association that was geared at domestic violence. These women activists also worked hard to get more women appointed to local commissions and boards that addressed domestic issues.

Yet, despite such local activism, domestic violence did not become a national mainstream concern until the 1990s, in part because of the sensationalism surrounding the murder of Nicole Brown Simpson—herself the victim of domestic violence at the hands of her ex-husband O. J. Simpson, who was later found not guilty of her murder in a riveting, televised trial. Feminists such as Jennifer Baumgardner and Amy Richards (2000) argue that while the Simpson trial did alert the consciousness of the nation to the issue of domestic violence, it had the unfortunate effect of ignoring "the grassroots organization that has named its reality and pioneered its treatment" (ibid., 60). Domestic violence remains a problem, as incidents involving well-known figures in recent years illustrate: in February 2009, the popular singer Rihanna's then-boyfriend, fellow singer Chris Brown, beat her and later pled guilty to felony assault charges and in 2014, the former Baltimore Ravens running back Ray Rice was caught on camera in a casino elevator beating his fiancé, now wife, Janay Palmer Rice, renewing a national dialogue about domestic violence and whether the NFL was complicit in downplaying this crime. Although the criminal justice system initially condoned a man's right to exercise violence in his home in his attempts to discipline his family, attitudes about domestic violence among law enforcement officials have changed (Johnson 2002). Judges, prosecutors, and police officers now view domestic violence as the serious crime it is, no doubt in part because of the organizing efforts of women at the grassroots to raise the profile of this issue.

### Women in the Labor Movement

Lastly, women are also active in labor relations at the local level, although most think of labor politics as a man's domain. In fact, women make up a growing percentage of union membership according to the Institute for Women's Policy Research, which reports that women make up roughly 45 percent of union members today (Institute for Women's Policy Research 2014). While the Bureau of Labor Statistics (2015) shows that men still have a higher union membership rate (11.7 percent) than women (10.5 percent) in the United States, women are predicted to be the majority of members of unions by 2025 (Jones, Schmidt, and Woo 2014).

In the past, women led the struggle against big business in rural areas such as Pike County in eastern Kentucky, where in the 1970s female hospital workers such as housekeepers, nurses' aides, cooks, and clerical workers engaged in a strike after owners of the Pikesville Methodist Hospital—one of the largest employers in the area—did little to address their concerns about heavy and erratic work schedules, lack of job security, and poor pay (Maggard 1998). More than 200 women strikers waged a picket line for 28 months and used a slogan that tapped into the class differences found between struggling workers and hospital owners: "We're fighting millionaires!" (ibid.). The women faced a business culture that viewed their employment as supplementary to men's earnings at the time, which meant that their work at the hospital was undervalued. After a protracted legal battle, the strikers were successful in 1980 when an appeals court refused to hear a final appeal by the hospital. The hospital was forced to reinstate the workers and compensate them for their losses.

Women have also led efforts to battle corporations that oppose labor organizing amidst their employees in the manufacturing sector. In 1988, General Electric (GE) waged a large-scale campaign against attempts by factory workers to unionize a large warehouse in rural Morristown, Tennessee, which was successful as workers rejected the union. One week later, however, GE executives suddenly closed the warehouse, moving to the next county and hiring subcontracted workers at almost half the price they paid workers in Morristown. Finding that they could only find new jobs through temporary agencies, women formed the grassroots organization Citizens Against Temporary Services (CATS). Although unsuccessful in a sex and age discrimination suit filed against the company (after their first lawyer withdrew, they could not afford a new one), they were successful in getting the state government to revoke GE's job training grants because it is illegal in Tennessee to train workers for jobs from which other workers have been laid off (Weinbaum 1997). Years later, CATS tried to get the state legislature to pass a bill that would define temporary work and regulate abuses of long-term temporary workers, but to no avail. Despite these setbacks, CATS has transformed previously apolitical women into engaged citizens and has become involved in other sorts of political movements in the area, including issues of environmental justice. As Weinbaum (1997) notes, CATS' example teaches that "women are taking on the most important and overwhelming political and economic issues facing the nation and resisting traditional categories, fighting the political elites, educating their communities and leading a movement" (Weinbaum 1997, 337).

These challenges remain even more daunting in the twenty-first century, particularly as they relate to the outsourcing of jobs. Women are disproportionately more likely than men to hold part-time, subcontracted work that is often the only type available after factories and manufacturing jobs leave town (Weinbaum 1997). Moreover, politically speaking, times for unions are difficult. Since 2001, six additional states have become what are known as "right to work" states, in which employees can decide if they want to financially support a union in a unionized workplace (National Right to Work Legal Defense Fund 2015). This status, now shared by 27 states—most of which are states that tend to vote Republican in the presidential elections or are swing states—makes it more difficult for unions to form and be financially sustainable. Moreover, union membership has witnessed serious declines in recent decades and, with that membership loss, less impact in American politics. Yet, women appear to be rising as leaders within the union movement (Sharp 2011) and research documents that women who are members of unions are most likely to earn higher wages and have better benefits than those who are not (IWPR 2015).

However, not all women are rising equally to leadership positions within organized labor. In January 2015, the Institute for Policy Studies released a survey of black women active in the labor movement. While African American women are more likely to be unionized (15.5 percent) compared with white women (11.4 percent), Asian women (12.6 percent), or Hispanic women (10.1 percent), the Institute found that fewer than 3 percent held elected leadership positions and that only one in four believed that unions invest resources in organizing black women workers (Lewis 2015).

The authors of the study argued that unions should promote and train women of color for such positions, in part because such women are the most reliable Democratic voters, and Democrats tend to prioritize the issues promoted by labor as compared with Republicans. As one of the authors of the study, Marc Bayard of IPS, put it, "If unions and the labor movement are to have a future, the future will not be male, pale, and stale" (quoted in Lewis, 2015).

## CONCLUSION

At the local level of government, women are making an impact as elected officials, bureaucrats, and activists in nongovernmental and grassroots organizations. Yet, women at this level do not always act in ways that differ greatly from those of their male counterparts, whether as mayors or as elected officials. Part of the reason that relatively few gender differences are found in local politics could be related to the demands and limits found in local governance. For instance, budgetary concerns are an overriding burden on all types of local government, whether located in rural, suburban, or city areas. Such financial worries often proscribe the ability of women to pursue public policies that they might otherwise follow, such as those that might give greater assistance to women and families in need. Also, handling the day-to-day functions of local governments, such as determining zoning requirements, handing out licenses, or picking up the garbage, has few, if any, gender components.

Despite these limitations, however, there are still a few ways that gender does become a factor in local politics. For example, one theme that emerges when examining the behavior of women and men elected officials and grassroots activists is the priority that women place on communication. Females involved in all sorts of local politics routinely stress the importance of bringing different voices to the political table, perhaps because for so many years their voices had been excluded. Women officials and activists at the local level are also more likely than men to notice the strain their positions or activism places on their family lives. Moreover, studies find that the public confidence in local government institutions grows as more women serve in them. As Jane Mansbridge's (1999) classic work on descriptive representation argues, having more women and individuals of color to represent such constituencies that heretofore have been underrepresented is important because it helps make the work of government, and the policies it prescribes, more legitimate. It also fosters more trust because elected representatives who look more like their constituents may be better situated to engage in meaningful dialogue with them. As Mansbridge writes, "Representatives and voters who share membership in a subordinate group can also forge bonds of trust based specifically on the shared experience of subordination" (641).

At the same time, however, women who do choose to become active in local politics are not monolithic. At the national and state levels, the majority of women tend to be Democrats and to have more liberal views than men. This chapter demonstrates that the same cannot necessarily be said about women in local politics. For example, women school board candidates are much more likely to be Republicans than Democrats. Moreover, although women's involvement at the grassroots level is often felt in progressive or liberal causes, the case involving mothers against busing in Boston as well as women's active participation in the Tea Party movement shows that many conservative women choose to become active in local politics, too. Women active at the local level of politics are ideologically quite diverse.

# REFERENCES

Adams, Kathy L. 2004. "Encouraged or Discouraged? Women Teacher Leaders Becoming Principals." *The Clearing House* 77(5): 209–12.

AFL-CIO. 2004. "Facts about Working Women." www.aflcio.org/yourjobeconomy/women/factsaboutworkingwomen.cfm.

Alozie, Nicholas O., and Lynne L. Manganaro. 1993. "Women's Council Representation: Measurement Implications for Public Policy." *Political Research Quarterly* 46(2): 383–98.

Alsop, Ronald. 2001. "Women See Few Role Models in Business School Faculties." *Wall Street Journal* (July 25): 1B.

American Association of State Colleges and Universities. 2009. Press Release. "Buffalo State College CEO Muriel Howard Appointed President of American Association of State Colleges and Universities." www.aascu.org/media/media_releases/release09march31.htm (accessed May 3, 2009).

American Association of University Women. 1992. *How Schools Shortchange Girls: The AAUW Report, A Study of Major Findings on Girls and Education.* Researched by the Wellesley College Center for Research on Women. Washington, DC: The American Association of University Women Foundation.

———. 1998. "Gender Gaps: Where Schools Still Fail Our Children." *Executive Summary.* www.aauw.org/research/GGES.pdf.

Antolini, Denise. 1984. "Women in Local Government: An Overview." In *Political Women: Current Roles in State and Local Government,* edited by Janet A. Flammang, 23–40. Beverly Hills: Sage Publications.

Aron, Hillel. 2013. "Why Are Women Practically Non-Existent on LA City Council?" *LA Weekly,* May 9. http://www.laweekly.com/news/why-are-women-practically-nonexistent-on-la-city-council-2613805

"Battered Women's Shelter." In *Political Women: Current Roles in State and Local Government,* edited by Janet A. Flammang, 221–41. Beverly Hills: Sage.

Baumgardner, Jennifer, and Amy Richards. 2000. *Manifesta: Young Women, Feminism, and the Future*. New York: Farrar, Strauss, and Giroux.

Beaty, LeAnn, and Trenton J. Davis. 2012. "Gender Disparity in Professional City Management: Making the Case for Enhancing Leadership Curriculum." *Journal of Public Affairs Education* 18(4): 617–32.

Beck, Susan Abrams. 2001. "Acting as Women: The Effects and Limitations of Gender in Local Governance." In *The Impact of Women in Public Office*, edited by Susan J. Carroll, 49–67. Bloomington, IN: Indiana University Press.

Benmayor, Rina, and Rosa M. Torreullas. 1997. "Education, Cultural Rights, and Citizenship." In *Women Transforming Politics: An Alternative Reader*, edited by Cathy J. Cohen, Kathleen B. Jones, and Joan C. Tronto, 187–204. New York: New York University Press.

Blair, Karen J. 1980. *The Clubwoman as Feminist: True Womanhood Redefined, 1868–1914*. New York: Holmes and Meier.

Blanchard, Paul D. 1977. "Women in Public Education: The Impact of Female School Board Members." *Journal of Humanics* 4: 64–69.

Bookman, Ann, and Sandra Morgen. 1988. *Women and the Politics of Empowerment*. Philadelphia: Temple University Press.

Boles, Janet. 2001. "Local Elected Women and Policy-Making: Movement Delegates or Feminist Trustees?" In *The Impact of Women in Public Office*, edited by Susan J. Carroll, 68–86. Bloomington, IN: Indiana University Press.

Boris, Eileen. 2002. "On Grassroots Organizing, Poor Women's Movements, and the Intellectual as Activist." *Journal of Women's History* 14(2): 140–42.

Bowman, Ann O'M., and Richard C. Kearney. 1999. *State and Local Government*. Boston: Houghton Mifflin.

Brown, Clyde, Neil R. Heighberger, and Peter A. Shocket. 1993. "Gender-Based Differences in Perceptions of Male and Female City Council Candidates." *Women & Politics* 13(1): 1–17.

Browning, Rufus P., Dale Rogers Marshall, and David H. Tabb. 1984. *Protest Is Not Enough: The Struggle of Blacks and Hispanics for Equality in Urban Politics*. Berkeley: University of California Press.

Bullock, Charles S. III, and Susan A. MacManus. 1991. "Municipal Electoral Structure and the Election of Councilwomen." *Journal of Politics* 53(1): 75–89.

Bureau of Labor Statistics. 2015. "Union Members—2014." January 23. http://www.bls.gov/news.release/union2.nr0.htm

California Women Lead. 2014. "Snapshot on the Status of Women in City Government." August. http://cawomenlead.org/wp-content/uploads/2014/08/Women-on-CA-City-Councils-report.pdf

Carendar, Keli. 2013. Personal interview by Melissa Deckman, by phone. April 1.

Carroll, Susan J., and Kira Sanbonmatsu. 2010. "Entering the Mayor's Office: Women's Decision to Run for Municipal Office." http://www.cawp.rutgers.edu/research/research_by_cawp_scholars/documents/Carroll_and_Sanbonmatsu_2010_MPSA-mayors.pdf

Center for American Women and Politics. 1992. Women in State Legislatures. www.cawp.rutgers.edu/Facts/StLegHistory/stleg92.pdf

———. 2016. Fast Facts. "Women Mayors in U.S. Cities 2016." January. www.cawp.rutgers.edu/fast_facts/levels_of_office/Local-WomenMayors/php

Congressional Research Service. 2009. "S. 1515: National Domestic Violence Volunteer Attorney Network Act." www.govtrack.us/congress/bill.xpd?bill=s110 -1515&tab=summary (accessed May 5, 2009).

Crow, Barbara A. 1997. "Relative Privilege? Reconsidering White Women's Participation in Municipal Politics." In *Women Transforming Politics: An Alternative Reader*, edited by Cathy J. Cohen, Kathleen B. Jones, and Joan C. Tronto, 435–46. New York: New York University Press.

Czubaj, Camilla Anne. 2002. "An Analysis of School Board Members." *Education* 122(3): 615–18.

Darcy, Robert, Susan Welch, and Janet Clark. 1994. *Women, Elections & Representation*. 2nd ed. Lincoln: University of Nebraska Press.

Dart, Tom. 2014. "Annise Parker Is Not Going Away." May 12. *The Advocate*. http:// www.advocate.com/politics/politicians/2014/05/12/annise-parker-not-going -away?page=0,1

Davey, Monica. 2006. "As Tribal Leaders, Women Still Fight Old Views." *New York Times*. February 4. http://www.nytimes.com/2006/02/04/us/as-tribal-leaders -women-still-fight-old-views.html.

Deckman, Melissa. 2004. *School Board Battles: The Christian Right in Local Politics*. Washington, DC: Georgetown University Press.

———. 2006. "Women at the School Board Level: Ideology, Party and Policy Concerns." *Journal of Women, Politics, and Public Policy* 28(1): 87–117.

———. 2007. "Gender Differences in the Decision to Run for School Board." *American Politics Research* 35(4): 541–63.

Donahue, Jesse. 1997. "It Doesn't Matter: Some Cautionary Findings about Sex and Representation from School Committee Conversations." *Policy Studies Journal* 25(4): 630–48.

———. 1999. "The Non-Representation of Gender: School Committee Members and Gender Equity." *Women & Politics* 20(3): 65–81.

Flammang, Janet. 1985. "Female Officials in the Feminist Capital: The Case of Santa Clara County." *Western Political Quarterly* 38(1): 94–118.

———. 1987. *Women's Political Voice: How Women Are Transforming the Practice and Study of Politics*. Philadelphia: Temple University Press.

Fox, Richard L., and Robert Schuhmann. 1999. "Gender and Local Government: A Comparison of Women and Men City Managers." *Public Administration Review* 59(3): 231–42.

———. 2000. "Gender and the Role of City Manager." *Social Science Quarterly* 81(20): 604–21.

"GenderGap in Government." 2004. www.gendergap.com/governme.htm

Goodmark, Leigh. 2011. "Legal System Fails Abused Women." *Baltimore Sun*, October 20. http://articles.baltimoresun.com/2011-10-20/news/bs-ed-domestic -violence-20111020_1_violence-statute-domestic-violence-dixie-shanahan

Hanna, John. 2011. "Domestic Violence Law Repealed by Lawmakers in Topeka, Kansas." *Huffington Post*, October 11. http://www.huffingtonpost.com/2011/10/11/ domestic-violence-law-topeka-kansas_n_1006203.html

Hardy-Fanta, Carol. 1993. *Latina Politics, Latino Politics: Gender, Culture, and Political Participation in Boston*. Philadelphia: Temple University Press.

———. 1997. "Latina Women and Political Consciousness: La Chispa Que Prende." In *Women Transforming Politics: An Alternative Reader*, edited by Cathy J. Cohen, Kathleen B. Jones, and Joan C. Tronto, 223–37. New York: New York University Press.

Hardy-Fanta, Carol, Pei-te Lien, Dianne M. Pinderhughes, and Christine Marie Sierra. 2006. "Gender, Race, and Descriptive Representation in the United States: Findings from the Gender and Multicultural Leadership Project." *Journal of Women, Politics & Policy* 28(3, 4): 7–42.

Hassett, Wendy L. 2004. "Career Advancement Choices of Female Managers in U.S. Local Governments." In *Gender and Women in Comparative Perspective*, edited by Heidi Gottfried and Laura R. Reese, 133–52. Lanham, MD: Lexington Books.

Herrick, Rebekah, and Susan Welch. 1992. "The Impact of At-Large Elections on the Representation of Black and White Women." *National Political Science Review* 3: 62–77.

Hess, Frederick. 2002. *School Boards at the Dawn of the 21st Century*. Alexandria, VA: American School Boards Association.

Holman, Mirya R. 2014. *Women in Politics in the American City*. Philadephia: Temple University Press.

Institute for Women's Policy Research. 2014. "Women in Unions." https://iwpr.org/issue/democracy-and-society/women-in-unions/

———. 2015. "Women in Unions." http://www.iwpr.org/initiatives/women-in-unions

Johnson, Richard. 2002. "Changing Attitudes About Domestic Violence." *Law & Order* 50(4): 60–65.

Jones, Janelle, John Schmitt, and Nicole Woo. 2014. *Women, Working Families, and Unions*. Washington, DC: Center for Economic and Policy Research. http://www.cepr.net/documents/women-union-2014-06.pdf.

Kansas Historical Society. n.d. "Susanna Madora Salter." https://www.kshs.org/kansapedia/susanna-madora-salter/12191

Kaplan, Temma. 1997. *Crazy for Democracy: Women in Grassroots Movements*. New York: Routledge.

Kay, Katty, and Claire Shipman. 2014. *The Confidence Code: The Science and Art of Self-Assurance: What Women Should Know*. New York: HarperCollins.

Kuruvilla, Carol. 2014. "Why Houston Is Forcing Pastors to Turn in Their Sermons." *Huffington Post*, October 15. http://www.huffingtonpost.com/2014/10/15/houston-pastor-sermon_n_5992044.html

Lawson, Melanie. 2015. "Houston Mayor Annise Parker Talks About Marriage, Children." *ABC-13 Eyewitness News*, March 29. http://abc13.com/politics/mayor-parker-talks-about-marriage-children/585574/

Lewis, Cora. 2015. "Labor Movement Pushes, Yet Again, to Get More Black Women in Charge." *Buzzfeed News*, May 10. http://www.buzzfeed.com/coralewis/labor-movement-pushes-for-more-black-women-in-charge#.exDdLb2Gn

MacManus, Susan A. 1999. "The Resurgent City Councils." In *American State and Local Politics*, edited by Ronald E. Weber and Paul Brace, 166–93. New York: Chatham House.

MacManus, Susan A., and Charles S. Bullock. 1993. "Women and Racial/Ethnic Minorities in Mayoral and Council Positions." *The Municipal Yearbook*, 70–84. Washington, DC: International City/County Management Association.

Maggard, Sally Ward. 1998. "We're Fighting Millionaires! The Clash of Gender and Class in Appalachian Women's Union Organizing." In *No Middle Ground: Women and Radical Protest*, edited by Kathleen Blee, 289–306. New York: New York University Press.

Maharaj, Nicole. 2004. U.S. Conference of Mayors Press Release. "Women Mayors Chair Mayor Shelia Young Brings More Structure to Group." www.usmayors.org (accessed February 9).

Mankiller, Wilma, and Michael Wallis. 1993. *Mankiller: A Chief and Her People.* New York: St. Martin's Press.

Manning, Richard D. 1988. "How Three Women Took Over Missoula County and the Gender Factor Became an Edge." *Governing* (May): 1–7.

Mansbridge, Jane. 1999. "Should Blacks Represent Blacks and Women Represent Women? A Contingent 'Yes.'" *The Journal of Politics* 61(3): 628–57.

Merritt, Sharyne. 1980. "Sex Differences in Role Behavior and Policy Orientations of Suburban Officeholders: The Effect of Women's Employment." In *Women in Local Politics*, edited by Debra W. Stewart, 115–29. Metuchen: Scarecrow Press.

Mezey, Susan Gluck. 1978. "Support for Women's Rights Policy: An Analysis of Local Politicians." *American Politics Quarterly* 6(4): 485–97.

Montjoy, Robert, and Douglas J. Watson. 1995. "A Case for Reinterpreted Dichotomy of Politics and Administration as a Professional Standard in Council-Manager Government." *Public Administration Review* 55(3): 231–39.

Moore, Margaret. 2009. Personal interview by Melissa Deckman, by phone. May 5.

Moulder, Evelina. 2015. Director of Survey Research, International City/County Management Association. Personal correspondence with author. June 1, 2015.

Mullins, Carolyn. 1972. "The Plight of the Board Woman." *American School Board Journal* 159(February): 27–30.

National Association of Counties. 2003. "A Brief Overview of County Government." Washington, DC: National Association of Counties.

National Coalition Against Domestic Violence. 2003. "Poll Finds Domestic Violence Is Women's Main Concern." www.ncadv.org/press_release.html

National Coalition Against Domestic Violence. n.d. "Domestic Violence Facts." http://www.ncadv.org/resources/FactSheets_221/html (accessed May 5, 2009).

National League of Cities. n.d. Research Brief on America's Cities. "The Faces of America's City Councils: America's City Councils in Profile." www.nlc.org

National Right to Work Legal Defense Fund. 2015. "Right to Work States." http://www.nrtw.org/rtws.htm

National School Boards Association. 2015. "Frequently Asked Questions: What Do We Know About School Board Members?" https://www.nsba.org/about-us/frequently-asked-questions

Palley, Marian Lief. 2001. "Women's Policy Leadership in the United States." *PS: Political Science & Politics* 34(2): 247–50.

Pennington, Bill. 2004. "Title IX Trickles Down to Girls of Generation Z." *New York Times* (June 29): D1.

Peterson, Paul. 1981. *City Limits.* Chicago: University of Chicago Press.

Piven, Frances Fox, and Richard A. Cloward. 1997. *The Breaking of the American Social Compact*. New York: The New Press.

Prindeville, Diane-Michele, and John G. Bretting. 1998. "Indigenous Women Activists and Political Participation: The Case of Environmental Justice." *Women & Politics* 19(1): 39–58.

Prindeville, Diane-Michele, and Teresa Braley Gomez. 1999. "American Indian Women Leaders, Public Policy, and the Importance of Gender and Ethnic Identity." *Women & Politics* 20(2): 17–32.

Robnett, Belinda. 1998. "African American Women in the Civil Rights Movement: Spontaneity and Emotion in Social Movement Theory." In *No Middle Ground: Women and Radical Protest*, edited by Kathleen Blee, 65–95. New York: New York University Press.

Ross, Bernard H., and Myron A. Levine. 2001. *Urban Power: Politics in Metropolitan America*. 6th ed. Itasca, IL: F.E. Peacock Publishers, Inc.

Saltzstein, Grace Hall. 1986. "Female Mayors and Women in Municipal Jobs." *American Journal of Political Science* 30(1): 140–64.

Schlozman, Kay Lehman, Nancy Burns, Sidney Verba, and Jesse Donahue. 1995. "Gender and Citizen Participation: Is There a Different Voice?" *American Journal of Political Science* 39(2): 267–93.

Schumaker, Paul, and Nancy Elizabeth Burns. 1988. "Gender Cleavages and the Resolution of Local Policy Issues." *American Journal of Political Science* 32(4): 1070–95.

Sharp, Kathleen. 2011. "Redefining the Union Boss." *New York Times*, November 19. http://www.nytimes.com/2011/11/20/business/women-are-becoming-unions -new-voices.html

Sierra, Christine. 2009. Interview with Melissa Deckman, by phone. April 21.

Silbermann, Rachel. 2014. "Gender Roles, Work-Life Balance, and Running for Office." Working Paper. https://dl.dropboxusercontent.com/u/9802842/Silber mann_WLB_Paper.pdf

Stewart, Debra. 1980. *The Women's Movement in Community Politics in the U.S: The Role of Local Commissions on the Status of Women*. New York: Pergamon Press.

Svara, James. 1990. *Official Leadership in the City: Patterns of Conflict and Cooperation*. New York: Oxford University Press.

Thomas, Sue. 1998. "Introduction." In *Women and Elective Office: Past, Present, and Future*, edited by Sue Thomas and Clyde Wilcox, 1–14. New York: Oxford University Press.

Thompson, Krissah. 2015. "Houston's Annise Parker, a gay mayor in a red state, ponders political future." *Washington Post*, March 17. http://www.washingtonpost .com/lifestyle/style/houstons-annise-parker-a-gay-mayor-in-a-red-state-ponders -political-future/2015/03/17/c06c8b3e-c7f1-11e4-a199-6cb5e63819d2_story .html

Tolleson-Rinehart, Sue. 2001. "Do Women Leaders Make a Difference?" In *The Impact of Women in Public Office*, edited by Susan J. Carroll, 149–65. Bloomington, IN: Indiana University Press.

Trounstine, Jessica, and Melody E. Valdini. 2008. "The Context Matters: The Effect of Single-Member versus At-Large Districts on City Council Diversity." *American Journal of Political Science* 52(3): 554–69.

Ulbig, Stacy. 2007. "Gendering Municipal Government: Female Descriptive Representation and Feelings of Political Trust." *Social Science Quarterly* 88(5): 1106–23.

U.S. Census Bureau. 2002. "Federal, State, and Local Governments: 2002 Census of Governments." www.census.gov/govs/www/cog2002.html

———. 2012. "Government Units in 2007." *US Census of Governments*, July. Washington, DC: Department of Commerce.

U.S. Department of Labor. 2002. "Facts on Working Women," November. www.dol .gov/wb/factsheets/wbo02.htm

Van Assendelft, Laura. 2014. "Entry Level Politics? Women as Candidates and Elected Officials at the Local Level." In *Women and Elective Office: Past, Present, and Future*. 3rd ed., edited by Sue Thomas and Clyde Wilcox, 199–215. New York: Oxford University Press.

Voorhies, Heidi, and Rachel Lange-Skaggs. 2015. "Women Leading Government: Why So Little Progress in 30 Years?" *PM Magazine*, January/February. http://icma .org/en/Article/105323/Women_Leading_Government

Watson, Douglas J., and Wendy L. Hassett. 2004. "Career Paths of City Managers in America's Largest Council-Manager Cities." *Public Administration Review* 64(2): 192–200.

Weber, Ronald E., and Paul Brace. 1999. "States and Localities Transformed." In *American State and Local Politics: Directions for the 20th Century*, edited by Ronald E. Weber and Paul Brace, 1–20. New York: Chatham House Press.

Weikart, Lynne A., Greg Chen, Daniel W. Williams, and Haris Hromic. 2006. "The Democratic Sex: Gender Differences and the Exercise of Power." *Journal of Women, Politics & Policy* 28(1): 119–39.

Weinbaum, Eve. 1997. "Transforming Democracy: Rural Women and Labor Resistance." In *Women Transforming Politics: An Alternative Reader*, edited by Cathy J. Cohen, Kathleen B. Jones, and Joan C. Tronto, 324–39. New York: New York University Press.

Wrigley, Julia. 1998. "From Housewives to Activists: Women and the Division of Political Labor in the Boston Antibusing Movement." In *No Middle Group: Women and Radical Protest*, edited by Kathleen Bree, 251–88. New York: New York University Press.

Wurr, Anne. 1984. "Community Responses to Violence Against Women: The Case of a Battered Women's Shelter." In *Political Women: Current Roles in State and Local Government*, edited by Janet A. Flammang, 221–41. Beverly Hills: Sage.

# 7

# Women in Congress and the State Legislatures

In the summer of 2013, the Senate Armed Services Committee held a very unusual hearing. The chairman of the Joint Chiefs of Staff and the uniformed chiefs of the Army, Navy, Air Force, Marine Corps, and Coast Guard all appeared before the committee to confront the problem of sexual assault in the military. It is rare for the heads of all the branches of the armed forces to jointly appear before Congress, and sexual assault is a difficult and uncomfortable topic of discussion. Some of the toughest questions came from the female senators on the committee (Whitlock 2013). The Pentagon had recently released a report demonstrating that the number of military personnel who were victims of sexual assault had increased by 35 percent between 2010 and 2012. The Pentagon's survey estimated that 26,000 troops experienced "unwanted sexual contact," but only 3,374 of these troops filed a report and of those, only 302 perpetrators were prosecuted (Carlson 2013). The release of the report came at a pivotal moment in the Senate. For the first time, there were seven women on the Armed Services Committee. Of these seven women, three served as subcommittee chairs, including Kirsten Gillibrand (D-NY), the chair of the Subcommittee on Personnel, which had jurisdiction over the issue. These women, both Republicans and Democrats, were willing to prioritize the issue of sexual assault even though it meant taking on the top military brass and pressing for changes in military procedures during a time of war (Carlson 2013; Stewart and Zengerle 2013).

Because these female senators were willing to expend political capital drawing attention to the issue and crafting policy solutions, Congress adopted several reforms including reforms to the military justice system that changed the procedures used to prosecute these crimes, eliminated the ability of military commanders to overturn jury convictions, and provided services and legal counsel to victims (Cassata and Pickler 2013). While the female senators agreed on the importance of the issue, they did not always agree on the necessary policy solutions. Indeed, the Senate was strongly divided over the question of whether the decision to prosecute a sexual assault should be taken out of the hands of military commanders and placed with independent prosecutors.

Democrat Kirsten Gillibrand (D-NY), supported by most of the Democratic women in the Senate, and two Republican women, Lisa Murkowski (R-AK) and Susan Collins (R-ME), championed a proposal to take this power out of the chain of command. Gillibrand argued that more victims would be willing to come forward if they could report the crime to someone outside the military chain of command. Moreover, the small number of cases prosecuted indicates that military leaders are not willing to bring cases against fellow soldiers under their command, and an independent group of military prosecutors is required (Peterson 2014). By contrast, fellow Democrat Claire McCaskill (D-MO), herself a former prosecutor with experience trying sexual assault cases, argued that commanders need to retain responsibility for these decisions and should be held accountable. Her proposal had the support of the female Republican members of the Armed Services committee, Kelly Ayotte (R-NH) and Deb Fischer (R-NE) as well as the Committee Chair, Carl Levin (D-MI) (Henneberger 2014). Ultimately, Gillibrand's proposal was defeated and the Senate passed McCaskill's bill. Both senators continue to work together to draw attention to the issue (Kaper 2014).

The long and continuing debate over how to curb sexual assault in the military demonstrates the importance of descriptive representation. While all senators want to keep our soldiers safe from sexual assault, members of Congress have multiple issues competing for their attention. It was the female senators who were willing to prioritize the issue and spend the time and political capital necessary to draw attention to the problem of sexual assault in the military, develop policy solutions, and build coalitions to pass their reforms into law. The fact that there were now 7 women on the Armed Services committee and 20 women in the Senate allowed the women senators to leverage their numbers to raise the awareness of the media, their male colleagues, and the Pentagon. While the female senators agreed that the military's policies on sexual assault require reform, their policy views are not monolithic. Influenced by their own party affiliations, constituent demands, and life experiences, they championed different solutions exemplified by the competing proposals of senators Gillibrand and McCaskill.

In this chapter, we look at the history of women's integration into the United States Congress and the 50 state legislatures. We also examine the similarities and differences in male and female legislators' policy activities and their leadership styles. We discuss the factors in the political

Senators Claire McCaskill (D-MO, top) and Kirsten Gillibrand (D-NY, bottom) hold dueling press conferences to build support for their competing proposals regarding sexual assault in the military. McCaskill is joined by cosponsors of her amendment and fellow Armed Services Committee members Deb Fischer (R-NE) and Kelly Ayotte (R-NH). Gillibrand is flanked by sexual assault survivors, Marine Corps veteran Sarah Plummer and Army veteran Kate Weber. Bill supporters, Senators Richard Blumenthal (D-CT) and Dean Heller (R-NV) stand behind them.
*Sources*: Top, Michael Reynolds, EPA European Pressphoto Agency b.v. / Alamy Stock Photo; bottom, AP Photo / J. Scott Applewhite.

environment that influence the ability and willingness of female legislators to work for policy changes on behalf of different groups of women.

## WOMEN AND REPRESENTATION

Today women are drastically underrepresented in Congress and the state legislatures, holding just under 20 percent of the seats in Congress and less than one quarter of state legislative seats (Center for American Women and Politics 2017a, 2017b). Does it matter that there are so few women in public office? Would policy or the nature of politics look any different if there were equal numbers of men and women serving in Congress and the state legislatures? The question of how to adequately represent the various interests in society has long preoccupied politicians and philosophers. Indeed, the question of representation was a major point of contention in the fight to ratify the Constitution. Campaigning against ratification, the anti-Federalists believed that the design of Congress would elevate the interests of the wealthy at the expense of the middle classes, particularly the virtuous yeoman farmers (Storing 1981). Supporters of the Constitution argued that the different classes of men had overlapping interests and the design of the electoral process would ensure the responsiveness of the representative regardless of the background of the elected official (Federalist 35). Thus, frequent elections in which all eligible citizens could vote would guarantee that a legislator would advocate for the needs of his/her district.

This debate over the contours of representation continues today with a focus on politically relevant social identities including gender, race, ethnicity, class, and sexual orientation. In her classic work, *The Concept of Representation* (1967), Hanna Pitkin draws a distinction between descriptive and substantive representation. She characterizes descriptive representatives as individuals who mirror certain social characteristics of their constituents such as race, class, or sex and thus are able to "stand for" those constituents. Meanwhile, substantive representatives "act for" the interests of the represented. Pitkin discounts the need for electing descriptive representatives to achieve substantive representation of constituent interests and asserts that the representative's descriptive characteristics will only be relevant if they affect the representative's actual actions and decisions.

More recently, feminist scholars have argued that increasing the descriptive representation of women and minorities in legislatures is a necessary but not sufficient condition for achieving the substantive representation of group interests (Phillips 1991, 1995, 1998; Mansbridge 1999; Dovi 2002). Political theorist Jane Mansbridge (1999) maintains that the election of minority group members will improve the representation of group interests by strengthening the relationship between legislators and their constituents and improving policy outcomes. With regard to the constituent-legislator relationship, Mansbridge argues that electing descriptive representatives will build trust between underrepresented groups and the government allowing policies to gain legitimacy in the eyes of minority group members. This improved communication between legislators and their constituents and enhanced trust is especially important in cases where there exists a history of discrimination between the majority and minority group. Furthermore, electing descriptive representatives provides role models, encouraging more women and minorities to see themselves as potential candidates and legislators, or symbolic representation. As more group representatives are elected, the majority group will also see these new groups as fit to rule, furthering their integration into the government and society.

Within the legislature, Mansbridge (1999) argues that expanding descriptive representation can improve the quality of deliberation among legislators and the nature of policy outcomes. Women and minorities will draw on their shared experiences as group members to bring new issues to the agenda that have not been adequately addressed by the majority. They will also provide a unique perspective on established debates by explaining how those issues will differentially impact various groups of women and/or minorities. When policy is being made, group members will be more likely to achieve inclusion of group interests in policy outcomes because of the moral authority they wield as group members and because of the vigorous advocacy they will bring to issues on the basis of shared life experiences.

While expanding descriptive representation can improve the quality of representation, there are also risks. Most significantly, advocates run the risk of essentializing a group, thereby creating the impression that group members always agree on policy positions and share the same interests (Mansbridge 1999; Dovi 2002). As we will see, representation is more complicated and women like men are influenced by their multiple identities including race, ethnicity, class, party affiliation, and more. With more women of differing backgrounds entering legislative office, they will bring a broader range of experiences to legislating and ensure that a greater diversity of viewpoints influences public policy.

## WOMEN'S REPRESENTATION IN LEGISLATIVE BODIES ACROSS THE WORLD

Compared to other countries, the United States ranks quite low in women's representation. Table 7.1 highlights the percentage of women serving in the lower houses of the national legislatures of countries around the world. A closer look at the electoral processes employed by these different countries reveals that the rules of the game matter. The countries with the highest levels of representation for women such as Sweden, Denmark, and the Netherlands have electoral systems that encourage broader representation for groups. These countries utilize proportional representation in which political parties are awarded legislative seats based on the percentage of the vote they garner in the election and where voters have the option of selecting more than one candidate in multimember districts (Inglehart and Norris 2003; Paxton and Hughes 2007; Krook 2009). By contrast, the United States relies on single-member districts where voters choose a single candidate rather than multiple candidates. The US system is candidate-centered rather than party-centered, meaning that instead of running as part of a party list in which the candidate's fate is tied to the performance of the party as a whole, American candidates must build their own campaigns, relying on their own networks to raise funds and canvass for votes. As a result, the

**Table 7.1. Women's Representation in the Lower or Single House of the National Legislature in Selected Countries Around the World**

| Country | Percentage of Women (%) |
| --- | --- |
| Rwanda | 61.3 |
| Bolivia | 53.1 |
| Iceland | 47.6 |
| Sweden | 43.6 |
| Mexico | 42.6 |
| Finland | 42.0 |
| Norway | 39.6 |
| Spain | 39.1 |
| Argentina | 38.9 |
| Belgium | 38.0 |
| Netherlands | 38.0 |
| Denmark | 37.4 |
| Germany | 37.0 |
| Portugal | 34.8 |
| New Zealand | 34.2 |
| Switzerland | 32.5 |
| Italy | 31.0 |
| Austria | 30.6 |
| United Kingdom | 30.0 |
| Australia | 28.7 |
| Israel | 27.5 |
| Canada | 26.3 |
| France | 25.8 |
| Ireland | 22.2 |
| United States of America | 19.1 |
| Greece | 18.3 |
| Japan | 9.3 |

*Source*: Inter-Parliamentary Union. 2016. "Women in National Parliaments: World Classification." www.iup.org/wmn-e/classif.htm. Data are percentages reported by countries as of December 1, 2016.

US system favors incumbents who have already established these networks of donors and supporters. These incumbents, who are mostly men, are reelected at rates above 90 percent, making it difficult for new groups to break into politics (Herrnson 2012; Jacobson 2013).

In addition to employing proportional representation, to enhance electoral opportunities for women, some established and new democracies have adopted statutory mechanisms such as gender quotas designating a minimum number of seats for women, or mandates that require parties to reserve a certain number of seats on their party list for women. The success of these laws depends on where women are ranked within the party lists and the severity of the sanctions for noncompliance (Inglehart and Norris 2003; Paxton and Hughes 2007; Krook 2009). A couple of examples illustrate the point. In 1991, Argentina adopted a gender quota law that required all parties contesting seats in the Chamber of Deputies to submit lists including a minimum of 30 percent women. Additionally, the law required that women be placed throughout the list, not clustered near the bottom. Party lists that did not comply with the law were rejected and the party was not allowed to compete in the district's election. Following the implementation of the law, the representation of women in the Chamber of Deputies rose from 4.6 percent in 1991 to 21.3 percent in 1993. Conversely, in 2000, France adopted a parity law that required parties to include 50 percent women in their lists or risk the loss of a percentage of their state funding. Although the law improved representation at the municipal level, in the 2002 election to the French National Assembly, women's representation rose by only 1.4 percent. This poor result was due to the fact that parties concentrated women in seats that could not be won or accepted the insubstantial financial penalty for noncompliance. As a result, women's representation in the French National Assembly continues to grow at a slow pace (Inglehart and Norris 2003; Paxton and Hughes 2007; Krook 2009; Norris and Krook 2014).

Many Latin American countries utilize gender quotas adopted as part of their constitutions or legislative statutes. Women now constitute the majority of legislators in the Chamber of Deputies, the lower house in Bolivia's parliament (see Table 7.1). In 2014, the country implemented a law requiring equal numbers of men and women on parties' candidate lists for the upper and lower houses of the Legislative Assembly. As a result, the proportion of women in the lower house rose from 22 percent elected in 2009 to 53 percent elected in 2014 (Etoniru 2014). Rwanda—the country with the largest number of women in the lower house (63.8 percent)—also has quotas requiring equal participation by women. These quotas, as well as bans on discrimination based on gender, race, ethnicity, and religion, were adopted after the Rwandan genocide. Rwanda is not a democracy. However, in many post-conflict countries, the disruption of gender roles and relations allows for the emergence of new women's movements and the demand for greater rights for women. These demands are reinforced by international organizations like the United Nations and World Bank that require compliance with international treaties regarding women's rights as a condition for receiving aid (Tripp 2013, 2015).

More common than statutory quotas are voluntary gender quotas. Many European, Scandinavian, and Latin American parties, particularly those on the left, have adopted voluntary gender quotas that are not prescribed by law but are adopted within party rules. Yet, scholars find that these quotas are a facilitating condition and the representation of women is more likely to advance in countries where electoral mechanisms coexist with political cultures in which the public holds more egalitarian views on gender roles and women's leadership. Additionally, the parties of the left that adopt gender quotas are already the parties that are most likely to accept women candidates (Inglehart and Norris 2003; Paxton and Hughes 2007; Krook 2009; Norris and Krook 2014).

## WOMEN'S REPRESENTATION IN CONGRESS AND THE STATE LEGISLATURES ACROSS TIME

The representation of women in Congress and the state legislatures has grown very slowly over time. In 2017, women constitute only 19.4 percent of the members of Congress and 24.8 percent (1,832) of state legislators (Center for American Women and Politics 2017a, 2017b). The number of women in office varies widely by state as women constitute 30 percent of the California congressional delegation including the minority leader of the House of Representatives, Nancy Pelosi (D-CA), while Mississippi and Vermont have never sent a woman to Congress (Center for American Women and Politics 2017a). Across the states, women hold 40 percent of state legislative seats in Vermont and Nevada while just under 13 percent of the state legislators in Wyoming and Oklahoma are women (Center for American Women and Politics 2017b) (see Figure 7.1). How do we explain why some states have more female officeholders than other states and why the growth of women in legislative office has been so slow over time?

The first women elected to state legislatures in the United States came from the western states that were the first to grant women suffrage. Women state legislators from Wyoming, Utah, Colorado, and Idaho were often elected with women's votes, as women voters often made up 40–50 percent of voter turnout in those states. In 1894, three women were elected to the Colorado House of Representatives: Clara Cressingham, Carrie C. Holly, and Francis Klock. In 1896, Martha Hughes Cannon, a doctor and woman's suffrage activist, became the first woman elected to a state senate when she beat several candidates including her husband, Angus, in an at-large

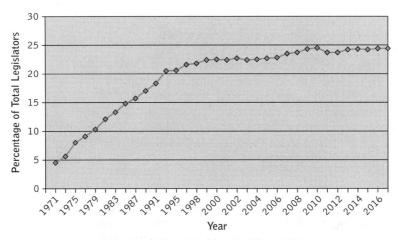

**Figure 7.1. Progress of Women in State Legislatures Since 1970.**
*Source*: "Women in State Legislatures 2017." Center for American Women and Politics 2017.

election for the Utah State Senate (Center for American Women and Politics 2004; Dolan 2004).

The greatest expansion in the number of women serving in state legislatures occurred after the passage of the Nineteenth Amendment granted women the vote, between 1920 and 1925. Women who ran for office in these early years faced numerous obstacles from voters, parties, and even the state itself as they had to fight to overturn provisions in state constitutions that only men could serve in the legislature (Dolan 2004). Once in office, these women entered a male bastion that was not accustomed to the presence of women. When Ida Sammis became one of two women to serve in the New York State Assembly in 1918, it was said that her "first unofficial act was to take her brass spittoon—each member of the assembly was allocated one—and polish it to a brilliant shine. She filled it with flowers and placed it on her desk" (Andersen 1996). By 1930, there were 149 women serving in state legislatures across the country. Women's representation across the states ebbed and flowed as social attitudes about women's participation in the public sphere changed, with more support for electing women during periods of social and economic prosperity and less during times of national crisis. Thus, the number of women serving in state legislatures decreased during the years of the Great Depression, increased during World War II, declined in the postwar 1950s as Americans sought a return to traditional values, and increased again after the Korean War (Werner 1968; Dolan 2004).

The percentage of women serving in state legislatures grew rapidly through the 1970s and 1980s, increasing from less than 6 percent in 1973 to more than 13 percent in 1983 as more women gained the educational and occupational qualifications associated with a run for office (see Figure 7.1). By 1993 women made up 21 percent of the membership of state legislatures. However, in the decade from 1994 to 2004, women's representation stagnated, hovering around 22 percent. The number of women serving state legislatures actually dropped between 2009 and 2011, declining from 24.3% to 23.7% after the Republican wave election of 2010. Currently, 24.8 percent of state legislators are women (Norrander and Wilcox 2014; Center for American Women and Politics 2017b).

How do we explain why women's progress has slowed so dramatically? Scholars point to a number of explanations: legislative structures, levels of professionalization and political culture within the state legislatures, and changing partisan dynamics. As already mentioned, one set of barriers is structural. The incumbency advantage and the high cost of campaigns make it difficult for new groups to make progress (Herrnson 2012; Jacobson 2013). Additionally, the elimination of multimember districts by many states, and the adoption of term limits, present further obstacles. Most state legislators are elected in single-member districts where voters select a single candidate to represent them. In multimember districts, more than one candidate is elected to represent citizens of a district. In those cases, voters are more likely to seek gender balance and vote for women when they can elect more than one candidate, and women may be more inclined to run if they are part of a team of candidates. Indeed, while the number of states using multimember districts declined from 13 in the 1990s to 10 in 2013, some of the states with the greatest number of women in office use multimember districts including Arizona, Maryland, New Hampshire, Vermont, and Washington (Norrander and Wilcox 2014; Sanbonmatsu 2014). Figure 7.2 identifies the states with the highest and lowest levels of women's representation in their state legislatures.

To reduce the power of incumbency and return power to citizen legislators, many political reformers of the 1990s advocated term limits. Today, 15 states place term limits on their legislators (NCLS 2015). It was thought that forcing out incumbents might also provide a path to office for new groups including women and racial minorities. However, particularly in the lower houses of legislatures, the number of women who are running for office has not kept pace with the number of women who are being kicked out when they reach their term limit. Whether it is because qualified women are less inclined to run for office than men or because the parties are not recruiting enough women to run, term limits have not been a path for expanding women's representation (Carroll and Jenkins 2001; Norrander and Wilcox 2014; Sanbonmatsu 2014). (See chapter 4 for further discussion of the reasons why there are fewer female than male candidates.)

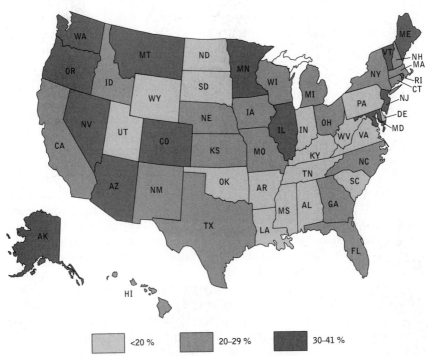

**Figure 7.2. Percentage of State Legislators Who Are Women.**
*Source*: "Women in State Legislatures 2017." Center for American Women and Politics 2017.

The number of women in the state legislature is also impacted by the level of professionalization of the legislature and the political culture of the state. More professionalized legislatures have paid staff, provide a higher salary, and meet year round. There is more competition for seats in more professionalized legislatures (Norrander and Wilcox 2014). The states with the highest levels of female representation generally do not have highly professionalized legislatures. For example, New Hampshire has a part-time legislature whose members are paid $100 per year compared to California, whose full-time legislators earn more than $95,000 per year. Overall, women hold the largest proportion of seats in legislatures with moderate levels of professionalism (Sanbonmatsu 2014).

States also vary in political culture. Research demonstrates that fewer women are elected in southern states with traditional political cultures. Indeed, women's voting participation in southern states lagged behind men's into the early 1970s (Norrander and Wilcox 2014). Women have also had difficulty breaking into politics in Mid-Atlantic states like New Jersey and Pennsylvania that have a history of strong political parties that controlled candidate recruitment. Meanwhile western states like Colorado have been friendlier to women politicians because they gave women the right to vote early, have political cultures that encourage participation, and they historically have weak party structures allowing for other avenues of political recruitment (Sanbonmatsu 2006, 2014; Norrander and Wilcox 2014).

Beyond political culture, the changing partisan dynamics in the country have also impacted women's representation. Throughout the 1990s and early 2000s, the Republican Party made gains at all levels of elective office. By 2002, the formerly solidly Democratic South had moved toward the Republicans, and the Republican Party controlled more state legislative seats than the Democrats for the first time since the 1950s (Jacobson 2013; Davidson et al. 2015). For most of the twentieth century, the Republicans did a better job of electing women to public office than did Democrats (Werner 1968; Cox 1996). Indeed, in a study of candidate recruitment to state legislatures, Sanbonmatsu (2002) finds that when Democrats have been the majority party in a legislature, they have recruited fewer women candidates. However, the contemporary parties are highly polarized, with Democrats trending more uniformly liberal and Republicans more conservative. In the 1980s and 1990s, the Republican Party included a growing and active socially conservative base with more traditional views about gender roles. The Tea Party movement that fueled the Republican electoral wave in 2010 called for a more conservative brand of politics that limits the role of government and scales back social welfare programs.

In the contemporary Republican Party, Republican women have not shared in the party's gains. Even as Republicans expanded their control of state legislatures from 41 percent of state legislative seats in 1993 to 53 percent of state legislative seats in 2011, the number of Republican women winning seats as a proportion of all Republicans remained stagnant or declined (Elder 2012; Carroll and Sanbonmatsu 2013; Norrander and Wilcox 2014). Indeed, Republican women and all women have their lowest levels of representation in the southern states that are currently the strongholds of the Republican Party. More Republican women are found in states with less professionalized legislatures. By contrast, as the Democratic Party has become more liberal and feminists have gained a more prominent foothold in the party, Democrats have placed a higher priority on recruiting women candidates and the gap between the parties has grown (Sanbonmatsu 2006, 2014; Elder 2008, 2012; Carroll and Sanbonmatsu 2013). As a result, in 2017, 60.4 percent (1,107) of female state legislators are Democrats while only 38.4 percent are Republicans (703) (Center for American Women and Politics 2017b). As we will see below, this partisan disparity in the number of women legislators persists at the congressional level.

## THE ADVANCEMENT OF WOMEN IN CONGRESS

In 1916, Jeannette Rankin (R-MT) became the first woman elected to Congress, and she ultimately went on to serve two terms (1917–1919 and 1941–1943). A political activist who worked for social justice, Rankin had traveled the country working for women's suffrage and peace and against child labor and poverty in America's cities. In her campaign for Congress, Rankin expressed her desire to act as an advocate for women and children. She once noted that the country spent $300,000 per year to study hog fodder but only $30,000 per year to study the needs of children. She asserted, "If the hogs of the nation are ten times more important than the children, it is high time that we [women] made our influence felt." Asked why a woman should be elected to Congress, she answered, "There are hundreds of men to take care of the nation's tariff and foreign policy and irrigation projects. But there isn't a single woman to look after the nation's greatest asset: its children." As a member of Congress, she worked for the national women's suffrage amendment, against child labor, and for programs to improve mothers' and children's health. However, she is best known as the only member of Congress who voted against both World War I and World War II (Kaptur 1996).

Rankin's path to office was unique since most of the small number of women who served in Congress as late as the 1960s came to office as widows. After the death of a politician, political parties often turned to the spouse who had name recognition and the sympathy of the voters but who did not have larger political ambitions. The widow would serve one or two terms until the party decided who the next representative would be or a candidate emerged, thus avoiding internal party strife. In fact, the first woman to be seated in the US Senate, Rebecca Latimer Felton (D-GA), served only one day. At 87 years old, she was appointed by the governor of Georgia to replace Senator Tom Watson after he died in office. She convinced the newly elected senator, Walter George, to delay taking the oath of office so that she could be seated and make a speech on the Senate floor. Felton was followed in the Senate by Hattie Carraway (D-AR) who replaced her deceased husband in 1931 and won election in her own right in 1932, serving until 1945 (Kaptur 1996). From 1916 to 1940, 54 percent of women who served in the House succeeded their husbands and from 1941 to 1964, 37 percent of women serving were widows. After 1964, the number of widows in office fell to 15 percent (Gertzog 1995; Dolan 2004). Today this method of gaining election is quite rare.

Several female members who began their service as widows went on to have more accomplished careers in Congress than did their husbands. Perhaps the most famous is Senator Margaret Chase Smith (R-ME) who was first elected to the House of Representatives after the death of her husband in 1940. She then became the first woman elected in her own right to the US Senate in 1948 and served there for an additional 24 years until she was defeated in the 1972 election. She is most well known for her Declaration of Conscience speech in which she was the first Republican to come out against the communist witch-hunt conducted by Senator Joe McCarthy (R-WI) in the 1950s. Numerous careers and lives were ruined by his unsubstantiated accusations and televised hearings in which he searched for communists in government and society. In 1964, Smith became the first woman to seek her party's presidential nomination, receiving 205,690 votes nationally and winning 27 delegates at the Republican National Convention. She spent only $25 on her campaign in the first primary state, New Hampshire, but her campaign practice of handing out recipes and muffins on the campaign trail and posing for photos while cooking gained so much publicity that Republican candidate Nelson Rockefeller felt compelled to respond by distributing his fudge recipe (Kaptur 1996). Current Maine Senator Susan Collins (R) credits Smith with inspiring her to run for public office. On a high school trip to Washington, DC, Smith brought Collins into her office and spoke to her for several hours about her Senate career. Today, Collins holds Smith's seat in the Senate (Mikulski et al. 2001).

By the 1970s, most women serving in Congress were professional politicians elected in their own right. However, their occupational backgrounds and paths to politics continued to differ from those of men. For example, women were more likely than men to have begun their political careers as community activists spurred to activism for or against a particular local project or as members of the PTA, the local school board, or other community groups. For example, Senator Barbara Mikulski (D-MD), the longest serving female senator, is a former social worker. Mikulski entered the political arena when she got involved in the fight to stop a highway project in her East Baltimore neighborhood. Similarly, when Patty Murray (D-WA) went to the state capitol to lobby against the elimination of a preschool program, a legislator dismissed her by saying, "You can't make a difference. You're just a mom in tennis shoes." In response, Murray organized a statewide parents' effort to revive the program. She was later elected to the school board and the Washington state Senate. When Murray ran for her first term in the US Senate, her campaign slogan was "just a mom in tennis shoes" (Mikulski et al. 2001).

Today, the educational and occupational backgrounds of male and female members of Congress continue to converge with more and more women entering Congress through the traditional pathways of law, business, or prior political office such as state legislator or city council member. However, elected women remain older and more likely to wait until their children are grown up before running for office (Burrell 1994, 2014).

Indeed, House Minority Leader Nancy Pelosi (D-CA) had been heavily involved in Democratic politics as a party fundraiser and activist, chairing the California Democrat Party in the 1980s. However, she waited until her five children were grown up before she first ran for the House of Representatives in a special election in 1987, at the age of 47 (Sandalow 2008). Today, there are more women with young children serving in Congress than ever before. Since power in Congress is derived from seniority, several women's PACs, such as the non-partisan Women Under Forty PAC, Democrat's EMILY's list, and the new Republican group Empowered Women, are focused on recruiting younger women to engage in politics and run for office (Cadei and Hunter 2009; Nelson 2015).

Compared to the 1970s, women in the contemporary Congress are more racially and ethnically diverse, with political views that span the ideological spectrum. They are also serving in a much more partisan and electorally competitive Congress. The number of women in Congress grew steadily but slowly throughout the 1970s and 1980s (see Figure 7.3). Similar numbers of Republican and Democratic women were elected to the House of Representatives throughout the 1980s. As late as 1991, there were only two women in the Senate, Republican Nancy Landon Kassebaum (R-KS) and Democrat Barbara Mikulski (D-MD) (Center for American Women and Politics 2017a). The paucity of women in Congress became an issue in the 1992 election when Anita Hill accused her former employer, Supreme Court nominee Clarence Thomas, of sexual harassment. The spectacle of Anita Hill being questioned by an all-male Judiciary committee prompted women across the country to run for Congress including current senators Dianne Feinstein (D-CA), Patty Murray (D-WA), and Barbara Boxer (D-CA) (Burrell 1994; Dolan 2001; Swers 2002). Referring to the fact that there were only two women in the Senate, Feinstein's campaign proclaimed that 2 percent was good enough for milk but not for women's representation in Congress (Feinstein 2006).

After the election, the number of women in Congress jumped from 32 to 54, the largest increase in a single election cycle, and the 1992 elections were dubbed "The Year of the Woman" (see Figure 7.3). Beyond the atypical focus on gender, there were structural features that facilitated the election of more women to Congress. Most importantly, the power of incumbency was weakened by the fact that 1992 was a redistricting year, and rather than facing election under new district lines, some incumbents decided to retire. Additionally, a series of congressional scandals reduced public trust in Congress, spurring more incumbent retirements. As a result, the election featured an unusually large number of open seats and more women ran in these competitive elections. With the public in the mood for a change, women capitalized on the fact that they were not part of the establishment (Burrell 1994; Dolan 2001; Swers 2002).

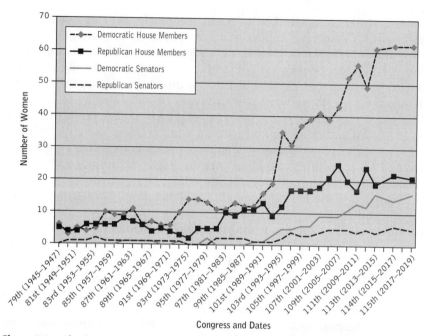

**Figure 7.3.   The Progress of Women in the House and Senate by Party.**
*Source*: "Women in the U.S. Congress 2017." Center for American Women and Politics 2017.

The elections of the early 1990s also brought increased racial diversity to Congress through the creation of majority/minority districts. As a result of amendments to the Voting Rights Act that sought to prevent dilution of the minority vote and ensure that minorities could elect a representative of their choice, the number of African Americans in Congress increased from 27 to 39 after the 1992 elections and the number of Hispanics in Congress rose from 10 to 17 (Manning and Shogan 2012; Bedolla, Tate, and Wong 2014). The first African Americans in Congress were elected during Reconstruction. However, when Reconstruction ended and Jim Crow laws were adopted to disenfranchise black voters, African Americans were excluded from Congress until Oscar DeLaPriest (R-IL) was elected to represent a Chicago area district in 1928 (Tate 2003; Manning and Shogan 2012).

The first African American woman did not come to Congress until the election of Shirley Chisholm (D-NY) in 1968. In that year, Chisholm was one of only ten women and nine African Americans in Congress. A former teacher and child care center director, she won her first election in her Brooklyn district with the campaign slogan "Unbought and Unbossed." This motto guided her career as she sought to serve the interests of groups that often go unheard, including the poor, children, women, and minorities. She was

Shirley Chisholm gives the victory sign after winning the Congressional election in Brooklyn's 12th District. She defeated civil rights leader James Farmer to become the first African American woman elected to Congress, November 5, 1968.
*Source*: © Bettmann / CORBIS.

not afraid to challenge the political establishment. Upon election to Congress, she protested against her assignment to the Agriculture Committee by objecting to her committee assignment on the floor of the House of Representatives. Rather than punishing her, the leadership decided to move her from that committee to the Veterans' Affairs Committee as a result of her actions. Satisfied with the result of her protest, she remarked, "There are a lot more veterans in my [Brooklyn, NY] district than there are trees" (Kaptur 1996).

Throughout her congressional career, Chisholm challenged the establishment and championed both civil rights and women's rights. She called the seniority system that guides the advancement of members of Congress to positions of power on committees, the "senility system" that left control of Congress to "a handful of old men." Yet, while she criticized existing power structures, she managed to avoid alienating her colleagues and was able to advance first to her desired assignment to the Education and Labor Committee and later to the powerful Rules Committee. By 1972, Chisholm decided to take her message of change nationally and she became the first woman and the first African American to run for the Democratic nomination for president. Although many of the male members of the Congressional Black Caucus actively opposed her candidacy, Chisholm was on the primary ballot in 12 states. Garnering less than 3 percent of the primary vote, she won 151 delegate votes at the Democratic National Convention (Kaptur 1996; Benenson 2005).

Hispanics first gained representation in Congress in 1822 when Florida was still a territory. The first Hispanic member to represent a state, Romualdo Pacheco (R-CA), entered Congress in 1877 (Office of the Historian and Office of the Clerk, United States House of Representatives 2013). It was more than 100 years later that the first Hispanic female, Ileana Ros-Lehtinen

(R-FL), was elected to Congress. Ros-Lehtinen continues to serve her Florida district and rose to chair the Foreign Relations Committee in the 112th Congress (2011–2012) where she fought against expanding relations with the Communist regime in Cuba (Center for American Women and Politics 2017c, 2017d).

While the creation of majority/minority districts helped expand representation for minority groups, almost all racial minorities in Congress represent a majority-minority district and there are few minority members elected outside of these types of districts (Davidson et al. 2015; Tate 2013). As a result, there are currently only 46 African Americans in the House of Representatives in the 115th Congress, a very small increase from the 39 elected after the introduction of majority-minority districts in the early 1990s. Because of the rapid population growth, the number of Hispanics in Congress has risen from 17 after the 1992 elections to 34 in the current House (Marcos 2016). Majority-minority districts also heavily vote Democratic. Therefore, most of the male and female racial minorities serving in Congress are Democrats. Indeed, the first African American Republican woman elected to Congress, Mia Love (R-UT), was elected in 2014 and she does not represent a majority-minority district.

Ileana Ros-Lehtinen (R-FL) chairs the House Foreign Affairs Subcommittee on Middle East and North Africa. Elected in 1989, Ros-Lehtinen is the first Hispanic woman to serve in Congress.
*Source*: Tom Williams / CQ Roll Call via AP Images.

Compared with their white female counterparts, minority women hold more seats in proportion to the number of minority men in the House of Representatives. Yet, very few minority women have been elected to the Senate. Elected in the 1992 "Year of the Woman" elections, Carol Moseley Braun (D-IL) was the first African American woman to serve in the Senate. After Moseley Braun lost her reelection bid in 1998, there were no women of color in the Senate until Japanese American Mazie Hirono (D-HI) was elected in 2012. The 2016 election marks a milestone for minority women in Congress. For the first time there will be more than one woman of color serving in the Senate, as three new minority women were elected. Kamala Harris (D-CA) is black and Indian American and Catherine Cortez Masto (D-NV) is the first Hispanic woman in the Senate. Tammy Duckworth (D-IL) is part Thai and is a veteran of the Iraq war (Marcos 2016). One of the first women to fly combat missions for the Army, Duckworth lost both of her legs when her helicopter was hit in battle (https://www.duckworth .senate.gov/content/about-tammy).

In addition to being more diverse, women in the contemporary Congress are much more likely to be Democrats than Republicans. In the 115th Congress, 78 women are Democrats compared to only 26 Republican women (Center for American Women and Politics 2017a). Almost all the minority women in Congress are Democrats. Of the 38 female minority members, only 3 are Republicans (Center for American Women and Politics 2017c). How do we explain this partisan disparity in which the gender gap in representation is larger than the gender gap in voting behavior?

The current partisan gap in women's representation did not emerge until after the 1992 elections (see Figure 7.3). While these elections were dubbed the "Year of the Woman," they were really the year of the Democratic woman, as the number of Democratic women in Congress rose from 22 in the 102nd Congress to 40 in the 103rd Congress, while only four more Republican women were elected to the 103rd Congress, taking their combined numbers in the House and Senate from 10 to 14 (Center for American Women and Politics 2017a). Since 1992, the gap between the number of Republican and Democratic women has only grown wider. The 1990s and 2000s have seen several volatile electoral cycles in which control of the House and Senate majority has shifted between Republicans and Democrats. In the years when Democrats have done well such as 2006 and 2008, the representation of Democratic women has also advanced. However, Republican women have not experienced concomitantly strong gains during Republican wave elections. Thus, in the 1994 Republican Revolution when Republicans took over the House majority for the first time in 40 years, the party gained 52 House seats but Republican women only expanded their presence from 12 to 17 seats. Similarly, in the wave election of 2010, Republicans won 63 House seats, but the representation of Republican women only increased by seven seats, from 17 to 24 House seats (Davidson et al. 2015; Center for American Women and Politics 2017a).

How can we explain these trends? Some scholars find that certain types of districts are more likely to elect women. These districts are generally more diverse, more urban, and have a higher median income. In contemporary politics, these types of districts are more likely to vote for Democrats (Palmer and Simon 2008; Pearson and McGhee 2013). Meanwhile, rural districts and the Southern states, which are the stronghold of the Republican Party, are also less likely to elect women (Elder 2008; Pearson and McGhee 2013). Dynamics within the parties also contribute to the disparity. The contemporary Democratic Party is a more liberal party and its voters are more likely to prioritize diversity and embrace positive stereotypes about female candidates (Burrell 2014; Elder 2014). Meanwhile, the Republican Party focuses more on candidate ideology than identity (Cooperman 2013; Elder 2014). Additionally, women's groups and civil rights organizations are more central to the Democratic coalition. These groups prioritize the election of more diverse candidates and are heavily engaged in efforts to recruit more women and minorities. EMILY's list is the most successful of these groups. They recruit women to run in primaries, raise money for candidates, and provide them with polling and other services that are important to campaigns. While Republicans have groups dedicated to electing more Republican women, including Maggie's List, their efforts lag behind the more established and successful Democratic groups (Crespin and Dietz 2010; Burrell 2014; Political Parity 2015). Looking more closely at candidate fundraising in the primary and general election as a potential cause of the partisan disparity in representation, Kitchens and Swers (2016) found that Democratic women actually raise more money than Democratic men. Among Republicans, Republican women generally raise as much money as Republican men. However, when the analysis is limited to quality candidates, meaning candidates with previous electoral experience, the Republican women raise less money than the Republican men. This suggests that the most viable female challenger and open seat candidates may have more trouble accessing Republican fundraising networks than the quality candidates who are Republican men.

Based on current trends, women will continue to grow their ranks in Congress and state legislatures. However, the partisan gap among legislators is likely to continue and grow. Moreover, as more women of color are elected, these women are disproportionately likely to be Democrats. As we will see below, the increasing concentration of female legislators in the Democratic Party has important consequences for the ability of female legislators to influence policy with women having more access to the levers of power in legislatures controlled by Democrats and less influence in Republican-controlled legislative bodies.

## WOMEN IN CONGRESS AND STATE LEGISLATURES: A DISTINCTIVE IMPACT ON POLICY?

The election of more women to Congress and the state legislatures raises the question of whether women legislate differently than men. Returning to the expectations of representation theory, do women espouse different policy priorities that focus more attention on the needs of women, children, and families? Do women exhibit a different leadership style or bring a unique perspective to existing policy debates that emphasizes how policy proposals will impact different groups of women? Examining the legislative activities of male and female members of Congress and the state legislatures, scholars find that the election of women does have a distinctive impact on policymaking.

One of the key arguments for descriptive representation is that descriptive representatives as members of the group will be more likely to understand group concerns based on shared life experiences and will prioritize policies that are important to group members. Examining legislators' perceptions of their representational roles, scholars find that female legislators in Congress and the state legislatures view women as a distinctive part of their constituency and feel a special responsibility to advocate for their interests (Reingold 1992, 2000; Thomas 1997; Carroll 2002). Surveys of legislators' policy priorities show that women are also more likely to consider women's issues an important part of their agenda than are their male colleagues (Dodson and Carroll 1991; Thomas 1994; Poggione 2004).

Gender differences in legislative behavior are most prominent at the agenda setting stage where members decide which causes to champion and work to craft bills and build coalitions to advance their policy proposals. Studies of bill sponsorship and cosponsorship demonstrate that women offer more bills on issues related to women, children, and families. This includes feminist or women's rights bills that promote role equity or role change for women such as bills concerning family leave, equal pay, sexual harassment, and reproductive rights. Female legislators also offer more initiatives on the social welfare issues that underlie the gender gap among voters such as health care and education. Generally, sex differences in legislative behavior are greater the more directly an issue can be connected to consequences for women as a group. Therefore, gender is a stronger predictor of which members will champion feminist initiatives such as reproductive rights than social welfare policies such as education reforms (Thomas 1994; Gelb and Palley 1996; Bratton and Haynie 1999; Reingold 2000; Wolbrecht 2000; Swers 2002, 2013, 2016a; Dodson 2006; Osborn 2012).

The advancement of more women into legislative office has also impacted the deliberative process among legislators. Women bring a distinctive perspective to policy debates based on their life experiences as mothers, daughters, and women of various backgrounds. In their committee activity and on the floor, women utilize their positions to advocate for women's concerns and influence how issues are framed and solutions are crafted. Congressional studies of policies ranging from welfare and health reform to violence against women and abortion indicate that women use their positions on key committees and within their party leadership to ensure that women's interests are included in legislation and to prevent the legislation from faltering at key points in the process. For example, during the development of welfare reform in the early 1990s, women in the Republican and Democratic parties who served on the House Ways and Means Committee and held positions in party leadership were pivotal in getting Congress to include child support enforcement and more funding for child care to support working mothers in the final bill (Swers 2002; Hawkesworth 2003; Dodson 2006; Johnson, Duerst-Lahti, and Norton 2007). When President Obama's health reform proposal was going through Congress, women in the House and Senate worked to ensure that women's health needs were included in the bill. For example, female senators pushed the administration to include broad coverage of contraception as part of a package of preventive services that insurance companies are required to offer (Swers 2013).

Analyses of floor speeches indicate that women act as vigorous advocates for women's interests. Women draw on their moral authority as women by referring to their roles as parents, mothers, and grandmothers. They are more likely to discuss the impact of policies on women and children (Shogan 2001; Cramer Walsh 2002; Levy, Tien, and Aved 2002; Swers 2002, 2013; Osborn and Mendez 2010; Pearson and Dancey 2011a). They highlight issues of women's rights in broader policy debates. Analyzing the Senate floor debates surrounding the nominations of John Roberts and Samuel Alito to the Supreme Court, Swers (2013) finds that among Democrats, Democratic women focused more attention than Democratic men on the nominees' positions on women's rights. The Democratic women were more likely than men to highlight women's rights issues outside of abortion such as equal pay, family leave policy, and the representation of women on the federal courts (see also Swers and Kim 2013).

There is some evidence that women have influenced the way that men view and discuss women's issues. For example, in a study of congressional debate on abortion since the 1970s, Levy, Tien, and Aved (2002) found that over time, women have moved the debate from one that emphasizes the morality of abortion to one that increasingly includes a focus on the health of the pregnant woman. As a result, both pro-choice and pro-life proponents frame their arguments with an eye to the impact on women and women's physical and mental health.

In sum, female legislators clearly prioritize women's interests in their work. They perceive themselves as representatives of women and women's interests. They have introduced more initiatives concerning women, children, and families to the legislative agenda and they act as vigorous advocates for these interests in the committees and on the floor. These findings reflect general trends in legislative behavior. There are numerous factors that affect whether an individual female legislator perceives herself as an advocate for women's interests and whether she has the ability to pursue these preferences in the legislative process. We turn now to the important political and institutional constraints that shape legislators' choices about what policies to champion.

## Party, Ideology, and Constituent Interests

Party affiliation, ideology, and constituent opinion are among the most important predictors of how representatives behave. In recent years, the Democratic and Republican Parties have become more ideologically homogeneous and further polarized from each other. As the formerly solid South moved away from the Democratic Party and liberal Northeastern Republicans left the Republican Party, commentators began referring to red states and blue states to represent the ideological divides in the country (Jacobson 2013). In response to this polarization, voting among members of Congress increasingly falls along party lines (Poole and Rosenthal 1997; Davidson et al. 2015).

In this partisan atmosphere, it is hard to see how gender might have an independent effect on legislative behavior. While early studies of voting in Congress suggested that female representatives are more liberal than their male colleagues, the voting records of male and female Democrats and Republicans in the House of Representatives converged by the early 2000s (Frederick 2009). Much of the gender difference in voting behavior stemmed from the more liberal voting records of moderate Republican women. However, there are few moderates left in Congress and the new women being elected from the South and West are just as conservative as their male counterparts (Frederick 2009; Thomsen 2015; Swers 2016b, 2017). Women in the Senate remain more liberal than their male colleagues (Frederick 2010). However, this may change as more conservative Republican women are elected to the Senate. Focusing on women's issues, scholars find that women often vote more liberally on policies regarding women's rights such as pay equity and abortion (Burrell 1994; Dolan 1997; Norton 1999; Swers 1998, 2002; Frederick 2009). However, this trend may be declining in line with the election of more conservative Republican women such as Deb Fischer (R-NE) and Joni Ernst (R-IA), both of whom have ties to the Tea Party movement (Swers 2016a, 2017).

Even in a partisan atmosphere, female members of Congress and state legislatures remain more committed to proposing and cosponsoring legislation related to women, children, and families. Numerous studies show that women are more likely to sponsor and cosponsor bills on women's issues even after accounting for the legislator's party affiliation, ideology, constituency effects, and committee position (Thomas 1994; Bratton and Haynie 1999; Wolbrecht 2000, 2002; Swers 2002, 2013; Dodson 2006; Osborn 2012; but see Reingold 2000).

Voters in a congressional or state legislative district have a general ideological view on issues. However, a legislator has wide discretion in choosing which specific policies to champion as long as they fall within the spectrum of policy views that his or her constituents can support. One would not expect a representative of a conservative district to support liberalized abortion laws. However, the member may advocate for increased funding for women's health research or programs to combat violence against women.

Analyzing bill proposals across ten state legislatures, Osborn (2012) finds that Democratic and Republican men and women advocate for distinct women's issues and offer different solutions to address specific problems. Democratic women offer the most bills regarding women's issues and their proposals span a wide range of women's interests. They are particularly aggressive advocates of policies regarding employment discrimination and women's health concerns ranging from cancer screening to services for pregnant women and breastfeeding mothers. Republican men offer the most bills to restrict abortion. Other proposals offered by Republican men focus on legal issues regarding marriage and divorce and efforts to increase punishment for sex offenders and expand child support enforcement. The bills of Democratic men span the range of issues and align more with the proposals of Democratic women, except in the areas of child support enforcement and sex offenders where they, like Republican men, focus more on punishment of offenders and less on victim's rights. Finally, Republican women offered the fewest proposals on women's issues. Their initiatives align more with the proposals of Republican men than Democratic women except in the area of women's health where their bills correspond more to the proposals offered by Democratic women including bills regarding breast cancer, services for pregnant women, and IVF insurance coverage. Republican women also offered more child care proposals than Republican men (Osborn 2012; Osborn and Kreitzer 2014). Thus, within the large category of women's issues, men and women from different parties have different ideas about what women need.

Beyond the policy preferences of individual legislators, the parties as a whole have developed reputations for expertise on particular issues. Women's issues have become a fault line between the parties. In a polarized era, women's rights issues are increasingly associated with the Democratic Party (Wolbrecht 2000; Winter 2010). Indeed, Osborn (2012) finds that more women's issue bills pass in state legislatures controlled by Democrats than in legislatures where Republicans are the majority party. Capitalizing on the party's presumed ownership of these issues and voter stereotypes concerning women's perceived expertise, Democratic women are generally the most active advocates of women's issue bills. When Democratic women advocate for expansion of equal pay or reproductive rights, they are pursuing legislation that both reflects their own policy priorities and helps the Democratic Party improve its standing with voters, particularly the activist base that donates to campaigns and mobilizes voters (Swers 2002, 2013; Dodson 2006). For example, Swers (2013) recounts how female Democratic senators were pivotal in drafting and building support for the Lilly Ledbetter Fair Pay Act. First brought to the floor in the run up to the 2008 presidential election, the media campaign female senators engaged in to build public support for the bill also served a dual purpose of portraying Republicans as opposing equal pay for women and acting against women's interests. Democratic women in Congress continue to combine their interest in seeking policies that expand women's rights with their roles as partisan warriors. In the 2012 and 2014 election cycles, Democratic women promoted additional pay equity proposals as well as contraception coverage and other benefits for women's health in the Affordable Care Act. As they promoted these policies, they also accused Republicans of engaging in a war on women in which Republican policy prescriptions would harm women's rights and their families (Swers 2013; Deckman and McTague 2014).

While advocating policies related to women's rights is generally a natural fit for Democratic women, the political calculus for Republican women is more complicated. Women's issues are not central to the platform of the Republican Party and many of these policies conflict with the views of social conservatives, an important constituency within the Republican Party. If Republican women advocate for women's rights legislation, they could alienate Republican Party colleagues and risk losing their support on other issues important to the legislator's constituency (Swers 2002, 2013). At the same time, in this era of tight electoral competition, women represent a key swing-voting group that both Republican and Democrats want to court in their efforts to become the majority party in Congress and across the state legislatures. Therefore, the leadership of both parties utilizes female legislators as spokespersons for the party's position on women's issues. Republican women are often asked to speak at press conferences and on the House and Senate floor to defend the party against charges that it is unfriendly to women's interests or to explain how Republican policies will help women (Swers 2002, 2013; Dodson 2006). Indeed, Republican Conference Chair Cathy McMorris Rodgers (R-WA) considers outreach to women voters and pushing back on the Democratic narrative of a war on women an important part of her job (Mimms 2015). Republican women hold press conferences to explain how small business tax cuts benefit women since women-owned

The 2016 elections brought three new women of color to the United States Senate: former state Attorney General Kamala Harris (D-CA); former U.S. Representative and veteran Tammy Duckworth (D-IL); and former state Attorney General Catherine Cortez Masto (D-NV).

*Sources (from left to right)*: ZUMA Press, Inc. / Alamy Stock Photo; ZUMA Press, Inc. / Alamy Stock Photo; dpa picture alliance / Alamy Stock Photo.

businesses are one of the fastest growing groups of small business owners. Pro-life Republican women are asked to speak on the floor when abortion is being debated to demonstrate that not all women are pro-choice and that Republicans are not anti-women (Swers 2002, 2013; Dodson 2006).

As the ranks of moderate Republican women continue to dwindle and more conservative women are elected, it remains an open question whether Republican women will choose to engage women's issues from a conservative perspective or whether they will prefer to focus on policies more central to Republican constituencies such as lowering taxes and rolling back regulations on business. Will they limit themselves to defending the party against Democratic attacks that characterize Republicans as anti-women or aggressively take up the banner of social conservatism (Swers and Larson 2005; Swers 2013)?

Since Republicans won control of the House in 2010, the Senate in 2014, and the presidency in 2016, Republicans have focused more aggressively on limiting abortion. Rather than simply voting with their party, conservative Republican women are taking leadership roles in these efforts. For example, Representative Diane Black (R-TN) and Senator Joni Ernst (R-IA) both sponsored bills to defund Planned Parenthood. Black's bill passed the House, while Ernst's bill was considered on the Senate floor but fell to a Democratic filibuster. When House Republican leadership decided to create a special committee to investigate Planned Parenthood's sale of fetal tissue for research, they appointed Marsha Blackburn (R-TN) to chair the committee, and half of the committee's members were Republican women, including Mia Love (R-UT), Vicky Hartzler (R-MO), and Diane Black (R-TN). Thus, it seems that the new generation of conservative women is more strongly engaged in women's issues, particularly abortion politics (Swers 2016b, 2017).

## Race, Ethnicity, and Social Class

Beyond party affiliations, women also differ from one another by race, ethnicity, and social class. Scholars are only beginning to examine the impact of intersectionality or overlapping social identities on the policy activities of legislators. Research demonstrates that women of color bring a different perspective to legislating, as they must confront both racism and sexism in their life experiences. With more women of color serving in the state legislatures since the 1990s, studies of policy priorities indicate that African Americans are more likely to sponsor progressive legislation than other legislators. They are also more likely to sponsor both a women's interest bill and a black interest bill than other legislators, indicating that black women focus on serving multiple groups in their legislative activities (Barrett 1995; Bratton and Haynie 1999; Bratton, Haynie, and Reingold 2006; Orey et al. 2006; Brown 2014). Similarly, studying the policy priorities of Latinos, Fraga et al. (2006) find that compared to their male Latino colleagues, Latinas place more emphasis on representing the interests of multiple minority groups, particularly African Americans and Asians. While Latino men and women identify similar policy priorities including education, health care, and economic development, Latinas are more likely than their male counterparts to propose and pass legislation reflecting their policy agenda (Fraga et al. 2008).

At the congressional level, case studies demonstrate that minority women legislators are aggressive advocates for the needs of women of color, particularly women in poverty. For example, Hawkesworth (2003) found that African American and Hispanic Democratic women were united in their opposition to welfare reform and used their floor time to speak against the stereotyping of welfare mothers as irresponsible, poor minority women. By contrast, minority men and white women in the Democratic Party were not unified on the welfare reform bill. Thus, minority women felt a greater responsibility to advocate for the interests of their poor minority women constituents than did minority men and white women (see also Barrett 1995; Reingold and Smith 2012; Garcia Bedolla, Tate, and Wong 2014). Similarly, Dodson (2006) finds that when Bill Clinton became president in 1992, abortion rights supporters hoped to achieve legislative victories after 12 years of Republican control of the presidency. She notes that white women focused their attention on the Freedom of Choice Act, a bill that would codify the right to abortion granted by *Roe v. Wade*. By contrast, minority women were more committed to overturning the Hyde amendment, which prevents federal Medicaid dollars from being used to fund abortions. These minority women placed a priority on facilitating access to abortion services for their poor and often minority constituents rather than codifying the abstract right. As more women from diverse backgrounds are elected to Congress and the state legislatures, researchers will continue to examine how the overlapping identities of race and gender influence members' policy priorities and the type of coalitions they build to support their initiatives.

## Institutional Position

The ability of members to advocate for women's issues also depends on their position in the institution. Legislatures are hierarchical bodies in which an individual's power depends on his or her level of seniority, committee position, and status as a member of the majority or minority party. Regardless of the promises legislators make in campaigns, if they do not have a seat at the table where decisions are made, they cannot influence the content and shape of the legislation (Hall 1996; Swers 2002, 2013; Davidson et al. 2015).

Being a member of the majority party is one of the most important determinants of a member's influence. The majority party controls the agenda in Congress and the state legislatures. Majority party leaders determine what proposals will be included in bills and which bills will be considered on the floor. Majority party members chair the committees and determine what issues the committee will consider. In a study of women in the House of Representatives, Swers (2002) found that the legislative priorities of women were strongly affected by whether they were in the majority or the minority party. Thus, Republican women were more active on feminist issues when they were in the minority party. As minority party members, these women were only expected to vote in favor of the feminist bills that the Democratic majority brought to the floor. When they were in the majority, promoting feminist legislation meant going against the policy convictions of other majority party members and important interest groups that supported the party. In this situation, Republican women put more of their political capital at risk by supporting feminist causes as these causes were not likely to be taken up by the Republican majority. Swers (2002) also found that congresswomen, both Democrats and Republicans, were more active on social welfare issues such as health care and education only when their party controlled the majority. This is because social welfare issues constitute a major fault line between the two parties. When their party controlled the majority, women had access to the legislative agenda and were more motivated to offer proposals on these issues because as majority party members they were now more likely to have an impact on the direction of policy in these areas (see also Dodson 2006).

In addition to majority party status, seniority and committee position are important determinants of a legislator's influence within the institution. In the Congress and the state legislatures, members have the most influence over policies that fall under the jurisdiction of their committees. This is because most policies are first formulated in the committees. By holding hearings to draw attention to issues and drafting legislation, committee leaders and rank and file members decide what issues will be important and what policy ideas will get attention. (Hall 1996; Swers 2002, 2013).

With the election of more women to Congress and the state legislatures in the 1990s, women are now gaining the levels of seniority necessary to gain seats on the more prestigious committees such as those that control taxing and spending, and they are advancing to committee and subcommittee chairmanships. Thus, the presence of seven women on the Armed Services committee and Kirsten Gillibrand's status as Personnel Subcommittee chair in the 113th Congress (2013–2014) gave these women the platform to aggressively pursue reforms of the military justice system (Henneberger 2014; Kaper 2014). Similarly, Norton (2002) found that women had limited influence on reproductive rights policies in Congress until they gained seats on the Appropriations Committee and other committees with jurisdiction over funding and restrictions. When the Violence Against Women Act first passed Congress, female members on key committees made sure that the bill moved through the legislative process and did not get stalled at one of the many points in the process where bills are killed (Swers 2002; Dodson 2006).

Given the power wielded by majority party members and committee leaders, it is important to note that the gender imbalance in women's representation, in which far more women serving in Congress and the state legislatures are Democrats, impacts the ability of women to influence policy. Because there are fewer female Republicans and many have little seniority after being elected in more recent elections, women as a group have less power when Republicans hold the majority. For example, when Democrats last controlled the House of Representatives in 2009–2010, Nancy Pelosi (D-CA) served as Speaker of the House. The most powerful position in the House, the Speaker sets the policy agenda, deciding what bills will be considered by the body, and plays a pivotal role in building coalitions and negotiating with the White House and the Senate leadership. Within the committees, three Democratic women chaired House committees and numerous female members held subcommittee chairs. When Republicans took control of Congress after the 2010 elections, only one Republican

Republican Conference Chair Cathy McMorris Rodgers (R-WA) speaks at a press conference on legislation to fight human trafficking, Jan. 27, 2015.
*Source*: Michael Reynolds, EPA European Pressphoto Agency b.v. / Alamy Stock Photo.

woman, Ileana Ros-Lehtinen (FL), chaired a committee, the Foreign Relations committee. After the 2012 elections, Cathy McMorris-Rodgers (WA) was elected to party leadership as Conference Chair and Candice Miller (MI) chaired the relatively weak House Administration Committee. In the new 115th Congress (2017–2018) Republican women are finally gaining more influence, as several Republican women are chairing important committees, including Diane Black (TN) as chair of the Budget Committee, Virginia Foxx (VA) as chair of the Education and Workforce Committee, and Kay Granger (TX) as chair of the Defense Appropriations Subcommittee, which decides the spending priorities of the military. Susan Brooks (IN) leads the Ethics Committee (Hawkings 2017).

The disparate power dynamics are even more stark in the Senate where the fact that there are only 100 senators compared to 435 House members means that individual senators advance to chairmanships more quickly and can hold multiple positions of power (Sinclair 1989; Swers 2013). When Democrats controlled the Senate in 2013–2014, women chaired eight committees including the powerful Appropriations Committee that allocates funding, the Budget Committee, which sets the parameters for the federal budget, and the Intelligence Committee that oversees the nation's spying programs. However, in the current Republican-controlled Senate, only two of the five women were elected before 2010, meaning they lack the seniority to advance to committee chairs. As a result, only two Republican women chair committees. Lisa Murkowski (R-AK) chairs the Senate's Energy and Natural Resources Committee and Susan Collins (R-ME) chairs the Special Committee on Aging (Center for American Women and Politics 2017d). Collins had chaired the Homeland Security and Governmental Affairs Committee from 2003 to 2007, where she passed legislation to reorganize government handling of terrorism threats based on recommendations of the 9/11 Commission. By virtue of their numbers and seniority, the partisan imbalance in women's representation means that women were in a better position to influence the Senate policy agenda on issues ranging from taxes to health care and foreign policy when Democrats held the majority.

### Gender, Race, and Institutional Norms

All institutions reflect the preferences and norms of the dominant group, and legislators who want to see their policy ideas enacted into law must understand and conform to the accepted rules and practices of the legislature. However, the standard operating procedures and accepted practices within legislatures are both raced and gendered (Acker 1992; Kenney 1996; Rosenthal 1998). The need to adapt to and negotiate these standards sets up additional hurdles for gaining acceptance within the institution (Duerst-Lahti 2002; Hawkesworth 2003). As a result of their underrepresentation and perceptions that it is more difficult for women to get elected, the women who win often feel they need to be more qualified and react to their minority status by trying to do more. Studies of legislative behavior indicate that in comparison to their male colleagues, female members of Congress secure more money in federal spending for their districts, they sponsor and cosponsor more bills, and they give more floor speeches to raise their visibility and draw attention to their policy priorities on a range of issues (Anzia and Berry 2011; Pearson and Dancey 2011b). While women sponsor more legislation, Volden et al. (2013) find that women are only more successful than men in passing legislation when they are in the minority party and their consensus building skills are an asset. However, they are less effective than men at keeping their bills alive when they serve in the majority.

As in business, women legislators sometimes feel that despite having a seat at the table, they are marginalized, finding it more difficult to get their contributions and policy views heard. For example, Swers (2013) finds that staffers for female members felt that Democratic women senators had to work harder than ideologically similar male colleagues to prove themselves on defense issues and they believed that they were taken less seriously by Pentagon officials. Additionally, an analysis of senators' appearances on the major Sunday talk shows demonstrated that women needed to achieve leadership positions on defense-related committees and within the party before they were viewed as experts and invited to talk about defense issues on the Sunday shows. By contrast, credentials did not play as significant a role in the appearances by male senators. While male senators who led important committees dominated the Sunday talk shows, other male senators who had not achieved leadership positions on foreign policy were also invited to speak on defense issues (Swers 2007).

Feelings of marginalization are particularly prevalent among women of color. Hawkesworth (2003) describes this experience as "race-gendering." Interviewing female members of Congress, she found that regardless of their level of seniority or committee leadership positions, minority women believed that their policy proposals were more likely to be ignored and their knowledge discounted by majority group members (both white men and women). In a case study of the passage of welfare reform in the 1990s, Hawkesworth finds that despite the importance of the issue to their constituents, minority women were excluded from Democratic task forces negotiating policy and their efforts to combat negative views of welfare recipients as welfare queens were ignored (see Smooth 2008, for similar findings in state legislatures). Uncovering the gender- and race-based norms within a legislature is a very difficult task, but these norms have very real consequences for members' legislative power.

## Critical Mass and Policy Influence

Given the gendered nature of institutions, it is possible that female legislators' desire to bring a distinctive point of view to policy deliberations and to advocate for legislation regarding women's interests depends on the number of other women in the legislature. To achieve their policy goals, legislators must build coalitions and find allies. Drawing on the theories of Rosabeth Moss Kanter (1977) concerning the impact of sex ratios on group behavior in corporate settings, scholars argue that when women constitute a small minority of legislators, they will be treated as tokens that represent their group, as symbols rather than as individuals. Feeling pressure to conform to male norms, these women will not feel comfortable representing and advocating for the concerns of women. Once these women constitute a "critical mass," at least 20–30 percent, they will feel more comfortable pursuing policy preferences based on gender (see also chapter 8).

Research on state legislatures has found some evidence to support the idea that legislative activity on women's issues increases as the proportion of women in the legislature increases. However, there are no clear threshold effects. For example, in her study of bill sponsorship and passage in the Arizona legislature, Saint-Germain (1989) shows that women's activity on behalf of women's interests, such as health care and education, increased as the number of women in the legislature increased. Similarly, in a study of 12 state legislatures in the 1980s, Thomas (1994) found that in states where the proportion of women in the legislature reached 20 percent, women were more likely to give priority to bills concerning women, children, and families and were more successful in passing these bills into law. At the congressional level, MacDonald and O'Brien (2008) note that between 1973 and 2003, congresswomen sponsored more bills on feminist and social welfare issues as the proportion of women in the House increased.

The proportion of women in the legislature can also impact policy outcomes. In a study of abortion policy, Berkman and O'Connor (1993) found that committees that included greater numbers of Democratic women were most successful in blocking restrictive abortion laws such as requirements for parental consent. Reingold and Smith (2012) demonstrate that since the enactment of welfare reform, states with higher proportions of women of color in the legislature have developed less punitive welfare policies allowing more flexibility in eligibility and work requirements and providing more generous cash benefits.

Yet, other scholars have questioned the value of critical mass arguing that women behave more distinctively when they are few in number and feel the responsibility for representing their group. For example, Crowley (2004) found that in state legislatures with few women, the female members played a pivotal role in passing child support legislation. Bratton (2005) argues that legislators must build a policy niche. Women's issue bills provide a natural fit for women in heavily male dominated legislatures and these women sponsored more women's issues legislation. However, when being a woman was not as distinctive and there were other women to share the burden, in some states sex differences in bill sponsorship diminished, as the legislature became more gender balanced. Examining sponsorship of black interest and women's interest bills, Bratton, Haynie, and Reingold (2006) note that women of color sponsored fewer women's interest bills as the overall number of women in the legislature increased. However, the proportion of minorities in the legislature did not impact their activism on black interest bills. This is likely due to the fact that both men and women are more likely to sponsor a women's interest bill than a black interest bill. Furthermore, across the ten state legislatures in their study, there were always more women's interest bills proposed than black interest bills.

Finally, focusing on critical mass ignores the legislator's position within the institution and the level of influence he or she wields. Therefore, Childs and Krook (2006) suggest that rather than looking at numbers of women, we should focus on the emergence of critical actors who build coalitions and mobilize support for policy change. These critical actors can be legislators with key committee or party leadership positions or individuals outside of the legislatures such as interest group and social movement leaders (see also Dahlerup 2006; Grey 2006; Beckwith 2007).

## Women in Leadership

Presence is only the first step to wielding power in the legislature. Members' length of service and their position in the institution impact their level of influence. Party leaders and committee chairs are the most powerful members of the legislature, wielding many formal and informal powers. Committee chairs craft the policy agenda for their committees, deciding which issues they want to highlight in hearings and drafting policy proposals (Hall 1996; Davidson et al. 2015). Party leaders set the legislative agenda for their chamber with an eye to expanding the electoral coalition of their party. They work to craft a message that will attract voters and serve as the major spokespersons for the party's platform in the media. The party leaders are also routinely involved in the final stages of negotiating policy with the president (or governor at the state level) (Rhode 1991; Davidson et al. 2015).

As women gain seniority and advance to leadership positions in their parties and on the committees, do they exhibit a different leadership style? Looking at committee chairs in state legislatures, male and female chairs exhibit different leadership styles, with women adopting more egalitarian leadership styles that value consensus and collaboration while men adopt more authoritative styles that emphasize competition and conflict (Kathlene 1994, 1995; Rosenthal 1997, 1998, 2000; Reingold 2000). However, Rosenthal (1998) notes that the female style of leadership is less prevalent in the legislatures that are more professionalized, meaning those that employ more staff, pay higher salaries, and meet over larger portions of the year. Thus, as more legislatures become professionalized, women may not continue expressing a different style of leadership. Rather than changing the institution, women may find that they need to adapt to the norms of the body to succeed.

In Congress, Volden et al. (2013) suggest that a consensus-oriented leadership style helps women build coalitions when they are in the minority party and these women are able to keep their bills alive through more stages of the legislative process. However, as Congress becomes more polarized, the ability to forge consensus is less valued and the parties work to sharpen the contrasts between them. As a result, Volden et al. (2013) find that in more recent years characterized by increased polarization, majority party women are less effective than men at pushing their bills through the legislative process and they compensate for this lack of success by introducing more legislation.

Indeed, the number of women in Congress increased most dramatically at the same time that Congress became more polarized, with Democrats becoming more uniformly liberal and Republicans more strongly

When Nancy Pelosi (D-CA) became the first female Speaker of the House, she invited all the children in the audience to come up and touch the gavel.
*Source*: Rich Lipski / *The Washington Post* / Getty Images.

conservative. It was in this atmosphere that Nancy Pelosi (D-CA) became the first woman to serve as Speaker of the House, a position she held from 2007 to 2010. With Democrats in the minority, Pelosi is currently the Minority Party Leader. The election of Pelosi as Speaker of the House marks the first time a woman has become the leader of her party and the institution in either house of Congress.

There is ample evidence that gender considerations influence Pelosi's leadership style. Pelosi speaks openly about the influence of her gender on her priorities. She often refers to herself as a mother of five and grandmother of six. This mantra has a dual purpose, as she wants to send the message that the needs of women and children are a priority for her but she also wants to counteract efforts by her political opponents to paint her as a San Francisco liberal whose policy views and values are outside the mainstream (Swers and Larson 2005; Rosenthal 2008; Sandalow 2008; Peters and Rosenthal 2010). After the election of President Barack Obama, Pelosi renewed her commitment to issues related to women and children. She played a key role in the decision to pass the Lilly Ledbetter Fair Pay Act as the first piece of legislation passed into law in the 111th Congress (Halloran 2009). She also pushed through an expansion of the State Children's Health Insurance Program (SCHIP), which provides health insurance to low-income children whose family incomes are above the poverty thresh-old necessary to qualify for Medicaid (Pear 2009). Pelosi led the fight to pass President Obama's comprehensive health care reform bill. Many of the president's advisors and the Senate leader Harry Reid (D-NV) believed that the president should scale back his health plan in the face of fierce Republican opposition, but Pelosi pushed Obama to utilize his Democratic majority in Congress and pursue comprehensive reform. When abortion politics threatened to derail the final bill, Pelosi brokered a deal to resolve the concerns of pro-life Democrats while keeping the support of her pro-choice colleagues (Bzdek 2010).

While studies of women in leadership emphasize women's roles as con-sensus builders (Kathlene 1994; Rosenthal 1998), Pelosi clearly has a very partisan leadership style. She prefers to sharpen the Democratic Party's message and highlight its differences with the Republican Party rather than compromising on legislation (Swers and Larson 2005; Rosenthal 2008; Peters and Rosenthal 2010). She is a prolific fundraiser and a favorite tar-get of Republicans looking to highlight the wrongheaded policies of the Democrats. However, within the Democratic caucus, Pelosi is viewed as a consensus builder who tries to take care of the needs of the various factions of the Democratic caucus. While Pelosi's own ideological views are in line with the progressive wing of the caucus, she took care to consult with the more moderate and conservative Democrats, placing these members on key committees and as advisors within the leadership ranks (Swers and Larson 2005; Rosenthal 2008; Sandalow 2008; Peters and Rosenthal 2010). As one staffer noted, "Pelosi is a consensus builder; on liberal things she acts as a facilitator organizing and working behind the scenes but she does not act as the public face because she knows she has to take care of the whole caucus" (Swers and Larson 2005). Pelosi is a consummate inside player who knows how to broker deals among factions within her party. She is less skilled at the outside game of media relations and has been criticized as having a wooden speaking style and a tendency to stick to, and repeat, a set of talk-ing points (Sandalow 2008; Peters and Rosenthal 2010).

Finally, Pelosi also used her power as Speaker and now minority leader to elevate more women within the party and committee leadership. Female Democrats were an important part of the coalition that helped elect Pelosi to leadership and she counts women, particularly members of the delega-tion of her home state of California as some of her strongest supporters and advisors. She has worked to expand gender and racial diversity across the committees, appointing more women and minorities to serve on presti-gious committees such as Appropriations and Ways and Means and expand-ing the number of committee and subcommittee chairs held by women and racial minorities (Swers and Larson 2005; Peters and Rosenthal 2010). Despite Pelosi's success, few women have advanced to the highest ranks of leadership within the parties. It remains to be seen how gender will impact a Republican female Speaker or a female Democratic or Republican Majority Leader in the Senate.

## CONCLUSION

The halls of power in the nation's legislatures remain overwhelmingly male. Yet, women continue to increase their presence in state legislatures and Congress. Research on the impact of electing women to office supports many of the expectations regarding descriptive representation. Women do bring a different perspective to legislating that focuses more attention in the deliberative process on the needs of women, children, and families. The presence of women yields more policy proposals related to women's interests and shapes the nature of policy outcomes. Still, the policy decisions of an individual legislator are shaped by the political context in which he or she serves. In addition to reflecting the interests of their constituency, today's female legislators serve in a more partisan and polarized environment in which more women elected to office are Democrats, and these Democratic women consider women's rights a priority and are eager to help their party reach out to women voters. Meanwhile, moderate Republicans are disappearing and a new generation of conservative women is slowly entering the field. Recent Republican activism to restrict abortion demonstrates that conservative women are taking leadership roles on that issue. However, it remains to be seen whether these conservative women will prioritize other women's issues from a socially conservative viewpoint or eschew these policies in favor of more traditional Republican priorities such as lowering taxes and cutting government spending.

Congress and the state legislatures are also becoming more diverse with more women of color entering the legislative arena. Even the US Senate, which had seen only two women of color elected in its history became more diverse after the 2016 elections. Research on women of color indicates that they govern differently than white women and minority men as their multiple group memberships drive their legislative agenda.

Looking to the future, women are increasingly gaining seniority and advancing to leadership positions in their committees. Will these women wield their power differently exhibiting a more consensus-oriented leadership style and/or advancing more policy priorities based on their interpretation of women's interests? While Nancy Pelosi's advancement to Speaker of the House marked a historic crack in what Pelosi called "the marble ceiling" (Marcus 2007), it remains to be seen how having more women in the highest echelons of party leadership will impact the direction of policy and the tone of politics.

# REFERENCES

Acker, Joan. 1992. "Gendered Institution: From Sex Roles to Gendered Institutions." *Contemporary Sociology* 21: 565–69.

Andersen, Kristi, 1996. *After Suffrage: Women in Partisan and Electoral Politics Before the New Deal.* Chicago: University of Chicago Press.

Anzia, Sarah, and Christopher R. Berry. 2011. "The Jackie (and Jill) Robinson Effect: Why Do Congresswomen Outperform Congressmen?" *American Journal of Political Science* 55: 478–93.

Barrett, Edith. 1995. "The Policy Priorities of African-American Women in State Legislatures." *Legislative Studies Quarterly* 20: 223–47.

Beckwith, Karen. 2007. "Numbers and Newness: The Descriptive and Substantive Representation of Women." *Canadian Journal of Political Science* 40: 27–49.

Benenson, Bob. 2005. "Former Rep. Shirley Chisholm Remembered for Opening Doors for Minorities and Women." *CQ Weekly* (January 10): 81.

Berkman, Michael B., and Robert E. O'Connor. 1993. "Do Women Legislators Matter? Female Legislators and State Abortion Policy." *American Politics Quarterly* 21: 102–24.

Bratton, Kathleen A. 2005. "Critical Mass Theory Revisited: The Behavior and Success of Token Women in State Legislatures." *Politics & Gender* 1: 97–125.

Bratton, Kathleen A., and Kerry L. Haynie. 1999. "Agenda Setting and Legislative Success in State Legislatures: The Effects of Gender and Race." *The Journal of Politics* 61: 658–79.

Bratton, Kathleen A., Kerry L. Haynie, and Beth Reingold. 2006. "Agenda Setting and African American Women in State Legislatures." *Journal of Women, Politics & Policy* 28: 71–96.

Brown, Nadia E. 2014. *Sisters in the Statehouse: Black Women and Legislative Decision Making.* New York: Oxford University Press.

Burrell, Barbara. *A Woman's Place Is in the House: Campaigning for Congress in the Feminist Era.* Ann Arbor: University of Michigan Press.

———. 2014. *Gender in Campaigns for the U.S. House of Representatives.* Ann Arbor: University of Michigan Press.

Bzdek, Vince. 2010. "Why Did Health-Care Reform Pass? Nancy Pelosi Was in Charge." *Washington Post* (March 28): B1.

Cadei, Emily, and Kathleen Hunter. 2009. "Political Gender Bias Remains Alive and Well." *CQ Weekly* (March 2): 459–61.

Carlson, Margaret. 2013. "Female Senators Battle Over Military Sex Assaults." *Bloomberg View*, November 20.

Carroll Susan J. 2002. "Representing Women: Congresswomen's Perception of Their Representational Roles." In *Women Transforming Congress*, edited by Cindy Simon Rosenthal, 50–68. Norman: University of Oklahoma Press.

Carroll Susan J., and Krista Jenkins. 2001. "Unrealized Opportunity? Term Limits and the Representation of Women in State Legislatures." *Women and Politics* 23(4): 1–30.

Carroll, Susan J., and Kira Sanbonmatsu. 2013. *More Women Can Run: Gender and Pathways to the State Legislatures.* New York: Oxford University Press.

Cassata, Donna, and Nedra Pickler. 2013. "Obama Orders Military to Review Sexual Assault." *Associated Press*, December 20.

Center for American Women and Politics. (CAWP). 2004. "Firsts for Women in U.S. Politics." New Brunswick: Center for American Women and Politics, Rutgers, The State University of New Jersey.

———. 2017a. "Fact Sheet: Women in State Legislatures 2017." New Brunswick: Center for American Women and Politics, Rutgers, The State University of New Jersey.

———. 2017b. "Fact Sheet: Women in the U.S. Congress 2017." New Brunswick: Center for American Women and Politics, Rutgers, The State University of New Jersey.

———. 2017c. "Fact Sheet: Women of Color in Elective Office 2017." New Brunswick: Center for American Women and Politics, Rutgers, The State University of New Jersey.

———. 2017d. "Fact Sheet: Women in Congress: Leadership Roles and Committee Chairs." New Brunswick: Center for American Women and Politics, Rutgers, The State University of New Jersey.

Childs, Sarah, and Mona Lena Krook. 2006. "Should Feminists Give Up on Critical Mass? A Contingent 'Yes.'" *Politics & Gender* 2(4): 522–30.

Cooperman, Rosalyn. 2013. "The Elephant in the Room: Conservative Women's PACs and Republican Women Candidates in U.S. House Elections, 2008–2012." Prepared for Presentation at the ECPR General Conference. Sciences Po Bordeaux, Domaine Universitaire.

Cox, Elizabeth M. 1996. *Women State and Territorial Legislators, 1895–1995: A State-by-State Analysis with Rosters of 6,000 Women.* Jefferson, NC: McFarland.

Cramer Walsh, Katherine. 2002. "Resonating to Be Heard: Gendered Debate on the Floor of the House." In *Women Transforming Congress*, edited by Cindy Simon Rosenthal, 370–96. Norman: University of Oklahoma Press.

Crespin, Michael H., and Janna L. Dietz. 2010. "If You Can't Join 'Em, Beat 'Em: The Gender Gap in Individual Donations to Congressional Candidates." *Political Research Quarterly* 63: 581-593.

Crowley, Jocelyn Elise. 2004. "When Tokens Matter." *Legislative Studies Quarterly* 29: 109–36.

Dahlerup, Drude. 2006. "The Story of the Theory of Critical Mass." *Politics & Gender* (2): 511–22.

Davidson, Roger H., Walter J. Oleszek, Frances E. Lee, and Eric Schickler. 2015. *Congress and Its Members*, 15th ed. Washington, DC: CQ Press.

Deckman, Melissa, and John McTague. 2014. "Did the 'War on Women' Work? Women, Men, and the Birth Control Mandate in the 2012 Presidential Election." *American Politics Research* 43: 3-26.

Dodson, Debra L. 2006. *The Impact of Women in Congress.* New York: Oxford University Press.

Dodson, Debra L., and Susan Carroll. 1991. *Reshaping the Agenda: Women in State Legislatures.* New Brunswick: Center for American Women and Politics, Rutgers, State University of New Jersey.

Dolan, Julie. 1997. "Support for Women's Interests in the 103rd Congress: The Distinct Impact of Congressional Women." *Women & Politics* 18: 81–94.

Dolan, Kathleen. 2001. "Electoral Context, Issues, and Voting for Women in the 1990s." *Women & Politics* 23(1-2): 21–36.

———. 2004. *Voting for Women: How the Public Evaluates Women Candidates.* Boulder: Westview Press.

Dovi, Suzanne. 2002. "Preferable Descriptive Representatives: Or Will Just Any Woman, Black, or Latino Do?" *American Political Science Review* 96: 745–54.

Duerst-Lahti, Georgia. 2002. "Knowing Congress as a Gendered Institution: Manliness and the Implications of Women in Congress." In *Women Transforming Congress,* edited by Cindy Simon Rosenthal, 20–49. Norman: University of Oklahoma Press.

Elder, Laurel. 2008. "Whither Republican Women: The Growing Partisan Gap Among Women in Congress." *The Forum* 6: Issue 1, Article 13.

———. 2012. "The Partisan Gap Among Women State Legislators." *Journal of Women, Politics & Policy* 33: 65–85.

———. 2014. "Women and the Parties: An Analysis of Republican and Democratic Strategists for Recruiting Women Candidates." Presented at American Political Science Association Conference, Washington, DC, August 28–31.

Etoniru, Nneka. 2014. "2014 Election Blog: A Look at Gender Quotas Ahead of Latin America's 2014 Legislative Votes." January 6. http://www.as-coa.org/blogs/2014-election-blog-look-gender-quotas-ahead-latin-americas-2014-legislative-votes (accessed June 23, 2015).

Feinstein, Dianne. 2006. "Women in Politics and Business." http://www.feinstein.senate.gov/public/index.cfm/speeches?ID=5aceabe1-7e9c-9af9-7152-0a03ca4a9fe6 (accessed June 3, 2015).

Fraga, Luis Ricardo, Linda Lopez, Valerie Martinez-Ebers, and Ricardo Ramirez. 2006. "Gender and Ethnicity: Patterns of Electoral Success and Legislative Advocacy Among Latina and Latino State Officials in Four States." *Journal of Women, Politics, & Policy* 28: 121–45.

———. 2008. "Representing Gender and Ethnicity: Strategic Intersectionality." In *Legislative Women: Getting Elected, Getting Ahead,* edited by Beth Reingold, 157–74. Boulder: Lynne Rienner Publishers.

Frederick, Brian. 2009. "Are Female House Members Still More Liberal in a Polarized Era? The Conditional Nature of the Relationship Between Descriptive and Substantive Representation." *Congress and the Presidency* 36: 181–202.

———. 2010. "Gender and Patterns of Roll Call Voting in the US Senate." *Congress and the Presidency* 37: 103–24.

Garcia Bedolla, Lisa, Katherine Tate, and Janelle Wong. 2014. "Indelible Effects: The Impact of Women of Color in the U.S. Congress." In *Women and Elective Office,* 3rd ed., edited by Sue Thomas and Clyde Wilcox, 235–52. New York: Oxford University Press.

Gelb, Joyce, and Marian Lief Palley. 1996. *Women and Public Policies: Reassessing Gender Politics.* Charlottesville, VA: University Press of Virginia.

Gertzog, Irwin. 1995. *Congressional Women: Their Recruitment, Integration, and Behavior.* 2nd ed. Westport, CT: Praeger Publishers.

Grey, Sandra. 2006. "Numbers and Beyond: The Relevance of Critical Mass in Gender Research." *Politics & Gender* 2(4): 492–502.

Hall, Richard. 1996. *Participation in Congress.* New Haven: Yale University Press.

Halloran, Liz. 2009. "House Approves Bills to Fight Gender Wage Gap." NPR.org, January 9, 2009.

Hawkesworth, Mary. 2003. "Congressional Enactments of Race-Gender: Toward a Theory of Raced-Gendered Institutions." *American Political Science Review* 97: 529–50.

Hawkings, David. 2017. "House Republican Women See a Boost in Authority." Roll Call, January 18.

Henneberger, Melinda. 2014. "Sen. McCaskill's Military Sexual-Assault Bill Is Meatier Than Advertised." *Washington Post*, March 9.

Herrnson, Paul S. 2012. *Congressional Elections: Campaigning at Home and in Washington*, 6th edition. Washington, DC: CQ Press.

Inglehart, Ronald, and Pippa Norris. 2003. *Rising Tide: Gender Equality and Cultural Change*. New York: Cambridge University Press.

Jacobson, Gary. 2013. *The Politics of Congressional Elections*. 8th ed. New York: Pearson.

Johnson, Cathy Marie, Georgia Duerst-Lahti, and Noelle H. Norton. 2007. *Creating Gender: The Sexual Politics of Welfare Policy*. Boulder: Lynne Rienner.

Kanter, Rosabeth Moss. 1977. "Some Effects of Proportions on Group Life: Skewed Sex Ratios and Responses to Token Women." *American Journal of Sociology* 82: 965–90.

Kaper. Stacy. 2014. "Kirsten Gillibrand Blames White House in Failure of Military Sexual-Assault Bill." *National Journal*, March 7.

Kaptur, Marcy. 1996. *Women of Congress: A Twentieth-Century Odyssey*. Washington, DC: Congressional Quarterly.

Kathlene, Lynn. 1994. "Power and Influence of State Legislative Policymaking: The Interaction of Gender and Position in Committee Hearing Debates." *American Political Science Review* 88: 560–76.

———. 1995. "Alternative Views of Crime: Legislative Policymaking in Gendered Terms." *Journal of Politics* 57: 696–723.

Kenney, Sally J. 1996. "New Research on Gendered Political Institutions." *Political Research Quarterly* 49: 445–66.

Kitchens, Karin E., and Michele L. Swers. 2016. "Why Aren't There More Republican Women in Congress? Gender, Partisanship, and Fundraising Support in the 2010 and 2012 Elections." *Politics & Gender* 12: 648–676.

Krook, Mona Lena. 2009. *Quotas for Women in Politics: Gender and Candidate Selection Reform Worldwide*. New York: Oxford University Press.

Levy, Dena, Charles Tien, and Rachelle Aved. 2002. "Do Differences Matter? Women Members of Congress and the Hyde Amendment." *Women & Politics* 23(1/2): 105–27.

MacDonald, Jason A., and Erin E. O'Brien. 2011. "Quasi-Experimental Design, Constituency, and Advancing Women's Interests: 'Critically' Reexamining the Influence of Gender on Substantive Representation." *Political Research Quarterly* 64: 472–86.

Manning, Jennifer E., and Colleen J. Shogan. 2012. "African-American Members of the United States Congress: 1870–2012." *Congressional Research Service*, November 26.

Mansbridge, Jane. 1999. "Should Blacks Represent Blacks and Women Represent Women? A Contingent 'Yes.'" *Journal of Politics* 61: 628–57.

Marcos, Cristina. 2016. "115th Congress Will Be Most Racially Diverse in History." *The Hill*, November 17.

Marcus, Ruth. 2007. "Grandma with a Gavel." *Washington Post* (January 10): A13.

Mikulski, Barbara, Kay Bailey Hutchison, Dianne Feinstein, Barbara Boxer, Patty Murray, Olympia Snowe, Susan Collins, Mary Landrieu, and Blanche L. Lincoln with Catherine Whitney. 2001. *Nine and Counting: The Women of the Senate.* New York: Harper Collins Publishers.

Mimms, Sarah. 2014. "A Ceiling of Her Making." *National Journal,* September 20.

National Conference of State Legislatures. 2015. "The Term-Limited States." http://www.ncsl.org/research/about-state-legislatures/chart-of-term-limits-states.aspx (accessed June 1, 2015).

Nelson, Rebecca. 2015. "The Conservative Answer to Feminism." *National Journal,* May 6.

Norrander, Barbara, and Clyde Wilcox. 2014. "Trends in the Geography of Women in the United States State Legislatures." In *Women and Elective Office,* 3rd ed., edited by Sue Thomas and Clyde Wilcox, 273–87. New York: Oxford University Press.

Norris, Pippa, and Mona Lena Krook. 2014. "Women in Elective Office Worldwide: Barriers and Opportunities." In *Women and Elective Office,* 3rd ed., edited by Sue Thomas and Clyde Wilcox, 288–306. New York: Oxford University Press.

Norton, Noelle H. 1999. "Committee Influence Over Controversial Policy: The Reproductive Policy Case." *Policy Studies Journal* 27: 203–16.

———. 2002. "Transforming Congress from the Inside: Women in Committee." In *Women Transforming Congress,* edited by Cindy Simon Rosenthal, 316–40. Norman: University of Oklahoma Press.

Office of the Historian and Office of the Clerk of the House of Representatives. 2013. *Hispanic Americans in Congress 1822–2012.* Washington, DC: United States Government Printing Office.

Orey, Byron D'Andra, Wendy Smooth, Kimberly S. Adams, and Kisha Harris-Clark. 2006. "Race and Gender Matter; Refining Models of Legislative Policy Making in State Legislatures." *Journal of Women, Politics & Policy* 28: 97–119.

Osborn, Tracy L. 2012. *How Women Represent Women: Political Parties, Gender, and Representation in the State Legislatures.* New York: Oxford University Press.

Osborn, Tracy L., and Rebecca Kreitzer. 2014. "Women State Legislators: Women's Issues in Partisan Environments." In *Women and Elective Office: Past, Present and Future,* edited by Sue Thomas and Clyde Wilcox, 181–98. New York: Oxford University Press.

Osborn, Tracy, and Jeanette Morehouse Mendez. 2010. "Speaking as Women: Women and Floor Speeches in the Senate." *Journal of Women, Politics, & Policy* 31: 1-21.

Palmer, Barbara, and Dennis Simon. 2008. *Breaking the Political Glass Ceiling: Women and Congressional Elections.* 2nd ed. New York: Routledge.

Paxton, Pamela, and Melanie M. Hughes. 2007. *Women, Politics, and Power: A Global Perspective.* Thousand Oaks, CA: Pine Forge Press.

Pear, Robert. 2009. "House Votes to Expand Children's Health Care." *New York Times,* January 15.

Pearson, Kathryn, and Logan Dancey. 2011a. "Speaking for the Underrepresented in the House of Representatives: Voicing Women's Interests in a Partisan Era." *Politics & Gender* 7: 493–519.

———. 2011b. "Elevating Women's Voice in Congress: Speech Participation in the House of Representatives." *Political Research Quarterly* 64(4): 910–23.

Pearson, Kathryn, and Eric McGhee. 2013. "What It Takes to Win: Questioning 'Gender Neutral' Outcomes in United SStates House Elections." *Politics & Gender* 9: 439–62.

Peters, Jr., Ronald M., and Cindy Simon Rosenthal. 2010. *Speaker Nancy Pelosi and the New American Politics.* Oxford: Oxford University Press.

Peterson, Kristina. 2014. "Senate Clears Way for McCaskill's Military Sex-Assault Bill." *Wall Street Journal,* March 6.

Phillips, Anne. 1991. *Engendering Democracy.* University Park: The Pennsylvania State University Press.

———. 1995. *The Politics of Presence.* Oxford: Oxford University Press.

———. 1998. "Democracy and Representation: Or, Why Should It Matter Who Our Representatives Are?" In *Feminism and Politics,* edited by Anne Phillips, 224–240. New York: Oxford University Press.

Pitkin, Hanna Fenichel. 1967. *The Concept of Representation.* Berkeley: University of California Press.

Poggione, Sarah. 2004. "Exploring Gender Differences in State Legislators' Policy Preferences." *Political Research Quarterly* 57: 305–14.

Political Parity. 2015. Primary Hurdles Report. Available at https://www.political parity.org/wp-content/uploads/2015/01/primary-hurdles-full-report.pdf.

Poole, Keith T., and Howard Rosenthal. 1997. *Congress: A Political-Economic History of Roll Call Voting.* New York: Oxford University Press.

Reingold, Beth. 1992. "Concepts of Representation Among Female and Male State Legislators." *Legislative Studies Quarterly* 17: 509–37.

———. 2000. *Representing Women: Sex, Gender, and Legislative Behavior in Arizona and California.* Chapel Hill: University of North Carolina Press.

Reingold, Beth, and Adrienne R. Smith. 2012. "Welfare Policymaking and Intersections of Race, Ethnicity, and Gender in United States State Legislatures." *American Journal of Political Science* 56: 131–47.

Rhode, David W. 1991. *Parties and Leaders in the Post-reform House.* Chicago: University of Chicago Press.

Rosenthal, Cindy Simon. 1997. "A View of Their Own: Women's Committee Leadership Styles and State Legislatures." *Policy Studies Journal* 25: 585–600.

———. 1998. *When Women Lead: Integrative Leadership in State Legislatures.* New York: Oxford University Press.

———. 2000. "Gender Styles in State Legislative Committees: Raising Their Voices in Resolving Conflict." *Women & Politics* 21: 21–45.

———. 2008. "Climbing Higher: Opportunities and Obstacles within the Party System." In *Legislative Women: Getting Elected, Getting Ahead,* edited by Beth Reingold, 197–222. Boulder: Lynne Rienner Publishers.

Saint-Germain, Michelle A. 1989. "Does Their Difference Make a Difference? The Impact of Women on Public Policy in the Arizona Legislature." *Social Science Quarterly* 70: 956–68.

Sanbonmatsu, Kira. 2002. "Political Parties and the Recruitment of Women to State Legislatures." *Journal of Politics* 64: 791–809.

———. 2006. *Where Women Run: Gender & Party in the American States.* Ann Arbor: University of Michigan Press.

———. 2014. "Women's Election to Office in the Fifty States: Opportunities and Challenges." In *Gender and Elections: Shaping the Future of American Politics,* Third Edition. Eds. Susan J. Carroll and Richard L. Fox. New York: Cambridge University Press 265-287.

Sandalow, Marc. 2008. *Madam Speaker: Nancy Pelosi's Life, Times, and Rise to Power.* New York: Modern Times.

Shogan, Colleen J. 2001. "Speaking Out: An Analysis of Democratic and Republican Women-Invoked Rhetoric of the 105th Congress." *Women & Politics* 23: 129–46.

Sinclair, Barbara. 1989. *The Transformation of the US Senate.* Baltimore: Johns Hopkins University Press.

Smooth, Wendy. 2008. "Gender, Race, and the Exercise of Power and Influence." In *Legislative Women: Getting Elected, Getting Ahead,* edited by Beth Reingold, 175–96. Boulder: Lynne Rienner Publishers.

Stewart, Phil, and Patricia Zengerle. 2013. "Senators, Military Brass Battle Over Curbing Sexual Assault." *Reuters,* June 4.

Storing, Herbert J. 1981. *The Anti-Federalist: Writings by Opponents of the Constitution.* Chicago: University of Chicago Press.

Swers, Michele L. 1998. "Are Congresswomen More Likely to Vote for Women's Issue Bills Than Their Male Colleagues?" *Legislative Studies Quarterly* 23: 435–48.

———. 2002. *The Difference Women Make: The Policy Impact of Women in Congress.* Chicago: University of Chicago Press.

———. 2007. "Building a Reputation on National Security: The Impact of Stereotypes Related to Gender and Military Experience." *Legislative Studies Quarterly* 32: 559–96.

———. 2013. *Women in the Club: Gender and Policy Making in the Senate.* Chicago: University of Chicago Press.

———. 2016a. "Pursuing Women's Interests in Partisan Times: Explaining Gender Differences in Legislative Activity on Health, Education, and Women's Health Issues." *Journal of Women, Politics & Policy* 37: 249-273.

———. 2016b. "Women & Legislative Leadership in the U.S. Congress: Representing Women's Interests in Partisan Times." *Daedalus* 145: 44–56.

———. 2017. "Gender and Party Politics in a Polarized Era" In *Party and Procedure in the United States Congress,* 2nd Edition, edited by Jacob R. Straus and Matthew E. Glassman. Lanham, MD: Rowman & Littlefield.

Swers, Michele L., and Christine C. Kim. 2013. "Replacing Sandra Day O'Connor: Gender and the Politics of Supreme Court Nominations." *Journal of Women, Politics, & Policy* 34: 23–48.

Swers, Michele L., and Carin Larson. 2005. "Women and Congress: Do They Act as Advocates for Women's Issues?" In *Women and Elective Office: Past, Present, and Future,* 2nd ed., edited by Sue Thomas and Clyde Wilcox, 110–28. New York: Oxford University Press.

Tate, Katherine. 2003. *Black Faces in the Mirror: African Americans and Their Representatives in the U.S. Congress.* Princeton: Princeton University Press.

———. 2013. *Concordance: Black Lawmaking in the U.S. Congress from Carter to Obama.* Ann Arbor: University of Michigan Press.

Thomas, Sue. 1994. *How Women Legislate.* New York: Oxford University Press.

———. 1997. "Why Gender Matters: The Perceptions of Women Officeholders." *Women & Politics* 17: 27–53.

Thomsen, Danielle M. 2015. "Why So Few (Republican) Women? Explaining the Partisan Imbalance of Women in the United States Congress." *Legislative Studies Quarterly* 40: 295–323.

Tripp, Aili Mari. 2013. "Women and Politics in Africa Today." *Democracy in Africa*, December 9. http://democracyinafrica.org/women-politics-africa-today/(accessed June 23, 2015).

———. 2015. *Women and Power in Post-conflict Africa*. New York: Cambridge University Press.

Volden, Craig, Alan E. Wiseman, and Dana E. Wittmer. 2013. "When Are Women More Effective Lawmakers Than Men?" *American Journal of Political Science* 57: 326–41.

Werner, Emmy E. 1968. "Women in the State Legislatures." *Western Political Quarterly* 21: 40–50.

Whitlock, Craig. 2013. "Military Chiefs Balk at Sexual-Assault Bill." *Washington Post*, June 4.

Winter, Nicholas J. G. 2010. "Masculine Republicans and Feminine Democrats: Gender and Americans' Explicit and Implicit Images of the Political Parties." *Political Behavior* 32: 587–618.

Wolbrecht, Christina. 2000. *The Politics of Women's Rights: Parties, Positions, and Change*. Princeton: Princeton University Press.

———. 2002. "Female Legislators and the Women's Rights Agenda." In *Women Transforming Congress*, edited by Cindy Simon Rosenthal, 170–97. Norman: University of Oklahoma Press.

# 8

# Women in the Executive Branch

As the Pentagon and Congress grapple with how to reduce sexual assault in the military, here's an idea that would transform and improve military culture: Recruit, retain and promote far more women to the upper ranks. (Anu Bhagwati, former Marine Corps Captain and Executive Director of Service Women's Action Network, 2013)

Sexual assault has been a serious problem in the US military for decades. In the spring of 2013, a few short months after Defense Secretary Leon Panetta opened most military combat positions to women, the Senate Armed Forces Committee held high-profile hearings on the subject. At issue was a bill proposed by Senator Kirsten Gillibrand (D-NY) aimed at reforming the way the military investigates and prosecutes allegations of military sexual assault. Senator Gillibrand cited statistics from the Department of Defense suggesting that approximately one percent of alleged perpetrators were ever held accountable for their crimes. Witnesses before the committee offered numerous recommendations for fixing a broken system, such as supplying victims with lawyers and other advocates, using civilian courts to prosecute members of the military, and redirecting prevention efforts toward stopping perpetrators rather than counseling potential victims to avoid assault.

Yet, Captain Bhagwati offered a much more profound solution: change the culture of the military by adding more women. In her testimony before the committee, Ms. Bhagwati stressed the additional importance of having a critical mass of women, noting that a sea change in military culture was necessary and would only emerge when women constituted about 20 percent of military personnel, offering that only then could we expect to see "climates start to shift when it comes to discrimination, harassment, and assault" (United States. Congress. Senate. Committee on Armed Services. 2013). Women today hold more than 14 percent of all military positions, but their share has remained virtually unchanged for the last 10 years, suggesting that reaching critical mass will take many years (Women's Research and Education Institute 2013).

Captain Bhagwati offered very similar solutions four years earlier when lamenting the quality of health care provided to female veterans seeking care in VA medical facilities. Testifying before a House Veterans Affairs Committee, Bhagwati argued that VA facilities would need to undergo "an enormous cultural shift" to recognize the specific medical needs of its female patients and to make strides in treating female patients with greater dignity and respect (United States. Congress. House. Committee on Veterans' Affairs. 2009). In a similar fashion, she emphasized how increasing the number of women in key health care positions would improve the quality of care provided to female veterans.

Captain Bhagwati's faith in the promise of increasing women's descriptive representation to improve women's experiences in these two masculine organizations reflects three themes that we draw upon in this chapter. First, many feminist scholars argue that the executive branch of government is the most masculine of the three branches of government and that this masculinity privileges men and disadvantages women (Brown 1998; Duerst-Lahti and Kelly 1995). Executive leaders are expected to demonstrate masculine traits such as assertiveness, decisiveness, and command. Feminist scholars argue that combined with gender role expectations about proper behavior for men and women, a preference for masculine leadership, or *masculinism*, creates significant barriers for women seeking to fit into and mold executive environments.

Second, and related to the first, women in the executive branch of government are particularly noticeable as "the other." Their small numbers, combined with individuals' greater visibility in hierarchical structures such as the executive, guarantee that they are outsiders in a man's world and must navigate multiple pressures associated with being perceived as tokens by dominants in the organization. For women of color, these pressures are often even greater: their status as racial and gender outsiders makes them especially visible. As Bhagwati and Rosabeth Moss Kanter (1977) contend, such pressures diminish only when groups in the minority reach critical mass status within an organization, when they are no longer such a visible minority among leadership.

Finally, despite these gendered challenges, female executives and public servants can and often do make a difference for women in their organizations and the larger population. Indeed, Bhagwati's belief that increasing the numbers of women in leadership positions will make the military and veterans' medical facilities more responsive to female service members is borne out by much contemporary research in the field of representative bureaucracy.

This chapter examines women's contributions to governance within the executive branch of government. After sketching out women's descriptive representation in executive positions, we turn our attention to the themes highlighted above to frame our discussion of substantive representation: Does policy look different, or is it more likely to consider the multitude of women's perspectives, when women wield executive branch positions? Do masculinism and tokenism work against women's inclinations to speak out or even recognize the ways in which policy differentially impacts women? Do these constraints get in the way of true responsiveness to the female citizenry? Will women at the helm of the executive branch lead differently than men, or has history created cultural norms and expectations that demand a particularly masculine type of leadership in these types of positions?

## WOMEN'S ACCESS TO THE EXECUTIVE BRANCH

### Masculinity, Power, and the Executive Branch

Captain Bhagwati's faith in the power of greater numbers of women in leadership ranks reminds us that the actions of public servants can make a real difference in the lives of the citizenry. These people rarely appear in the spotlight, but nonetheless play important roles in shaping government responsiveness to reflect public desires. Often referred to as the fourth branch of government, the executive branch is staffed by a multitude of individuals who serve alongside the president and state governors. Who are these executive branch individuals? How well have women fared in penetrating the ranks of the executive branch? What can we learn about women's symbolic and descriptive representation by focusing on the executive branch?

As discussed in chapter 4, women lag far behind men in terms of putting themselves forward as candidates for elected office, with the effect that women are underrepresented in the vast majority of elected offices. But in the executive branch, typically it is only those at the very top of the hierarchy, such as presidents and governors, who achieve their positions through elections. The majority of executive branch officials receive their positions through presidential or gubernatorial appointment or civil service merit-based systems. Even so, women remain underrepresented in most executive branch positions. Why?

Many feminist scholars point to *gender power* or *masculinism* to explain the paucity of women at the top (Duerst-Lahti and Kelly 1995; King, 1995; Stivers 2002). Masculinism is a system of formal and informal power arrangements that privilege masculine character traits, customs, and operating procedures over feminine ones. The presidency is a particularly good example of gender power at work. Since only men have been presidents in the United States, they have essentially defined what it means to be president. Donald Trump not so subtly invoked masculinism in his presidential campaign, criticizing Hillary Clinton for not having that "presidential look" and attacking Republican candidate Carly Fiorina's appearance, asking "Can you imagine that, the face of our next president?" He could do so because women seeking the presidency will always be "the other" and judged by the masculine standards established by their male predecessors. Women entering such masculine domains do not have the liberty to change the rules of the game, but rather must go along to get along. The American populace expects the president to be assertive, commanding, and tough and will likely judge all future presidents, male and female, by these standards.

Many feminist writers have further argued that masculinism is especially prevalent in hierarchical organizations, with the consequence that females working in hierarchical organizations such as the executive branch have to manage their femaleness to succeed, whereas men face no comparable challenge. Because their femaleness sets them apart, they risk being punished if they do not abide by the gendered standards and norms of their organizations. The Department of Defense is one such example of an executive branch organization, one with an environment particularly imbued with the masculine values of discipline, order, and hierarchy. Cynthia Enloe (1983) argues that women entering masculine domains such as the military are constantly reminded of their outsider status such that "women may serve the military, but they can never be permitted to *be* the military" (15). The military has relied on women for years, as nurses, military wives, civilian workers, soldiers, and prostitutes but has kept them on the periphery to preserve the essentially masculine nature of the military. According to Enloe, such a sexual division of labor is a mechanism for keeping women marginal to the core masculine identity of the military. Sexual harassment and assault of female members serve a similar purpose, reminding women that they are interlopers into a masculine environment where men have always set the standards for behavior and have no interest in relinquishing this power. Sharon Mastracci and Lauren Bowman (2015), in their analysis of gendered public organizations, argue that such behavior is typical, that "organizational norms and practices are rooted in those of their founders, who in older public organizations were almost exclusively male, and those structures are resistant to change" (866).

Women's difficulties in reaching the high-ranking and influential positions in the executive branch have been studied extensively by public administration scholars, who employ two metaphors to illustrate women's career advancement struggles in public organizations: glass ceilings and glass walls. As the name glass ceiling suggests, the higher up the hierarchy one goes, the fewer women one finds. Popularized in the 1990s to explain why few women were serving as CEOs in corporate boardrooms and in positions as top government executives, the glass ceiling metaphor suggests that women can rise only so high in organizations before an invisible barrier precludes further advancement. Glass walls, on the other hand, keep women segregated in particularly feminine occupations or within agencies whose functions are most consistent with feminine gender stereotypes such as health care and education and underrepresented in agencies with masculine foci such as defense, foreign affairs, and law enforcement (Duerst-Lahti and Kelly 1995). If all agencies and positions were equally powerful, such occupational sorting would cause little concern. But according to Meredith Newman (1995), these patterns result in female administrators being placed in relatively less powerful positions that afford less influence and discretion on the job than afforded to their male colleagues.

Hillary Clinton famously drew on the glass ceiling metaphor in her 2008 bid for the Democratic nomination, quipping that "although we weren't able to shatter that highest, hardest glass ceiling this time . . . it's got about 18 million cracks in it" (Milbank 2008). She was speaking as the most formidable female presidential candidate in the history of the United States, coming closer to the office of the presidency than had any woman before her (see also chapter 5). Eight years later, Barack Obama heaped high praise on Clinton during his convention speech, arguing "there has never been a man or a woman . . . more qualified than Hillary Clinton to serve as president of the United States of America." Yet despite winning the popular vote, she suffered defeat at the hands of a man with zero political experience who regularly claimed that he alone could solve America's problems. For all of the women who have ever been skipped over for a promotion only to see a less qualified man rise to the position, the glass ceiling metaphor rang all too true. Clinton's status as one of the most experienced politicians in America, however, did not protect her from the obstacles faced by many other women banging up against the glass ceiling, such as subtle discrimination as well as gendered stereotypes about her capacity to lead (see also preface).

Despite women's historic omission from the US presidency, a growing number of women are building executive experience in other venues, including governors' mansions, presidential and gubernatorial administrations, and state and local governments. We turn now to women's descriptive representation in these domains.

## Descriptive Representation

### Governors

Female descriptive representation in the governor's mansions reached an all-time high of 18 percent in 2009, when women were at the helm of nine

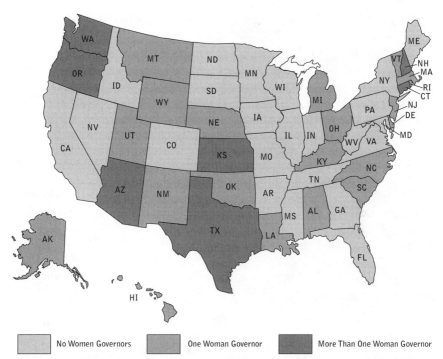

No Women Governors      One Woman Governor      More Than One Woman Governor

**Figure 8.1.   How Women Have Fared as Governors Across the States, 1925–2017.**
*Source*: Center for American Women and Politics, State Fact Sheets. Accessed online at
http://www.cawp.rutgers.edu/fast_facts/resources/state_fact_sheet.php.

states. In the history of the United States, a total of 37 women have served
as their states' governors, with Democratic women enjoying a slight historic
advantage. Yet, only about half of the states have ever elected a female head
of state (see Figure 8.1). Women of color were entirely absent from governors' mansions until 2010, when two Republican women made history by
becoming the first female governors in their respective states as well as the
first two women of color to win governors' seats in the history of the United
States. Susana Martinez became the first Latina governor in the country
when New Mexico overwhelmingly chose her over her male opponent and
Nikki Haley became the first Asian American woman to lead a state when
elected in the same year by the voters of South Carolina (Center for American Women and Politics 2015a).

Seven different states have sent more than one woman to the governor's
mansion. A girl born in Arizona in 1997 might erroneously conclude that
female governors were the norm as three different female governors
ruled the state of Arizona for 18 consecutive years from 1997 to 2015.
This historic feat is not likely to be matched anytime soon—no other state

On January 19, 2011, Nikki Haley became the first female Governor of South Carolina and the first Asian American woman elected governor in the United States. She thanks her family as she delivers her first State of the State address at the South Carolina Statehouse in Columbia, South Carolina. She currently serves as Donald Trump's Ambassador to the United Nations.

*Source*: AP Photo / Brett Flashnick.

has ever elected sequential female governors.

Women are clearly faring better in reaching these top political positions in the states compared to their failed attempts at the US presidency, yet their representation lags behind that of their sisters in the legislative and judicial branches of government, where women constitute closer to 25 percent of positions (see chapters 7 and 9). What accounts for this difference? Consistent with masculinism discussed earlier, some scholarship suggests that women seeking executive positions have greater difficulty convincing the public they are cut out for the job. The general public typically assumes that women's stereotypical strengths are better suited for legislative arenas than executive positions (Rosenwasser and Dean 1989). When the public thinks of a successful executive, it typically lists qualities such as strength, aggression, decisiveness, and the ability to get things done. But the same public typically gives women credit for being compassionate, sensitive, and cooperative (Huddy and Terkildsen 1993; Kahn 1996).

Consistent with this explanation, the first three female governors in the United States were not originally elected to their posts, but gained their positions when their husbands could no longer serve. The very first woman to hold this position was Nellie Tayloe Ross, a Democrat from Wyoming. Her husband fell ill and died while serving as governor, prompting the Wyoming Democratic Party to ask Ross to run in his stead. She was their unanimous choice and agreed to run to continue her husband's work. She won a special election to fill his seat by a margin of over 8,000 votes, no small feat for a state that was then, and continues to be, strongly Republican (Scharff 1995). Two years later, she lost her reelection bid to serve a second term. In retrospect, she lamented that she should have done more to court the women's vote. Wyoming became the first territory in the country to grant full female suffrage (in 1869), but Ross explained that she was wary of making her gender a focus of the campaign and did little to reach out to women's organizations (Scharff 1995). As we discuss later in the chapter, executive women are often reluctant to place too great an emphasis on gender, worrying that doing so will only remind others of their status as outsiders playing a man's game.

Texas elected Miriam "Ma" Ferguson in the same electoral cycle in 1924, but Nellie Ross enjoys the distinction of being the very first female governor in the United States because she was inaugurated some 15 days before Mrs. Ferguson. Ferguson succeeded her husband Governor Jim Ferguson when he was prohibited from running for his old seat because he had been impeached, convicted, and removed from office for corruption. Ironically, the Fergusons were opposed to female suffrage on the grounds that women's greatest contributions to society were in the home. Accordingly, the candidacy of "Ma" Ferguson emphasized her virtues as a feminine, traditional woman, as someone who would largely serve as a stand-in while Jim Ferguson ran the show behind the scenes (Sallee 1996).

# THE FIRST WOMAN GOVERNOR
*Wyoming's Governor*
## THE WOMAN WHO MADE GOOD

NELLIE TAYLOE ROSS

Businesslike—Able—Courageous. She Has Earned Re-election

Nellie Tayloe Ross became the first female governor in the United States in 1925 when she won a special election to succeed her deceased husband in office.
*Source*: Nellie Tayloe Ross Collection, American Heritage Center, University of Wyoming.

Lurleen Burns Wallace became the third female governor almost 40 years later. Again, her husband preceded her in office and she ran to take his place because Alabama state law prohibited him from serving two consecutive terms as governor. In a strange twist of fate, Lurleen Wallace was hospitalized with a cancerous tumor while in office and her husband effectively took over all her official responsibilities during and after the hospitalization (Stineman 1980).

What can we glean about women's representation in governors' offices, offices that often serve as a stepping-stone to the US presidency? These first three female governors were largely symbolic placeholders, not true power brokers who demonstrated women's rightful place in presiding over the states. Women have come a long way since they were expected to be stand-ins for their husbands. But the fact that so few females serve as governor at any given time ensures that they remain highly visible and held up as symbols for all to see. Former Governor Ann Richards recognized that she was unusual for a Texas governor and playfully compared herself to a two-headed cow, offering, "Some people are willing to let me into their office and talk to me just because they want to see the genuine article" (Cook 1993). She symbolized a new breed of politicians for Texas: the female variety. When elected in 2010, South Carolina Governor Nikki Haley was hailed as the "new face of the south" and many pundits suggested that her election symbolized a new Republican party, more open and inclusive to women and racial minorities than ever before (Campo-Flores 2010). Across the country in New Mexico, Susana Martinez became the first Latina governor in the United States, and the Republican party soon thereafter appointed her to co-chair its "Future Majority Project" to recruit, train, and support more diverse candidates, focusing especially on Latinos and women (Republican State Leadership Committee n.d.; Sanbonmatsu 2013).

## Presidential and Gubernatorial Cabinets

Soon after election day, one of the first orders of business for the president-elect is to begin assembling his or her administration. Each president has responsibility for appointing thousands of individuals to work in the executive branch assisting him or her in fulfilling the constitutional responsibility to "faithfully execute the laws of the Nation." According to the latest version of the Plum Book, the federal government's listing of the top policymaking positions in the federal government, President Barack Obama made approximately 8,000 federal appointments after winning reelection in 2012. Many of these positions are fairly routine: only about 1,000 of them actually require Senate confirmation (Garcia 1997) and most receive very little public attention.

The most highly publicized and scrutinized executive branch appointments go to the members of the president's cabinet, at minimum composed of the vice president and the heads of the 15 executive departments. Most presidents also bestow cabinet rank on a few additional positions, such as the White House chief of staff, the administrator of the Environmental Protection Agency, the director of the Office of Management and Budget, the chair of the Council of Economic Advisers, the US Trade Representative, and the US Ambassador to the United Nations.

Most presidents seek to improve upon the record of their predecessor when it comes to appointing women and minorities, if not by increasing their sheer numbers, then by making history by increasing the diversity of the federal service by making appointment "firsts." These appointees often symbolize that the president is responsive to all the people, and that his administration will "look like America." In her analysis of presidential cabinets going back to Franklin Delano Roosevelt, MaryAnne Borrelli (2002) argues that presidents historically tapped women to serve in positions distant from the president's agenda with few opportunities to influence policy, more valuable for their symbolic than substantive impact.

Yet women's fortunes began improving under the Clinton administration. President Bill Clinton became the first president to appoint a woman to the inner cabinet, the most prestigious positions that consist of the heads of Treasury, State, Defense, and Justice. He selected Janet Reno as his Attorney General, and his two successors, George W. Bush and Barack Obama, followed suit by appointing Condoleezza Rice and Hillary Clinton as their Secretaries of State. In addition, all three of these presidents appointed women of color to posts they had never held before, selected women for positions central to their policy agendas, and chose women with substantial backgrounds in their designated areas so that they would be able to hit the ground running (Borrelli 2010; Dolan 2012). For example, Barack Obama appointed Janet Yellen as the very first female head of the Federal Reserve System, arguably one of the most influential positions in the world, let alone in Washington. She came to the position with extensive experience in the financial sector, including previous stints as the chair of the Council of Economic Advisers and a board member of the Federal Reserve System (Mui 2014).

As of this writing, Donald Trump appears willing to break ranks with his predecessors, nominating only white men to serve in his inner cabinet and selecting women for positions relatively distant from his agenda. Despite his promises to serve as a president for all the people, Donald Trump's initial cabinet looks a lot more like himself than America. Especially noteworthy are the number of billionaires with no government experience he has called to serve. One of these individuals is his pick for Secretary of Education, billionaire philanthropist Betsy DeVos. A strong proponent of private school vouchers who has no government experience, DeVos's nomination met with scathing opposition from the largest teachers' union in the country, who objected to her corporate approach and "cookie-cutter solutions" for improving public education (Markon, Costa, and Brown 2016; Berman 2017).

At this juncture, Donald Trump's record in terms of appointing women is a mixed bag. Although he has nominated fewer women to cabinet-level positions than did Barack Obama in either of his two terms, his selection of women for 20% of these positions is similar to the records of his three Republican presidential predecessors (see Figure 8.2). Nor is Trump breaking new ground by appointing important "firsts" to his cabinet or by creating a particularly racially diverse cabinet. His selection of two women of color to join the cabinet, Nikki Haley as Ambassador to the United Nations and Elaine Chao as Secretary of Transportation, places him on par with both Democratic and Republican presidents going back to Bill Clinton, at least in terms of numbers (see Figure 8.2). Yet Chao already made history as the first Asian American woman to serve in a presidential cabinet when George W. Bush tapped her to be his Secretary of Labor in 2001. The Department of Transportation has never been led by a woman of color, so Chao's appointment is a historic first. Nikki Haley, the first female governor of South Carolina, follows in the footsteps of a number of other women in her role as Ambassador to the UN. Neither is she the first woman of color in the position: that honor belongs to Susan Rice, an African American woman who served in Obama's first administration.

Finally, none of Trump's female appointees are poised to be particularly influential in his administration, suggesting his choices reflect more symbolism than substance. None serve in the inner cabinet nor in positions that are key to implementing his campaign promises to crack down on

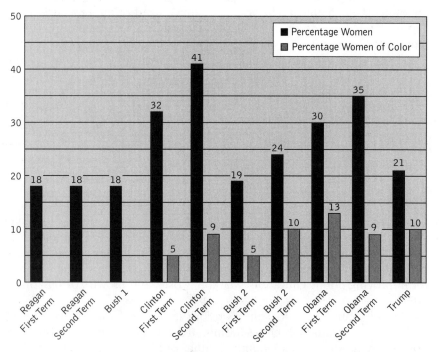

**Figure 8.2. Women Appointed to Presidential Cabinets.**
*Sources*: Center for American Women and Politics. Accessed online at http://www.cawp .rutgers.edu/fast_facts/levels_of_office/documents/prescabinet.pdf. "PowerPost: Here Are the People Donald Trump Has Chosen for His Cabinet." 2017. *Washington Post*. Available at https://www.washingtonpost.com/graphics/politics/trump-administration-appointee -tracker/

illegal immigration, bring law and order, or re-create manufacturing jobs in the United States.

While glass ceilings do not appear to be keeping women out of the cabinet, at least in most recent presidential administrations, there is some evidence that glass walls remain. As of this writing, three cabinet departments have never been led by a woman: the Departments of Defense, Treasury, and Veterans Affairs. Each is a highly masculine domain, supporting feminist scholars' contention that these types of departments are the least amenable to women's leadership. Women have cracked into the ranks below Cabinet Secretary, however. Barack Obama appointed Army veteran Tammy Duckworth to the position of Assistant Secretary for Veterans Affairs shortly after he assumed office in 2009 and appointed women to roughly one-third of the other available slots in the Department of Veterans' Affairs (data collected by authors).

Because most cabinet positions have now been held by women, perhaps gender power will be less problematic for women as presidential administrations become more and more gender integrated. As women prove their mettle in executive branch positions, they may begin to reshape dominant gender norms, shed the mantle of outsiders, and wield the levers of power like their male colleagues. Yet the masculinism inherent in Trump's key nominations should give us pause; it reflects what many critics predicted during his campaign: that his vision for "making America great again" relies disproportionately on white men holding the reins of power.

### Career Civil Service/State and Local Bureaucracies

High-ranking positions such as presidential appointees receive a great deal of media attention but represent only the tip of the iceberg in terms of the sheer numbers of individuals working in the executive branch of government. The federal and state governments employ thousands more individuals through their civil service systems. These individuals, often referred to as bureaucrats or public administrators, are responsible for implementing government programs and delivering public services to American citizens. Michael Lipsky (2010) calls public-service workers who interact directly with citizens "street-level bureaucrats" and argues that they are important policy actors because "the discretionary actions of public employees are the benefits and sanctions of government programs and determine access to government rights and benefits."

At lower levels of the bureaucracy where jobs are much more plentiful, women tend to be very well represented. For example, women constitute 83 percent of the nurses working for Veterans' Affairs medical facilities and 81 percent of public elementary school teachers (Bureau of Labor Statistics 2014; US Office of Personnel Management 2014). Yet, consistent with theories about gender power and patterns discussed earlier, women's access to state and local government positions remains uneven and shaped by glass ceilings and glass walls: women are least well represented at the highest rungs of these organizations and tend to have the greatest career success in agencies and departments that deal in women's issue areas.

To illustrate, we examine two particularly gendered areas of public service in state and local bureaucracies: teaching and policing. Women are greatly overrepresented among the ranks of teachers, while men constitute a disproportionate share of the nation's police and firefighting forces. Consistent with gender stereotypes about the strengths of the sexes, men are called on to protect and serve, while women are tapped to caretake and teach.

Kenneth Meier and Vicky Wilkins (2002) describe school districts as "classic glass ceiling organizations," noting that while women predominate at the lower levels, they have trouble reaching higher administrative posts. At the highest ranks, women constitute about 24 percent of school superintendents (Kowalski et al. 2010), but their numbers are noticeably higher at lower levels of the hierarchy. Women recently achieved parity in principal positions, making up 52 percent of school principals in 2011 (Bitterman, Goldring, and Gray 2013), and they have always dominated the ranks of teachers by nearly a three-to-one margin over their male colleagues. But even so, gendered patterns of leadership persist. Male teachers are found disproportionately at the high school level while female teachers are disproportionately represented in elementary and middle schools (Bureau of Labor Statistics 2014).

Why are women not better represented at the top of this ostensibly feminine field? One national study of school superintendents found that women are not typically well positioned to become high-level education administrators, as few administrators come from the ranks of elementary school teachers, nor do they have

Appointed by Barack Obama in 2015, Loretta Lynch is the first African American woman to serve as US Attorney General.
*Source*: The U.S. Department of Justice, http://www.justice.gov/ag/meet-attorney-general.

as much experience in fiscal management as men—a stereotypically masculine criterion that boards of education increasingly consider when hiring superintendents (Glass 2000). Consistent with our previous discussion of glass walls, female superintendents also face discrimination in their fields as they are more likely to be assigned to work in less desirable locations and for lower pay than male superintendents (Wolverton 1999). One result of having so few women superintendents is that some often feel the need to distance themselves from their gender, as they must overcome perceptions from co-workers that they are somehow different or more emotional than male superintendents (Gardiner, Enomoto, and Grogan 2000). For these women, even in a female-dominated field, managing their femaleness in high-ranking positions remains a necessity.

Tammy Duckworth, former assistant secretary of the US Department of Veterans Affairs, arrives at the World War II Memorial in Washington for a ceremony honoring World War II veterans who fought in the Pacific. Duckworth lost her legs after her Blackhawk helicopter was shot down during a mission in Iraq, and was awarded a Purple Heart for her service. President Obama appointed her assistant secretary in 2009, where she served until 2011. She was elected to the US House in 2012 and the US Senate in 2016.
*Source*: AP Photo / Cliff Owen.

Although the field of education is in many ways dominated by women, the same cannot be said for policing, where in 2008, women made up just 20 percent of all sworn law enforcement personnel in the United States. According to a 2010 study by the Department of Justice, women fared best in the largest police departments with more than 500 sworn personnel, of which 21 percent were female. By contrast, women comprised just 10 percent of personnel in small and rural police departments (Langton 2010).

At higher organizational levels, some argue that a "brass ceiling" exists that keeps women out of the top job of police chief. Of the 18,000 police departments across the United States, the National Center for Women and Policing (NCWP)'s Director Margaret Moore estimated that in 2009, only about 224 police departments, or less than 1 percent, had female chiefs (Moore 2009). A more recent CNN article suggests little to no progress: in 2013 there were 220 female police chiefs across the country. Although progress is slow, women are breaking into the top law enforcement positions across the country. In 2007, for example, Cathy Lanier was named Chief of the Metropolitan Police for the District of Columbia and women have recently served as police commissioners in cities as large as San Francisco, Boston, Detroit, and Houston (Drexler 2013).

The NCWP argues that the lack of female representation among police officers is due to a widespread gender bias in police hiring, which keeps the number of women officers artificially low. They believe that too much emphasis is placed on masculine characteristics such as physical prowess, which might keep otherwise qualified women from serving (Lonsway et al. 2002). Yet, some changes underway offer a more welcoming environment for female recruits than in previous years. According to many, the policing field has begun to shift its emphasis away from a paramilitary structure in the wake of police brutality scandals to one that more prominently emphasizes more stereotypically feminine skills such as communication and community relations—a structure in which women officers can potentially excel ("Women Rise to Top Police Ranks in U.S. Cities" 2004). Studies show that women officers rely on a less physical style of policing and are better at de-escalating violent confrontations with citizens; they are particularly effective in dealing with domestic violence issues (Lonsway 2000).

Whether as presidential appointees, police officers, school teachers, or a myriad of other positions in public administration, women have the potential to influence public policy in many ways. Women have made great strides in terms of their overall representation in elected executive branch positions throughout American government, but still lag behind in many areas, particularly in leadership roles. Can they still make a substantive difference? We turn next to this question.

## LINKING DESCRIPTIVE AND SUBSTANTIVE REPRESENTATION: DO WOMEN MAKE A DIFFERENCE?

The executive branch provides many pathways for enacting substantive representation. Executive branch officials shape policy outputs through agenda setting that enables them to place certain items on the agenda while keeping others off, as well as through their ability to decide how best to implement and enforce existing laws, rules, and regulations. But because most of these individuals are not elected, their responsiveness to the public is cause for concern.

Representative bureaucracy theorists offer a solution for keeping unelected bureaucrats accountable and responsive to the public: make the bureaucracy descriptively representative of the public. If the government is a true microcosm of the people it serves, the theory is that those in charge of making decisions will better reflect the wishes and demands of an increasingly diverse citizenry. The theory stresses that individuals' life experiences differ according to race, gender, sexual orientation, and, potentially, other characteristics. Such life experiences, in turn, shape their political attitudes and perspectives (Dolan and Rosenbloom 2003).

As chapter 3 discussed, women and men do have slightly different political attitudes, arguably shaped by their different life experiences in a gendered world. As bureaucrats exercising discretion to implement public policy, for example, making decisions about which motorists should be pulled over for traffic violations, which students should be assigned to gifted or remedial classes, and which small businesses should qualify for government loans, these life experiences and attitudes are thought to come to bear. If women's experiences differ from men's, the theory posits that women will bring different perspectives to the table and ultimately shape government outcomes to better reflect the experiences of women in their organizations as well as in the larger population. Captain Bhagwati's conviction that adding more women to the leadership ranks of the military would reduce sexual assaults nicely illustrates the logic of the theory: not only would women better understand the effects of sexual assault on women, but would more likely devote time and energy toward fixing the problem.

Many executive women agree that women's presence in government changes policy processes and outcomes. When asked if they think women's presence in the federal government significantly changes the way policy is made, almost two-thirds of the female members of the Senior Executive Service (SES), the highest ranking members of the federal career service, agreed that it does. They were nearly three times more likely than their male colleagues to voice such sentiments (SOFE 1997). Former Vermont Governor Madeline Kunin stresses that women bring something different to governing and that democracy is more legitimate with greater numbers of women sitting at the table:

> More women in public life may not immediately turn swords into plowshares, but women do bring a different and diverse set of life experiences to the process—and for democracy to be truly representative, it is only just that we [women] be equally represented. (Kunin 1987, 212)

Former Governor Ann Richards voiced a similar sentiment, noting that women tend to better understand the concerns and experiences of other women:

> The most sympathetic and sensitive of our men friends, no matter how hard he tries, cannot hear with a woman's ear or process information through a woman's experience. (quoted in Dow and Tonn 1993, 294)

As these examples suggest, women's presence brings new understandings and perspectives to bear on policy conversations and government actions. For men who have never experienced or been threatened by military sexual assault, it is unlikely that they will truly understand and appreciate the devastating effects it has on victims. Few male health care providers will understand how the masculine environment of a VA medical facility affects women's comfort levels and their willingness to seek care as a woman might. As one female veteran apprehensive about seeking care in the VA explained, the VA "is a very, very anti-woman organization . . . the whole Veterans' Administration is geared to men, period" (Heikkila 2011, 127).

But understanding is only the first step. Does any evidence suggest that such attitudes and perspectives shape women's behavior in the executive branch? Do they ultimately serve as advocates or spokespersons for women? On these questions, the scholarship is mixed. In contrast with the wealth of studies on women's impact in the legislative and judicial branches, scholarship on executive women is more limited. A great deal of this literature focuses on the conditions that facilitate greater descriptive representation for women, but only a few demonstrate a link between descriptive and substantive representation. Much anecdotal evidence confirms that many executive women advocate on behalf of their female clientele, however.

Perhaps the most visible way in which female executives have left a unique impact on policy is through challenging some of the dominant values of public organizations, especially by making their organizations more attentive and responsive to women's often overlooked needs and perspectives. Former Reagan appointee Amoretta Hoeber reminded her male Army colleagues that women and men in the military are not interchangeable. When the US Army was planning to purchase new combat boots for the troops, Hoeber noticed that the test group assembled to try out the new boots was composed entirely of men. She argued for including women in the group, emphasizing that women's feet are different than men's, and believes that including women in the group ultimately made a difference in the choice of boots (McGlen and Sarkees 1993). Senior Executive Service women are also significantly more likely than their male colleagues to consider the differential impact of policy decisions on women and men in their own work (SOFE 1997).

Pioneering women working for the Veterans Health Administration illustrate these perspectives at work. Two Florida VA hospitals, one in Bay Pines and another in Tampa, are often held up as exemplars in providing quality care to female veterans. According to VA official Connie LaRosa, female veterans deserve the credit for instigating significant changes at each. As she explains, change occurred in these facilities because "strong women Veterans . . . saw the need for other women Veterans to get the health care they themselves wanted from the VA" (Department of Veterans Affairs 2012). Three female nurses who served in the Vietnam War returned to work at the Bay Pines facility and were instrumental in reshaping the facility to better serve women: Joan Furey, the first Director of the Center for Women Veterans, Mary "Toni" Lawrie, a frequent witness at congressional hearings on women veterans health care, and Sara McVicker, a member of the Advisory Committee on Veterans Affairs. In the Tampa facility, Peggy Mikelonis spearheaded the opening of one of the nation's first Women's Health Centers in the VA. Despite her success, Mikelonis acknowledged the obstacles along the way, offering, "It's not easy building a women's program in a male-dominated system." As female veterans themselves, these women were acutely aware of the unique challenges women face in a male-dominated system and brought meaningful change to their facilities. In addition, both Lawrie and Mikelonis began hosting week-long training programs for other women working across the VA, providing guidance for establishing a women's program and getting their male colleagues to buy in to the changes (Department of Veterans Affairs 2012).

Additional evidence suggests that female executives use their positions to alter public policy to include previously excluded or marginalized women. Appointed as the first woman to head the National Institutes of Health (NIH), Director Bernadine Healy advocated women's health issues from the beginning of her tenure and launched a $625 million project to study breast cancer, osteoporosis, and heart disease in 160,000 women shortly after taking office. NIH funds clinical research studies to assess the efficacy of various medical treatments, but for years routinely excluded female patients from clinical trials. Consistent with the theory of masculinism, middle-aged men were considered the "normal" patient despite the obvious biological and physiological differences between the sexes, women's longer life expectancies, and their dissimilar responses to medical treatments. Healy presided over a shift in NIH policy, championing the importance of including the previously excluded half of the population in such important research studies (Glazer 1994).

From their seats in the inner cabinet, both Secretaries of State Hillary Clinton and Madeleine Albright prioritized women's rights during their tenure. Two months after taking office as the first female Secretary of State, Madeleine Albright instructed US diplomats to make women's rights central to American foreign policy (Lippman 1997). In her very first meeting with leaders from the Persian Gulf states, Albright led the charge herself, suggesting that women's rights be on the agenda for their next meeting (Gross 2003). Secretary of State Hillary Clinton similarly prioritized the needs of women and funded 67 programs across the globe to further the rights of women. She also appointed Melanne Verveer as special ambassador to shepherd efforts promoting the welfare of women (Calabresi 2011; "What Hillary Did Next; American Diplomacy" 2012). In her 2016 presidential campaign, Clinton again stressed her commitment to women's rights and vowed to be a champion for those marginalized by the current economy, advocating, among other things, family-friendly policies that facilitate women's participation in the workforce (Gearan and Rucker 2015).

At lower levels of the hierarchy, additional findings corroborate that greater descriptive representation of women in government bureaucracies and as street-level bureaucrats leads to substantive representation for women. In the female-dominated area of teaching, greater percentages of female school teachers and administrators are positively related to positive educational outcomes for female students (Keiser et al. 2002), suggesting that female staff use their discretion to improve the quality of the learning environment for their female students. Drawing from another feminine domain, the higher the percentage of female supervisors in child support enforcement offices, the greater the amount of child support dollars collected for female-headed families (Wilkins and Keiser 2006).

In a more masculine policy domain, Meier and Nicholson-Crotty (2006) find a positive relationship between the number of policewomen in a department and the number of rape reports and arrests for rape offenders. Using data from the 1990s, the authors estimate that increasing the numbers of women in police departments by around 5 percent would result in an almost 12 percent increase in the number of reported sexual assaults. But in another masculine domain, female farmers are no more likely to have their federal farm loans approved by Farmers Home Administration offices employing higher percentages of female loan officers than those with fewer female staff (Selden 1997).

In sum, the evidence suggests that having women in bureaucratic positions of power is oftentimes helpful to women in the population, but is no guarantee that the diversity of women's voices will be heard or acted upon. Although representative bureaucracy scholars have made good faith efforts to untangle the ways in which female bureaucrats provide substantive representation for women in the population, the ways in which executive women do or do not provide substantive representation to American women remains unsettled. The masculinism of the executive branch often creates real obstacles for those who bring feminine viewpoints or values to the table, prompting many questions for future scholars: Is women's substantive representation more common in departments that are more heavily skewed toward "women's issues"? In departments that have a larger female clientele than others? Where there is an office dedicated to women's concerns? We are just beginning to tackle these questions to better understand whether descriptive and substantive representation are linked in the executive branch.

## Challenges to Providing Substantive Representation

Forty years ago, Rosabeth Moss Kanter (1977) highlighted the difficulties faced by demographic groups who are vastly outnumbered in an organization. She argues that when women or racial minorities are few and far between in an organization, or when they comprise 15 percent or less of the whole, they are regarded as tokens and face all sorts of performance pressures not experienced by dominants in the organization. These women are highly visible, their differences from men are exaggerated, and their behavior is often perceived as typical for all women. One effect of their status as tokens is unique performance pressures that make it more difficult for them to carry out their jobs without having every action highly scrutinized for how well it fits the dominant values of the organization.

For executive women, the pressures of being a token are especially acute. For one, executive positions are often more highly visible than are legislative or judicial positions. Political executives usually sit at the apex of some hierarchy as the top official in charge of their respective organizations: head of the state, head of a large government department or agency, and so on. Such positioning is likely to invite increased attention and publicity for both men and women. But being a woman in such a position further heightens this attention. Positions such as governor, attorney general, and cabinet secretary tend to conjure up images of male politicians. When women achieve these positions, the public often has difficulties in reconciling their images of power with a female face. As Madeleine Kunin explains it,

> In conversation, when I was introduced, I noticed that people didn't hear the word "Governor" before my name. They smiled and nodded, as they would to anyone who had just joined the circle, and promptly resumed their conversation. They had not heard the word "Governor" because their eyes had not

Then Secretary of State Hillary Rodham Clinton checks her BlackBerry from a desk inside a C-17 military plane bound for Tripoli, Libya. The photo became an Internet meme: Hillary Rodham Clinton, wearing sunglasses, staring at her BlackBerry.
*Source*: AP Photo / Kevin Lamarque, Reuters Pool.

prepared them for it . . . men were governors and women were not. (1994, 349–50)

For women of color, these pressures are often even more acute. When Nikki Haley was running for the Republican party nomination for South Carolina's open gubernatorial seat in 2010, a disgruntled fellow party member took a racist swipe at her Indian family's Sikh religious background by referring to her as a "raghead" and lamented that "people going into politics today are different than the people I always served with," not so subtly hinting that an outsider like Haley, a woman of color, was unqualified for the job. In a state with the lowest percentage of women serving in the state legislature and few elected officials of color, Haley clearly stood apart (Green 2011).

Like Haley, most high-ranking executive women are so visible that everything they do is subjected to heightened scrutiny. Because female politicians are anomalies, they cannot simply blend into the woodwork. Others are constantly watching their behavior to see if they behave as expected or contrary to stereotypical presumptions. Many political women attest to the increased attention their status as women in a man's world brings. When

Carla Anderson was undergoing Senate confirmation hearings after being nominated by President Ford as only the third woman ever to serve as a US cabinet secretary, Senator William Proxmire (D-WI) indirectly challenged her qualifications for the job, suggesting that gender sealed her nomination (Stineman 1980).

Such treatment is par for the course, according to MaryAnne Borrelli (2002), who argues that women nominees are often presumed less competent during Senate confirmation hearings than are men, a consequence of being judged by a "heroic man" standard. While male secretaries are routinely portrayed as heroic men who arrive ready to save the day, women are depicted as considerably less heroic and, consequently, as less capable of fulfilling their executive duties. Female cabinet nominees are often portrayed as possessing the same character traits as men do, but as exhibiting them only passively or failing to use them in a powerful fashion. Even though both male and female secretary nominees are described in newspaper coverage as "confident," only women are tagged as "unnervingly confident." While both male and female cabinet nominees often have families, only female nominees are faulted for "abandoning" them, while male nominees are praised for their sacrifice (Borrelli 2002). When the standard for success is so infused with masculinity, women have a difficult time proving their capacity to measure up.

In practice, heightened visibility often means that token women are presumed to speak and stand for all women. Many executive women have explained that they were cognizant of the fact that they would be held up as a standard by which all future executive women would be judged. The very first female governor, Nellie Tayloe Ross, remarked that if elected, she would conduct her administration so "that it might never be said that women were unfitted (sic) for executive office" (Scharff 1995, 93). Over 80 years later, Susana Martinez acknowledged the same pressures, adding that her status as a Latina invited additional scrutiny. "I'm often introduced as the first Latina governor. With that comes an enormous responsibility," she says. "Those little girls watching me have to see me deliver my promises" ("How to Grab Them; New Mexico's Governor" 2011). After losing her bid to be the first female vice president in the United States, Geraldine Ferraro voiced a similar sentiment: "It is a sorry fact in this country that the defeat of one woman is often read as a judgment on all women" (quoted in Watson and Gordon 2003).

According to Kanter (1977), token individuals sometimes take special pains to demonstrate they have adopted the dominant values of the organization, and one way of exhibiting such loyalty is by avoiding any actions that appear to benefit their own social group. As Kanter explains, sometimes "the price of being 'one of the boys' is a willingness to occasionally turn against the girls" (79). In their analysis of high-ranking women working for the Department of Defense, Nancy McGlen and Meredith Reid Sarkees (1993) find evidence of such behavior. Women who have risen above the glass ceiling at Defense differ very little from their male colleagues when asked about their policy attitudes, but they do evince more conservative ideology than their male colleagues. McGlen and Sarkees (1993) surmise that Defense women are highly conscious of their minority status within the organization and adjust their attitudes to better align with the strongly conservative culture of the department. Dolan (2002) finds corroborating evidence among senior executive women at Defense, showing that they align quite closely with their male colleagues when it comes to attitudes about gendered policy issues such as sexual harassment. Although the majority of male and female senior executives in the Defense Department agree that more should be done to combat sexual harassment in the federal government, greater numbers of *men* than women hold such opinions. In addition, women at Defense are somewhat *less* likely to consider how their own decisions might differentially impact women than their male colleagues, which suggests that advocating for women in a highly masculine environment is fraught with difficulty (SOFE 1997).

Yet, when women achieve a critical mass within an organization, token pressures typically dissipate—dominants can no longer assume that any one woman stands for all women, and women consequently feel less constrained in their own actions. As Captain Bhagwati's comments at the beginning of this chapter suggest, the military culture will not likely change until women achieve a critical mass. Whether women will feel more comfortable looking out for other women or men will become more sensitized to female service members' needs is not entirely clear, but the evidence suggests that critical mass is important. For example, Dolan (2000) finds that senior executive women are more likely to show support for a variety of gendered policy initiatives when they work for agencies and departments where women wield a critical mass of leadership positions. Similarly, women working in these types of agencies are more likely to consider how their policy decisions affect women and to agree that women's presence in government changes policymaking. When men work with greater numbers of influential women, they also agree that policymaking changes. Yet, these men are no more likely than men working elsewhere in the federal government to consider how their own policymaking decisions potentially affect women and men differently (SOFE 1997). These findings suggest, at least provisionally, that women who rise above the glass ceiling in organizations like the Department of Defense will bear a disproportionate burden in advocating for women.

Even though women continue to increase their numbers across all branches of government, simply having a seat at the table is no guarantee that their voices and perspectives will be heard. Perhaps recognizing their status as outsiders, some argue that women develop distinct and feminine leadership styles or even eschew adopting an advocacy role for other women. If women are greatly outnumbered and perceive that their minority status has negative implications concerning their ability to get the job done, do they try to open up the process for other outsiders? Take special pains to include others who might have previously been excluded? Employ power-to rather than power-over leadership?

### Power and Leadership Style

Hillary Clinton's tenure as Secretary of State was evaluated in a recent article published in *Foreign Affairs*, a leading foreign policy magazine. In the article, author Michael Hirsh characterized Clinton's approach as one of "soft power." As Hirsh (2013) explained,

> Her most lasting legacy will likely be the way that she thrust soft diplomacy to the forefront of U.S. foreign policy. . . . She set out to create . . . a new kind of people-to-people diplomacy, one designed to extend Washington's influence in an Internet-driven world in which popular uprisings, such as the Arab Spring, could quickly uproot the traditional relationships between governments.

A *Time* magazine article similarly highlighted Clinton's strengths in mending broken relationships with other countries, arguing that her efforts to build deeper relationships and boost cooperation with nongovernmental organizations had won praise from Democrats and Republicans alike (Calabresi 2011). Perhaps Secretary John Kerry's tenure will be described in similar terms, but for female leaders, a great deal of scholarship suggests that Clinton's approach is typical, that many female leaders employ feminine styles of leadership that emphasize consensus, collaboration, and empowerment rather than masculine or "power over" leadership that stresses competition, command and control, an emphasis on individual accomplishment, and hierarchy (Eagly and Johnson 1990; Jalalzai 2013).

One study of male and female governors finds that women are more likely than men to express an empowerment motivation in their positions (Barth and Ferguson 2002). Similarly, various scholars studying the rhetoric of former Governor Ann Richards conclude that her speaking style and rhetoric were very much geared toward empowering others, especially women (Dow and Tonn 1993; Kaml 2000). According to these scholars, Richards used public speaking occasions to draw connections with her audience, to encourage them to connect their experiences as average citizens with hers, and to draw on their own instincts in judging politicians and the political process. They characterize her rhetoric as particularly feminine because she focuses on empowering others rather than boosting her own profile.

Former Secretary of State Madeleine Albright similarly suggests that consensus comes more easily for women and that women have a more difficult time with confrontation, but she acknowledges that the job sometimes necessitates as much.

> Men are capable of having strong personal disagreements or arguments about a subject and then walk out of a room and go and play golf or have a drink or something. And I think women do take it more personally. And I don't think we like to have face-to-face confrontations, but I sure learned that it was essential to state my views very clearly and not care whether I was liked or not. And it took me a while to learn it. But I think others will testify to the fact that I did learn it. (Gross 2003)

Other evidence suggests that many female governors adopt a consensus style of leadership (Kunin 1994; Barbara Lee Family Foundation 2001). Former New Jersey Governor Christine Todd Whitman's speeches are peppered with references to government decision making being an open process, based on consensus (Sheeler 2000). She credits her style to growing up on a farm, where people need to work cooperatively to get things done, and points out that others criticize her for too much consensus building (Beard 1996). Former Republican Governor Jane Dee Hull agrees that consensus is part of women's repertoire more often than it is for men: "Women tend to want to put people around the table and talk. Men order things, like ordering dinner" (Clift and Brazaitis 2000, 283).

But not all executive women lead by consensus. Research on women and men in state government executive positions finds that women do not necessarily have any special claims to using consensus-based leadership styles (Duerst-Lahti and Kelly 1995). While serving as Secretary of State under George W. Bush, Condoleezza Rice explained that her approach was more hierarchical than consensus based:

> Nor do I believe you can do everything by consensus. At the Pentagon, I learned that if you seek consensus you get a third of a tank, a third of a plane, and a third of an aircraft carrier. If you don't drive the process from the top, you get across-the-board cuts and everyone gets weaker. (quoted in Dowd 2000, 102)

Perhaps Rice's position reflects a fundamental difference between the Democratic and Republican parties, with the Republican Party placing a higher value on hierarchy whereas Democrats lean more heavily toward a consensual approach (Freeman 1986). As many other chapters in the book confirm, we are just beginning to better understand the ways in which political party shapes political women's approaches to campaigning and legislating. Whether political party similarly shapes their overall leadership style is a question for future scholars.

# CONCLUSION

As this chapter demonstrates, women have made great strides in terms of their overall representation in executive branch positions throughout American government. With the exception of the Trump administration, the numbers of women in presidential cabinets have generally increased with each successive president who takes office; women of color continue breaking new ground in cabinets and governors' positions; and women continue to make inroads into masculine positions such as police chiefs and Secretary of Homeland Security. The evidence suggests that glass ceilings and glass walls persist, but are showing signs of weakening.

Yet, many contemporary stories suggest that although women are gaining seats at the executive table, they are not yet fully fledged members of the club. As outsiders breaking into new territory, women are often cognizant that they are playing by someone else's rules. Because men have always been in charge, they have developed the rules, customs, and mores of the place. When women arrive, they cannot help but be reminded of the masculinism of the place—the executive branch is imbued with male power, male values, and men at the helm.

The evidence presented in this chapter suggests that there is often a link between descriptive and substantive representation such that women are more attentive to the needs and perspectives of other women than are their male colleagues in executive roles. On this score, Captain Bhagwati is on solid ground in suggesting that greater numbers of women in leadership will facilitate a culture change that is more attentive to the needs of its female service members. Yet, the highly masculine nature of the executive branch and the military, in particular, reminds us that women seeking to exercise influence in these domains face considerable constraints. They may avoid championing women's interests to avoid being defined by their gender or wait until a critical mass of women hold leadership positions before pressing for change. With the passage of time and with additional research, scholars will hopefully develop a more comprehensive understanding of when executive women are most likely to advocate for other women and whether some circumstances make substantive representation more likely than others.

# REFERENCES

Barbara Lee Family Foundation. 2001. *Keys to the Governor's Office: Unlock the Door.* Brookline, MA: Barbara Lee Family Foundation. http://www.barbaraleefoundation .org/wp-content/uploads/Keys-to-the-Governors-Office.pdf

Barth, Jay, and Margaret R. Ferguson. 2002. "Gender and Gubernatorial Personality." *Women & Politics* 24(1): 63–82.

Beard, Patricia. 1996. *Growing up Republican: Christie Whitman, the Politics of Character*. New York: HarperCollins Publishers.

Berman, Russell. 2017. "The Donald Trump Cabinet Tracker." *The Atlantic*, as updated January 11. Available at https://www.theatlantic.com/politics/archive/2017/01/trump-cabinet-tracker/510527/

Bitterman, Amy, Rebecca Goldring, and Lucinda Gray. 2013. "Characteristics of Public and Private Elementary and Secondary School Principals in the United States: Results from the 2011–12 Schools and Staffing Survey. First Look. NCES 2013-313." *National Center for Education Statistics.* http://eric.ed.gov/?id=ED544176 (accessed May 27, 2015).

Borrelli, MaryAnne. 2002. *The President's Cabinet: Gender, Power and Representation.* Boulder, CO: Lynne Rienner Publishers.

Borrelli, MaryAnne. 2010. "The Contemporary Presidency: Gender Desegregation and Gender Integration in the President's Cabinet, 1933–2010." *Presidential Studies Quarterly* 40(4): 734–49.

Brown, Wendy L. 1998. *Manhood and Politics: A Feminist Reading in Political Theory.* Totowa, NJ: Rowman & Littlefield Publishers.

Bureau of Labor Statistics. 2014. *Women in the Labor Force: A Databook.* Washington, DC: Bureau of Labor Statistics.

Calabresi, Massimo. 2011. "Head of State." *Time* 178(18): 26.

Campo-Flores, Arian. 2010. "Woman on the Verge. (Nikki Haley)(COVER STORY)." *Newsweek* 156(2).

Center for American Women and Politics. 2015a. *History of Women Governors.* Rutgers University, New Brunswick, NJ: Eagleton Institute of Politics.

———. 2015b. *Women Appointed to Presidential Cabinets.* Eagleton Institute of Politics: Rutgers University. http://www.cawp.rutgers.edu/fast_facts/levels_of_office/documents/prescabinet.pdf

Clift, Eleanor, and Tom Brazaitis. 2000. *Madam President: Shattering the Last Glass Ceiling.* New York: Scribner.

Cook, Alison. 1993. "Lone Star: [Biography]." *New York Times, Late Edition (East Coast):* A22.

Department of Veterans Affairs. 2012. "Pioneers of Women's Health." *Vanguard* 63(2): 8–10.

Dolan, Julie. 2000. "The Senior Executive Service: Gender, Attitudes, and Representative Bureaucracy." *Journal of Public Administration Research and Theory* 10(3): 513–29.

———. 2002. "Representative Bureaucracy in the Federal Executive: Gender and Spending Priorities." *Journal of Public Administration Research and Theory* 12(3): 353–75.

———. 2012. "Women in the Obama Administration: Insiders or Outsiders Looking In?" In *Women and Executive Office: Pathways and Performance,* edited by Melody Rose, 75–87. Boulder, CO: Lynne Rienner Publishers.

Dolan, Julie, and David H Rosenbloom. 2003. *Representative Bureaucracy : Classic Readings and Continuing Controversies.* Armonk, NY: M.E. Sharpe.

Dow, Bonnie J., and Mari Boor Tonn. 1993. "Feminine Style and Political Judgment in the Rhetoric of Ann Richards." *Quarterly Journal of Speech* 79(3): 286–302.

Dowd, Ann Reilly. 2000. "Is There Anything This Woman Can't Do?" *George* 5: 86–91+.

Drexler, Peggy. 2013. "Opinion: When the Top Cop Is a Woman—CNN.com." *CNN.* http://www.cnn.com/2013/09/17/opinion/drexler-shooting-women/index.html (accessed June 3, 2015).

Duerst-Lahti, Georgia, and Rita Mae Kelly, eds. 1995. *Gender Power, Leadership, and Governance.* Ann Arbor: University of Michigan Press.

Eagly, Alice H., and Blair T. Johnson. 1990. "Gender and Leadership Style: A Meta-Analysis." *Psychological Bulletin* 108(2): 233–56.

Enloe, Cynthia. 1983. *Does Khaki Become You?* London: Pluto Press.

Freeman, Jo. 1986. "The Political Culture of the Democratic and Republican Parties." *Political Science Quarterly* 101(3): 327.

Garcia, Rogelio. 1997. *Women Appointed by President Clinton to Full-Time Positions Requiring Senate Confirmation, 1993–96.* Congressional Research Service, Library of Congress.

Gardiner, Mary E., Ernestine Enomoto, and Margaret Grogan. 2000. *Coloring Outside the Lines: Mentoring Women into School Leadership.* Albany, NY: State University of New York Press. http://site.ebrary.com/id/10021842 (accessed June 25, 2015).

Gearan, Anne, and Philip Rucker. 2015. "Democracy Not 'Just for Billionaires,' Hillary Clinton Tells Crowd in N.Y." *The Washington Post.* http://www.washington post.com/politics/democracy-not-just-for-billionaires-hillary-clinton-tells-crowd -in-ny/2015/06/13/346e3318-11fb-11e5-a0fe-dccfea4653ee_story.html (accessed June 23, 2015).

Glass, Thomas E. 2000. "Where Are All the Women Superintendents?" *School Administrator* 57(6): 28–32.

Glazer, Sarah. 1994. "Women's Health Issues: Will Women Benefit from Increased Research Funding?" *CQ Researcher by CQ Press* 4: 409–32.

Green, J. 2011. "Good Ol' Girl: Does Nikki Haley, the New Governor of South Carolina, Signal a Fundamental Change in the GOP's Relationship with Women, and in the GOP Itself?" *Atlantic Monthly* 307(1): 56–63.

Gross, Terry. 2003. "Former Secretary of State Madeleine Albright." *Fresh Air.* http://www.npr.org/templates/story/story.php?storyId=1432866 (accessed June 25, 2015).

Heikkila, Kim. 2011. *Sisterhood of War: Minnesota Women in Vietnam.* St. Paul, MN: Minnesota Historical Society Press.

Hirsh, Michael. 2013. "The Clinton Legacy: How Will History Judge the Soft-Power Secretary of State?" *Foreign Affairs* 92(3): 82–91.

"How to Grab Them; New Mexico's Governor." 2011. *The Economist* 401(8764): 42.

Huddy, Leonie, and Nayda Terkildsen. 1993. "The Consequences of Gender Stereotypes for Women Candidates at Different Levels and Types of Office." *Political Research Quarterly* 46(3): 503–25.

Jalalzai, Farida. 2013. *Shattered, Cracked or Firmly Intact? Women and the Executive Glass Ceiling Worldwide.* New York: Oxford University Press.

Kahn, Kim Fridkin. 1996. *The Political Consequences of Being a Woman: How Stereotypes Influence the Conduct and Consequences of Political Campaigns.* New York: Columbia University Press.

Kaml, Shannon Skarpho. 2000. "The Fusion of Populist and Feminine Styles in the Rhetoric of Ann Richards." In *The Rhetoric of Female Governors*, edited by Brenda DeVore Marshall and Molly A. Mayhead. Westport, CT: Praeger Publishers Inc.

Kanter, Rosabeth Moss. 1977. "Some Effects of Proportions on Group Life: Skewed Sex Ratios and Responses to Token Women." *American Journal of Sociology* 82(5): 965–90.

Keiser, Lael R., Vicky M. Wilkins, Kenneth J. Meier, and Catherine A. Holland. 2002. "Lipstick and Logarithms: Gender, Institutional Context, and Representative Bureaucracy." *The American Political Science Review* 96(3): 553–64.

King, Cheryl Simrell. 1995. "Sex-Role Identity and Decision Styles: How Gender Helps Explain the Paucity of Women at the Top." In *Gender Power, Leadership and Governance*. edited by Georgia Duerst-Lahti and Rita Mae Kelly, 67–92. Ann Arbor: University of Michigan Press.

Kowalski, Theodore J. et al. 2010. *The American School Superintendent: 2010 Decennial Study*. Totowa, NJ: Rowman & Littlefield Education.

Kunin, Madeleine M. 1987. "Lessons from One Woman's Career. (Political Equality Is Essential to True Equality)." *Journal of State Government* 60(5): 209–12.

———. 1994. *Living a Political Life*. New York: Knopf: Distributed by Random House.

Langton, Lynn. 2010. *Women in Law Enforcement*. http://books.google.com/books?hl=en&lr=&id=nqW3BgAAQBAJ&oi=fnd&pg=PA355&dq=%22and+size+of+agency+(number+of+full-time+sworn%22+%22to+the+reorganization+of+several+large%22+%22Service+(USPIS)+and+the%22+%22Fish+and+Wildlife%22+%22Force+Protection+Agency+did+not+provide+1998+data+on+the+sex+of+officers%3B+these+four%22+&ots=CDhxQFEjw6&sig=nT_v2_qYke7jy_b_VD0bNisaQ_k (accessed May 27, 2015).

Lippman, Thomas W. 1997. "State Dept. Seeks Gains for Women." *The Washington Post*. http://www.washingtonpost.com/archive/politics/1997/03/25/state-dept-seeks-gains-for-women/2bddd98e-6b79-45a9-8346-0a466e30de32/(accessed June 25, 2015).

Lipsky, Michael. 2010. *Street-Level Bureaucracy: Dilemmas of the Individual in Public Services*, 2nd ed. New York: Russell Sage Foundation.

Lonsway, Kim et al. 2002. "Equality Denied." http://womenandpolicing.org/PDF/2002_Status_Report.pdf (accessed June 25, 2015).

Lonsway, Kimberly A. 2000. "Hiring & Retaining More Women: The Advantages to Law Enforcement Agencies." http://eric.ed.gov/?id=ED473183 (accessed June 25, 2015).

Markon, Jerry, Robert Costa, and Emma Brown. 2016. "Trump Nominates Two Prominent GOP Women." *Washington Post*, November 23.

Mastracci, Sharon, and Lauren Bowman. 2015. "Public Agencies, Gendered Organizations: The Future of Gender Studies in Public Management." *Public Management Review* 17(6): 857–75.

McGlen, Nancy E., and Meredith Reid Sarkees. 1993. *Women in Foreign Policy: The Insiders*. New York: Routledge.

Meier, Kenneth J., and Jill Nicholson-Crotty. 2006. "Gender, Representative Bureaucracy, and Law Enforcement: The Case of Sexual Assault." *Public Administration Review* 66(6): 850–60.

Meier, Kenneth J., and Vicky M. Wilkins. 2002. "Gender Differences in Agency Head Salaries: The Case of Public Education." *Public Administration Review* 62(4): 405–11.

Milbank, Dana. 2008. "A Thank-You for 18 Millions Cracks in the Glass Ceiling." *Washington Post* (8 June): A1.

Moore, Margaret. 2009. Personal interview by Melissa Deckman, by phone. May 5.

Mui, Ylan Q. 2014. "Janet Yellen Confirmed as Federal Reserve Chairman." *The Washington Post.* http://www.washingtonpost.com/business/economy/janet-yellen-confirmed-as-next-fed-chief/2014/01/06/14b38582-76f2-11e3-8963-b4b654bcc9b2_story.html (accessed June 23, 2015).

Newman, Meredith Ann. 1995. "The Gendered Nature of Lowi's Typology; or Who Would Guess You Could Find Gender Here?" In *Gender Power, Leadership and Governance,* edited by Georgia Duerst-Lahti and Rita Mae Kelly, 141–66. Ann Arbor: University of Michigan Press.

"PowerPost: Here Are the People Donald Trump Has Chosen for His Cabinet." 2017. *Washington Post.* Available at https://www.washingtonpost.com/graphics/politics/trump-administration-appointee-tracker/

Republican State Leadership Committee. n.d. *The Future Majority Project and "Right Women, Right Now."* Washington, DC: Republican State Leadership Committee. Accessed at http://rslc.gop/wp-content/uploads/2015/01/FMP-Report-FINAL.pdf

Rosenwasser, Shirley Miller, and Norma G. Dean. 1989. "Gender Role and Political Office." *Psychology of Women Quarterly* 13(1): 77–85.

Sallee, Shelley. 1996. "'The Woman of It': Governor Miriam Ferguson's 1924 Election." *The Southwestern Historical Quarterly* 100(1): 1–16.

Sanbonmatsu, Kira. 2013. "The Candidacies of U.S. Women of Color for Statewide Executive Office." Chicago, IL: Social Science Research Network. http://papers.ssrn.com/abstract=2300783 (accessed May 15, 2015).

Scharff, Virginia. 1995. "Feminism, Femininity, and Power: Nellie Tayloe Ross and the Woman Politician's Dilemma." *Frontiers: A Journal of Women Studies* 15(3): 87.

Selden, Sally Coleman. 1997. *The Promise of Representative Bureaucracy: Diversity and Responsiveness in a Government Agency.* Armonk, NY: M.E. Sharpe.

Sheeler, Krista Horn. 2000. "Christine Todd Whitman and the Ideology of the New Jersey Governorship." In *Navigating Boundaries: The Rhetoric of Women Governors,* edited by Brenda DeVore Marshall and Molly Mayhead, 99–122. Westport. CT: Praeger Publishers Inc.

Stineman, Esther. 1980. *American Political Women: Contemporary and Historical Profiles.* Littleton, CO: Libraries Unlimited, Ltd.

Stivers, Camilla. 2002. *Gender Images in Public Administration: Legitimacy and the Administrative State.* Thousand Oaks: Sage Publications.

Survey of Federal Executives. 1997. Original survey data collected by Julie Dolan.

United States. Congress. House. Committee on Veterans' Affairs. 2009. (House) *Eliminating the Gaps: Examining Women Veterans' Issues.* Washington, DC: Government Printing Office. http://www.gpo.gov/fdsys/pkg/CHRG-111hhrg51873/pdf/CHRG-111hhrg51873.pdf

United States. Congress. Senate. Committee on Armed Services. 2013. (Senate) *Sexual Assaults in the Military.* http://www.armed-services.senate.gov/hearings/oversight-sexual-assaults-in-the-military (accessed April 27, 2014).

U.S. Office of Personnel Management. 2014. Fedscope. Accessed at http://www
.fedscope.opm.gov/

Watson, Robert P., and Ann Gordon. 2003. *Anticipating Madam President*. Boulder,
CO: Lynne Rienner.

"What Hillary Did Next; American Diplomacy." 2012. *The Economist* 402(8777): 31.

Wilkins, Vicky M., and Lael R. Keiser. 2006. "Linking Passive and Active Representation by Gender: The Case of Child Support Agencies." *Journal of Public Administration Research and Theory* 16(1): 87–102.

Wolverton, Mimi. 1999. "The School Superintendency: Male Bastion or Equal
Opportunity?" *Advancing Women in Leadership Journal*. www.advancingwomen
.com/awl/spring99/Wolverton/wolver.html

Women's Research and Education Institute. 2013. *Women in the Military: Where
They Stand*, 8th ed. Washington, DC: Women's Research and Education Institute.
http://www.wrei.org/WIM2013e.pdf

"Women Rise to Top Police Ranks in U.S. Cities." 2004. *msnbc.com*. http://www
.nbcnews.com/id/5076267/ns/us_news/t/women-rise-top-police-ranks-us-cities/
(accessed June 25, 2015).

# 9

# Women in the Judiciary

In May 2009, President Barack Obama announced Judge Sonia Sotomayor to fill the Supreme Court vacancy left by retiring Justice David Souter—the first opportunity Obama had to replace a sitting justice upon his election in 2008. Sotomayor, a judge with 17 years' experience on the US Appellate Court and a Yale Law School grad, is not only the third woman to be appointed to the Supreme Court, but she is also the first Hispanic and has a compelling life story, having been raised by a widowed mother in public housing in the Bronx. Sotomayor graduated from Princeton University (on a full scholarship) *summa cum laude* in 1976 and after law school worked as a prosecutor in New York City and in private practice before her first judicial appointment by President George H. W. Bush in 1991.

Her selection did not elicit overwhelming support from Republican senators, many of whom expressed alarm at a speech that Sotomayor gave in 2001 as a sitting federal appellate judge at the University of California at Berkeley's School of Law. In that speech, addressing the role that her background played in her jurisprudence, she remarked, "I would hope that a wise Latina woman with the richness of her experiences would more often than not reach a better conclusion than a white male who hasn't lived that life" (quoted in Savage, 29). Sotomayor's 2001 comments challenged a sentiment that was often invoked by former Supreme Court Justice Sandra Day O'Connor—the first woman to be appointed to the Supreme Court in 1981—that "a wise old woman and a wise old man will reach the same conclusion." In her Berkeley Law School address, Sotomayor stated that she was unsure whether O'Connor was right in her statement, saying, "Whether born from experience or inherent physiological or cultural

271

differences . . . our gender and national origins may and will make a difference in our judging."

Sotomayor's comments sparked much debate on both sides of the political aisle. Former Republican United States House Speaker Newt Gingrich
stated that Sotomayor's speech indicated that she was a "Latina woman racist," although he later backtracked from such language. Most conservatives
expressed concern that the statement, combined with her previous ties with
left-leaning Hispanic advocacy groups that actively promote affirmative
action policies,[1] indicated that she would let her personal bias influence her
judicial decision making. President Barack Obama defended his nominee,
arguing that, while she may have used a poor choice of words, "she was
simply saying that her life experiences will give her information about the
struggles and hardships that people are going through—that will make her
a good judge" (quoted in Kirkpatrick 2009, A1). Sotomayor sought to dif-
fuse the controversy over those specific words, saying in her testimony at

---

[1]Affirmative action policies are designed to give preferential treatment to racial minorities in
issues such as college admissions as a way to overcome past discrimination.

In May 2009, President Barack Obama nominated Sonia Sotomayor, the third woman—
and first Latina—to serve on the United States Supreme Court.
*Source*: AP Photo / Alex Brandon.

the hearings for her confirmation that the words were "a rhetorical flourish that fell flat" and that they had been misinterpreted (quoted in Baker and Lewis 2009, A1). She said, "It was bad because it left an impression that life experiences command a result in a case. But that's clearly not what I do as a judge" (ibid.). Ultimately, Sotomayor won the confirmation and has successfully launched her career as a Supreme Court justice, but her 2001 comments, along with Sandra Day O'Connor's famous words, raise a fascinating question: To what extent should a judge's gender and background impact his or her decision making?

This issue for Sotomayor once again emerged publicly in the aftermath of a 2014 Supreme Court decision, *Schuette v. Coalition to Defend Affirmative Action*. In a 6-2 decision, the Court upheld Michigan's ban on affirmative action, which voters passed in a 2006 ballot initiative.[2] In a stinging dissent, Sotomayor used very personal language to dismiss the majority's decision that racial-based preferences perpetuate racial discrimination, calling on the Supreme Court to consider the "simple truth that race does matter." She writes,

> Race matters, in part, because of the long history of racial minorities being denied access to the political process. Race also matters because of persistent racial inequality in society—inequality that cannot be ignored and that has produced stark socioeconomic disparities. And race matters for reasons that really are only skin deep, that cannot be discussed in any other way, and that cannot be wished away. . . . Race matters because of the slights, the snickers, the silent judgments that reinforce the most crippling of thoughts: "I do not belong here."

Legal analysts, such as *Slate's* Dahlia Lithwick (2014), noted that Sotomayor's dissent painted a picture "that looks a lot like her own life." For instance, Joan Biskupic's biography of Sonia Sotomayor recounts how she once lodged a complaint against a partner in the Washington law firm where she worked for telling colleagues and prospective hires that Sotomayor was only admitted to Yale Law School because she was Latina (Biskupic 2014). Storied liberal publications such as *The New Yorker* and *The New Republic* described her *Schuette* dissent as eloquent and courageous. It is precisely because of Sonia Sotomayor's passionate rebuttal of attacks on affirmative action, drawing from a unique perspective as a woman of color and employing "practical language"—dubbed by *New Republic's* legal analyst David Fontana (2014) as the "Sotomayor Style"—that her supporters

---

[2]Michigan voters passed the ban, which barred any preferential treatment for racial minorities in terms of admission to public colleges, hiring of government personnel, or the awarding of government contracts, by 58 percent of the vote. Justice Elena Kagan recused herself from the case, having worked on the case while she was Solicitor General serving in the Obama administration.

believe Sotomayor to be the ideal person to talk about fairness and equality under the law.

Yet, conservative critics used extremely pointed language to express their disapproval of Sotomayor's dissent in *Schuette*. The *National Review* wrote that Sotomayor's opinion was "illiterate and logically indefensible," adding "the still-young career of this self-described 'wise Latina' on the Supreme Court already offers a case study in the moral and legal corrosion that inevitably results from elevating ethnic-identity politics over the law" (*National Review* 2014). Steve Hayes of *The Weekly Standard* described Sotomayor's dissent on a Fox News panel as "a decision written by somebody who was writing about emotion," language that feminist critic Marcie Bianco argues is often used as code to discredit or marginalize women and minorities (Bianco 2014).

The fallout after the *Schuette* decision once again brings up fundamental questions about the nature of representation and politics. Recall Sandra Day O'Connor's statement that she believes that wise women and wise men serving as judges will make similar decisions. Sotomayor, however, has taken a different stance, arguing that her experiences, both as a woman and a Latina, while not totally dictating her jurisprudence, do play a part in her decision making.

That two such prominent women who have reached the pinnacle of the legal profession hold differing perspectives on the role that one's sex or ethnicity should play in judicial decision making reminds us that elite political women are far from monolithic on the question of substantive representation. Interestingly, however, O'Connor has been outspoken in her advocacy for having more women serve as judges, despite her belief that a judge's gender will not affect the quality of decisions, saying that "there are cases where our experience as women might bring some perspective to the situation before the court" (quoted in Blackburn 2010). Of course, this begs a fundamental question: Does the behavior of women jurists differ from that of male jurists? Do women judges make different decisions than their male counterparts in certain areas of the law that have particular relevance for women, such as sex discrimination? Does gender actually make a difference on the bench? Would we even want such personal qualities to impact decision making on the bench, given that the American legal system, as many legal scholars maintain, is built upon precedent and objectivity?

Before examining the scholarly literature that considers how (or if) gender affects judicial decision making, this chapter takes a look at the number of women currently serving as judges nationwide, with a nod to the history of women in the judiciary. Before discussing women's roles as judges, however, this chapter briefly examines the role of the courts in American politics, considering how gender may potentially impact this branch of government.

## WHY THE COURTS ARE IMPORTANT

Although different than the legislative and executive branches, the courts hold an important place in our political system. The judiciary handles a variety of disputes between two parties—whether those parties are private citizens or the government, or the dispute under question is civil or criminal in nature. One result is that the courts play a significant role in the lives of everyday Americans, as they provide one of the most frequent contacts between people and their governments, particularly at the state and local levels.

Verdicts made by the courts, especially when one of the parties involved is the government, can also have important political and policy ramifications. Nowhere is this more evident than at the United States Supreme Court. The job of the Supreme Court is to maintain national supremacy in the law by ensuring uniformity in the interpretation of national laws. One way that it does so is by examining the constitutionality of acts of Congress or, more frequently, state legislation. For example, if a state legislature passes a law that places certain limits on a woman's ability to obtain an abortion, the United States Supreme Court may decide to hear challenges to the law to decide if it violates liberties or guarantees provided in the United States Constitution. However, few such challenges make it all of the way to the Supreme Court and, as a result, the lower federal courts and state supreme courts have also come to play an important role in determining public policy.

In recognition of the increasing role of courts in policymaking, interest groups and citizens often turn to the courts—both federal and state—when the legislative process is not accessible or does not produce desired results. In that vein, the courts are often viewed as the institutions that protect the rights of minorities. Women have turned to the courts to expand their rights (O'Connor 1980). For example, in the late 1960s and 1970s, Congress passed several pieces of legislation that banned sex discrimination in the workplace and in higher education. Given that determining what constitutes discriminatory behavior can be nebulous at times, various women (often with the backing of women's legal and political organizations) have brought their individual cases regarding discrimination before the courts. Most recently, in 2015, the Supreme Court expanded the rights of pregnant women facing employer discrimination in *Young v. United Postal Service*. Peggy Young, a former UPS truck driver, was placed on unpaid leave as a result of her high-risk pregnancy after doctors told her she could not lift packages of more than 20 pounds. Young had petitioned instead for lighter duty, which she argued had been given to other workers who became sick and required lighter job responsibilities (Liptak 2015). Young sued UPS under the 1978 Pregnancy Discrimination Act, which amended the Civil Rights Act to outlaw "discrimination on the basis of pregnancy, childbirth, or related medical conditions." Under the law, employers must treat women affected by pregnancy in the same manner as "employees who are similar in their ability or inability to work" (EEOC n.d.). While an appellate court had dismissed Young's lawsuit, claiming that UPS had also denied light duty requests from other temporarily disabled employees—in essence, claiming that their policy was "pregnancy-blind"—the Supreme Court disagreed, remanding Young's case back to the lower courts and giving her the chance to prove that UPS had, in fact, discriminated against her because of her pregnancy (Grossman and Brake 2015). Notably, UPS has since changed its policy to routinely allow lighter duty for pregnant workers (Liptak 2015).

While women and other minorities have often sought relief in the courts for their grievances, the judiciary is restricted in its ability to make policy compared with the legislative or executive branches. Unlike legislators or administrators, for example, judges cannot make decisions that will affect policy unless a case appears before them in their dockets. Judges are often circumscribed from such behavior by the norms of their profession because they are expected to be impartial and detached from the cases that they hear, relying on evidence in a case before making a decision. Judges are also constrained by the nature of law. As Martin and Pyle (2000) note: "The law itself, statutes and precedents, the facts of the case, the requirements of evidence, the possibility of being overturned on appeal, even the nature of the adversarial system, all restrict the freedom of judicial discretion" (1211).

Yet, many who study the courts also acknowledge that the act of adjudication is potentially influenced by the personal characteristics of judges. It is in this capacity that the gender of judges could potentially make a difference in judicial decision making. As research in political science finds that women differ from men politically, both in terms of their activism and their attitudes, many political observers believe that women judges may also differ in important ways from men judges. Proponents of increasing the presence of women on the bench argue that it is only fair to have a judiciary that is made up of both men and women. They contend that recruiting representatives with more diverse backgrounds and experiences to the bench would result in a judiciary that would be a fairer institution—one that would more effectively use the talents of all citizens (Bratton and Spill 2002; Kenney 2013).

## WOMEN IN THE JUDICIARY

In the early twentieth century, a few women were appointed to specialized courts with limited jurisdictions (Morrison 2002).[3] For example, Georgia

---

[3] History records indicate that Esther Morris was the first woman to serve as a jurist, who in 1869 became a part-time justice of the peace in Wyoming at the South Pass Mining Camp (Hermann and Kelly 1988). In 1886, Carrie Burnham Kilgore (the first female graduate of the University of Pennsylvania Law School) was appointed a master in chancery (essentially,

Bullock served on the Los Angeles Women's Court, which began in 1914 (Cook 1993). The court was developed during the Progressive Era, with the idea being that such a specialized court would help "fallen" women to learn and conform to the cultural gender role norms of the day if they were given special and separate treatment from male defendants. Judge Bullock believed that it was her duty as a judge on this court to help rather than merely punish women for small offenses, in the hope of reclaiming such women to society. Moreover, it was a duty that she believed was specially required of women at the time, remarking at the end of her first session: "The salvation of women must be through women" (Cook 1993, 146). Bullock later parlayed her experience on the women's court, along with the many connections she had made with various women's organizations of the day, to an appointment as a municipal judge in California in 1926 and then won election to the superior court in Los Angeles in 1932—a seat that she held for 25 years (Cook 1993).

One of the first women appointed to the federal bench was Burnita Shelton Matthews, appointed to the District Court for the District of Columbia by President Truman in 1949. She was the first woman to serve as a federal trial court judge. An active suffragist, Matthews attended classes at National University (now George Washington University) while working in the Veterans' Administration. Upon her graduation in 1920, she could not find work in any law firm, so she began her own practice in Washington, DC (Ginsburg and Brill 1995). She also worked as counsel to the National Woman's Party, the suffragist organization founded by Alice Paul that later introduced the original text for the ERA. Upon announcement of her selection to the federal bench, one fellow judge was reported to have said, "Mrs. Matthews would make a good judge, [but there's] just one thing wrong; she's a woman" (ibid., 285). To show her faith in her fellow women, Matthews would only hire women as her law clerks (ibid.). For more on the first woman to be appointed to the Federal Appellate Bench, Florence Allen, see Box 9.1.

It was not until the 1960s that President John F. Kennedy appointed additional women to the federal bench, including Sarah Hughes in 1961 (Mezey 2000). Hughes later became famous as the federal judge who swore in Lyndon Baines Johnson after Kennedy's assassination in 1963. In 1968, President Johnson appointed Shirley Mount Hufstedler to the United States Court of Appeals for the Ninth Circuit. She is perhaps best known, however, as being the first Secretary of Education, after President Carter enlisted her to be the head of this newly created cabinet-level department in

the administrative head of the court), making her the first woman to serve in a state judiciary (O'Connor 2000). The first elected woman judge was Catherine McCullough, who became a justice of the peace in Evanston, Illinois, in 1907 (Hermann and Kelly 1988).

**Box 9.1. Florence Allen, First Federal Judge**

The first woman to be appointed to the federal courts, Florence Allen grew up in rural Utah where her father was a surveyor for a mining company. A professor of Latin and Greek as well, Clarence Allen became Utah's first congressman while Florence was a young teenager. After studying the piano as an undergraduate, Allen pursued legal studies, graduating from New York University's law school in 1913 and settling in Ohio, where she was admitted to the bar in 1914. An active suffragist, in 1919, she was appointed as assistant county prosecutor in Cuyahoga County, Ohio, and when women were franchised in 1920, she ran for judge for the court of common pleas, which she won. However, she soon refused an assignment as a judge in a newly created divorce division of the court, as she was not only more interested in criminal law but also felt unqualified to judge divorce cases as an unmarried woman. Her refusal of the appointment brought her acclaim, as did her attitude that it was important to have women serve as judges. As Allen herself wrote, "When women of intelligence recognize their share in and their responsibility for the courts, a powerful moral backing is secured for the administration of justice" (Allen 1965, 48). Allen parlayed this popularity into a successful election onto the Ohio Supreme Court. After 11 years on the Ohio Supreme Court, she was appointed by Franklin Delano Roosevelt to the Sixth Circuit Court of Appeals in 1934—a decision that was not supported by several male members of the circuit. Allen writes in her memoirs that when her appointment to the court was announced, one of her fellow judges went to bed for two days. She quickly won her colleagues' admiration, however, with her conscientious work. She garnered national attention as the author of the three-judge panel ruling that the federal government's action of erecting dams and reservoirs in the Tennessee Valley Authority was constitutional. The United States Supreme Court later affirmed her judgment (Ginsburg and Brill 1995).

*Photo source*: Library of Congress / The Standiford Studio, Cleveland.

1979 (Ginsburg and Brill 1995). Upon Carter's defeat in 1980, Hufstedler returned to private practice.

Under President Jimmy Carter's administration in the late 1970s, women began to have more than a token presence in the federal judiciary. Presidents Nixon and Ford only managed to appoint two additional women to the federal bench. But under Carter's watch, 40 women were nominated and approved. Carter also actively sought out qualified people of color. Carter was willing to reach deeper into the qualified pool of potential judges to ensure that more women were selected, in part because his deputy White House counsel, Margaret McKenna, prioritized this outcome by having the White House take control over judicial nominations from the Justice Department (Kenney 2014). McKenna and the White House encouraged Carter to forgo the traditional route of judicial selection: senatorial courtesy, in which senators of the president's party from states with openings in the judiciary make recommendations to the president. Instead, Carter established merit commissions to select potential nominees that included not just senators but also state bar association members, practicing attorneys, non-lawyers, women's and minority's organizations, sitting judges, and the ABA (Martin 1987). The result was that Carter's nontraditional nominees (both females and nonwhite males) were younger and less likely to be partners in traditional law firms. Carter was also helped in this endeavor by the creation of 152 new judgeships by Congress under the Omnibus Judgeship Act (Mezey 2000) (see Figure 9.1).

President Ronald Reagan did not continue Carter's affirmative action policy toward women or minorities. Compared with Carter, for whom 15.5 percent of judicial appointees were women, Reagan appointed just 7.6 percent of women as federal judges (ibid.). The reasons for this were varied, but many believed it was due to Reagan's emphasis on ideology in selecting judges. Because Reagan made conservatism an important factor in his decision to appoint judges, there were likely fewer potential women nominees to select. Also, Reagan abandoned the merit system put in place by Carter, reverting to the more traditional system of senatorial courtesy (Martin 1987).

Reagan's successor, George H. W. Bush, did a much better job of appointing women to the federal bench, in part because he relied less on ideological purity as a factor for appointments. Bush was also aided, as Carter had been, by the establishment of more judicial positions nationwide. Bush appointed women to more than 19 percent of federal judgeships during his one term in office (Mezey 2000). President Bill Clinton further increased the judicial appointments in terms of women in the judiciary. Making it a top priority to diversify the bench, and also aided by the establishment of new judgeships by Congress, Clinton more than doubled the number of

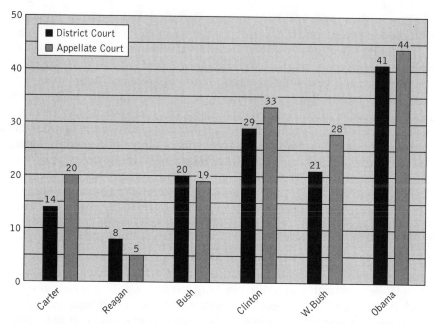

**Figure 9.1. Presidential Appointments: Percentage of Women Appointed to Federal Courts.**
*Sources*: Goldman, Federal Judicial Center.

women serving in the federal judiciary in his time in office (Palmer 2001). For his first term, 52.1 percent of his appointments were nontraditional (either female or nonwhite). Clinton named 87 women (28.5 percent) as district court appointees. The percentage of female appointees under Clinton to the circuit court or court of appeals was even higher—32.8 percent. When Clinton began office, approximately 1 in 10 federal judges was female; when he left, the number was 1 in 5 (Goldman et al. 2001). Unlike Reagan, Clinton cared less about the ideology of judges and concentrated more on diversity. One result is that Clinton's nontraditional appointees (including minority men) were more likely to come from diverse backgrounds than the traditional ones. For example, they were more likely to have backgrounds in government or the state judiciary or to have prosecutorial experience than white males (ibid.). One study found, however, that despite having impeccable credentials, Clinton's female judicial nominees, under divided government, were delayed longer in their processing under the GOP Senate than were his male nominees (Hartley 2001).

President George W. Bush also had a good track record of appointing women to the bench—coming close to, but not quite matching, Clinton's numbers in terms of women. During his two terms in office, out of 327 judicial appointments, 77 (23.5 percent) were women (Federal Judicial Center 2017). In their examination of the diversity of the federal bench from Carter through George W. Bush's first term, political scientists Rorie Spill Solberg and Kathleen Bratton (2005) systematically identify several factors that help explain what influences the appointment of women and minorities. Their multivariate analysis finds that larger courts tend to predict gains made by women and African Americans across administrations, which suggests that it is politically easier to appoint a woman to a single seat on a large court. Also, they find that women are more likely to be appointed to all-male courts. In other words, presidents face particular political pressure to appoint women (and judges of color) in courts that lack diversity. While scholars of judicial appointments often note that Senatorial courtesy is an important consideration in determining who gets appointed to the federal bench, Solberg and Bratton find that "liberal senatorial delegations do not generally increase the likelihood that a woman, African American, or Hispanic judge will be selected" (130). Moreover, the partisanship of the Senate delegation from states in which judges were appointed was also not a significant factor in predicting appointment diversity. The size of the court and the existing diversity of the court, then, trump political factors when it comes to predicting when women and minorities will be tapped to serve on the federal courts.

Turning to the Obama presidency, Obama has the strongest record of judicial appointment of women by far. In addition to the appointment of two women to the United States Supreme Court, as of the summer of 2015, 40.9 percent of Obama's appointments to the district court level and 43.4 percent of his appointments to the appellate courts were women. Of those appointments, a significant number were women of color: Obama appointed 38 non-white women (37 percent) to the district courts and 4 non-white women (17 percent) to the appellate courts. Among other notable appointments, Obama tapped the first Asian American woman, Jacqueline Nguyen, to serve on the US Appellate courts (see Box 9.2). As of 2014, women make up approximately 25 percent of all active federal judges (Federal Judicial Center 2017).

### Women on the Supreme Court

Presidents Reagan, Clinton, and Obama share the distinction of appointing the only four women to serve on the United States Supreme Court. In 1981, keeping a promise he made while campaigning for president (in part to appeal to women voters), Reagan appointed Sandra Day O'Connor as the first female justice of the Supreme Court. Born in 1930, Sandra Day O'Connor grew up on the Lazy B cattle ranch on the Arizona–New Mexico border (Lane 2004). During the school year, she lived with her grandparents

**Box 9.2.  Jacqueline Nguyen, First Asian American U.S. Appellate Court Judge**

President Barack Obama made history in 2012 when he appointed Jacqueline Nguyen to a seat on the United States Court of Appeals for the Ninth Circuit in Pasadena, California, as she became the first Asian American woman to serve on any American federal appellate court. She is also the nation's first Vietnamese-American federal judge. Nguyen arrived in the United States at the age of ten after the fall of Saigon during the Vietnam War. Growing up, she worked in her family's donut shop and helped her mother peel and chop apples to earn extra money. After she won a scholarship to Occidental College, where she majored in English, she went to law school. After a brief time in private practice, she pursued her passion for public service by working for the United States Attorney's office, which led to her eventual appointment as a California Superior Court judge in 2002 (Egelko 2012). Featured in a profile at the Federal Judicial Center's "Pathways to the Bench" video series, Nguyen tells prospective attorneys (and judges) that no opportunity is too small to pass by and inspires young people to "have the courage and work ethic to accept opportunities that will shape your life." The American Bar Association awarded Nguyen its 2015 Spirit of Excellence Award, which recognizes her commitment to racial and ethnic diversity in the legal profession (ABA 2014). *Photo source*: United States Courts for the Ninth Circuit 2012 Annual Report, p. 10, http://www.ce9.uscourts.gov/publications/AnnualReport2012.pdf.

and attended private school in El Paso, Texas, but she returned to the ranch during the summers—where she grew up learning to ride horses and spent time with her father and his cowboys during their work, which no doubt made her comfortable working and competing with men (Lane 2004). Upon graduating high school at age 16, O'Connor attended Stanford University in 1946, earning a joint B.S. in economics and law degree in a six-year program. It was at Stanford Law that she met her husband and she was a classmate of former Chief Justice William Rehnquist. Despite graduating magna cum laude, the only job offer she received upon completing law school was as a legal secretary.

Instead of private practice, O'Connor sought work in the public sector upon returning with her husband to Arizona. She found work as a deputy county attorney—but only because she volunteered to work for free until a paid position opened (Lane 2004). Later, she took leave from practicing law to raise her three small sons from 1960 to 1965. While raising her family, O'Connor was active in state Republican Party politics and in community service organizations such as the Junior League. In 1965, she returned to work full-time as a state assistant attorney general—a position she gained from her political contacts—and was later appointed to a vacant seat in the State Senate in 1969. Her time in the Senate was successful, as she won reelection twice and was the first woman to be elected nationally as majority leader in a State Senate (Maveety 1996). In 1975, she was elected as a county judge and was elevated to Arizona's highest court—the State Court of Appeals—in 1979.

Reagan tapped O'Connor to be the first woman on the Supreme Court because despite her short time as a state Supreme Court justice in Arizona, O'Connor had developed a reputation as a solid conservative on many issues that were important to the Reagan administration, especially federalism. Yet, she was a moderate on issues such as abortion, which led women's organizations to support her nomination while pro-life groups opposed her (Palmer 1991). The National Association of Women Judges, which was formed in 1979 in part to advocate for the appointment of a woman to the United States Supreme Court, was also pleased with O'Connor's nomination. After her confirmation hearings, the United States Senate confirmed O'Connor unanimously.

In 1993, President Bill Clinton appointed Ruth Bader Ginsburg as his first nominee to the Supreme Court. At the time, Ginsburg was serving her twelfth year as an appellate judge on the federal Court of Appeals for the District of Columbia Circuit. Ginsburg was brought to Clinton's attention as a possible nominee, in part because of the efforts of her husband Martin Ginsburg, a prominent tax attorney and law professor at Georgetown University. To help publicize his wife as a possible candidate, Martin Ginsburg began a letter-writing campaign, contacting various dignitaries and legal scholars to call or write to the White House in support of Ginsburg's candidacy as a Supreme Court justice. Upon his wife's nomination, Martin Ginsburg told the *Washington Post:* "If there was something that I could have done to be helpful, I would have done it, because I think my wife is super, and the President couldn't have made a better appointment than the one he just made" (O'Connor and Palmer 2001, 264).

In some ways, Ruth Bader Ginsburg's personal story differs dramatically from O'Connor's—but in other ways, it is very similar. Ginsburg was born in Brooklyn in 1933, and was taught by her mother to be independent and scholarly despite the gender norms that pervaded their ethnic neighbor-hood (Campbell 2002). Ginsburg's academic success in New York's public schools earned her a scholarship to Cornell University, where she met her husband Martin Ginsburg, whom she married in 1954 after graduating first in her class. Ginsburg followed her husband to Harvard Law School—he had just completed his first year there—where she was one of just nine women in a law class of 500 (Ginsburg 1997).

Ginsburg excelled at Harvard, and she earned a coveted spot on the *Harvard Law Review*. Her academic performance was all the more remark-able because not only was she the mother of a young child at the time, but also in her second year, her husband developed testicular cancer. She maintained her high level of work while also taking notes for him when he missed classes and typing his papers. When Martin Ginsburg accepted a job at a New York law firm, she transferred to Columbia Law School for her final year, graduating at the top of her class.

Similar to the situation faced by Sandra Day O'Connor, not a single law firm would hire Ginsburg upon her graduation and, despite recommenda-tions from her Columbia professors, she was denied a chance to clerk with Supreme Court Justice Felix Frankfurter. She accepted a position as a clerk with a federal district court judge in New York and then went into academia, becoming a law professor at Rutgers University. She later became the first tenured woman faculty member at Columbia Law School (Ginsburg 1997).

Unlike Sandra Day O'Connor, Ginsburg did not work in the public sector nor was she involved in electoral politics. Instead, in addition to becoming a notable law professor, she also was founder and general counsel to the American Civil Liberties Union's (ACLU) Women's Rights Project (Campbell 2002). While still teaching at Rutgers, and realizing that women faculty members were paid less than men, Ginsburg took part in a class action lawsuit that brought women's salaries on par with men (Ginsburg 1997). At the same time, the ACLU was beginning to hear similar complaints about discriminatory behavior from other women in different fields, and they recruited Ginsburg to help with these sex discrimination cases under the auspices of the Women's Rights Project. As part of the ACLU, Ginsburg helped in 34 cases at the Supreme Court level (Campbell 2002).

Moreover, she successfully argued five out of six such cases in front of the Supreme Court, including the pivotal 1971 *Reed v. Reed* case, which was the first decision to establish that laws that segregated on sex-based differences were "entitled to some sort of scrutiny under the Fourteenth Amendment" (O'Connor and Clark 1999, 273). In other words, this case called into ques-tion the constitutionality of statutes that allowed for gender discrimination. Given Ginsburg's successful and prodigious record as a litigator, professor, and legal scholar, she was appointed to the United States Court of Appeals for the District of Columbia Circuit in 1980 by Jimmy Carter.

Upon joining the Supreme Court as the second female justice, Ginsburg quickly became a close friend of O'Connor, despite their ideological and partisan differences. Ginsburg was solidly in the liberal camp of the Court, whereas O'Connor leaned more to the conservative side, although she was typically the key deciding vote on a number of issues on the Court. Both women, however, shared a similar voting record when it came to issues that affected women disproportionately, such as abortion and sex discrimination. In 2006, O'Connor retired from the bench to spend time with her ailing husband, who was suffering from Alzheimer's disease and who passed away in 2009, although she still hears oral arguments occasionally as a substitute judge in the federal appellate courts, following in the tradition of other retired Supreme Court justices (Brust 2008). In February 2009, Ginsburg took a brief leave of absence to undergo pancreatic cancer surgery, which doctors deemed successful, and returned to work by the end of the month. At 84, and in fairly good health, Ginsburg shows no signs of slowing down. If anything, her popularity is at an all-time high (see Box 9.3), particularly with a younger generation of millennial women who

**Box 9.3. Notorious RBG**

Who says octogenarians can't be hip? Supreme Court Justice Ruth Bader Ginsburg, 84, has acquired an entirely new generation of fans through the tumblr meme known as Notorious RBG (notoriousrbg .tumblr.com), created by NYU Law student Shana Knizhnik, with the subtitle "Justice Ruth Bader Ginsburg, in all her glory." The popularity of the meme inspired Knizhnik and MSNBC reporter Irin Carmon to pen a new biography called *Notorious RBG: The Life and Times of Ruth Bader Ginsburg*, described by Carmon as an "irreverent celebration" of Ginsburg's life and legacy for feminism. Or, as they write on their tumblr site, they are taking their "national RBG girl crush to the next level." For her part, Ginsburg is a big fan of the website, telling reporter Katie Couric that the meme is something she enjoys: "Most of it is very funny. I haven't seen anything that isn't pleasing or funny on that website."

*Photo source*: Cover image from *NOTORIOUS RBG: The Life and Times of Ruth Bader Ginsburg* by Irin Carmon and Shana Knizhnik. Reprinted with permission from the authors.

are discovering Ginsburg's pioneering role as a crusader for women's legal rights and who respect her outspoken dissents championing women's legal rights. Ginsburg's popularity has spawned a Tumblr meme as well as a new biography—with the tagline "The Notorious R.B.G"[4] (Schwartz 2015).

## O'Connor, Ginsburg, and Beyond

When Sandra Day O'Connor announced her retirement in July 2005, it set off a frenzy of speculation about who should replace the first female Supreme Court justice. Female senators, women's groups, and even First Lady Laura Bush pressured President George W. Bush to appoint another female justice. Instead, President Bush first nominated John Roberts but elevated him to nomination for Chief Justice after Chief Justice William Rehnquist died around the same time. Bush then tried to nominate a woman, his White House Counsel, Harriet Miers, but a revolt within the Republican Party over her qualifications led Miers to withdraw her nomination and Bush ultimately nominated current Supreme Court justice Samuel Alito. O'Connor herself expressed disappointment that President Bush did not select a woman to replace her (Greenburg 2007).

In the years since Ronald Reagan appointed O'Connor to the court, the nature of Supreme Court nomination politics has drastically changed. Once the president selects a nominee, a majority of senators must vote to confirm the nomination. The polarization of the Democratic and Republican parties has made the ideology of the president and the presumed ideological leanings of the nominee more central to confirmation (Epstein and Segal 2005; Binder and Maltzman 2009). Speculation about the ideological views of a justice is even more intense on critical nominations where, as in the case of the O'Connor replacement, the new justice could swing the balance of opinion in a more liberal or conservative direction (Ruckman 1993).

Moreover, issues of race and gender now permeate the debate over nominees. While presidents and senators maintain that there is no litmus test for a potential justice, a nominee's position on *Roe v. Wade* is heavily scrutinized. The court plays an important role in determining the scope of women's rights, from reproductive rights to employment discrimination (Scherer 2005). The confirmation battle over Clarence Thomas's elevation to the Supreme Court in 1991, which included accusations of sexual

---

[4]The Notorious R.B.G. is a tweak of the moniker used by the late rapper Christopher "Notorious B.I.G" Wallace. In 2014, a student at NYU Law School launched the notoriousrbg.tumblr.com, a website where fans of Ginsburg post doctored art work inspired by her legacy, famous Ginsburg quotes, links to interviews of Ginsburg, and photos of Ginsburg with famous political leaders and celebrities.

harassment by his former work colleague Anita Hill, focused even more attention on gender and jurisprudence. As the country has become more diverse and more women and minorities have achieved the educational and employment credentials that qualify them for a seat on the federal bench, the parties compete to claim credit for increasing diversity on the courts or appointing the first member of a particular group to the Supreme Court or one of the federal appellate or district courts (Goldman 1997; Scherer 2005). This partisan conflict often exacerbates the controversy surrounding a particular female or minority nominee (Bell 2002; Soloweij, Martinek, and Brunell 2005).

Finally, there has been a change in the makeup of the Senate since O'Connor was first nominated to the court. Demonstrating the importance of descriptive representation, there are now more female senators who have a seat at the table and are able to weigh the records of nominees and cast confirmation votes. When O'Connor was nominated in 1981, there were only two women in the Senate. When the Senate considered O'Connor's replacement, 14 women senators weighed in on the nomination. Analyzing the floor debate and the votes senators cast on the nominations of John Roberts and Samuel Alito, Michele Swers (2013) found that in this polarized era, partisanship dominated confirmation votes. Members of the president's party, in this case Republicans, almost always supported the president's nominees. For the opposition party Democrats, a senator's ideological distance from the president and the nominee strongly impacted the vote as the most liberal senators were the most likely to oppose Roberts and Alito. Still, even after accounting for ideology, Swers found that among the more moderate senators, female Democrats were more likely to oppose the nominees than their moderate male counterparts. The most striking impact of the presence of women in the Senate, however, was their influence on the deliberative process. Analyzing senators' floor speeches explaining their votes on the nominations, Swers found that Democratic women were much more likely than their male Democratic colleagues to prioritize Roberts's and Alito's positions on women's rights when making their vote decisions. Furthermore, the female senators were also more likely to consider the nominees' positions on a range of women's rights issues beyond abortion including equal pay, employment discrimination, and family leave (Swers 2013).

In the years following O'Connor's departure from the court, Ruth Bader Ginsburg lamented the fact that she was the only woman on the Supreme Court. In high-profile decisions on partial birth abortion and employment discrimination, Ginsburg took the unusual step of reading her dissents from the bench and criticizing her colleagues for not understanding the social position of women. Thus, following the Lilly Ledbetter pay discrimination case, Ginsburg stated, "The court does not comprehend, or is indifferent to, the insidious way in which women can be victims of pay discrimination" (quoted in Barnes 2007).

Hence, when Barack Obama was elected president, there was a great deal of focus on whether he would appoint a woman or even the first Hispanic woman to the next Supreme Court vacancy. That moment arrived fairly soon in his presidency, when Justice David Souter announced in April 2009 his intention to step down from the Supreme Court. In May 2009, Obama announced Judge Sonia Sotomayor, a US Appellate Court judge with 17 years' experience, to be his pick for the Supreme Court. Her Supreme Court appointment was met (largely) with enthusiasm from both women's rights organizations and Latino groups (less so from conservative organizations). She was confirmed in August 2009, although she did not receive overwhelming support from Republican senators, many of whom stated their objections over her past support of affirmative action (see earlier discussion in this chapter).

Former Justice Sandra Day O'Connor also lauded Sotomayor's appointment to the Supreme Court:

> I am very happy that another woman is being appointed. I think that's very important. I was terribly disappointed when I retired in 2006 not to be replaced by a woman. We have to remember that slightly more than 50 percent of us in this country have two X chromosomes and I think it doesn't hurt to look at our national institutions and see women represented. I don't think two females on the Supreme Court is enough, but it is certainly better than one. (quoted in Lodge 2009)

In April 2010, Justice John Paul Stevens, who had served on the nation's highest court since his appointment by President Gerald Ford in 1975, again gave President Barack Obama the chance to make another appointment to the Supreme Court. The following month, Obama selected a second woman nominee, Elena Kagan, whom he had appointed US Solicitor General in his early months in office. The US Solicitor General is considered the government's top lawyer, tasked with the job of representing the United States in cases that appear before the United States Supreme Court, and hence is often referred to as the "10th Justice" given the frequency with which he or she interacts with the nation's highest court.

Elena Kagan grew up in a middle-class Jewish family in New York City to an educator mother and lawyer father. Like Sotomayor, Kagan attended Princeton University, graduating *summa cum laude* in 1981, attended Oxford to earn a master's degree, and then completed law school at Harvard, graduating in 1986, where she served on the law review. Unlike other Supreme Court justices, Kagan's early career encompassed both politics *and* law. For instance, she clerked with former Justice Thurgood Marshall in 1988 and also served as an advisor for the 1988 presidential campaign for Democratic nominee and former Massachusetts Governor Michael Dukakis. After a brief time in private practice, Kagan became a law professor at the University of Chicago law school, but left this position to serve as a domestic policy assistant to Bill Clinton (Goldstein, Leonning, and Slevin 2010). Obama was not the first president to appoint Kagan to the federal bench—Clinton nominated her to the DC Circuit Court of Appeals in 1999, but her nomination got mired in judicial politics in the Senate Judiciary Committee, so she opted to return to academia, becoming a full law professor at Harvard and ultimately the first woman Dean of Harvard Law School in 2003 (Dillon 2003). Upon Obama's election as president, she was confirmed to be the first female Solicitor General.

Unlike Sotomayor's appointment, Obama's selection of Kagan was met with less overt drama that followed Sotomayor after her "wise Latina" comment became more widely known. Of course, some conservatives pointed to her previous political background in a Democratic White House as a

The first woman to serve on the Supreme Court, retired Justice Sandra Day O'Connor (left), visits the three current female justices residing on the Court: Justice Sonia Sotomayor, Justice Ruth Bader Ginsburg, and Justice Elena Kagan.
*Source*: Steve Petteway, *Collection of the Supreme Court of the United States.*

potential problem while others were concerned that she had never served as a judge—although up until the 1970s, it was not unusual for many Supreme Court justices to come to the bench from outside of the judiciary. However, some proponents of Ms. Kagan believed her lack of judicial experience was helpful to her prospects, given that she had no "judicial paper trail" to defend during her confirmation hearings (Baker and Zeleny 2010). Kagan was easily confirmed, mainly because the Democrats had a filibuster-proof 60-vote majority. She managed to obtain the votes of 5 Republicans as well as 2 Independents and all but one of the Democratic Senators, resulting in a 63-to-37 vote. However, Kagan received fewer votes than did Sotomayor at her confirmation, when she was confirmed 68-to-31. By contrast, Sandra Day O'Connor was confirmed unanimously, and Ruth Bader Ginsburg had only 3 votes cast against her. Of course, Samuel Alito, who had been nominated to replace O'Connor in 2005, was only confirmed by a majority of 58-to-42 votes, which reflects the growing political polarization of fights over nominees to the judicial branch. On January 31, President Donald Trump appointed Neil Gorsuch to fill the seat of former Justice Antonin Scalia, who unexpectedly passed away in February 2016. Gorsuch was a Bush-appointed Appellate Court Judge for the Tenth Circuit. If confirmed, he will be the Court's 109th male justice.

### Women in the State Judiciary

Most Americans will never have a case heard in front of the Supreme Court. Any personal interaction—if any—Americans may have with the judiciary is most likely to occur at the state level, which, similar to the federal judicial system, is composed of state courts of last resort, intermediate appellate courts, and trial courts, where there are approximately 11,800 judges, and some (but not all) states have non-attorney courts, or state limited and special jurisdiction courts, which have approximately 4,900 judges (National Association of Women Judges [NAWJ] 2016). As political scientist Sally J. Kenny (2013) notes, women remain somewhat underrepresented as judges compared to their composition in the qualified labor pool—that is, the percentage of women as state judges is consistently lower than the proportion of women lawyers who have the requisite backgrounds to be eligible to serve. Data compiled by the NAWJ from the 2016 *American Bench*, the annual biographical references on America's judges and courts, show that women make up 31 percent of America's judiciary. Breaking down the data by type of court, NAWJ reports that women constitute 35 percent of judges on state courts of last resort, 35 percent of judges on state intermediate appellate courts, 30 percent of judges on state general jurisdiction courts, and 33 percent of judges on state limited and special jurisdiction courts (see Figure 9.2).

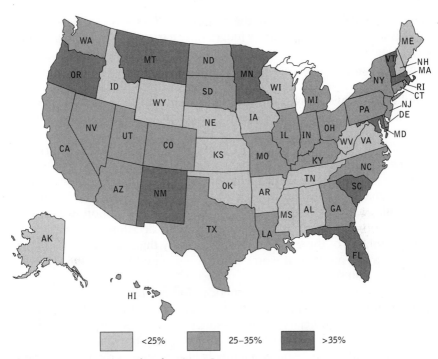

**Figure 9.2. Women Appointed to State Courts.**
*Source*: National Association of Women Judges, https://www.nawj.org/statistics/2016-us -state-court-women-judges

Unlike at the federal level, where judges are appointed by the president and approved by the Senate, selection of judges varies by state—although selection generally boils down to two major methods: election and appointment.[5] In 26 states, all or most judgeships are decided by either partisan (9 states) or nonpartisan (17 states) elections. In reality, many of these elections are non-contested, with incumbents carrying an extraordinary advantage. Moreover, in many cases, the governor often appoints incumbent judges, as vacancies on the bench frequently occur prior to elections. Thus, even in states with no appointive system, governors have a large hand in shaping the judiciary. The other states use some sort of appointment selection process. In 4 states, all or most judgeships are done by gubernatorial appointment, whereas 2 others use legislative appointment. The most popular method of judicial selection at the state level, however, is the merit selection or Missouri Plan used by 18 states. This plan involves a merit

[5]See the National Center for State Courts for information about how states select their judges. http://www.judicialselection.us/judicial_selection/methods/selection_of_judges.cfm?state=.

panel that makes suggestions to the governor for nominees for state judicial vacancies. Once appointed, these judges serve a trial one-year term and then face a retention election asking voters whether they should be retained in office (they face no opposition). Rarely do these appointed judges lose such retention elections.

Political scientists have examined whether the method of judicial selection at the state level—appointment or election—is related to the number of women serving on the bench. One theory is that appointive systems in general tend to depress diversity in state courts, because such systems tend to "favor the status quo by perpetuating the dominance of elites in the judiciary, thus decreasing judicial opportunities for political minorities who may not have the conventional legal backgrounds or experience" (Hurwitz and Lanier 2001, 86). Alternatively, others argue that appointive systems could be more beneficial to women because elite decision makers might be more cognizant of the need for greater diversity than voters, leading to an increase in the number of women in the judiciary (Alozie 1996; Hurwitz and Lanier 2003).

A study by scholars from the American Judicature Society examined all women and minority appellate court judges serving in 2008 to determine which method of judicial selection resulted in the most diverse bench and their findings are mixed. The most common selection method for both minority members and women members of state supreme courts was merit or appointive selection: roughly half of minority judges (54.3 percent) and women judges (48.5 percent) serving in 2008 were chosen through some sort of merit plan (Reddick, Nelson, and Caulfield 2009). However, at the intermediate appellate courts, partisan elections placed slightly more women on such courts than other selection processes, although merit selection remained the more typical avenue for minority judges. Their analysis also finds that party plays a factor when it comes to gender diversity on the state bench: women are more likely to be appointed by Democratic governors than Republican governors for appellate courts AND are more likely to be elected to both types of courts in majority-Democratic states than in majority-Republican states (ibid.).

The American Judicature Society study, while thorough, does not consider how other factors, such as state characteristics, the size of the court, and pools of potential candidates, may work in conjunction with style of selection to either promote or inhibit women's ascension to state courts. For example, research by Margaret Williams (2007) suggests that the merit system actually depresses women's representation on the bench when controlling for other factors, at least at the appellate court level. Williams writes that "states using merit selection to fill the appellate judiciary, on average, see three fewer women on the appellate bench relative to similar states using partisan elections to fill the appellate bench" (1199). However, the appointment system does appear to boost gender diversity on state supreme courts in one case: when such courts are all male. Yet, once women have been appointed to a vacancy in an all-male state Supreme Court, and their appearance as token women is solidified, "the chance that a woman will be appointed to the bench drops significantly once the court achieves any degree of gender diversity" (Bratton and Spill 2002, 516). Kenney and Windett's 2012 study finds further that women are more likely to be appointed to state Supreme Courts when the sitting governor is a woman rather than a man. Moreover, their work finds that state culture matters—states that have higher indices of gender equality are more likely to have women serving on their state's courts of last resort. What appears to count more than selection method when it comes to the presence of women on state courts of last resort is the number of judges on the bench, as scholars have noted a positive relationship between the size of the court and female presence on it (Alozie 1996; Bratton and Spill 2002; Hurwitz and Lanier 2003). The more seats that are available to be filled, the more opportunities women have to serve on the bench.

Women have not only increased their presence in the eligibility pool from which judges are considered, but the criteria for their eligibility have also expanded in recent years. For instance, women and men state Supreme Court justices often take a different path to the bench, with women being more likely to serve in the public sector, and men more likely to come from a private law practice. Moreover, women justices are less likely than their male counterparts to have served in elected political office (Martin and Pyle 2002). These findings suggest that the traditional eligibility pool has shifted to allow for people with more diverse backgrounds, especially women and minorities, to be considered for service on the high court. Many proponents of increasing the number of women are optimistic that women's increased presence in law school—as of 2016, women made up more than half (52 percent) of law school students (ABA 2017)—will eventually result in more qualified women to be tapped to serve as judges or in their taking the plunge and running for judicial office in states that have an elected judiciary. Yet, despite women's higher presence in law schools, women continue to make up far less of the percentage of practicing attorneys—approximately 36 percent (ABA 2017). Moreover, women's representation as leaders within the legal profession is also disproportionately low. For example, women make up only 22 percent of partners in law firms nationwide (ibid.). Political scientist Sally Kenney (2013) warns that the tendency of women to "trickle up" from the labor pool of qualified potential judges has not materialized as quickly as many proponents of women judges had hoped, suggesting that something other than simply the number of qualified women has kept women from serving as judges. As of 2016, however, the national data as indicated in Figure 9.3 show that at least one woman serves on every state's

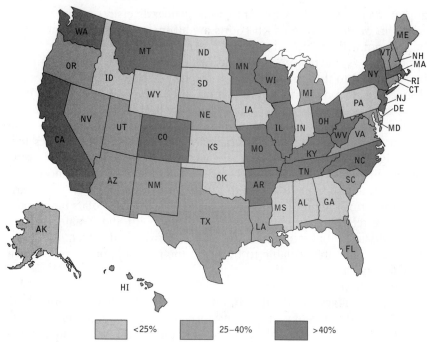

**Figure 9.3. Women Appointed to State Courts of Last Resort.**
*Source*: National Association of Women Judges, http://www.nawj.org/statistics/2016-us
-state-court-women-judges and The American Bench 2014, Foster-Long, LLC.

court of last resort, with the exception of Idaho. In most cases, at least two women serve on their state's most prestigious courts and in seven states—California, New Jersey, New York, North Carolina, Ohio, Tennessee, and Wisconsin—women make up 50 percent or more of the bench.

The impact of type of judicial selection system on women's representation in state courts is also dependent on the *level* of the court under consideration and whether the election was partisan or nonpartisan. For instance, Margaret Williams's 2007 analysis finds that more women sit on state trial courts chosen by non-partisan elections than on courts chosen by partisan elections. State ideology and the presence of female attorneys in a state is also linked to women's representation on state trial courts—women fare better in more liberal states and where more women practice law. For general jurisdiction courts, scholars from the American Judicature Society found the following breakdown of women's pathway to trial courts in their random sample of trial court judges: 30 percent came through merit selection, 28 percent came from judicial appointment, 24 percent came from partisan elections, 12 percent from non-partisan elections, and the remaining 5 percent came from legislative or court appointment. However, given that these data are derived from a random sample of courts, when the authors conducted tests to determine if such selection methods were significantly different, they found that they were not. In other words, at this level, it appears that women are just as likely to be appointed or elected to serve on the trial court bench (Reddick, Melson, and Caufield 2009).

Turning more specifically to judicial elections, several studies that analyze the impact of sex on such elections find in multivariate analyses that there is no systematic bias against women candidates (Hall 2001; Reid 2010). Indeed, Frederick and Streb's (2008) study of the success of female and male candidates running in state intermediate appellate court elections from 2000 to 2006 suggest that women candidates had a slight *advantage* over men candidates, as their regression models suggest that women are more likely to win their races than men. However, Traciel Reid (2010), a leading scholar of gender and judicial elections, notes that while regression analyses that predict success in judicial elections or success in raising funds for such campaigns often find that the impact of gender is not statistically significant, scholars of judicial elections should not assume that gender does not impact these races. Reid's assessment of general elections for state Supreme Court judgeships held between 1996 and 2006 suggests that women face specific challenges that their male counterparts do not. For example, male judicial candidates who are incumbents enjoy a significant fundraising advantage compared with female judicial candidates who are incumbents. Campaign spending also has less impact on women's vote shares than on men's vote shares in judicial elections. Moreover, Reid's research finds that while a higher percentage of women who ran in state judicial elections had judicial experience, this indicator of quality did not boost the electoral chances of women. She writes, "Even having stronger credentials and more money, women [judicial candidates] were unable to parlay electoral assets into sizable electoral gains" (469). In other words, Reid contends that comparable to the work on women who run for other political offices (Lawless and Fox 2005), women who run for judgeships have to be *better* candidates in order to achieve similar electoral results.

Few studies have examined the gender dimensions of judicial campaigns among states that use elections to select state Supreme Court justices. However, McCarthy (2001) found that although some female judicial candidates did campaign on the theme that more women should be elected to help diversify state Supreme Courts in the 1980s and early 1990s, as more women came to serve on state Supreme Courts by the late 1990s, the gender of the candidate rarely became an issue in campaigns. McCarthy's analysis of judicial campaign platforms in the late 1990s found that candidates stressed their professional experience and judicial philosophy during campaigns—not their gender (or the gender of their opponent). However, McCarthy questioned whether such campaign themes actually had an impact on the outcome of elections given the relatively low salience of judicial campaigns at the time.

Increasingly, though, judicial elections appear to have become more politicized, in part because of a 2002 Supreme Court decision, *Republican Party of Minnesota v. White*, which overturned a state ban restricting judicial candidates from announcing their political and legal views on disputed issues as a violation of judicial candidates' First Amendment free speech rights. Given that state courts of last resort increasingly decide cases with important political and policy implications, many interest groups, parties, and corporations have a vested interest in shaping the makeup of the court. In recent years, spending on judicial campaigns has also increased as a result of the Supreme Court's 2010 *Citizens United* decision, which allows for unlimited spending from corporations in political campaigns—as long they are not directly coordinated with those campaigns. The increased spending has trickled into many political races, with the Brennan Center for Justice (2014) reporting that more than $9 million was spent on political advertising in states with judicial elections.

Given the increasing prominence of judicial elections in American politics, and the fact that slightly more judges in the American states will be elected rather than appointed, political scientist Sally Kenney (2010) calls on scholars of women and politics to consider how gender intersects with such election results and also the initial decision to run for judgeships. One study, which draws on the work of Richard Fox and Jennifer Lawless on political ambition, analyzed a pool of "potential judges" (attorneys) in Texas to consider whether similar gender differences emerged in terms of ambition for seats on the state judiciary (Williams 2008). Fascinatingly, while controlling for other factors, women attorneys actually express *more* ambition for judicial office than men. This study suggests that women may appear more ambitious than men with respect to judicial elections because many of them believe that women actually face more barriers than men in legal careers as opposed to becoming a judge. Yet, while women express somewhat greater ambition to run for judicial office in Texas than men, the opportunity structure may still prevent women from taking the additional step of running for judgeships. Still, these results—while limited to just one state—suggest that scholars of women and politics should consider that there is variation in the ambition of women to run for office across political offices including judicial elections.

## THE DIFFERENCE WOMEN JUDGES MAKE

Scholars focus on two primary questions when it comes to comparing men and women judges (Palmer 2001). First, do women judges use a different style or "voice" when it comes to legal reasoning? Second, do women judges make different decisions than men, especially when it comes to policy issues that are potentially of greater interest to women? For example, are they more sensitive to issues of sex and race discrimination?

### Do Women Judges Use A "Different Voice"?

Few books in recent years have had as much of an impact on various fields in the social sciences (or have been as controversial) as Carol Gilligan's *In a Different Voice: Psychological Theory and Women's Development* (1982). A thorough analysis of Gilligan's work is beyond the scope of this chapter, but an overview of her theory and how it could apply to the judiciary is relevant here. Gilligan's theory grapples with moral development among men and women, and how men and women often differ when it comes to speaking and thinking about moral problems and the relationship between oneself and the larger community. Through interviews about conceptions of self and morality, Gilligan found that women often thought about such problems differently than men, regardless of their age or social status. For most men, morality is viewed in terms of fairness, with a concern rooted in individual rights. For most women, caretaking rather than fairness is more important, and they tend to place greater emphasis not on the formal rules of society in deciding what is moral but more on an understanding of responsibilities that they have toward the larger community.

Gilligan argues that these conceptions of morality are rooted in childhood, as studies that focus on how girls and boys play show that when quarrels arise during games, boys are preoccupied—in a legal sense—with the rules of games, whereas girls are more tolerant in their attitudes toward the rules (Gilligan 1982). Boys care more about competition, and girls care more about cooperation. Over time, Gilligan argues that men and women begin to see larger moral problems differently. For women, she writes:

> The moral problem arises from conflicting responsibilities rather than from competing rights and requires for its resolution a mode of thinking that is contextual and narrative rather than formal and abstract. This conception of morality as concerned with the activity of care centers moral development around the understanding of responsibility and relationships, just as the conception of morality as fairness ties moral development to the understanding of rights and rules. (19)

In essence, to solve problems men seek an answer available in existing rules, whereas women seek solutions that maintain their relationships. While Gilligan notes that most people use both "moral" voices at one time or another, women and men tend to emphasize one voice much more often.

Given its emphasis on reason and decision making, legal scholars interested in the impact of gender on decision making have analyzed whether Gilligan's theory has any applicability to jurisprudence. If Gilligan is correct, then we may find that women judges reach their decisions in a different manner than do men, bringing to the bench a different perspective. For example, Suzanna Sherry (1986) has argued that women could bring to the bench a "feminine" (*not* feminist) perspective, closely linked to what in political philosophy is known as the classical republican tradition. Unlike the modern, liberal philosophy that supports the current legal system, with its emphasis on individual rights and liberties, this classical tradition is communitarian and contextual. A feminine legal paradigm, according to Sherry, would be one that emphasizes connectedness, context, and responsibility rather than autonomy or rights.

A virtual cottage industry developed around whether this "different voice" was evident in the jurisprudence of the Supreme Court's first female justice, Sandra Day O'Connor. While O'Connor generally sided with her fellow conservatives on the High Court, her tendency to write concurring and separate opinions that rejected the reasoning of her colleagues led some scholars to speculate that she worked from a "feminine" perspective (Sherry 1986; Behuniak-Long 1992; Palmer 2001). Sherry (1986) writes that in many of her decisions, especially those regarding freedom of religion, "O'Connor often rejects bright-line rules and occasionally makes explicit her preference for contextual determinations" (ibid., 605). Sherry's legal analysis of several of O'Connor's decisions shows that, in some cases, O'Connor favored the concerns of the community over the rights of the individual. Other scholars point to her decisions in abortion cases as more evidence of O'Connor's unique feminine voice. Rather than asserting a woman's clear right to have an abortion—as feminist scholars would have hoped—O'Connor upheld some state restrictions on abortion, but only if they did not present an undue burden on a woman's fundamental right to seek an abortion (Sullivan and Goldzwig 1996). This "balancing-of-interests" approach to abortion is an attempt, according to some, to "circumvent the divisive polarity of her colleagues' ideologically driven tests" on the controversial issue (Maveety 1996, 33). Those who maintain that O'Connor spoke with this accommodationist, feminine voice criticized her from both sides of the spectrum: some on the right believe she inhibited the Court's ability to form a solid conservative majority, whereas others on the left believe she undermined any potential for a more feminist jurisprudence on the Court (Behuniak-Long 1992).

Still others question whether O'Connor's voice on the High Court was truly distinct, and, if so, if it was colored mainly by her gender. On 40 different equal protection cases, for example, Aliota (1995) finds that O'Connor's voice or voting pattern was not unique from that of fellow justices—in direct contrast to Sherry's work on O'Connor that focused on far fewer cases. O'Connor's proclivity to disagree with her fellow conservatives, some argue, may not have stemmed from any feminine voice but could have been because she was simply less conservative in these areas (Davis 1993; Maveety 1996). Moreover, others argue that her centrist or accommodationist tendencies in some cases may have stemmed more from her political experiences as a former majority leader in the Arizona State Senate than from her gender (Maveety 1996; Palmer 2001; Lane 2004).

Extending the "different voices" theory to other judges has also yielded few corroborating findings. Sue Davis (1992–1993) compared the legal reasoning of a group of women and men appellate judges from the Ninth Circuit Court of Appeals. For example, in discrimination cases, she looked for evidence that women judges, embodying a female voice according to Gilligan's theory, would be more likely to emphasize the importance of full membership in the community in their decisions, with the notion that exclusion (through discrimination) is unacceptable. Alternatively, a "male" voice in discrimination cases would show up in the decisions of judges when discrimination was discussed in terms of the "denial of personal autonomy of the victims," treating equality not in terms of connection but in terms of independence. Yet, while Davis found that sometimes women do speak in a different voice in their decisions, so do men. Therefore, she found little evidence to suggest that "the presence of women judges will transform the very nature of law" (171). David Allen and Diane Wall (1993) also looked for, but failed to find, evidence of a different voice among women judges at the state Supreme Court level by examining whether women justices were more likely to pen dissenting decisions, which would indicate that there was a lack of common ground between women and men on the bench. Although women were somewhat more likely to write dissents than men, particularly in criminal rights and economic liberty cases, there was no pattern that suggested that women state Supreme Court justices consistently used different legal reasoning to decide cases—although they did find that women justices were uniformly more supportive of expanding women's rights, regardless of party.

Generally speaking, empirical studies have not gathered much evidence to verify that women judges have a different voice when it comes to legal reasoning. Why not? Gilligan's theory itself might be flawed, or may not be appropriate for application to jurisprudence. Palmer (2001) argues that failure to find a unique, different voice among women judges could be linked to socialization experiences women face in law school: law school is structured to teach students to think about law in similar ways, and women who might otherwise wish to use any alternative approach to legal reasoning—one that is more contextual than abstract—may abandon it to become successful in their field. Moreover, once women become judges, the nature of the legal process, whereby judges "examine the facts of a legal dispute, identify the features of those facts, determine what legal principles should apply, and apply those principles to the facts" may subvert any sex-based differences (Davis 1992–1993, 151).

Notably, both retired Supreme Court Justice Sandra Day O'Connor and Ruth Bader Ginsburg put little stock in the theory that women judges decide cases differently than do male judges merely because they are women. As political scientist Sally Kenney points out in her book, *Gender & Justice* (2013), O'Connor believes there is little evidence to suggest that "gender differences lead to discernible differences in rendering judgment" (5). Moreover, Kenney cites the following quote from Ruth Bader Ginsburg, who has said of such studies that try to isolate sex as a variable in analyzing jurisprudence: "I certainly know that there are women in federal courts with whom I disagree just as strongly as I disagree with any man" (ibid., 5). Yet, both women have argued for having more women serve as judges and, at least in certain areas of the law such as sex discrimination or women's rights, they have discussed why a woman's perspective is useful on the courts. As we shall see, for Ruth Bader Ginsburg, in particular, women judges may be essential for protecting the unique legal rights of women. It is to the question of whether having women judges advances women's legal rights that we now turn.

### Empirical Studies: The Impact of Sex on Jurisprudence

One argument in support of having more women appointed or elected to the judiciary is that it would enhance women's representation in government. This argument, though, is predicated on the assumption that women judges will do a better job of "acting for" or representing other women's interests than men judges. Although some empirical evidence suggests that female legislators are more inclined to initiate or support policies that disproportionately affect women or children (see chapter 7 on Women in Congress and the State Legislatures), can the same be said for female judges? This question has less to do with the reasoning of cases—unlike those empirical studies reviewed earlier that analyzed whether Gilligan's "different voice" theory was applicable to judicial decision making—and more to do with whether the actual outcomes of cases favor the interests or rights of women. For instance, do women jurists make judgments that can be interpreted as more liberal or more conservative? Do women judges decide cases in such a way that women's rights or other minority rights are expanded? Given that women are most frequently the victims of harassment, for example, women judges may be more sympathetic to victims of discrimination than men judges.

Early studies found few differences among men and women judges—or found that women judges were *less* likely to make decisions that disproportionately affected the interests of women in the ways that feminists had hoped. For example, one study of local trial judges in a large northeastern city who served from 1971 through 1979 found that men and women judges did not differ with respect to conviction or sentencing behavior—with one exception (Gruhl, Spohn, and Welch 1981). Male judges were much less likely than women trial court judges to sentence women to prison, causing the authors to label their behavior as "paternalistic" (ibid.). Another study focused on men and women on the federal bench, examining 12 matched sets of judges appointed by President Carter (Walker and Barrow 1985). These judges served in the same district and were of the same race. The idea behind the study was that if differences were found between the matched pairs of judges, the likely explanation for such differences would be their gender since they were similar in most other respects. Walker and Barrow found no real evidence that these female district court judges were more likely to "act for" other women when it came to cases involving sexual harassment, gender discrimination, maternity rights, or affirmative action. Although female district judges were more likely to be liberal on economic regulation cases, in that they deferred more often to the government's position in such cases, they were actually *less* supportive than male district judges of personal rights claims (at least in some cases).

Why did early studies find that women judges were not more likely than men judges to represent the interests of women in their decision making? On the one hand, given their minority status within the judiciary—both at the state and federal levels—there is some concern that women judges would not want to stand out or appear too different from their male counterparts. As "tokens" on the court, women judges may feel pressured to conform to a more male model of judicial behavior, causing them to act more conservatively in such cases (Martin 1993). On the other hand, the early findings that show a lack of support among women judges for female litigants could simply be a result of having too few female judges to examine.

Later studies of women judges, which have come about as their numbers have greatly increased, have shown mixed results when it comes to gender differences among judges. One study of state Supreme Court justices found that women judges vote more liberally than male judges on two types of cases not necessarily associated with women's issues: obscenity and death penalty sentencing. However, those gender differences appeared only among Democratic judges, as Republican men and women of the bench tended to vote the same (Songer and Crews-Meyer 2000). The preponderance of evidence from empirical studies that isolate the impact of sex on decision making on cases not directly germane to women's rights shows that gender is not significant.

Yet, turning to studies that specifically isolate analyses to discrimination cases, most—but not all—show that women judges have been found to be more supportive of plaintiffs in employment discrimination cases (even after controlling for party) whether at the United States Court of Appeals (Davis, Haire, and Songer 1993; Songer, Davis, and Haire 1994; Boyd, Epstein, and Martin 2010) or on state Supreme Courts (Gryski, Main, and Dixon 1986; Allen and Wall 1993). For instance, in Boyd, Epstein, and Martin's (2010) comprehensive study of the effects of sex on judging in all sex discrimination cases in the United States Appellate courts from 1995 to 2002, they find that the probability of a male judge deciding favorably for a female plaintiff in a sex discrimination case is 10 percent less than a female judge, even controlling for ideology.

The presence of at least one female judge on courts can also influence the behavior of the male judges on the bench, resulting in the court being more likely to find the presence of sex discrimination in noncriminal cases at the state Supreme Court level (Gryski, Main, and Dixon 1986). At the United States Appellate Court level, in which a three-judge panel typically hears appeals, having a woman on the panel significantly increases the likelihood that a male judge will rule in favor of a female plaintiff (Peresie 2005; Boyd, Epstein, and Martin 2010). Although difficult to isolate exactly why this effect occurs, some scholars believe that having a woman on a panel sensitizes her male colleagues to issues of gender equality through the deliberation process, in which judges have to come to a consensus on a decision.

On the other hand, studies of justices on the Michigan Supreme Court, one of the few state high courts to have had a majority of women serve on its bench, find that although women justices generally do make more liberal decisions than men, on "feminist" issue cases, party matters more than gender. One exception is for cases concerning divorce, in which women justices are more likely than men to support a woman's claim (Martin and Pyle 2000). Segal (2000) used the same research design employed by Walker and Barrow in their study of Carter appointees. In this case, Segal selected 13 matched gender pairs of Clinton appointees, and found, like Walker and Barrow, few gender differences among Clinton appointees. If anything, Clinton's female appointees were more likely to rule against women's claims than were his male appointees in those districts, leading Segal to conclude that Clinton's female appointees "are not inclined to support a judicial role that is particularly sensitive to the claims of various outgroups in American society" (149). Finally, one study of trial judges found that although younger judges and Democratic judges were more likely to rule in favor of plaintiffs in sexual discrimination cases, gender was not a significant predictor in statistical models that examined such cases (Kulik, Perry, and Pepper 2003).

## Gender and the Supreme Court: Why Gender Matters

At the Supreme Court level, the appointment of both Sandra Day O'Connor and Ruth Bader Ginsburg led to increased support among male justices for sex discrimination cases (Palmer 2002; O'Connor and Yanus 2010). Further analysis of the impact of O'Connor and Ginsburg on sex discrimination cases shows that both justices wrote a disproportionate number of majority opinions in the areas of women's rights: between 1993 and 2000, they wrote on half of the 12 cases in this area (Palmer 2002). Even though O'Connor and Ginsburg differed with respect to many of their decisions—in their 12 years (1993–2005) of serving together, they agreed only 52 percent of the time with respect to decisions handed down from the bench (O'Connor and Yanus 2010)—on gender discrimination cases and abortion cases, they agreed 90 percent of the time.

While O'Connor and Ginsburg were serving together, the Supreme Court heard 14 sex discrimination cases, and the women justices were on the same side of the decision making in 12 of those cases. One of the most well-known sex discrimination cases was *United States v. Virginia et al.*, the 1996 decision that required the Virginia Military Institute (VMI)—an all-male military academic funded by the state—to open its doors to women cadets as the Court ruled that all categorical exclusion of women from state-funded colleges was unconstitutional. In a 7–1 decision penned by Justice Ginsburg, the Court held that "Virginia's categorical exclusion of women from the educational opportunities VMI provides denies equal protection to women."

After O'Connor's departure, the Court headed in a more conservative direction with respect to women's rights, leaving Ginsburg as the sole female voice until Obama's appointment of Sotomayor in 2009. In 2007, the Supreme Court, in *Ledbetter v. Goodyear*, narrowly upheld a lower court decision that prevented women from seeking back pay over pay discrimination alleged to have occurred years earlier. In a stinging dissent, Justice Ginsburg argued that the majority was either indifferent to or failed to recognize the "insidious" way that women can be subject to pay discrimination and she called on Congress to pass legislation that would allow victims of past pay discrimination to be able to seek justice under Title VII of the Civil Rights Act (Barnes 2007). (Congress did, in fact, pass such legislation, and the Lilly Ledbetter Fair Pay Act—named after the plaintiff of the Supreme Court case—was the first piece of legislation President Barack Obama signed in January 2009.) Moreover, in the heated arena of abortion politics, the Supreme Court upheld a federal abortion statute, the Partial Birth Abortion Ban Act, that banned a certain abortion procedure to be used in late-term abortions in *Gonzalez v. Carhart* (2007). Seven years earlier, with Justice O'Connor still serving, the Supreme Court had struck down a similar

Nebraska statute, so the Court took the rare path of essentially overturning a similar decision (O'Connor and Yanus 2010).

The addition of two other women to the Supreme Court, however, has not stemmed the more conservative trend of decision making when it comes to women's rights. In the court's *Burwell v. Hobby Lobby* (2014) decision, which challenged a provision in the Affordable Care Act that requires employers' insurance plans to provide free contraception as part of its comprehensive health care guidelines, the court sided with the owners of the craft shop Hobby Lobby, who objected to the provision on religious grounds. In a contentious 5–4 decision, the court's majority held that the ACA provision violated the religious rights of a privately held corporation under the federal Religious Freedom Restoration Act. For the first time, the Supreme Court recognized that for-profit businesses are "persons" capable of exercising religion. As the National Women's Law Center notes about the majority decision, there was no discussion of the "important role that birth control plays in women's lives" (NWLC 2014).

In a sharply worded dissenting decision, Justice Ginsburg expressed alarm at the implications the case may have for women's rights. In the dissent, she wrote, "In a decision of startling breadth, the Court holds that commercial enterprises, including corporations, along with partnerships and sole proprietorships, can opt out of any law (saving only tax laws) they judge incompatible with their sincerely held religious beliefs" (1). She later added that the exemption sought by Hobby Lobby and other privately held corporations whose owners had religious objections to providing certain forms of birth control would "deny legions of women who do not hold their employers' beliefs access to contraceptive coverage that the ACA would otherwise ensure" (*Burwell v. Hobby Lobby* 2014). Moreover, Ginsburg took the relatively unusual step of publicly speaking out about the *Hobby Lobby* decision in ways that highlight the unique perspective that women judges can bring to jurisprudence. In an interview with the Associated Press (2014) following the end of the 2013–2014 term, Ginsburg said, "I have no doubt that if the court had been composed of nine women the result would have been different in *Hobby Lobby*."

On *Hobby Lobby* and on most other cases, Ginsburg, Sotomayor, and Kagan typically voted together. In the time since Obama appointed Elena Kagan through the end of the 2014 term, Justices Sotomayor and Kagan voted together 94 percent of the time. Ginsburg and Sotomayor voted together 90 percent of the time while Kagan and Ginsburg voted together 93 percent of the time (Bowers, Liptak, and Willis 2014). Justice Stephen Breyer, a Clinton appointee, also voted with all three female justices at very high levels: 88 percent with Ginsburg, 88 percent with Sotomayor, and 89 percent with Kagan, showing that shared ideology is likely a stronger predictor of vote choice than gender on the Supreme Court. Moreover, it is also worth noting that the Supreme Court is often united in its decision making, making many unanimous decisions. Indeed, as a *New York Times* analysis shows, since Kagan was appointed in 2010, "even the members of the court least likely to agree voted together 66 percent of the time" (ibid.).

## Beyond the Essentialist Argument: Why Gender Still Matters

Do women, then, make a difference when it comes to serving as judges? Yes and no. Clearly, many female judges themselves believe that it is important to have women serving in the judiciary because women bring a unique view and much-needed qualities to the bench—including raising awareness about issues such as gender discrimination in their male brethren. Some studies find, in addition, that women judges are more liberal in their decision making when it comes to some issues of greater relevance to women, such as sexual harassment. Yet, other studies find little evidence that women judges decide cases differently from men. For example, there is not much indication that women judges have a unique decision-making style, or "different voice," compared with men when it comes to their jurisprudence. Although women can potentially make distinctive contributions in some limited areas of the law while serving on the bench, they are limited in the changes they can pursue by the constraints of the judiciary itself. More often than not, women decide cases in similar ways to men because they are socialized in law school and later in the profession to think like lawyers and judges. Judges are also constrained in their decision making by their needs to consider precedent, the rule of law, and fact patterns in their cases. Some scholars, in fact, believe it may not be a bad thing that there are few consistent data to show that women judges routinely act differently than their male counterparts—even in sexual harassment cases. Studies that find few differences between men and women judges are an indication that most judges apply consistent standards in their decisions, regardless of gender (Kulik, Perry, and Pepper 2003). That one's personal characteristics such as gender take a back seat to the more relevant situational or behavioral factors in court cases can raise our confidence about judges—regardless of their gender or personal background—and about the judiciary more generally.

But some feminist scholars believe that having more women serve on the judiciary, even if women and men make similar decisions, is important for other reasons. In her work *Gender & Justice,* political scientist Sally J. Kenney (2013) makes what she calls the "nonessentialist case" for having more women in the judiciary. Noting that women make up a "far cry from half" of sitting judges on the federal and state courts, she argues that making the bench more gender diverse should not be based on the fact that women and men have essential differences—an argument, notably, that feminism emerged to challenge, which often kept women and men in separate spheres and justified women's exclusion from public life. Instead, she writes that the most persuasive arguments to increase gender diversity on the bench appeal to democracy and legitimacy. The argument for having more women serve as judges—and more minorities, as well—goes beyond mere window dressing or symbolism. Sally Kenney writes:

> The presence of women [in the judiciary] disrupts the normal assumption that heterosexual white men are the only citizens capable of performing the core ritual of rendering objective judgment, that only privileged men are naturally suited to assume authority on behalf of the state and to exercise their parochial care on behalf of society. (176)

To return to the controversy surrounding Supreme Court Justice Sonia Sotomayor's confirmation hearings, Kenney writes that they "clearly triggered anxiety about expanding the deciders to include women of color. Privilege and authority are joined in ways that seem natural and proper, and appointments such as Sotomayor's disrupt those naturalized links and enable us to see exclusion" (176–77). Sotomayor's comments about a "wise Latina" making better judgments than a "white man who hasn't lived that life" struck a nerve and challenged the notion that judging can be entirely objective and neutral, made in a vacuum without reference to life's experiences. Her passionate dissent in the *Schuette* decision, which upheld a state ban on affirmative action, further illustrates that a judge's life history, rooted in his or her racial, gender, or social class identities, perhaps brings something valuable to rendering judgment. Simply put, there are many reasons why a bench that looks more like America is important, just, and fair.

## CONCLUSION

From the pioneering days of early female judges such as Florence Allen, the first woman appointed to the federal judiciary, women have made huge strides in the legal profession. Women now make up about 26 percent of all federal judges and 31 percent of all state judges. At the upper pinnacle, women make up one-third of the United States Supreme Court and 35 percent of state Supreme Court justices. With more than half of all law students currently being female, it is likely that more women will make their impact felt both as attorneys and as judges in this crucial third branch of government. Having more women represented as judges is important, for in the words of Ruth Bader Ginsburg, "A system of justice will be richer for diversity of background and experience. It will be poorer, in terms of appreciating what is at stake and the impact of its judgments, if all its members are cast from the same mold" (quoted in Martin 1993, 126).

Although the representation of more women in the judiciary is important with respect to democratic norms, and may also inspire future generations of girls and boys by providing more diverse judges as role models, whether the inclusion of more women on the bench actually leads to the enhanced representation of women or women's interests is more debatable. For instance, although some studies show that female judges are somewhat more sympathetic to the victims of sexual or racial discrimination (who tend to be female or minority), most studies show that women and men judges largely decide cases in the same manner. Moreover, the hypothesis that women would potentially use a different, "feminine" voice in terms of their jurisprudence has not been borne out. On the bench, women largely decide cases in the same way as men—which likely reflects their common legal training and the conservative nature of law itself. Some believe that the finding that gender has little effect on the way that judges make decisions actually boosts our confidence in women's ability to perform this demanding job—and supports the notion that more women should be selected to serve in the judiciary.

## REFERENCES

Aliota, Jilda M. 1995. "Justice O'Connor and the Equal Protection Clause: A Feminine Voice?" *Judicature* 78(5): 232–35.

Allen, David, and Diane Wall. 1993. "Role Orientations and Women State Supreme Court Justices." *Judicature* 7(3): 156–65.

Allen, Florence. 1965. *To Do Justly.* Cleveland: The Press of Western Reserve University.

Alozie, Nicholas. 1996. "Selection Methods and the Recruitment of Women to State Courts of Last Resort." *Social Science Quarterly* 77(1): 110–26.

American Bar Association (ABA). 2017. "A Current Glance at Women in the Law." http://www.americanbar.org/content/dam/aba/marketing/women/current _glance_statistics_january2017.authcheckdam.pdf

———. 2014. "California judge Jacqueline Nguyen to receive ABA diversity 2015 Spirit of Excellence Award." http://www.americanbar.org/news/abanews/aba -news-archives/2014/10/california_judgejac.html

The Associated Press. 2014. "Ginsburg: Court Right to Void Buffer Zones." *New York Times.* August 1. http://mobile.nytimes.com/aponline/2014/08/01/us/politics/ap -us-supreme-court-ginsburg.html?ref=politics&_r=0&referrer

Baker, Peter, and Neil A. Lewis. 2009. "Republicans Press Judge About Bias and Activism." *New York Times* (July 15): A1.

Baker, Peter, and Jeff Zeleny. 2009. "Obama Chooses Hispanic Judge for Supreme Court Seat." *New York Times* (May 27): A1.

———. 2010. "Obama Picks Kagan as Justice Nominee." *New York Times* (May 9): A1.

Barnes, Robert. 2007. "Over Ginsburg's Dissent, Court Limits Bias Suits." *Washington Post* (May 30): A1.

Bazelon, Emily. 2009. "The Place of Women on the Court." *New York Times Magazine* (July 12): 22.

Behuniak-Long, Susan. 1992. "Justice Sandra Day O'Connor and the Power of Maternal Legal Thinking." *Review of Politics* 54(3): 417–44.

Bell, Lauren Cohen. 2002. "Senatorial Discourtesy: The Senate's Use of Delay to Shape the Federal Judiciary." *Political Research Quarterly* 55: 589–607.

Bianco, Marcie. 2014. "Sexist Critics Dismiss Justice Sotomayor's Impassioned Affirmative Action Dissent as 'Emotional.'" *Identities.Mic*, April 24. http://mic.com/articles/88297/sexist-critics-dismiss-justice-sotomayor-s-impassioned-affirmative-action-dissent-as-emotional

Binder, Sarah A., and Forrest Maltzman. 2009. *Advice and Dissent: The Struggle to Shape the Federal Judiciary.* Washington, DC: Brookings Institution.

Biskupic, Joan. 2014. *Breaking In: The Rise of Sonia Sotomayor and the Politics of Justice.* New York: Sarah Chricton Books.

Blackburn, Bradley. 2010. "Justices Ruth Bader Ginsburg and Sandra Day O'Connor on Life and the Supreme Court." abcnews.com. October 26. http://abcnews.go.com/WN/diane-sawyer-interviews-maria-shriver-sandra-day-oconnor/story?id=11977195

Bowers, Jeremy, Adam Liptak, and Derek Willis. 2014. "Which Supreme Court Justices Vote Together Most and Least Often." *New York Times.* July 3. http://www.nytimes.com/interactive/2014/06/24/upshot/24up-scotus-agreement-rates.html?_r=0&abt=0002&abg=1

Boyd, Christina, Lee Epstein, and Andrew D. Martin. 2010. "Untangling the Causal Effects of Sex on Judging." *American Journal of Political Science* 54(2): 389–411.

Bratton, Kathleen A., and Rorie L. Spill. 2002. "Existing Diversity and Judicial Selection: The Role of the Appointment Method in Establishing Gender Diversity in State Supreme Courts." *Social Science Quarterly* 83(2): 504–19.

Brennan Center for Justice. 2014. "TV Ad Spending in Judicial Races Surpasses $9.1 Million." http://www.brennancenter.org/press-release/tv-ad-spending-judicial-elections-surpasses-91-million

Brust, Richard. 2008. "A Cowgirl Rides the Circuit." *ABA Journal* 94(4): 26–28.

*Burwell v. Hobby Lobby.* 2014. 573 U.S. 354 Dissent.

Campbell, Amy Leigh. 2002. "Raising the Bar: Ruth Bader Ginsburg and the ACLU Women's Rights Project." *Texas Journal of Women and the Law* 11(20): 157–244.

Cook, Beverly Blair. 1984. "Women on the State Bench: Correlates of Access." In *Political Women: Current Roles in State and Local Government,* edited by Janet A. Flammang, 191–218. Beverly Hills: Sage.

———. 1993. "Moral Authority and Gender Difference: Georgia Bullock and the Los Angeles Women's Court." *Judicature* 77(3): 144–55.

Davis, Sue. 1992–1993. "Do Women Speak in a Different Voice? Carol Gilligan, Feminist Legal Theory, and the Ninth Circuit." *Wisconsin Women's Law Journal* 81(1): 143–73.

———. 1993. "The Voice of Sandra Day O'Connor." *Judicature* 77(3): 134–39.

Davis, Sue, Susan Haire, and Donald R. Songer. 1993. "Voting Behavior and Gender on the United States Courts of Appeal." *Judicature* 77(3): 129–33.

Dillon, Sam. 2003. "First Woman Is Appointed as Dean of Harvard Law School." *New York Times*, April 4. http://www.nytimes.com/2003/04/04/us/first-woman-is -appointed-as-dean-of-harvard-law.html

Egelko, Bob. 2012. "Jacqueline Nguyen Confirmed for 9th Circuit Court." *SF Gate*, May 8. http://www.sfgate.com/politics/article/Jacqueline-Nguyen-confirmed -for-9th-Circuit-court-3541241.php

Epstein, Lee, and Jeffrey A. Segal 2005. *Advice and Consent: The Politics of Judicial Appointments*. New York: Oxford University Press.

Equal Employment Opportunity Commission. n.d. "Facts about Pregnancy Discrimination." http://www.eeoc.gov/eeoc/publications/fs-preg.cfm

Federal Judicial Center. 2017. *Federal Judges Biographical Database*. www.fjc.gov/ public/home.nsf/hisj

Fontana, David. 2014. "Sonia Sotomayor Is a National Treasure." *New Republic*, April 24. http://www.newrepublic.com/article/117501/sonia-sotomayor-schuette -dissent-national-treasure

Frederick, Brian, and Matthew J. Streb. 2008. "Women Running for Judge: The Impact of Candidate Sex in State Intermediate Appellate Court Elections." *Social Science Quarterly* 89(4): 937–54.

Gilligan, Carol. 1982. *In a Different Voice: Psychological Theory and Women's Development*. Cambridge, MA: Harvard University Press.

Ginsburg, Ruth Bader. 1997. "Remarks on Women's Progress in the Legal Profession in the United States." *Tulsa Law Journal* 33: 13–21.

———. 2001. "The Supreme Court: A Place for Women." *Vital Speeches of the Day* 67(14): 420–25.

Ginsburg, Ruth Bader, and Laura W. Brill. 1995. "Address: Women in the Federal Judiciary: Three Way Pavers and the Exhilarating Change President Carter Wrought." *Fordham Law Review* 64: 281–90.

Goldman, Sheldon. 1997. *Picking Federal Judges: Lower Court Selection From Roosevelt Through Reagan*. New Haven: Yale University Press.

Goldman, Sheldon, Elliot Slotnick, Gerald Gryski, and Gary Zuk. 2001. "Clinton's Judges: Summing up the Legacy." *Judicature* 84(5): 220–54.

Goldstein, Amy, Carol D. Leonning, and Peter Slevin. 2010. "For Supreme Court Nominee Elena Kagan, a History of Pragmatism over Partisanship." *Washington Post*. May 11. http://www.washingtonpost.com/wp-dyn/content/ article/2010/05/10/AR2010051002787.html?sid=ST2010080505264

Greenburg, Jan Crawford. 2007. *Supreme Conflict: The Inside Story of the Struggle for Control of the United States Supreme Court*. New York: The Penguin Press.

Grossman, Joanna L., and Deborah L. Brake. 2015. "Forceps Delivery: The Supreme Court Narrowly Saves the Pregnancy Discrimination Act in *Young v. UPS*." *Verdict*. https://verdict.justia.com/2015/03/31/forceps-delivery-the-supreme-court -narrowly-saves-the-pregnancy-discrimination-act-in-young-v-ups

Gruhl, John, Cassia Spohn, and Susan Welch. 1981. "Women as Policymakers: The Case of Trial Judges." *American Journal of Political Science* 25(2): 308–22.

Gryski, Gerald S., Eleanor C. Main, and William J. Dixon. 1986. "Models of State High Court Decision Making in Sex Discrimination Cases." *Journal of Politics* 48(1): 143–55.

Hall, Melinda Gann. 2001. "State Supreme Courts in American Democracy: Probing the Myths of Judicial Reform." *American Political Science Review* 95:315–30.

Hartley, Roger E. 2001. "A Look at Race, Gender, and Experience." *Judicature* 84(4): 191–97.

Hermann, Ria, and Rita Mae Kelly, with the assistance of Donna Langston and Julie Greenburg. 1988. "Women in the Judiciary." In *Women and the Arizona Political Process*, edited by Rita Mae Kelly, 84–108. Lanham, MD: University Press of America.

Hulse, Carl. 2010. "Senate Confirms Kagan in Partisan Vote." *The New York Times*, August 5. http://www.nytimes.com/2010/08/06/us/politics/06kagan.html

Hurwitz, Mark, and Drew Noble Lanier. 2001. "Women and Minorities on State and Federal Appellate Benches, 1985 and 1999." *Judicature* 85(2): 84–92.

———. 2003. "Explaining Judicial Diversity: The Differential Ability of Women and Minorities to Attain Seats on State Supreme and Appellate Courts." *State Politics & Policy Quarterly* 3(4): 329–52.

Kenney, Sally J. 2010. "Critical Perspectives on Gender and Judging." *Politics & Gender* 6: 433–95.

———. 2013. *Gender & Justice: Why Women in the Judiciary Really Matter*. New York: Routledge.

———. 2014. "Judicial Women." In *Women in Elective Office: Past, Present and Future*, 3rd ed., edited by Sue Thomas and Clyde Wilcox, 216–34. New York: Oxford University Press.

Kenney, Sally J., and Jason Windett. 2012. "Diffusion of Innovation or State Political Culture? Explaining the First Women State Supreme Court Justices." Paper prepared for 2012 State Politics and Policy Conference. http://2012sppconference.blogs.rice.edu/files/2012/02/Kenney_Windett_SPPC_Draft.pdf

Kirkpatrick, David D. 2009. "A Judge's Focus on Race Issues May Be Hurdle." *New York Times* (30 May): A1.

Kulik, Carol T., Elissa L. Perry, and Molly B. Pepper. 2003. "Here Comes the Judge: The Influence of Judge Personal Characteristics on Federal Sexual Harassment Case Outcomes." *Law and Human Behavior* 27(1): 69–86.

Lane, Charles. 2004. "Courting O'Connor: Why the Chief Justice Isn't the Chief Justice." *Washington Post Magazine* (July 4): W10.

Lawless, Jennifer L., and Richard L. Fox. 2005. *It Takes a Candidate: Why Women Don't Run for Office*. Cambridge: Cambridge University Press.

Liptak, Adam. 2015. "UPS Worker's Pregnancy Discrimination Suit Reinstated by Supreme Court." *New York Times*, March 25. http://www.nytimes.com/2015/03/26/us/ups-workers-pregnancy-discrimination-suit-reinstated-by-supreme-court.html

Lithwick, Dahlia. 2014. "What We Talk About When We Talk About Talking About Race." April 24. http://www.slate.com/articles/news_and_politics/jurisprudence/2014/04/race_and_the_supreme_court_what_the_schuette_decision_reveals_about_how.html

Lodge, Sally. 2009. "Q&A with Sandra Day O'Connor." *Publisher's Weekly*, May 28. www.publishersweekly.com/article/CA6660760.html

Martin, Elaine. 1987. "Gender and the Judicial Selection: A Comparison of the Reagan and Carter Administrations." *Judicature* 71(3): 136–42.

———. 1993. "Women on the Bench: A Different Voice?" *Judicature* 77(3): 126–28.

Martin, Elaine, and Barry Pyle. 2000. "Gender, Race, and Partisanship on the Michigan Supreme Court." *Albany Law Review* 63: 1205–36.

———. 2002. "Gender and Racial Diversification of State Supreme Courts." *Women & Politics* 24(2): 35–52.

Maveety, Nancy. 1996. *Justice Sandra Day O'Connor: Strategist on the Supreme Court.* Lanham, MD: Rowman & Littlefield.

McCarthy, Megan. 2001. "Judicial Campaigns: What Can They Tell Us About Gender on the Bench?" *Wisconsin Women's Law Journal* 16: 87–112.

Mezey, Susan Gluck. 2000. "Gender and the Federal Judiciary." In *Gender and American Politics*, edited by Sue Tolleson-Rinehart and Jyl Josephson, 205–26. London: M.E. Sharpe.

Morrison, Linda. 2002. "The National Association of Women Judges: Agent of Change." *Wisconsin Women's Law Journal* 17: 291–93.

National Association of Women Judges. 2016. https://www.nawj.org/statistics/2016 -us-state-court-women-judges.

National Review. 2014. "Half a Win on Racial Discrimination." April 22. http:// www.nationalreview.com/article/376340/half-win-racial-discrimination-editors

National Women's Law Center. 2014. "Fact Sheet: *Burwell v. Hobby Lobby Stores, Inc. and Conestoga Wood Specialties v. Burwell:* Supreme Court Allows Some Closely Held Corporations to Use Religion to Undermine Women's Health and Equality." August. http://www.nwlc.org/sites/default/files/pdfs/hobby_lobby_supreme _court_decision_factsheet.pdf

O'Connor, Karen. 1980. *Women's Organizations' Use of the Courts.* Lexington, MA: Lexington Books.

O'Connor, Karen, and Patricia Clark. 1999. "Women's Rights and Legal Wrongs: The United States Supreme Court and Sex Discrimination." In *Women in Politics: Outsiders or Insiders?*, edited by Lois Duke Whitaker, 262–77. Upper Saddle River, NJ: Prentice Hall.

O'Connor, Karen, and John R. Hermann. 1995. "United States Supreme Court Law Clerk Participation before the Supreme Court." *Judicature* 78(5): 247–52.

O'Connor, Karen, and Barbara Palmer. 2001. "The Clinton Clones: Ginsburg, Breyer, and the Clinton Legacy." *Judicature* 84(5): 262–73.

O'Connor, Karen, and Alixandra Yanus. 2010. "Judging Alone: Reflections on the Importance of Women on the Court." *Politics & Gender.* 6(3): 441–52

O'Connor, Sandra Day. 2000. "Remarks Delivered by Sandra Day O'Connor." University of Pennsylvania School of Law. November 17. https://www.law.upenn .edu/alumni/alumnijournal/Spring2001/feature1/oconnorremarks.html.

Palmer, Barbara. 1991. "Feminist or Foe? Justice Sandra Day O'Connor, Title CVII Sex Discrimination, and Support for Women's Rights." *Women's Rights Law Reporter* 13(2 and 3): 159–70.

———. 2001. "Women in the American Judiciary." *Women & Politics* 23(3): 89–99.

———. 2002. "Justice Ruth Bader Ginsburg and the Supreme Court's Reaction to Its Second Member." *Women and Politics* 24(1): 1–23.

Parloff, Roger, 2007. "The War Over Unconscious Bias." *Fortune* 156(8): 90–102.

Peresie, Jennifer. 2005. "Female Judges Matter: Gender and Collegial Decision Making in the Federal Appellate Courts." *Yale Law Journal* 114: 1759–90.

Reddick, Malia, Michael J. Nelson, and Rachel Paine Caulfield. 2009. "Racial and Gender Diversity on State Courts." *The Judges' Journal* 48(3): Summer. American Bar Association. http://www.judicialselection.com/uploads/documents/Racial_and_Gender_Diversity_on_Stat_8F60B84D96CC2.pdf

Reid, Traciel. 2010. "Women Candidates and Judicial Elections: Telling an Untold Story." *Women & Politics* 6(3): 465–74.

Ruckman Jr., P. S. 1993. "The Supreme Court Critical Nominations, and the Senate Confirmation Process." *Journal of Politics* 55: 793–805.

Savage, Charlie. 2009. "A Judge's View of Judging Is on the Record." *New York Times.* May 14.

Scherer, Nancy. 2005. *Scoring Points: Politicians, Activists, and the Lower Federal Court Appointment Process.* Stanford: Stanford University Press.

Schuette v. COALITION TO DEFEND AFFIRMATIVE ACTION, 134 S. Ct. 1623, 572 U.S., 188 L. Ed. 2d 613 (2014).

Schwartz, Hunter. 2015. "Ruth Bader Ginsburg Goes Full Notorious RBG." *Washington Post.* April 16. http://www.washingtonpost.com/blogs/the-fix/wp/2015/04/16/ruth-bader-ginsburg-goes-full-notorious-rbg/

Segal, Jennifer A. 2000. "Representative Decision Making on the Federal Bench: Clinton's District Court Appointees." *Political Research Quarterly* 53(1): 137–51.

Sherry, Suzanna. 1986. "Civic Virtue and the Feminine Voice in Constitutional Adjudication." *Virginia Law Review* 72: 543–615.

Solberg, Rorie L., and Kathleen A. Bratton. 2005. "Diversifying the Federal Bench: Presidential Patterns." *The Justice System Journal* 26(2): 119–33.

Soloweij, Lisa A., Wendy L. Martinek, and Thomas L. Brunell. 2005. "Partisan Politics: The Impact of Party in the Confirmation of Minority and Female Federal Court Nominees." *Party Politics* 11: 557–77.

Songer, Donald, Sue Davis, and Susan Haire. 1994. "A Reappraisal of Diversification in the Federal Courts: Gender Effects in the Courts of Appeals." *Journal of Politics* 56(2): 425–39.

Songer, Donald R., and Kelley A. Crews-Meyer. 2000. "Does Judge Gender Matter? Decision Making in State Supreme Courts." *Social Science Quarterly* 81(3): 750–62.

Spill, Rorie, and Kathleen A. Bratton. 2001. "Clinton and the Diversification of the Federal Judiciary." *Judicature* 84(5): 256–61.

Sullivan, Patricia A., and Steven R. Goldzwig. 1996. "Abortion and Undue Burdens: Justice Sandra Day O'Connor and Judicial Decision Making." *Women & Politics* 16(3): 27–54.

Swers, Michele L. 2013. *Women in the Club: Gender and Policy Making in the Senate.* Chicago: University of Chicago Press.

US Census Bureau. 2013. "How Do We Know: America's Changing Labor Force." https://www.census.gov/how/pdf/EEO_infographic.pdf

Walker, Thomas G., and Deborah J. Barrow. 1985. "The Diversification of the Federal Bench: Policy and Process Ramifications." *Journal of Politics* 47(2): 596–617.

Williams, Margaret. 2007. "Women's Representation on State Trial and Appellate Courts." *Social Science Quarterly* 88(5): 1192–1204.

———. 2008. "Ambition, Gender, and the Judiciary." *Political Research Quarterly* 61(1): 68–78.

# Appendix A

## "Declaration of Sentiments" and "Resolutions" Adopted by the Seneca Falls Convention of 1848

When, in the course of human events, it becomes necessary for one portion of the family of man to assume among the people of the earth a position different from that which they have hitherto occupied, but one to which the laws of nature and of nature's God entitle them, a decent respect to the opinions of mankind requires that they should declare the causes that impel them to such a course.

We hold these truths to be self-evident: that all men and women are created equal; that they are endowed by their Creator with certain inalienable rights; that among these are life, liberty, and the pursuit of happiness; that to secure these rights governments are instituted, deriving their just powers from the consent of the governed. Whenever any form of government becomes destructive of these ends, it is the right of those who suffer from it to refuse allegiance to it, and to insist upon the institution of a new government, laying its foundation on such principles, and organizing its powers in such form, as to them shall seem most likely to effect their safety and happiness. Prudence indeed will dictate that governments long established should not be changed for light and transient causes; and accordingly all experience hath shown that mankind are more disposed to suffer, while evils are sufferable, than to right themselves by abolishing the forms to which they were accustomed. But when a long train of abuses and usurpations, pursuing invariably the same object evinces a design to reduce them under absolute despotism, it is their duty to throw off such government, and to provide new guards for their future security. Such has been the patient sufferance of the women under this government, and such is now the necessity which constrains them to demand the equal station to which they are entitled.

The history of mankind is a history of repeated injuries and usurpations on the part of man toward woman, having in direct object the establishment of an absolute tyranny over her. To prove this, let facts be submitted to a candid world.

He has never permitted her to exercise her inalienable right to the elective franchise.

He has compelled her to submit to laws, in the formation of which she had no voice.

He has withheld from her rights which are given to the most ignorant and degraded men—both natives and foreigners. Having deprived her of this first right of a citizen, the elective franchise, thereby leaving her without representation in the halls of legislation, he has oppressed her on all sides.

He has made her, if married, in the eye of the law, civilly dead.

He has taken from her all right in property, even to the wages she earns.

He has made her, morally, an irresponsible being, as she can commit many crimes with impunity, provided they be done in the presence of her husband. In the covenant of marriage, she is compelled to promise obedience to her husband, he becoming, to all intents and purposes, her master—the law giving him power to deprive her of her liberty, and to administer chastisement.

He has so framed the laws of divorce, as to what shall be the proper causes, and in case of separation, to whom the guardianship of the children shall be given, as to be wholly regardless of the happiness of women—the law, in all cases, going upon a false supposition of the supremacy of man, and giving all power into his hands.

After depriving her of all rights as a married woman, if single, and the owner of property, he has taxed her to support a government which recognizes her only when her property can be made profitable to it.

He has monopolized nearly all the profitable employments, and from those she is permitted to follow, she receives but a scanty remuneration. He closes against her all the avenues to wealth and distinction which he considers most honorable to himself. As a teacher of theology, medicine, or law, she is not known.

He has denied her the facilities for obtaining a thorough education, all colleges being closed against her.

He allows her in Church, as well as State, but a subordinate position, claiming Apostolic authority for her exclusion from the ministry, and, with some exceptions, from any public participation in the affairs of the Church.

He has created a false public sentiment by giving to the world a different code of morals for men and women, by which moral delinquencies which exclude women from society are not only tolerated, but deemed of little account in man.

He has usurped the prerogative of Jehovah himself, claiming it as his right to assign for her a sphere of action, when that belongs to her conscience and to her God.

He has endeavored, in every way that he could, to destroy her confidence in her own powers, to lessen her self-respect, and to make her willing to lead a dependent and abject life.

Now in view of this entire disfranchisement of one-half the people of this country, their social and religious degradation—in view of the unjust laws above mentioned, pressed, and fraudulently deprived of their most sacred rights, we insist that they have immediate admission to all the rights and privileges which belong to them as citizens of the United States.

In entering upon the great work before us, we anticipate no small amount of misconception, misrepresentation, and ridicule; but we shall use every instrumentality within our power to effect our object. We shall employ agents, circulate tracts, petition the State and National legislatures, and endeavor to enlist the pulpit and the press on our behalf. We hope this Convention will be followed by a series of Conventions embracing every part of the country.

*The following resolutions were discussed by Lucretia Mott, Thomas and Mary Ann McClintock, Amy Post, Catharine A. F. Stebbins, and others, and were adopted.*

WHEREAS, The great precept of nature is conceded to be, that "man shall pursue his own true and substantial happiness." Blackstone in his Commentaries remarks, that this law of Nature being coeval with mankind, and dictated by God himself, is of course superior in obligation to any other. It is binding over all the globe, in all countries and at all times; no human laws are of any validity if contrary to this, and such of them as are valid, derive all their force, and all their validity, and all their authority, mediately, and immediately, from this original; therefore,

*Resolved*, That such laws as conflict, in any way, with the true and substantial happiness of woman, are contrary to the great precept of nature and of no validity, for this is "superior in obligation to any other."

*Resolved*, That all laws which prevent woman from occupying such a station in society as her conscience shall dictate, or which place her in a position inferior to that of man, are contrary to the great precept of nature, and therefore of no force or authority.

*Resolved*, That woman is man's equal—was intended to be so by the Creator, and the highest good of the race demands that she should be recognized as such.

*Resolved*, That the women of this country ought to be enlightened in regard to the laws under which they live, that they may no longer publish their degradation by declaring themselves satisfied with their present position, nor their ignorance, by asserting that they have all the rights they want.

*Resolved,* That inasmuch as man, while claiming for himself intellectual superiority, does accord to woman moral superiority, it is pre-eminently his duty to encourage her to speak and teach, as she has an opportunity, in all religious assemblies.

*Resolved,* That the same amount of virtue, delicacy, and refinement of behavior that is required of woman in the social state, should also be required of man, and the same transgressions should be visited with equal severity on both man and woman.

*Resolved,* That the objection of indelicacy and impropriety, which is so often brought against woman when she addresses a public audience, comes with a very ill-grace from those who encourage, by their attendance, her appearance on stage, in the concert, or in feats of the circus.

*Resolved,* That woman has too long rested satisfied in the circumscribed limits which corrupt customs and a perverted application of the Scriptures have marked out for her, and that it is time she should move in the enlarged sphere which her great Creator has assigned her.

*Resolved,* That it is the duty of the women of this country to secure themselves their sacred right to the elective franchise.

*Resolved,* That the equality of human rights results necessarily from the fact of the identity of the race in capabilities and responsibilities.

*Resolved, therefore,* That, being invested by the Creator with the same capabilities, and the same consciousness of responsibility for their exercise, it is demonstrably the right and duty of woman, equally with man, to promote every righteous cause by every righteous means; and especially in regard to the great subjects of morals and religion, it is self-evidently her right to participate with her brother in teaching them, both in private and in public, by writing and by speaking, by any instrumentalities proper to be used, and in any assemblies proper to be held; and this being a self-evident truth growing out of the divinely implanted principles of human nature, any custom or authority adverse to it, whether modern or wearing the hoary sanction of antiquity, is to be regarded as a self-evident falsehood, and at war with mankind.

*At the last session Lucretia Mott offered and spoke to the following resolution:*

*Resolved,* That the speedy success of our cause depends upon the zealous and untiring efforts of both men and women, for the overthrow of the monopoly of the pulpit, and for the securing to women an equal participation with men in the various trades, professions, and commerce.

*Source:* Shanley, Mary Lyndon. 1988. *Women's Rights, Feminism, and Politics in the United States.* Washington, DC: American Political Science Association.

# Appendix B

## National Organization for Women's Bill of Rights and Redstockings Manifesto

### BILL OF RIGHTS

Adopted at NOW's first national conference, Washington, DC, 1967.

   I. Equal Rights Constitutional Amendment.
   II. Enforce Law Banning Sex Discrimination in Employment.
   III. Maternity Leave Rights in Employment and in Social Security Benefits.
   IV. Tax Deduction for Home and Child Care Expenses for Working Parents.
   V. Child Day Care Centers.
   VI. Equal and Unsegregated Education.
   VII. Equal Job Training Opportunities and Allowances for Women in Poverty.
   VIII. The Right of Women to Control Their Reproductive Lives.

### WE DEMAND

   I. That the US Congress immediately pass the Equal Rights Amendment to the Constitution to provide that "Quality of rights under the law shall not be denied or abridged by the United States or by any State on account of sex," and that such then be immediately ratified by the several States.
   II. That equal employment opportunity be guaranteed to all women, as well as men, by insisting that the Equal Employment Opportunity Commission enforces the prohibitions against sex discrimination in

employment under Title VII of the Civil Rights Act of 1964 with the same vigor as it enforces the prohibitions against racial discrimination.

III. That women be protected by law to ensure their rights to return to their jobs within a reasonable time after childbirth without loss of seniority or other accrued benefits, and be paid maternity leave as a form of social security and/or employee benefit.

IV. Immediate revision of tax laws to permit the deduction of home and child-care expenses for working parents.

V. That child-care facilities be established by law on the same basis as parks, libraries, and public schools, adequate to the needs of children from the pre-school years through adolescence, as a community resource to be used by all citizens from all income levels.

VI. That the right of women to be educated to their full potential equality with men be secured by Federal and State legislation, eliminating all discrimination and segregation by sex, written and unwritten, at all levels of education, including colleges, graduate and professional schools, loans and fellowships, and Federal and State training programs such as the Job Corps.

VII. The right of women in poverty to secure job training, housing, and family allowances on equal terms with men, but without prejudice to a parent's right to remain at home to care for his or her children; revision of welfare legislation and poverty programs which deny women dignity, privacy, and self-respect.

VIII. The right of women to control their own reproductive lives by removing from the penal code laws limiting access to contraceptive information and devices, and by repealing penal laws governing abortion.

*Source:* Shanley, Mary Lyndon. 1988. *Women's Rights, Feminism, and Politics in the United States.* Washington, DC: American Political Science Association. Also available in the Early Documents section of the Feminist Chronicles online at www.feminist.org/research/chronicles/early4.html.

## REDSTOCKINGS MANIFESTO

I. After centuries of individual and preliminary political struggle, women are uniting to achieve their final liberation from male supremacy. Redstockings is dedicated to building this unity and winning our freedom.

II. Women are an oppressed class. Our oppression is total, affecting every facet of our lives. We are exploited as sex objects, breeders, domestic servants, and cheap labor. We are considered inferior beings, whose only purpose is to enhance men's lives. Our humanity is denied. Our prescribed behavior is enforced by the threat of physical violence.

Because we have lived so intimately with our oppressors, in isolation from each other, we have been kept from seeing our personal suffering as a political condition. This creates the illusion that a woman's relationship with her man is a matter of interplay between two unique personalities and can be worked out individually. In reality, every such relationship is a *class* relationship, and the conflicts between individual men and women are *political* conflicts that can only be solved collectively.

III. We identify the agents of our oppression as men. Male supremacy is the oldest, most basic form of domination. All other forms of exploitation and oppression (racism, capitalism, imperialism, etc.) are extensions of male supremacy: men dominate women, a few men dominate the rest. All power structures throughout history have been male-dominated and male-oriented. Men have controlled all political, economic, and cultural institutions and backed up this control with physical force. They have used their power to keep women in an inferior position. *All men* receive economic, sexual and psychological benefits from male supremacy. *All men* have oppressed women.

IV. Attempts have been made to shift the burden of responsibility from men to institutions or to women themselves. We condemn these arguments as evasions. Institutions alone do not oppress; they are merely tools of the oppressor. To blame institutions implies that men and women are equally victimized, obscures the fact that men benefit from the subordination of women, and gives men the excuse that they are forced to be oppressors. On the contrary, any man is free to renounce his superior position provided that he is willing to be treated like a woman by other men.

We also reject the idea that women consent to or are to blame for their own oppression. Women's submission is not the result of brainwashing, stupidity, or mental illness but of continual, daily pressure from men. We do not need to change ourselves, but to change men.

The most slanderous evasion of all is that women can oppress men. The basis for this illusion is the isolation of individual relationships from their political context and the tendency of men to see any legitimate challenge to their privileges as persecution.

V. We regard our personal experience, and our feelings about that experience, as the basis for an analysis of our common situation. We cannot rely on existing ideologies as they are all products of male supremacist culture. We question every generalization and accept none that are not confirmed by our experience.

Our chief task at present is to develop female class consciousness through sharing experience and publicly exposing the sexist foundation of all our institutions. Consciousness-raising is not "therapy," which implies the existence of individual solutions and falsely assumes that the male–female relationship is purely personal, but the only method by which we can ensure that our program for liberation is based on the concrete realities of our lives.

The first requirement for raising class consciousness is honesty, in private and in public, with ourselves and other women.

VI. We identify with all women. We define our best interest as that of the poorest, most brutally exploited woman.

We repudiate all economic, racial, educational, or status privileges that divide us from other women. We are determined to recognize and eliminate any prejudices we may hold against other women.

We are committed to achieving internal democracy. We will do whatever is necessary to ensure that every woman in our movement has an equal chance to participate, assume responsibility, and develop her political potential.

VII. We call on all our sisters to unite with us in struggle.

We call on men to give up their male privileges and support women's liberation in the interest of our humanity and their own.

In fighting for our liberation we will always take the side of women against their oppressors. We will not ask what is "revolutionary" or "reformist," only what is good for women.

The time for individual skirmishes has passed. This time we are going all the way.

July 7, 1969

*Source:* Shanley, Mary Lyndon. 1988. *Women's Rights, Feminism, and Politics in the United States.* Washington, DC: American Political Science Association.

# Index